# Democracy and the Rule of Law

The question posed in this book is why governments do or do not act according to laws. The traditional answer of jurists has been that law has an autonomous causal efficacy: law rules when actions follow anterior norms; the relation between laws and actions is one of obedience, obligation, or compliance. Contrary to this normative conception, the authors defend a positive interpretation according to which the rule of law results from the strategic choices of relevant actors. Rule of law is just one possible outcome in which political actors process their conflicts using whatever resources they can muster: only when these actors seek to resolve their conflicts by recourse to law, does law rule. What distinguishes "rule of law" as an institutional equilibrium from "rule by law" is the distribution of power. The former emerges when no one group is strong enough to dominate the others and when the many use institutions to promote their interests. Conflicts between rule of majority and rule of law are simply conflicts in which actors use either votes or laws as their instruments of power.

José María Maravall is Academic Director and Professor of Political Sociology at the Juan March Institute in Madrid. He is the author of *Dictatorship and Political Dissent* (1979), *The Transition to Democracy in Spain* (1982), and *Regimes, Politics, and Markets* (1997).

Adam Przeworski is Carroll and Milton Petrie Professor of Politics at New York University. He is coauthor of *Democracy and Development* (Cambridge, 2000) and *Sustainable Democracy* (Cambridge, 1995) and coeditor of *Democracy, Accountability, and Representation* (Cambridge, 1999).

Together, Professors Maravall and Przeworski also coauthored (with L. C. Bresser Pereira) *Economic Reforms of New Democracies* (Cambridge, 1993).

CAMBRIDGE STUDIES IN THE THEORY OF
DEMOCRACY


General Editor

ADAM PRZEWORSKI    New York University


OTHER BOOKS IN THE SERIES

John Elster, ed., *Deliberative Democracy*
Adam Przeworski, Susan Stokes, and Bernard Manin, eds.,
*Democracy, Accountability, and Representation*
Adam Przeworski et al., *Democracy and Development:
Political Institutions and Well-Being in the
World, 1950–1990*
Robert Barros, *Constitutionalism and Dictatorship:
Pinochet, the Junta, and the 1980 Constitution*

# Democracy and the Rule of Law

Edited by

**José María Maravall**

*Juan March Institute*

**Adam Przeworski**

*New York University*

PUBLISHED BY THE PRESS SYNDICATE OF THE UNIVERSITY OF CAMBRIDGE
The Pitt Building, Trumpington Street, Cambridge, United Kingdom

CAMBRIDGE UNIVERSITY PRESS
The Edinburgh Building, Cambridge CB2 2RU, UK
40 West 20th Street, New York, NY 10011-4211, USA
477 Williamstown Road, Port Melbourne, VIC 3207, Australia
Ruiz de Alarcón 13, 28014 Madrid, Spain
Dock House, The Waterfront, Cape Town 8001, South Africa

http://www.cambridge.org

First published 2003

Printed in the United States of America

*Typeface* Centennial Light 9.5/12.5 pt.     *System* LATEX 2$_\varepsilon$   [TB]

*A catalog record for this book is available from the British Library.*

*Library of Congress Cataloging in Publication data*

Democracy and the rule of law / edited by José María Maravall, Adam Przeworski.
      p.   cm. – (Cambridge studies in the theory of democracy)
      Includes bibliographical references and index.
      ISBN 0-521-82559-8 (hardback) – ISBN 0-521-53266-3 (pbk.)
      1. Rule of law – Congresses.   2. Democracy – Congresses.
   I. Maravall, José María.   II. Przeworski, Adam.   III. Series.
   K3171.A6 D46   2003
   340′.11–dc21                                                    2002035189

ISBN 0 521 82559 8 hardback
ISBN 0 521 53266 3 paperback

# Contents

# Contributors

**Robert Barros,** Visiting Professor, Department of Humanities, Universidad de San Andrés

**John Ferejohn,** Carolyn S. G. Munro Professor of Political Science and Senior Fellow of the Hoover Institution, Stanford University

**Biancamaria Fontana,** Professor of the History of Political Thought, Université de Lausanne

**Roberto Gargarella,** Professor of Constitutional Theory and Political Philosophy, Universidad Torcuato Di Tella and Universidad de Buenos Aires

**Carlo Guarnieri,** Professor of Political Science, Università di Bologna

**Stephen Holmes,** Professor of Law and Political Science, New York University

**José María Maravall,** Professor of Sociology, Universidad Complutense de Madrid, and Academic Director, Centro de Estudios Avanzados en Ciencias Sociales (Instituto Juan March)

**Pasquale Pasquino,** Director of Research in Political Theory, Centre National des Recherches Scientifiques, Paris, and Professor in Politics and Law, New York University

**Adam Przeworski,** Carroll and Milton Petrie Professor of Politics, New York University

**Ignacio Sánchez-Cuenca,** Professor of Political Science, Centro de Estudios Avanzados en Ciencias Sociales (Instituto Juan March)

**Catalina Smulovitz,** Professor, Department of Political Science and Government, Universidad Torcuato Di Tella, and Researcher (Consejo Nacional de Investigaciones Científicas y Tecnológicas)

**Michel Troper,** Professor, Université de Paris X–Nanterre, Member of the Institut Universitaire de France, and Director of the Centre de Théorie du Droit

**Barry R. Weingast,** Senior Fellow, Hoover Institution, and Ward C. Krebs Family Professor and Chair, Department of Political Science, Stanford University

# Acknowledgments

We wish to acknowledge the contribution of the Juan March Institute to the different stages of the publication of the book. José Luis Yuste and the members of the Scientific Committee of the Institute encouraged us to organize a workshop and eventually to edit a book. The workshop was held at the Institute in Madrid in June 2000. Magdalena Nebreda of the Institute provided invaluable help in organizing the conference and in the subsequent editing of the book.

# Introduction

Our central question is why governments do or do not act according to laws.

The traditional answer to this question has been that the law has an autonomous causal efficacy. People obey the law because it is the law: actions follow prior norms. This view is now being contested by arguments that law cannot be treated as an exogenous constraint on actions. In some situations, the actions that individuals want to and do undertake are stable and predictable even if they do not implement any antecedent laws.

The normative conception of the rule of law is a figment of the imagination of jurists. It is implausible as a description. Moreover, it is incomplete as an explanation. Why do people obey laws? Why do they obey a particular law? Would they obey any norm just because it is a law?

By a normative conception, we mean only the following. First, a set of rules constitutes law if and only if it satisfies some formal conditions. Second, the rules that satisfy these formal conditions are obeyed. Hence, law rules when actions follow anterior norms. The question whether the law rules is thus one of obligation, obedience, or compliance.

Lists of the formal requirements for a set of rules to qualify as law converge. According to a standard formulation (Fuller 1964: ch. 2), laws are norms that are (1) general, (2) publicly promulgated, (3) not retroactive, (4) clear and understandable, (5) logically consistent, (6) feasible, and (7) stable over time. Moreover, these norms must have a hierarchical structure (Raz 1979: 210–29), so that particular norms conform to general ones.

Law rules if "those people who have the authority to make, administer, and apply the rules in an official capacity . . . do actually administer the law consistently and in accordance with its tenor" (Finnis 1980: 270). This implies that they also abstain from undertaking actions not

**1**

empowered by rules. As Solum (1994: 122) observes, when law rules, no extralegal commands are treated as obligatory.

In the strongly normative conception, the law is the source of its own normativity. The relation between laws and actions is seen as one of obligation. If norms qualify as laws, then it is the duty of public officials to follow them and it is the duty of everyone to obey orders of public officials justified by these norms. But even if the motivation to act according to the law is not moral, a conception is normative as long as actions are distinguished by their consistency with preexisting norms.

Regardless of the motivation for compliance, the most valuable effect of the rule of law is that it enables individual autonomy. Rule of law makes it possible for people to predict the consequences of their actions and, hence, to plan their lives. To cite Raz, "In curtailing arbitrary power, and in securing a well-ordered society, subject to accountable, principled government lies the value of the rule of law" (1994: 361).

In our view, this conception confuses a description for an explanation. Situations in which actions can be described in terms of the normative conception may transpire even when these actions do not implement any anterior norms. Regularity need not be an effect of rules; it is the regularity of actions that makes them appear as if they implemented prior norms. Moreover, actions of government that are predictable, stable over time, and limited generate the conditions for individual autonomy attributed to the rule of law by the normative conception, whether or not these actions follow anterior norms.

To develop a positive conception of the rule of law, one must start with political forces, their goals, their organization, and their conflicts. To advance their goals, actors use the instruments they can muster. These instruments may be economic, military, or ideological. But they also include specifically state powers. The instruments available to Silvio Berlusconi as an owner of mass media are distinct from those at his disposal as the president of AC Milan. And both are different from the instruments available to an Italian prime minister.

The state is a system of institutions, each with somewhat specific prerogatives. These prerogatives are instruments, rather than prescriptions (Gregg 1999: 366–7). As such, they are a source of specifically institutional power. Citizens can vote; the legislature can pass laws; courts can issue orders to put people in jail; in almost all countries the executive can propose the budget. A private firm can buy votes, legislators, or judges, but it cannot issue laws. Neither can the courts.

State institutions are populated, which means that some people have specifically institutional powers. The state as a whole may use this power with regard to private actors – for example, when the legislature imposes taxes, the bureaucracy collects them, and the courts sanction those who evade them. But the particular state institutions may confront one another, as when the legislature votes against the executive or when courts sentence a minister to jail. Moreover, because these institutional powers are valuable to private actors, they may try to utilize them in conflicts in the private sphere or in their relation to a particular state agency. Thus, private interests may seek to influence the legislature; citizens may seek recourse in courts to counteract an arbitrary decision of the bureaucracy.

Whenever everyone is doing what is best for him or her, given what everyone else does, actions are predictable and, unless some exogenous event occurs, stable. Hence it is not stability that distinguishes the rule of law but the distribution of power. When power is monopolized, the law is at most an instrument of the rule of someone. Only if conflicting political actors seek to resolve their conflicts by recourse to law, does law rule.

An autocracy, a situation in which one political force monopolizes power and rules unbounded, may entail what both Barros and Holmes, following Montesquieu, refer to as "rule by law." Here, law is the instrument of the sovereign, who, by definition of sovereignty, is not bound by it. Moreover, because this state of affairs is based on a monopoly of force, nothing compels the sovereign to rule by law. Extralegal commands are as forceful as those dressed as law.

As Holmes puts it, "rule of law and rule by law occupy a single continuum and do not present mutually exclusive options." What distinguishes them is not the nature of the law, whether it operates as a tool or as a framework, but the power system to which they respond. In Holmes's words, "the powerful will cede power only to rival powerful forces." Rule of law emerges when, following Machiavelli's advice, self-interested rulers willingly restrain themselves and make their behavior predictable in order to obtain a sustained, voluntary cooperation of well-organized groups commanding valuable resources. In exchange for such cooperation, rulers will protect the interests of these groups by legal means. Rule of law can prevail only when the relation of political forces is such that those who are most powerful find that the law is on their side or, to put it conversely, when law is the preferred tool of the powerful.

To cite Holmes again, "To say that 'law is a tool of the powerful' ... is not to embrace or promote cynicism." If such well-organized groups cannot use laws to their advantage, they will promote their interests by extralegal means. If they can, an institutional equilibrium ensues in which all relevant forces find it useful to channel their public actions through political institutions, and conflicts are processed on the terrain of institutions. Those who have the votes use the legislature, those who have laws on their side use courts, those who have access use the bureaucracy. The difference between rule by law and rule of law lies then in the distribution of power, the dispersion of material resources, the multiplication of organized interests; in societies that approximate the rule of law, no group becomes so strong as to dominate the others, and law, rather than reflect the interests of a single group, is used by the many.

In any institutional equilibrium, actions are predictable, understandable, stable over time, and limited. Hence, individuals can anticipate the consequences of their own behavior; everyone can autonomously plan one's life. As Troper argues, the "constraints on individual actions are different from legal obligations and taking them into account is different from obedience. Nevertheless, one could claim that the result is similar to that expected of the *Rechtsstaat*.... citizens are politically free, because they can predict the consequences of their actions."

If citizens are to be able to predict actions of public officials, they must know what to expect of them. What enables citizens to forecast actions of governments is not whether these actions are described by laws. For example, to anticipate whether the legislature will raise taxes, private economic agents need to know that only the executive can initiate tax legislation, which means that the project must enjoy support of the ruling party or coalition, that the bill must be approved by a parliamentary committee, and that it must be passed by a majority of those voting in the legislature as a whole. Note that some steps in this example are not described by laws: the approval of the executive committee of the ruling party is not. Indeed, in some countries taxes can be raised only if the initiative is approved by a Confederation of Industry. To form predictions, economic agents treat the written and unwritten rules in the same way – specifically, they consider the need for approval by the ruling party or by interest groups as equally necessary as the approval by the legislature. To be able to say "This will never happen because the logging interests oppose it" is as good a base for predicting what the government will do as a constitutional provision against takings.

But if regularities arise endogenously, so that laws are codifications of the actions that political actors choose to pursue given what others do, why do we write some of these descriptions down as "laws"?

First, in some situations there are multiple ways in which the political life of a society can be structured. We can, for example, elect one, two, or more legislators in a district, and each of these electoral systems may induce regular and predictable, but not necessarily the same, actions on the part of voters and of political parties. Yet to make these actions consistent, we need to pick one among the several possible rules. Otherwise, parties will offer two candidates in a district and voters will vote to elect three. As Kornhauser (1999: 21) puts it, "The legal structure identifies which of many equilibria the players will in fact adopt. The enactment of a law results in the institution of a new equilibrium."

Second, laws indicate to citizens when to act against governments. By coordinating expectations, they facilitate collective actions that impose sanctions on governments. Weingast attributes a particular importance to the constitution: if a government acts in ways that are not predictable from the constitution, citizens have a reason to treat these acts of government as particularly undesirable and to single out these deviations for punishment. Hence, laws serve as focal points facilitating coordination among citizens.

Finally, we write laws only with regard to those actions to which we intend to apply the coercive power of the state. This is why many regularities are not dressed as legal norms: consulting the São Paulo Confederation of Industry on tax legislation is not. Even if in some societies people customarily wear black at funerals while in others they wear white, such customs are not codified as laws. Even if everyone attends a church, church attendance is rarely a matter of legislation. But if you do not pay taxes, you go to jail.

In sum, laws inform people what to expect of others. Even if it were to deviate from the announced course of action, the state announces what it plans to do, including what it intends to punish. Such announcements provide safety for individuals. At the same time, they facilitate coordination of sanctions against a government that deviates from its own announcements. In this sense, publicly promulgated rules provide an equilibrium manual. And because citizens value predictability, and the security it affords, they may care that the government would not violate laws even if they do not care about the actions that constitute violations. For example, people may condone the fact that political parties finance their activities by imposing an informal tax on public contracts, yet condemn these actions because they violate the law.

In what sense are equilibria institutional? One way to think about this question is to follow Calvert (1995a,b), asking whether the same equilibrium, the same set of interactions, could and would emerge in a situation without or with a particular institution. Calvert compares two situations. In one, randomly selected pairs of individuals repeatedly play a game in which everyone "defects," generating outcomes that are collectively undesirable. In the second, everything is the same except that there is one individual, called the "director," who is informed about the outcome of each interaction and who, in turn, informs everyone about the past record of the partner with whom one happens to be matched. Now everyone "cooperates," and collectively desirable outcomes ensue. Thus, what induces cooperation is the institution of the "director." Everyone uses the institution of the director while his actions change the relation between current actions and future consequences, inducing everyone to cooperate. Cooperation would not occur without the institution of the director; hence cooperation is not an equilibrium of the preexisting situation. The equilibrium is institutional because it is constructed by exercise of institutional power.

Institutions orient actions because they shape incentives and expectations. A proper set of incentives can induce political forces to behave in conformity with the institutional framework.

Some rules are impossible to break. In the view of Searle (1969, 1995), echoed in this volume by Sánchez-Cuenca as well as Troper, this is a property of "constitutive" rules. Physical possession does not constitute property unless the parties who transfer the possession sign a specific piece of paper, a "contract." A command is not a law unless it is properly adopted by a legislature. A ballot for two candidates in a single-member district is not a vote. Even if I wanted to break such rules, I cannot. I cannot break the rule about what constitutes property or a vote because, regardless of my intentions, others understand my action in terms of this rule. If I cast two votes in a single-member district, my action will be meaningless to others; I will have cast an "invalid" vote. If I appropriate a piece of land without a "valid" contract, others will not recognize it as my property.

Constitutive rules do not preclude actions from being taken. The executive may issue a command and call it a law. But if the executive does not submit a bill to the legislature and have it properly approved, the command will not be recognized by courts as law. A political party that won fewer votes than its opponent may force its way into office. But it will not have won the election. If the constitutive rule is that what counts as winning is obtaining a majority of votes, usurpation of office by a minority will not be recognized as an electoral victory.

Thus, how actions are understood depends on constitutive rules, whereas whether particular actions are undertaken is a matter of incentives. But constitutive rules shape incentives. If the constitutive rule defines as law an act of the legislature, and if the executive wants its commands to be recognized as law, it has an incentive to obtain a legislative majority.

Incentives include rewards and punishments. By creating new powers, institutions make it attractive to use these powers. In Calvert's example, the "director" has the power of fingering people who defected in the past, thus condemning them to privately administered punishments. In equilibrium, everyone wants to inform the director about the outcome of an interaction and everyone finds it useful to ask the director about the past record of the current partner. A general heading a dictatorship may want to become an elected president, even if he faces the risk of being defeated in elections. In turn, the formation of the Ministerio Público in Brazil will make public officials think more than twice before they engage in corruption.

Finally, institutions induce equilibria by imposing coherence on justifications of actions. A decision by an institution is seen by others as conforming to the institutional framework only if it can be predicted. Hence, institutional actors must provide reasons that would be seen by others as consistent with their institutional prerogatives. These reasons are not unique. But they must be recognized by others as valid. Within the legal context, this implies that they must be couched in a particular language. A higher court would not want to say "We did it because it is Friday" because the lower courts would not follow this ruling. Judges can speak to judges only in the language of law, even if they may have full discretion in what they are saying. (Besides his chapter in this volume, see Troper 1995.)

Thus far we have done nothing but distinguish the possible states of affairs. Our emphasis throughout is that situations that appear to conform to the normative model of the rule of law may and do arise even when political actors, some of whom have specifically institutional prerogatives, do not implement any anterior rules. Moreover, to repeat for the final time, such situations generate all the virtuous effects attributed to the rule of law in the normative conception. The question now is, Under what conditions should we expect such situations to transpire?

Can any institutional equilibrium emerge and survive under any conditions? This question was central in the Marxist debates about the "relative autonomy of instances." The instrumental version of Marxism maintained that political institutions, including the law, can only be a reflection of underlying economic power. Only some political and legal institutions are compatible with the capitalist organization of production. One mechanism by which this correspondence is generated is that those endowed with economic power utilize it to gain political power and use laws to perpetuate their economic power. As a result, democracy is just the best shell for what is in effect always a dictatorship of the bourgeoisie (Lenin 1932: 14). This version was contested by Althusser (1965a,b) and Poulantzas (1964, 1967). Even if "in the last instance," whatever that means, the legal system could not undermine the economic system of capitalism, each of the "instances" has a logic of its own. Specifically, the law cannot be used as an instrument of particular interests of capitalists because the legal system must be general and internally coherent to constitute law. As Barros shows, even rule by law must respect the specificity of law as an instrument of rule.

Another way to pose this question is to ask to what extent institutions can constrain the power of organized groups. What matters from our point of view is that unless political, including legal, institutions are at least somewhat independent from military or economic power, the effect of institutions cannot be distinguished from that of what Sánchez-Cuenca refers to as "brute power." The rule of law is conceivable only if institutions tame or transform brute power.

Holmes argues that political actors act within the institutional framework only to the extent that institutions constitute effective means for pursuing organized interests. In our terms, the equilibrium is institutional only if all the powerful interests channel their conflicts through the institutions. Hence, the chances of political forces when they use institutions must not diverge too far from the power of organized interests. The legal system must recognize this power; otherwise it will not be used. Thus, those groups that have the capacity to defend their interests by extralegal means are also those best protected by the law. Yet once law becomes an effective instrument of some interests, more and more people will organize to avail themselves of this instrument. As organized interests multiply, a society will come closer to the rule of law, power will not be monopolized, and the law will not used by the few against the many. "Power politics incubates the rule of law," according to Holmes; his optimistic conclusion is that all interests become organized, power is dispersed, and the law is an instrument used by everyone.

Democracy cannot exist unless at least one rule is followed – namely, that which regulates who should occupy office given the results of elections. Przeworski argues that this rule is obeyed when political actors have too much at stake to risk being defeated when they seek to establish a dictatorship. And because the stakes are larger in countries that are affluent, he concludes that in wealthy countries this rule is implemented even if electoral chances diverge from "brute power," whereas in poor countries only if the two correspond.

In institutional equilibria occupants of governmental offices undertake those and only those public actions which are expected of them. Hence, their actions are limited. It bears repetition that we are not saying that these actions implement some anterior norms but only that they are sufficiently regular so that they can be described by norms. How then does something that looks as if it were an implementation of anterior norms emerge out of conflicts in which political forces use institutions as tools?

The generic answer is that the institutional actors anticipate that a deviation from the expected behavior would subject them to punishment from other actors. The main distinction here is between sanctions that are external and internal to the government. External sanctions are those administered by actors outside the government as a whole: the mechanisms through which these sanctions are applied are often referred to as "vertical." Elections are a vertical accountability mechanism: they reward or punish the incumbent government conditional on its actions while in office (Przeworski, Stokes, and Manin 1999). Internal sanctions are those inflicted by one government agency upon another. These are "horizontal" mechanisms (O'Donnell 1994, 1999).

Taking issue with the core tenet of liberalism, Gargarella claims that horizontal mechanisms are not necessary to induce limits on majority rule. In his view, the majority can control itself and, even if the majority does not manage to exercise self-restraint, it must anticipate sanctions by the people. For its own good, the majority does not want to act hastily or foolishly, and it can prevent itself from acting precipitously by institutional devices that promote rational deliberation. And the people can control their representatives by frequent elections, recall, or imperative mandates. Hence, there is no intrinsic conflict between majoritarianism and the rule of law.

According to Weingast, citizens can prevent major transgressions by the government if they agree about the proper limits of state action and act together whenever the government transgresses these limits. The constitution plays an important role in this explanation. But the constitution matters not because governments feel a duty to obey it. Rather, it serves as the focal device, enabling particular individuals to guess what others will consider as major transgressions and thus to agree when to act. Actions of groups with different interests must be coordinated. Specifically, those who may be advantaged by a particular transgression must act against it alongside those who are hurt by it. Even though

Weingast characterizes this readiness to act against transgressions by the state as a "duty," it is induced by the possibility that in the future the government may change the beneficiaries and the victims.

But must actions of citizens be coordinated for the government to fear external sanctions? If the government knows who is organized, it can collude with some organized interests against other interests. In turn, if challenges to transgressions by the state arise spontaneously from the civil society, the government cannot anticipate when transgressions will meet with opposition. According to Smulovitz, such decentralized, uncoordinated enforcement is more effective than coordinated actions.

Whether the majority restrains itself or anticipates reactions from the civil society, actions of government are limited in these views even when the state is a unitary actor. In the classical liberal view, however, only a divided government can be a limited one. Divided and limited powers can be stable and avoid the unconstrained will of rulers; as Hampton (1994) and Kavka (1986) argue against Hobbes, this is the foundation of the rule of law: a sovereign whose powers are circumscribed. Moreover, a mere separation of powers is not enough, because separation of powers leaves unlimited latitude to the legislature, decisions of which must be implemented by all other branches of government. What is needed is a system of checks and balances that makes it impossible for any particular authority to undertake actions unilaterally, without the cooperation or consent of some other authorities (Manin 1994).

The Madisonian theorem asserts that a government divided in this manner will be a limited, moderate one. Whereas the theory of the separation of powers defends functional boundaries between the different public authorities, defined with precision in order to prevent interferences from one branch of government in the functions assigned to another, the theory of checks and balances sustains that each branch of government should exercise some influence on the others (Vile 1967). Only then would limited government be a self-enforcing equilibrium. To quote Manin (1994: 57), "Each department, being authorized to exercise a part of the function primarily assigned to another, could inflict a partial loss of power to another if the latter did not remain in its proper place.... each would be discouraged from encroaching upon the jurisdiction of another by the fear of retaliation.... the initial distribution of power would hold: no relevant actor would want to deviate from it." As one agency counters another agency, actions of the government as a whole become predictable and moderate.

Institutional design – what Troper calls the "mechanical conception" – obviously matters. The particular agencies must have the means and the incentives to check one another. In particular, if the government as a whole is to be limited, there must be no "unchecked checkers," agencies that can check others without being subject to checks by them. If the courts can dictate to other branches of the government, and these branches cannot control the courts, the power of the judiciary is unchecked. Moderation emerges in this conception only if every action of any branch requires cooperation of some other branch to be effective.

But what is the source of power of government agencies? Why would the legislature accept decisions of the courts? Why would the executive implement instructions of the legislature? The experience of the only dictatorship discussed in this volume is particularly eye-opening. It shows that a government may be limited even if the divided powers that check one another are not institutional. It is sufficient that they have real power. In Chile, the four branches of the armed forces, which together formed the Junta de Gobierno, had a long tradition of autonomy and strong corporatist interests. None of the four military branches wanted another to dominate the government. Hence, from the beginning of the dictatorship, Junta decisions had to be taken by unanimity, so that each branch checked the others. The result was that even though the Junta as a whole had the capacity to act at will, internal differences led it to conform to the constitutional document it originated and even to decisions of the Constitutional Tribunal it created. Hence, Barros argues, any division of power is sufficient to generate limited government as long as these powers are separate and real. Note that even though the Constitutional Tribunal was appointed by the military, it soon assumed autonomy and at various occasions ruled against the Junta. The opposition to the military regime thus found in the tribunal an institution to constrain the Junta.

Conversely, it is sufficient to look at communist constitutions to see that a formal division of institutional powers is not sufficient to limit the government. While some of these constitutions would satisfy any liberal, communist rulers used the single party to control all the institutional powers. Divided powers were just a facade. Institutions are effective only if there is some distinct external power behind them. The Italian judiciary, described by Guarnieri, became an effective check only when it was backed by big business and the media (Burnett and Mantovani 1998: 261–3). In turn, the Venezuelan Congress and the Supreme Court found themselves powerless against the president when Hugo Chávez could muster overwhelming popular, as well as military, support.

Hence, a system of checks and balances leads the government as a whole to act in ways that are predictable and moderate when (1) these institutions have means and incentives to check one another and (2) when their institutional prerogatives are backed by support from organized interests.

We have been speaking generically of "institutional" equilibria because we see the domination by the legislature and the domination by the courts as modalities of situations that satisfy all the requirements attributed exclusively to the rule of law in the normative conception. Needless to say, this is not the view of most legal scholars, who see the rule of law as qualitatively different from the rule of majority. For example, according to Raz (1994: 260), "Legislatures because of their preoccupation with current problems, and their felt need to secure re-election by a public all too susceptible to the influences of the short term, are only too liable to violent swings and panic measures" and "The rule of law functions in modern democracies to ensure a fine balance between the power of a democratic legislature and the force of tradition-based doctrine" (1994: 361). Dworkin (1986: 376) goes even further: "Any competent interpretation of the Constitution as a whole must therefore recognize ... that some constitutional rights are designed exactly to prevent majorities from following their own conviction about what justice requires." For such views, as Guarnieri observes, "Submitting the performance of public functions to the scrutiny of independent judges becomes an effective and essential check on the exercise of political power, ensures the supremacy of the law and guarantees citizens' rights."

This opposition of democracy and the rule of law is typically posed in conceptual, almost logical terms, as a conflict between abstract principles of popular sovereignty and of justice. We do not see it as such. What are the grounds to juxtapose intemperate legislators to oracles of "the law," "tradition," or even "justice"? Are we asked to believe that judges have no interests other than to implement "the law," that their decision power is nondiscretionary, that independence guarantees impartiality of decisions? Because the legitimacy of nonelected authorities rests on their impartiality, the courts have an institutional self-interest in appearing to be impartial, or at least nonpartisan. But there are no grounds to think – indeed, as both Guarnieri and Maravall evidence, there are reasons to doubt – that independent judges always act in a nondiscretionary, impartial manner. The rule of judges need not be the rule of law. And, to cite Guarnieri, "If the interpretation of the laws becomes the exclusive domain of self-appointed bureaucrats, the risk for democracy is evident."

Examining a historically distant situation turns out to be particularly enlightening. Fontana illustrates the difference between the rule of law and the rule of judges with the experience of France in the second half of the sixteenth century. The judiciary was generally seen as the most important of powers, independent and unchecked; this position was reinforced by a chaotic and contradictory legal system. But justice was not impartial: it was "sacrificed to greed, stupidity, social privilege and empty legal forms." Fontana writes that "In his *Essais* Montaigne accused repeatedly the Robe of corruption and described justice itself as a commodity sold for a prize to those who could afford it"; "he simply could not believe that the independence of the judiciary would be beneficial to the country as a whole if magistrates turned into a moneyed cast bent on the protection of its own privileges, an institution which abused its autonomy to serve the interests of an advantaged minority." Different attempts to reform the system of justice failed due to "the incapacity of the magistracy to promote its own reform." Legal order could only be rebuilt at the end of the century through politics, with the Nantes agreements.

The relation between democracy, understood in this context as the rule of majority, and the rule of law is always and everywhere a concrete relation between two populated institutions: the legislatures and the courts. "Where legal institutions successfully claim broad authority to regulate and structure social interaction," Ferejohn and Pasquino observe, "democratic rule seems somewhat restricted. And the converse seems true as well: where parliament claims sovereign authority to make whatever law it chooses, judicial institutions are relegated to a subservient status – judges become, at best, agents of the legislature and interpreters of its commands." Legislatures, courts, the executive, and the regulatory and the investigative authorities may or may not be in conflict. The legislature may find that its action is deemed by a court contrary to the constitution and may desist from pursuing it further. But it may push through a constitutional amendment or simply change the rules by which the courts are regulated. The courts will have it in the first case; the legislature in the second. This is what the relation between democracy and the rule of law is about. No more than that: a world of populated institutions in which actors may have conflicting interests and different powers behind them. And as Tushnet (1999: 56) puts it, "The Supreme Court at its best is clearly a lot better than Congress at its worst. But Congress at its best is better than the Court at its worst."

Constitutional courts and governments may come into conflict over ideological issues. But even when they are not divided by ideology, both politicians and judges desire to expand their institutional authority. Each of these conflicts, as Ferejohn and Pasquino see them, is "political in the sense that it is rooted in desires to maintain or increase authority and is not necessarily connected to norms of legality themselves." And judges have a natural advantage vis-à-vis politicians since, given the hierarchical organization of the judiciary, they can solve their collective action problems easier than competing politicians.

The general consensus is that during recent times the victors in these conflicts have been the courts. This trend is being generally described as a "judicialization" of politics. Yet it is necessary to distinguish the enhanced judicial authority over legislation – "constitutionalization" – from judicial actions against politicians, "criminalization."

Ferejohn and Pasquino describe the trend toward the displacement of the political by the juridical, of elective and accountable organs by nonaccountable courts. They argue that courts acquire extensive authority over legislation whenever the political system is fragmented, indecisive, or gridlocked. In the Kelsenian model, specialized tribunals acquire direct legislative prerogatives, because constitutional adjudication is a positive legislative function. But even in the United States, where judges are limited to applying laws to particular controversies and cannot repeal statutes, they render decisions of the legislature invalid when they decide not to apply them on constitutional grounds.

Maravall argues that criminalization of politics is a response to collusion among politicians. When politicians collude, successfully hiding their actions from the public, electoral as well as parliamentary accountability mechanisms fail. This is when groups in the civil society, whether business, unions, or media, with interests of their own, seek to activate judicial action. For example, a revolt against what was in effect an illegal tax imposed by different political parties to finance their activities led business groups in Italy, France, and several other countries to seek judicial intervention. In the end, the courts prevailed.

But the lines of conflict do not necessarily juxtapose legislatures and courts. Courts can be used by politicians as instruments in partisan struggles. Even if the courts are independent, they need not be impartial. When the partisan opposition sees no chance to win elections, it may seek to undermine the government by provoking judicial actions against incumbent politicians. To consolidate its partisan advantage, the incumbent government may use friendly judges to harass the opponents. Courts are instruments in this conflict. The rule of law means simply compliance with judicial decisions. And, as Maravall observes, losers may comply not because they recognize the decision as legal or just but only because they do not want to threaten the institutions.

The conflict between rule of majority and rule of law is just a conflict between actors who use votes and laws as their instruments. Whether legislatures or courts prevail in particular situations is a matter of politics. Rule of law is just one possible outcome of situations in which political actors process their conflicts, using whatever resources they can muster. When law rules, it is not because it antecedes political actions. We wrote this book because we believe that law cannot be separated from politics.

## References

Althusser, Louis. 1965a. *Pour Marx*. Paris: Maspero.

   1965b. *Lire le Capital*. Paris: Maspero.

Burnett, Stanton, and Luca Mantovani. 1998. *The Italian Guillotine*. Lanham, Md.: Rowman & Littlefield.

Calvert, Randall. 1995a. "Rational Actors, Equilibrium and Social Institutions." In Jeffrey S. Banks and Eric A. Hanushek (eds.), *Modern Political Economy*. Cambridge: Cambridge University Press.

   1995b. "The Rational Choice Theory of Social Institutions: Cooperation, Coordination, and Communication." In Jack Knight and Itai Sened (eds.), *Explaining Social Institutions*. Ann Arbor: University of Michigan Press.

Dworkin, Ronald. 1986. *Law's Empire*. Cambridge, Mass.: Belknap Press.

Finnis, John. 1980. *Natural Law and Natural Rights*. Oxford: Clarendon Press.

Fuller, Lon. 1964. *The Morality of Law*. New Haven: Yale University Press.

Gregg, Benjamin. 1999. "Using Legal Rules in an Indeterminate World." *Political Theory* 27, 3: 357–78.

Hampton, Jean. 1994. "Democracy and the Rule of Law." In Ian Shapiro (ed.), *The Rule of Law. Nomos XXXVI*. New York: New York University Press.

Kavka, Gregory. 1986. *Hobbesian Moral and Political Theory*. Princeton: Princeton University Press.

Kornhauser, Lewis A. 1999. "The Normativity of Law." *American Law and Economics Review* 6: 3–25.

Lenin, Vladimir. 1932. *State and Revolution*. 1917. Reprint, New York: International Publishers.

Manin, Bernard. 1994. "Checks, Balances and Boundaries: The Separation of Powers in the Constitutional Debate of 1787." In Biancamaria Fontana (ed.), *The Invention of the Modern Republic*. Cambridge: Cambridge University Press.

O'Donnell, Guillermo. 1994. "Delegative Democracy." *Journal of Democracy* 5, 1: 56–69.

   1999. "Horizontal Accountability and New Polyarchies." In Andreas Schedler, Larry Diamond, and Marc Plattner (eds.), *The Self-Restraining State: Power and Accountability in New Democracies*. Boulder: Lynne Rienner Publishers.

Poulantzas, Nicos. 1964. "L'examen marxiste de l'État et du Droit actuels." *Temps Modernes*, 219–20.

   1967. "À propos de la théorie marxiste du Droit." *Archives de Philosophie du Droit* 12.

Przeworski, Adam, Susan Stokes, and Bernard Manin (eds.). 1999. *Democracy, Accountability, and Representation*. Cambridge: Cambridge University Press.

Raz, Joseph. 1979. *The Authority of Law*. Oxford: Clarendon Press.

  1994. *Ethics in the Public Domain*. Oxford: Clarendon Press.

Searle, John. 1969. *Speech Acts*. Cambridge: Cambridge University Press.

  1995. *The Construction of Social Reality*. New York: Free Press.

Solum, Lawrence. 1994. "Equity and the Rule of Law." In Ian Shapiro (ed.), *The Rule of Law*. *Nomos XXXVI*. New York: New York University Press.

Troper, Michel. 1995. "La liberté d'interpretation du juge constitutionnel." In Paul Amselek (ed.), *Interpretation et Droit*. Brussels: Bruyland.

Tushnet, Mark. 1999. *Taking the Constitution Away from the Courts*. Princeton: Princeton University Press.

Vile, M. J. C. 1967. *Constitutionalism and the Separation of Powers*. Oxford: Clarendon Press.

Part One

**Chapter One**

# Lineages of the Rule of Law

This chapter elaborates a highly stylized and simplified account of the emergence of two features of the rule of law as commonly understood: predictability and equality. Legal historians would stress the role of economic, demographic, technological, scientific, religious, and cultural factors in bringing about and stabilizing institutional innovations as startlingly novel as legal certainty and equality before the law. When describing the role of important social actors in promoting or inhibiting such developments, they would weave into their story a variety of factors, including ideology, irrational passions, improvisation within inherited institutions, and the unexpected consequences of habitual behavior in a changed setting. My objective, in what follows, is both more modest and more theoretical.

I aim to clarify the reasons why powerful political actors might furiously resist or warmly embrace the rule of law. We cannot explain why the rule of law does or does not emerge in a specific historical context by invoking nothing but the strategic calculations of powerful political actors. But the self-interested reasons why powerful members of a society might encourage or discourage such a development are undoubtedly relevant and deserve a focused treatment.

I ask, first, why governments, with the means of repression in their hands, might be induced to make their own behavior predictable. For help in answering this question, I turn to Machiavelli. His thesis, essentially, is that governments are driven to make their own behavior predictable for the sake of cooperation. Governments tend to behave as if they were "bound" by law, rather than using law unpredictably as a stick to discipline subject populations, less because they fear rebellion than because they have specific goals (such as fending off attempts by foreign invaders to seize their territory) that require a high degree of voluntary cooperation from specific social groups possessing specific skills (soldiers) and assets (the tax base). Along similar lines, the acceptance by political rulers of other basic features of constitutional government, such as freedom of speech and parliamentary immunity, can be explained as a by-product of their attempt to obtain the information, essential to effective governance, that is locked inside the heads of knowledgeable citizens and that cannot be dislodged by repressive measures. They may also, presumably, recognize their own tendency, when shielded from criticism, to overlook dangers and make irreparable errors.

For the sake of parsimony, I assume that "the political ruler" is internally coherent, capable of acting upon rational calculations, and already in full control of the means of repression. All of these traits are historical achievements, however, and would have to be explained in a fuller account. On this simplified assumption, I examine the claim that "the political ruler" first submits to regularized constraints when he perceives the benefits of so doing. At first, this claim sounds almost trivial. But it is not trivial because it generates the testable hypothesis that the rule of law will emerge or not emerge, be strengthened or weakened, be extended or contracted, as the goals and priorities of political rulers and the parameters of their calculations change. (Systems that restrain rulers constitutionally can become self-sustaining, this analysis also implies, if they manage, on an ongoing basis, to allocate power to individuals with a strong incentive to keep the system in place.)

Any attempt to explain the emergence of constitutional restraints raises the question of why most governments in the past and present remain largely unbounded by law. One possible answer is that political rulers are hopelessly myopic, emotional, and incapable of acting on their own long-term interest. Alexis de Tocqueville defended exactly this position: "If remote advantages could prevail over the passions and needs of the moment, there would have been no tyrannical sovereigns or exclusive tyrannies."[1] Machiavelli, my guide in what follows, thinks about the matter somewhat differently. He suggests that political rulers cleave to unconstitutional methods when they anticipate that the returns to making their behavior predictable are lower than the returns to making it unpredictable. Repressive and acquisitive elites are unlikely to favor a shift toward the rule of law if they suspect that it will unhorse them. Bullies and plunderers – who could never flourish if the rules of the game were crystal clear and reliably enforced – cannot be expected to promote or embrace a system that will radically devalue the rude skills

---

[1] Tocqueville, *Democracy in America* (1969: 210).

of acquisition and domination they have perfected in the state of nature. (I have drawn this conclusion after studying the Russian case.)

Keeping things fluid can be an especially appealing strategy for a certain type of ruler. That is presumably an important reason why the rule of law is historically rare. Injecting uncertainty into social situations is a well-known mechanism of control: if a subject population never knows what is going to happen to it, it is unlikely to present a serious challenge to the government. Moreover, a government may continuously choose to destabilize property rights if it fears that stable patterns of ownership would provide a platform from which to launch attacks upon itself. In effect, whether political rulers choose to govern by predictability or unpredictability depends on a number of specific factors that change over time: their goals, their personal habits and skills, the obstacles and enemies they face, their privileged social partners, the resources directly available to them without mobilizing cooperation from the citizens at large, and the skills, wealth, and organizational capacity of their subject populations.

This Machiavellian analysis, while suggestive, remains incomplete because it focuses only on legal certainty as the offspring of regularized constraints on state power. We ordinarily associate the rule of law not only with predictability but also with a roughly equal treatment of social groups. Liberal theory expresses this ideal of equality before the law in its fantasy of a society made up of individuals rather than organized interests. Distributive outcomes, however, are determined not by head counts but by power asymmetries among organized interests. In no society is power dispersed equally among disassociated individuals. As a result, no state, however liberal or democratic, treats all citizens equally before the law. One reason for this ubiquitous deviation from ideal justice has already been suggested: a political authority that submits to constitutional restraints to obtain voluntary social cooperation has no incentive to treat all groups equally, because it needs the cooperation of some groups more than the cooperation of others. In particular, it needs the cooperation of well-organized groups with assets that can be easily mobilized for war and other state purposes.

The rights of big landowners were secured long before the rights of orphans for the banal reason that governments are selectively responsive to groups with political leverage, that is, to those whose cooperation they think they need. Historically, well-organized interests able to defend themselves and achieve their goals by extralegal means are also the first to gain the effective right or capacity to defend themselves and achieve their goals by legal means. A government's favoritism to groups

**21**

especially useful to itself results in law enforcement that operates on two tracks. Law can become highly predictable for privileged social strata while remaining maddeningly erratic for the less well-off. What looks on paper like an impartial system behaves in practice like a "dual state." The question then arises of how privilege ("private law") ever evolves into something more inclusive. Formulated differently, why and when does special-interest legislation – as well as bias in prosecution, adjudication, and so forth – give way to a legal system that, roughly speaking, serves all citizens equally? For the answer to this second question, I turn to Rousseau.

His answer, in effect, is that inequality before the law never gives way to equality before the law. No legal system treats all citizens equally. Even the most advanced *Rechtsstaat* remains to some extent a *Doppelstaat*. That is to say, if we define the rule of law in such a way as to exclude the disproportionate influence of organized interests on the making, interpreting, and applying of law, we have identified a system that has never existed and can never exist. But this does not mean that we should junk the concept or dismiss it as useless for descriptive purposes. The rule of law can still be distinguished from rule by law, and not only because some governments, for their own purposes, choose to make their behavior more or less predictable and other governments, for their own purposes, do not. If we identify the rule of law with that point of ideal justice where all citizens are treated equally, says Rousseau, then we have to admit that the rule of law can never be achieved. But it can be approximated. The circle of those able to protect their interests reliably by legal means can be doggedly expanded. Liberal justice is approximated, Rousseau argues, in precisely those societies where many roughly equal groups making up a large proportion of the population all gain some leverage over the government and its privileged social partners.

When a broad and diverse plurality of groups possesses some degree of political leverage, ordinary citizens will be able to add legal instruments to the extralegal means that they usually employ to protect their interests. Such a pluralistic society is as close as we can get to the rule of law, although it remains highly imperfect. A government that attempts to become responsive to such a cacophony of complaints and aspirations, for one thing, risks collapsing into incoherence. But the most conspicuous disorder of such a system, according to Rousseau, is asymmetrical pluralism. Written law may declare otherwise, but members of politically influential groups receive, in reality, much better legal protection than members of politically insignificant groups.

Group power can never be fully equalized. But if the majority of citizens in a highly pluralistic order nevertheless belongs to groups with some political leverage, these citizens will, on a predictable basis, be able to use law to pursue their goals and safeguard their assets to some extent. They will be able, for instance, to count on the police to protect them from private predators. Tenants will be able to use law against landlords, employees against employers, wives against husbands, debtors against creditors, consumers against producers, not to mention criminal suspects against the police. Moreover, competitive relations between members of the political and economic elite may confer a modest "tipping power" on ordinary citizens, who are thereby additionally enabled to defend their interests despite their relatively modest resources.

Rousseau's conceptualization here, while just as stylized as Machiavelli's, helps clarify variations among liberal societies and within the same liberal society over time. In particular, it helps explain what we mean when we say that a nominally liberal government, while continuing to rule *through* law, is retreating from the rule *of* law. This happens when the contest between strong and weak grows more lopsided, that is, when a few well-organized social networks monopolize political access and turn law into an instrument increasingly useful to themselves but decreasingly useful to fellow citizens who belong to poorly organized and politically voiceless strata. One explanation for why this might occur is that the government, given its shifting goals, problems, and resources, is sometimes strongly motivated to play favorites.

To regain their abraded capacity to use the law in such a situation (i.e., to restore, to some extent, the rule of law), groups whose legal rights have been diluted or destroyed have to change the incentives facing political rulers and their unjustly privileged social partners. But collective action problems may fatally undermine the bargaining power of certain poorly positioned citizens and thereby prevent them from securing much legal certainty, as well as participatory rights and economic security, from the rich and powerful. Moreover, the incentives facing political and economic elites do not depend exclusively on the organizational capacity of the excluded. Other decisive factors include the culturally shaped priorities of the dominant forces, their inner cohesiveness, the assets independently at their disposal, and, above all, the international context. If the international context is sufficiently hostile, and power and privilege palpably depend on physical control of a piece of territory, the rich and the powerful have a strong motive to provide the citizens at large, including the poor, with some degree of political participation, legal certainty, and economic transfers. If not, not.

## Lineages of Self-Restraint

I begin at the beginning, with the simple question: why do people with power accept limits to their power? An even more pointed formulation is: why do people with guns obey people without guns? An economic twist is: why would the rich ever voluntarily part with a portion of their wealth? In legal theory, the parallel question runs: why do politicians sometimes hand power to judges? Why do politicians allow judges, who control neither purse nor sword, to overturn and obstruct their decisions and sometimes even to send officeholders to jail? Such questions are too broad, not to mention too vague, to be answered with any degree of finality or comprehensiveness. But they can serve as clumsy levers to pry loose some important insights about the origins, developments, and setbacks of the rule of law.

Self-restraint is usually explained in one of two ways. People are thought to restrain themselves either when they are in the grip of moral norms or when they anticipate the advantages of self-restraint. Normative answers focus on the inherently binding power of norms (such as fairness) or on a somewhat ineffable sense of "legitimacy." Some legal theorists suggest that politicians are cowed and silenced by the sheer professionalism of judges, by their persuasive reason giving, by their splendid impartiality, or perhaps by their special intimacy with uncriticizable higher principles. Because politics does not satisfy the public's hunger for justice, the argument sometimes goes, politicians are subtly pressured by their constituents to cede some of their powers to judges.

The idea that norms have an independent causal force may be true or false, but it does not help pinpoint conditions under which the rule of law is likely to emerge. For the same reason, it contributes little to understanding why established rule-of-law systems sometimes expand generously and sometimes contract tightfistedly the legal protections they offer to disadvantaged groups. Whatever the merit of the normative approach to law's binding character, it is also true that individuals often adapt their behavior to novel and complex rules because they anticipate gaining some advantage thereby. True, "man is a sociable animal." People like to spend time in each other's company and, indulging a natural gregariousness, enjoy making and keeping promises to each other. Nonetheless, people also keep their promises to each other, even though this may involve costly self-restraint, because they want to maintain their reputations as promise keepers, an asset that is likely to prove useful in the future. Statesmen and constitution makers can reason in a similar way. In designing a constitution, they can place the power to break treaties "beyond the lawful reach of legislative acts."[2] A government operating under such a constitution may manage to renounce a small short-term benefit, such as the chance to escape from a bad treaty ratified imprudently in the past, for the sake of a greater long-term benefit, namely, the chance to win the confidence of other states with whom many mutually useful treaties may be signed in the future.

The capacity or power to make a promise that one cannot easily break is exactly that – a capacity and a power. It may look like a restriction or restraint from the viewpoint of one's later self, but that is an incomplete perspective. If promises were not a means for social actors to assert themselves and pursue their interests, or if individuals and governments acted as if they had no continuous identity over time, promises would have no afterlife, no binding power. As things stand, individuals sometimes repay onerous loans, and governments sometimes abide by galling treaties. And they do so, when they do, at least partly because publicly observable compliance with promises is palpably in their long-term interest. Though not the whole story, similarly banal calculations of expediency presumably help explain why politicians defer to judges and even why people with guns obey people without guns. The larger implications of this theme are suggested by the following observation. From Voltaire to Max Weber, continental intellectuals urged their own autocratic regimes to imitate British political institutions on the grounds that limited government, on the British model, would increase the military power and economic wealth of their countries. Self-restraint is a tool and it can be explicitly advertised and consciously embraced because it furthers desired ends. To drive this prudential, rather than moral, lesson home, those assigned in the past to educate the children of political rulers repeatedly stressed the miserable fate of wicked "tyrants" who, refusing to accept limits, were destroyed by overreaching and hubris.

## Lineages of Judicial Independence

The decision of politicians to cede some of their power to judges is mysterious only if we assume that power wielders are exclusively concerned to maximize power. If we start with a different premise, say, that politicians want to maximize deniability as well as power, the mystery begins to fade.

For human, as opposed to divine, beings, omnipotence is unappealing, as well as unattainable. For one thing, it would occupy too many

---

[2] *Federalist Papers* 64.

evenings. (Indeed, it would occupy an infinite number of evenings, which is more than we have at our disposal.) Shedding responsibilities, downsizing goals to match capacities, is a prudent step for the most Herculean of bosses, commanders, rulers, panjandrums, chiefs. Downsizing one's aims to fit one's resources is therefore a classical definition of "freedom." Ceding power over some domains is necessary in order to get full control of others. Monopolizing power is especially unattractive in situations swarming with unsolvable problems. The mighty will typically ditch responsibility for intractable dilemmas on which they hesitate to squander scarce time and effort to no avail. To improve the ratio of assets at their disposal to liabilities on their shoulders, they pare down their duties, burdens, and charges – the problems for which they are personally answerable.

Similarly pedestrian considerations are relevant to the more general question of the origins of the separation between executive and judicial power. Many legal historians interpret the gradual development of independent courts in England as an evolving division of labor whereby the king's court slowly cast aside aggravating and time-consuming burdens. No one is surprised that today's White House and Congress pay no attention to a child custody case (so long as Cuban-American relations are not involved), nor does anyone ask why politicians would "cede power to judges" in such a context. Politicians cede this power because they do not want it, and they do not want it because they have better things to do. The independence of the judiciary has to be real, and not apparent merely, Montesquieu adds. If the ruler pulls strings behind the curtains, people will notice where ultimate decision-making power lies, and the steps of the ruler's palace will again swarm with harassing crowds hoping to influence upcoming decisions of the court. Formulated differently, powerful people long to reduce the clutter in their in-boxes. Any sensible political ruler will want to delegate the donkey work. He will "get off my case"; that is to say, he will support the independence of the judiciary.

That advantages of specialization played some role in the emergence and stabilization of the rule of law is highly likely. More interesting is the insight that the powerful are especially eager to shed specific powers, namely those that are liable to excite lasting hatred and resentment. To exercise power is to create winners and losers. Winners may or may not feel appreciative; but losers almost certainly feel aggrieved. It is dangerous to wield power because the powerful are eye-catching targets for the vengeance of those whom they have really or supposedly harmed. To diminish the danger of reprisal, power wielders typically seek deniability by yielding, in reality as well as appearance, some key elements of decision-making power. To choose a trivial example, when an editor rejects an article for his journal, he blames his anonymous editorial board and claims that his "hands are tied." For similar reasons, the judiciary itself may claim to be the least dangerous branch, to avoid rousing resistance, attracting the attention of critics, and awakening sleeping dogs. In general, protests of impotence resound most loudly just where you would expect: in the corridors of power.

Tom Schelling could explain why. But so could Alexander Hamilton, who defends the jury system on the grounds that tying the judge's hands improves his position: "The temptations to prostitution which the judges might have to surmount must certainly be much fewer, while the co-operation of a jury is necessary, than they might be if they had themselves the exclusive determination of all causes."[3] Judges (and their families) would be exposed by their own unshackled power to frightening threats as well as alluring bribes. To blunt this danger, the judge's verdict can be made to hinge upon the independent decision of twelve randomly selected citizens. These jurors are much less vulnerable to bribes and threats than sitting judges because the former are suddenly plucked out of the anonymous body of people and just as abruptly dispersed back into the multitude: "[T]here is always more time and better opportunity to tamper with a standing body of magistrates than with a jury summoned for the occasion."[4] By hinging the judge's choices on the decision of the jury, the judge's power is, yes, somewhat diminished, but in exchange he achieves a degree of security greater than what the most vigilant bodyguards could provide. And a judge's credibility and therefore public acquiescence in his decisions are also enhanced by an arrangement that makes bribery manifestly more difficult.

Although perennially controversial, Machiavelli remains a subtle and provocative guide to the enigma of political support for the autonomy of law. He traces the origins of the separation of executive and judicial power to what he claims to be an important but neglected fact of human psychology. It is best for the prince to shed judicial power, and not only – though this factor remains supremely relevant – because punished parties will despise their punisher and their families will plot cruel revenge against his. The esoteric truth ostensibly explaining why politicians welcome judicial independence is that *justice does not stimulate loyalty or mobilize political support*. In Machiavelli's words, "when a man receives those honors and useful things that he believes he merits, he will not

---

[3] *Federalist Papers* 83.
[4] Ibid.

acknowledge any obligation to those who reward him."[5] People treated justly feel that they deserve it and do not give their benefactor any credit for treating them that way. Thus, judicial power has substantial negative consequences (the resentment of the punished) without producing, in recompense, any positive consequences (no loyalty from those who are treated justly). Hence, the shrewd prince will forfeit powers that are resented, such as punishment, and retain powers that engender gratitude, such as the power to pardon: "Princes must make others responsible for imposing burdens, while handing out gracious gifts themselves."[6] Loyalty and political support are excited by gifts that are undeserved and even unhoped-for, not by benefits that recipients fully merit and therefore expect and believe to be their due. The far-seeing ruler, as a consequence, will create a genuinely autonomous judicial body for whose actions the political branches receive neither credit nor blame. His courts will specialize in punishing malefactors and dispensing justice, while he, the prince, will retain for himself the discretionary power to issue pardons and confer other unjustifiable benefits, which presumably stir gratitude in, and secure political support from, the lucky beneficiaries.

### Lineages of Reliability

According to Adam Przeworski (Chapter 5 in this volume), the primary check on the behavior of the powerful is fear of revolt. Unless they are made to quake in their boots, those who control the means of repression will never behave with decent moderation. Machiavelli made the same point when he explained that the principal brake on the cruelty and extravagance of princes is not Christian morality but the fear of assassination. The fundamental lesson of *The Prince*, in fact, is that a rational ruler will visibly benefit his people, keep them content, and rule in such a way that they are not strongly motivated to slit his throat. Roman history, as he reconstructs it in the *Discourses*, suggests that constitutional restraints on power developed when the privileged few panicked at the prospect of deadly urban riots.

To these considerations we could add that an important check on the extravagance and insouciance of the rich is the realization that even the poorest can get their hands on matches. Like assassination and insurrection, arson is an extreme version of refractory behavior that can

[5] Machiavelli, *Discourses on Livy*, I.16.
[6] Machiavelli, *The Prince*, XIX.

harm the interests of the rich and powerful. The privileged, if they think ahead (which they do not necessarily do), naturally wish to avoid a dangerous backlash by "the beast with many heads."[7] But fear of a backlash is an acknowledgment of power. To say that the weak and poor can extract concessions from the rich and powerful by threatening arson or revolt is to confess that the rich and powerful are not the only ones who wield power. The weak comply with the law because they must, whereas the powerful comply with the law only when it serves their purposes. This is true, but strong-weak is a continuous not a dichotomous variable. *All organized interests are weak to some extent.* None has God-like power. This is exactly Machiavelli's point. The powerful will cede power only to rival powerful forces, including the uncooperative or insurrectionary "street." Similar reasoning lay behind Montesquieu's famous claim, all-important to the American Framers, that freedom can be sustained only where "power arrests power."

The credible threat of violent retaliation, as in assassination or revolt, is not the sole source of power. A more important source of power is the credible threat to withdraw urgently needed cooperation. The threat to withdraw cooperation, in fact, provides a more enduring motivation for the regularization of governmental power than the threat to inflict physical harm noted by Machiavelli and stressed by Przeworski. The prince who concedes benefits to diffuse an ongoing revolt may withdraw these concessions as soon as the rebels have been disarmed; he will keep his word only so long as it is useful. The prince who concedes benefits to maintain the loyalty of his troops, by contrast, will be unable to withdraw his generous concessions so long as he has enemies abroad. Moreover, no one will be duped by the populist gestures of a ruler who offers a sop to citizens just when they are threatening to revolt. By contrast, a ruler who provides benefits to past, present, and future soldiers will be easily understood to be acting for a clear purpose that he genuinely shares with his community, namely defense against conquest by foreigners.

Fear of violent rebellion, moreover, gives the ruler a strong motivation to maintain his subject population in a state of paralysis, resignation, docility. To guard against insurrection, he may choose to deploy divide-and-rule strategies and to govern by forcing his subjects to live in uncertainty. The first order of business of a ruler who fears bodily harm from his own subjects is to keep them apprehensive, disorganized, groveling, quarreling, uneducated, and incapable of resistance. He would not

---

[7] Shakespeare, *Coriolanus*, IV.1.

necessarily apprehend any great benefit in granting them the freedom to associate, cooperate, and communicate among themselves. Fear of violence from below, therefore, does not explain why a ruler who controls the means of repression would voluntarily accept regularizing restraints on his own power. Quite the contrary.

According to Machiavelli, the principal reason why people with power voluntarily agree to render their own behavior predictable is that even the most powerful people need cooperation to attain their ends. If a ruler with great ambitions alienates and irritates his citizens, he is breaking his tools. To say that people pay their debts because they want to remain eligible for future loans is to say that they submit to restraints on their current freedom of choice for the sake of cooperation now and in the future. The same logic applies to a political ruler. He can attain his objectives, under some conditions, only if he distributes rights and resources downwards, in a way "best calculated to conciliate the confidence of the people."[8]

But under what conditions is this likely to occur? The rich and powerful are often shielded in their privileges by collective action problems afflicting the poor and the weak. Uncoordinated action is futile; and joint action is difficult to organize. Indeed, the privileged can successfully scheme to exacerbate the collective action problems of the disadvantaged, or prevent their alleviation, by various strategies of divide and rule. But even when the poor and the weak have a negligible capacity for collective action, the rich and the powerful may be "compelled" to surrender some degree of wealth, if not power, in their favor. Even when lower-class rebellions have no chance of succeeding, for instance, they can give a big headache to ruling groups, who may therefore decide that subsidizing bread and circuses is an efficient way to preempt messy urban disorder.

An example of political leverage – meaning a capacity to extract beneficial concessions – without any capacity for coordinated action is contagious disease. Although the lucky few generally have the best doctors that money can buy, they cannot protect themselves effectively from contagious diseases that incubate in poor neighborhoods. As a result, they may willingly invest in public health programs aimed at reducing the incidence of those contagious diseases against which they cannot selectively inoculate themselves. For similar reasons, French and British colonial armies spent money inoculating local populations. They did this not from a generous spirit of compassion and charity but strategically

---

[8] *Federalist Papers* 70.

to protect European troops. Such redistributions are not eleemosynary but prudential.

Such a stylized analysis is obviously a gross simplification of historically complex processes. But Machiavelli's presentation of its basic logic can nevertheless help us focus on otherwise neglected factors that may play a significant role in legal change. Reduced to fundamentals, Machiavelli's thesis is the following. Faced with foreign enemies, the rich and the powerful have no choice but to arm ordinary citizens because, when adversity strikes, every political elite needs "partisan friends" or *partigiani amici*.[9] Because foreign mercenaries can betray their paymaster at any moment, a prudent ruler will rely solely on domestic troops, who have a personal stake in protecting the homeland. Once ordinary citizens have arms, however, the rich and the powerful can no longer treat them any way they like. In particular, political rulers must restrain themselves from seizing the women and looting the property of potential recruits. They also have an incentive to engage in defensive democratization, that is, to grant citizen-soldiers some influence over political decision making as well as access to legal forums where their grievances can be heard and remedied.

"Men will always be bad unless, by necessity, they are compelled to be good."[10] Political rulers, in particular, behave morally only when they are forced. The "necessity" that forces rulers to be good, however, is less the prospect of rebellion than their need, given their ambitions, for social cooperation. The principal source of the political leverage of the poor and the weak, following this analysis, is the existence of violent foreign predators and land grabbers. Ultimately, the power and privileges of a society's political and economic elite depend on that society's tenuous hold upon a piece of real estate located in a perilous international environment. Citizen soldiers have leverage, therefore, because they can credibly threaten to refuse to fight (or fight tenaciously) in the face of an invasion. This threat is more credible than the threat of workers to refuse to work, for workers always need income to survive. And the threat of soldiers not to fight cannot be easily deflected by the prospect of punishment, as can, to some extent, threats of assassination, arson, and even insurrection. The high morale and tenacity essential to an effective fighting force cannot be elicited by fear of harsh penalties. If the government arms soldiers who do not feel any particular stake in the system, the soldiers may simply sell their weapons to the enemy and desert.

---

[9] Machiavelli, *Discourses on Livy*, I.21, 60.
[10] Machiavelli, *The Prince*, XXIII.

A ruler who needs to raise a citizen army cannot keep his subjects apprehensive, disorganized, demoralized, mutually distrustful, passive, and incapable of collective resistance. So what is he to do? To secure the voluntary cooperation of ordinary citizens in war, according to Machiavelli, a shrewd ruler will provide the poor and the weak with fair legal procedures, democratic participation, and property rights. This is not utopian aspiration, but a historically observable pattern. Political rulers, in special circumstances, have made their own behavior predictable for what they perceived to be their own benefit. That a foreign threat changes the incentives of the elite is suggested by many historical examples, such as: "[I]n time of war the landholding class accepted a fairly steep tax on its property, even though it was the most influential political group in the country" (Strayer 1970: 108). That war between mass armies boosts the leverage of less affluent and less prestigious citizens is also suggested by the observation that, during World War II, and despite a ban on strikes, American unions organized and grew much faster than they had through plant sit-ins and mass picketing in the late 1930s. Finally, the central role of veterans benefits in the original emergence of both property rights and the welfare state suggests that transfer programs, too, are rooted in this ur-form of the social contract, namely, the exchange of combat service for legal protection and opportunities for "voice." If this Machiavellian explanation holds up, then redistributive politics represents a strategic gamble by political and economic elites trying to nail down today the popular cooperation they will need tomorrow when foreign armies are on the march.

According to Machiavelli, citizens will exert themselves only if they have a reasonable chance of capturing some benefits from such exertion. "Riches multiply and abound," he argues, when property rights become secure: "For everybody is eager to acquire such things and to obtain property, provided that he be convinced that he will enjoy it when it has been acquired."[11] By contrast, economic growth will be thwarted by an unpredictable ruler who seizes assets without reason or notice and without providing any mechanisms for legal redress. Citizens become attached to a rule-of-law regime not only because it allows them to accumulate assets but also, more generally, because it makes it possible for them to predict the consequences of their actions, to pursue remedy when wronged, and generally to plan their lives.

The rule of law will be established and maintained when political and economic elites understand the vital contribution it makes to national

---

[11] Machiavelli, *Discourses on Livy*, II.2.

security. That is the crux of Machiavelli's analysis. The security of acquisitions and transactions, when combined with political citizenship, contributes enormously to a republic's military strength:

> [A]ll towns and all countries that are in all respects free, profit by this [freedom] enormously. For, wherever increasing populations are found, it is due to the freedom with which marriage is contracted and to its being more desired by men. And this comes about where every man is ready to have children, since he believes that he can rear them and feels sure that his patrimony will not be taken away, and since he knows that not only will they be born free, instead of into slavery, but that, if they have virtue, they will have a chance of becoming rulers.[12]

Just as a dwindling population is a military liability, so a surging population, if organized and rewarded correctly, can be a military asset. Rulers introduce freedom (*il vivere civile* or *il vivere libero*) today in order to increase the supply of citizen stakeholders tomorrow. Citizens will produce more children (i.e., future soldiers) if they are convinced that their hereditary property rights are secure and that their children will enter a system of political promotion open to talents.

Extending this analysis, Machiavelli also traces Rome's power to its free trade and open immigration policy. Because its "constitution" welcomed foreigners who introduced unknown products and new arts, Rome soon "thickened with inhabitants."[13] This choice for an open economy and an open demography, highly displeasing to nativists and xenophobes, also had significant military consequences. Sparta, which closed itself off from trade and immigration, could barely muster 20,000 soldiers, while Rome could easily put 280,000 into the field. Some people were offended by Rome's "tumultuous" city life (often contrasted to the austere order of Sparta); but the uproar was an inevitable side effect of the mixing of peoples that led to Rome's astonishing military success.

Unpredictable rule, it should be said, has certain significant advantages. Above all, a ruler whose behavior is erratic and unpredictable will keep his enemies off balance. On the other hand, under certain conditions, unpredictable rule can be self-defeating. That is Machiavelli's point. A hyperalert prince who rules with a knife constantly in his hand, who pales when a citizen passes him in the streets, who cannot turn his back on his own bodyguards, will soon be physically exhausted. A

---

[12] Ibid.
[13] Ibid., II.3.

rapacious ruler who cannot restrain himself from making off with the women and plundering the property of his subjects will be surrounded by conspiring enemies. And having offered nothing to ordinary citizens, he will find it very difficult to raise an effective and loyal army. A tyrant keeps his subjects poor, uneducated, and helpless so that they cannot cause him any trouble or thwart his will. But by crushing potential sources of political resistance, he also myopically deprives himself of potential sources of political support. If citizens are granted some measure of freedom, by contrast, they will resist foreign conquerors with civic ferocity. If ordinary people are instead consigned to passivity and subordination (*il vivere servo*), they will yield pliantly to foreign conquerors who, upon arrival, will gladly take the ruler's life.

By extending to previously disenfranchised groups the power to elect political representatives, a ruling elite can purchase the cooperation of ordinary citizens. That is how Machiavelli explains Rome's remarkable success in expansion and annexation: the city expelled its haughty princes and granted property rights and political influence to the plebeians. Citizens will fight for a community in which they possess a palpable stake. Jumping across the centuries, we discover a similar argument made in similar words by Max Weber. In one of the few passages where he drops his usual insistence on the gulf between morality and politics, Weber (1994) thundered against the attempt by German landowners to withhold full voting rights from demobilized German soldiers who fought in the Great War to defend, among other things, the property of the rich. To those being asked to risk their lives to protect the homeland, and therefore also the private rights of its richest inhabitants, the government cannot morally or safely deny basic liberties. And, in fact, when poor citizens fight for their country, they often demand and receive the right to vote.

This raises the question of why poor citizens are not everywhere and always granted democratic liberties, legal access, and economic support. Machiavelli did not believe that history was foreseeable. His theory of defensive democratization has no predictive value, therefore. The mechanism it describes depends on a number of variables that appear or do not appear for unknown reasons. By far the most important of these variables is the motivation of "the ruler," who may be seeking glory or not, may be interested in future generations or not, may be looking forward to a peaceful retirement or not, and so forth. Machiavelli's theory does not, as would be absurd, predict a universal tendency toward liberal democracy. It says, instead, that under certain specified conditions (as when rulers feel threatened by a neighboring country's army) liberalization and democratization are likely to occur, whereas under contrary conditions (such as the rise of push-button warfare with a diminished role for citizen armies) de-democratization and a retrenchment of civil liberties are much more likely.

## The Lawful Management of Conflict

Human beings, according to Machiavelli, while naturally enjoying each other's company, are also naturally myopic, unfocused, aimless, undisciplined, and basically uncooperative. If left to their own devices – if laissez-faire prevails – they will inevitably work at cross purposes and fall into incoherence, wasteful disputatiousness, and mutual paralysis. Contrary to what Rawls would lead us to expect, they may agree quite easily on "the good" (e.g., the defeat of an enemy) but they will be unable to cooperate because they have different ideas of "the right." This is because, as Machiavelli explains, people who live together inevitably rub each other the wrong way, and the ill-will that arises from such mutual chafing is usually associated with – whether caused by or causing, he does not specify – conflicting ideas of what is just and what is unjust.

Self-defeating patterns of behavior are universal. But the difficulties they present for creating a coherent polity and an effective fighting force are exacerbated by the emotions and conflicting narratives of injustice associated with class conflict. Anger can become especially virulent in societies where class divisions run deep, for the envy of the poor is regularly enflamed by the insolence of the rich, who, according to Machiavelli, are seldom capable of resisting the temptation to humiliate publicly their social inferiors. Rulers should want to be feared, not hated. If they were rational, therefore, they would avoid insolence. If they were rational, they would also avoid repressive measures, which are more likely to kindle hatred than fear. Being less than perfectly or consistently rational, they often succumb to the puerile pleasures of insolence. Insolence is a problem because it stirs hate, and hate works faster than fear. The hatred of low-status citizens for the high and mighty bursts instantly into their aggrieved minds. By contrast, apprehension of further retaliation that might restrain the injured from launching an attack kindles only gradually.

For Machiavelli, one of the few social contexts in which these self-defeating passions can sometimes be brought under control is war. Because they, too, need talented generals, the poor and weak have a good reason, in time of war, to put aside their normal peacetime envy of the rich and powerful. Similarly, the rich and powerful need infantry in wartime and will therefore, if ruled by reason, curb their habitual insolence toward the poor and the weak. If rational, both sides will moderate their nasty impulses for their common good, but of course they do not always or even usually behave rationally. The political and economic elite is no more likely to be ruled by reason than the multitude. The poisonous interaction of insolence and envy, which according to Machiavelli is the key to the self-destructive class politics of the ancient city, poses an acute challenge to institutional design. What institutions can mitigate the self-weakening class conflict that manifestly exposes the whole city to foreign conquest? Machiavelli's answer is: the rule of law.

To defend against external threats, prescient political rulers will create, train, and finance a military establishment. To defend against internal conflicts (which are militarily weakening), they will create, train, and finance a judicial establishment. This at least is how Machiavelli explains the origins of the criminal justice system in both ancient Rome and the Italian republics. Constitution makers introduced fair trials because they understood them to be an indispensable *tool of governance*, that is to say, a powerful mechanism for dampening the emotionally charged class antagonisms that expose a republic to foreign conquest.

Mutual distrust and animosity among citizens can never be eradicated. But they can be domesticated by the skillful design of judicial institutions. Rather than allowing such self-defeating passions to fester outside the system, constitution makers channel them inside standing governmental bodies. Machiavelli is thinking specifically of public trials where ordinary citizens, feeling injured, can openly lodge accusations against members of the elite who have purportedly injured them: "[W]hen these humors do not have an outlet by which they may be vented ordinarily, they have recourse to extraordinary modes that bring a whole republic to ruin."[14] By inviting the politically destabilizing desire to avenge perceived wrongs to vent itself inside the system, a forum for public accusations reduces the poisonous influence of anonymous denunciations and the demand for back-street ambushes. It can help cauterize class resentment and the desire for vengeance before they spiral out of control.

The rich and powerful will be sorely tempted to claim immunity from such prosecutions. But this would be a fatal mistake, destabilizing for the polity and personally endangering its political and economic elite. The rich and powerful must renounce immunity in the short run to establish an effective method for managing class tensions in the long

[14] Ibid., I.7.

36

run. That they *can* do so, Roman history strongly suggests. A politically and economically dominant group has a powerful incentive to expose itself in this way. For to give the desire of the many for revenge against the few a public platform is also to impose upon such class resentment a consequential discipline. Unlike the disseminator of venomous rumors behind the backs of the slandered or the organizer of a private ambush, the public accuser has to appear personally, face his enemy, and prove his case to the satisfaction of third parties. He must give the accused a chance to rebut unfavorable testimony and dispute fabricated evidence. The rule of law, in this sense, emerges as a two-edged sword, as a joint tool of both the many and the few, and therefore as a means for advancing the city's general good. A society that manages, in this way, to channel internal hatreds inside public institutions will be more cohesive in the face of external foes. To achieve the social cohesion necessary for war, Machiavelli asserts, the elite must renounce its immunity and expose itself to legal challenges. This is how power politics, if the elite is sufficiently prudent, can incubate the rule of law.

## The Systole and Diastole of Justice

Pure democracy is the ideal end point on a spectrum where all oligarchical elements vanish. This utopian condition, or regulative ideal, is never fully realized in practice. Unlike ideal democracy, partial and reversible democratization exists and can be studied. It implies a widening of the circle of consultation, an enlarging of the number of participants who wield influence over the making, interpreting, and applying of laws. When government by freewheeling debate first arises, it is naturally a practice reserved to a few privileged insiders. Subsequently and gradually it becomes more inclusive. Those with special access naturally craft laws that favor themselves. As time goes by, "voice opportunities," and the chance to influence the shape of law, are either extracted by or voluntarily granted to previously disenfranchised groups. As the participatory circle widens, laws begin to reflect broader social concerns. But why have certain political systems at times become moderately or even radically more inclusive? According to Machiavelli, democratization occurs when the ins need the cooperation of the outs and therefore let them come (partly) in. The reel can also be run backwards. De-democratization occurs when, for whatever reason, the circle of consultation constricts. If the rich and the powerful suddenly come to believe that they no longer require the cooperation of the weak and the poor (because, say, high-tech weaponry reduces the utility of mass

**37**

armies), they may connive to disenfranchise ordinary citizens or at least to reduce their influence over legislation and especially over the distribution of wealth.

Human beings are not motivated by material incentives alone. They are also motivated, for example, by fairness. As anyone who has run an office knows, unfair treatment of co-workers destroys morale and therefore undermines efficiency. Hence, a boss who aims at maximizing productivity has a good reason to treat his workers fairly. Because the same logic applies to political organizations, including states, we may question Machiavelli's claim that justice never generates political loyalty. But, whatever he says about justice, Machiavelli never doubts that *injustice* courts subversion and resistance. And he also argues, quite explicitly, that perceived equity in the tax code is positively correlated with efficient tax collection.[15] The observation that people will stand patiently in line so long as they detect no presumptuous latecomers unfairly vaulting ahead suggests the value of equal treatment for the smooth functioning of social organizations. But none of this implies that fairness will automatically be forthcoming. Machiavelli's analysis suggests only that a political elite will treat fairly those groups whose cooperation it thinks it needs. "Selective impartiality" sounds like an oxymoron; but this is the principle upon which, following his analysis, all political organizations are based, presumably including territorial nation-states.

Democracy waxes and wanes. The determining factor is the perceived need of the political elite for cooperation from larger or smaller numbers of ordinary citizens. Machiavelli would want the emphasis here to fall on "perceived." A political elite may think it needs cooperation from ordinary citizens when it does not, although this is not very likely. It is much more common for the rich and powerful to be deluded into believing that they will never need the voluntary cooperation of the poor and the weak. Such myopia can be fatal, as progressives love to point out. But it can also happen that the rich and the powerful really do not need a great deal of active cooperation from ordinary citizens and know it.

The assumption that injustice is always politically destabilizing is equivalent to the pious belief that evildoers are automatically punished. As it turns out, the maintenance of injustice may actually be less destabilizing politically than a well-meaning attempt to alleviate the miseries of the worst off, who may ratchet up their demands unreasonably

---

[15] Ibid., I.55.

if their conditions abruptly improve. Unjust distributions of power and privilege do not necessarily trigger a healthy process of readjustment for a simple reason. While a political system may seem unfair to most people, most people do not necessarily count. And those who decidedly do count, the country's elite, often have a lucrative stake in maintaining current injustices. Poverty and injustice can be stabilized, if losers are kept disorganized and sedated into passivity, repressive organs are well nourished, spoils are distributed intramurally, and potential centers of opposition to the current dispensation are crushed or co-opted as they arise. Therefore, liberal democracy is far from being the preordained destiny of mankind. Under certain circumstances, nevertheless, it can emerge and become fairly stable. In trying to explain why and when, Machiavelli stresses the importance of foreign threats. But other factors may conceivably produce similar effects.

## The Sweetness of Self-Inflicted Wounds

Force is sometimes described as a scarce resource because no political ruler has enough of it to work his will by repressive means against all his subjects simultaneously. At the very least he will have a hard time imposing himself on his own praetorian guard by threats of violence. The strongest is not strong enough if he does not manage to turn might into right. So the power of compulsion must always be supplemented by some other sources of power. Because the too-frequent use of force also has numerous unpleasant side effects, especially a tendency to spin out of control, political rulers, if given the choice, prefer that citizens obey the law voluntarily. This is an important reason why a prudent autocrat might willingly impose a degree of predictability on his own exercise of power.

To elicit the voluntary compliance from citizens that he plainly needs, a political ruler may voluntarily accept the discipline ordinarily associated with the rule of law. He can agree, for example, that his own commands assume a certain form. According to the standard list, a constitutional government maintains its legitimacy, and thereby ensures a relatively high degree of compliance, by issuing its commands in the form of general rules (not ad hoc instructions) that are spelled out publicly and in advance, that are understandable, that are mutually consistent, that are stable over time (though changeable), that are not retroactive, and that are enforced reliably by the various professional agencies that make up the system of justice, including an independent judiciary. Public readiness to comply also seems to increase if the government observably obeys its own rules, that is to say, if officials themselves pay taxes, go to jail for crimes, and so forth, and also cleave broadly to the constitution. Finally, it makes a difference if the public believes that rules are being enforced fairly, so that privileged groups with special access are not allowed to exempt themselves egregiously from laws that should apply to all.

In Rousseau's famous definition: "[O]bedience to a law one prescribes to oneself is freedom."[16] Machiavelli makes the same point, formulating it as an observation about the perversity of human psychology. Important actors will tend to accept a decision if they had a hand in making it. To increase the likelihood that the consuls would accept the authority of the dictator, the Roman "constitution" gave the consuls the right to choose the dictator. The rationale behind this assignment of the appointment power to important individuals, according to Machiavelli, was that "wounds and every other ill that a man does to himself spontaneously and by choice hurt much less than those that are done to you by someone else."[17] Hamilton makes the same point in a more familiar way: "Men often oppose a thing merely because they have had no agency in planning it."[18] By extrapolating on this pungent reasoning, we discover a possible reason why, under certain conditions, rulers with the means of repression in their hands might voluntarily embrace an extension of the suffrage.

Political rulers themselves are unlikely to ask, Why do political rulers submit themselves to constitutional restraints? However, they could ask another question, namely, Why do citizens sometimes freely agree to comply with the law? If citizens comply voluntarily with law when it is in their perceived self-interest to do so, then the prudent ruler, who wants to husband his resources, will try to make obedience to law seem to be, if not to be, in the self-interest of citizens. But, as Tocqueville follows Machiavelli in arguing, this is not a complete account of the most common rationale for citizen compliance with law. People also comply with the law for psychologically more subtle reasons, most notably because they are given a voice in the law-making process.[19] Just as no one will attack the institution of private property if he owns property himself, so the less fortunate members of society can be induced to respect authority by being given a small piece of authority. Rules agreed

[16] Rousseau, *The Social Contract*, I.8.
[17] Machiavelli, *Discourses on Livy*, I.34.
[18] *Federalist Papers* 70.
[19] Tocqueville, *Democracy in America* (1969: 240–1, 238, 224).

upon through consultations between regulators and regulated tend to work better than rules imposed by unilateral diktat. Such rules are better adapted to "reality on the ground" and are more likely to elicit cooperation from groundlings at the stage of implementation.

Even when laws thwart private interests, a degree of compliance can sometimes be obtained simply by a generous expansion of the suffrage, by granting all groups a "voice" in the legislative assembly. This is the democratic motive for compliance stressed by Tocqueville. Parental pride can to some extent replace self-interest as a motivation for adapting one's behavior to previously unknown, complex, and burdensome regulations. In America, Tocqueville claimed to discover that citizens were emotionally attached to their government because they took part in it and that they obeyed their laws because they participated in creating them.[20] More soberly, he adds that people who participate, even indirectly, in making laws (and in applying laws directly as jurors) are more likely to know what the laws actually say.[21] Active political participation also makes it more likely that citizens will understand the basic rationale behind new laws. Such an understanding significantly increases the likelihood of compliance. Finally, participants in the law-making process may comply, even if their interests are momentarily ignored, because they know that they will have a chance to change the law in the future. They submit to the law today because they believe they could change it tomorrow.[22] It is easier to tolerate a nuisance if one expects that, with enough effort, it could be removed. Analogously, ordinary people defer to the authority of public officials because they know they could oust them from office in the next election.[23]

## Sequencing Rights

The rich and the powerful often need the cooperation of the poor and the weak, but not always to the same degree. A ruler's strategic choice of means depends on, among other things, his changing beliefs, commitments, and goals. To the extent that a political ruler has a clear grasp of his situation, he will support extending private and political rights to ordinary citizens when he expects to need their cooperation not

---

[20] Ibid., 241, 237.
[21] Ibid., 304. The original reads: "C'est en participant à la législation que l'Américain apprend à connaître les lois."
[22] Ibid., 248, 241.
[23] Ibid., 205.

on a one-shot basis but over time. But he will eventually withdraw these rights, if he can, when he sees no enduring reason why such cooperation will prove particularly useful to him in the future. If Machiavelli's theory of the origins of the social contract is correct, we should expect that the development of push-button weaponry would reduce to some extent the concern of rulers for the well-being of the ruled, causing back-pedaling and a certain unraveling of the social contract.

But gated communities and prison-building programs cannot utterly decouple the serenity of the castle from the misery of the cottage, the prosperity of the suburb from the penury of the ghetto. As a result, even the most militant enemies of the welfare state, such as Thatcher and Reagan, did little to reduce the overall size of government transfer programs. Why not? A Machiavellian hypothesis would be that redistribution, far from being an expression of class warfare, is an alternative to it. Political and economic elites can embrace regulation in favor of workers and consumers as well as redistribution in favor of the disadvantaged because they see such arrangements as politically stabilizing. After all, as Aristotle commonsensically remarked, "when there are many who have no property and no honors they inevitably constitute a huge hostile element in the state."[24] Entitlements are the property of the poor. An extensive transfer system gives to even the worst-off members of the community a stake in the system of private property. When universal suffrage arrives, they have little interest in destroying a system of which they, too, are minor beneficiaries. Perhaps conservative politicians, as opposed to libertarian ideologues, remain wedded to certain forms of redistribution for this reason. An alternative hypothesis, which may not be so different, is that transfer programs serve the interests of groups with clout in the widest sense, which includes the ability to pester the truly mighty and keep them awake at night.

But before the poor come the rich. How and why are the property rights of the well-to-do protected from political authorities? This brings us back to that opening question, Why do people with guns obey orders from people without guns? Why do not the military and the police simply confiscate the property of wealthy and unarmed civilians? Why would a political ruler allow property rights to become entrenched? This is not necessarily a rational move. Not only does it require the ruler to sacrifice the short-term pleasures of rapacity, but if rich men feel supremely confident in their impregnable fortune, they may begin to give grief to those in power.

[24] Aristotle, *Politics*, 1281b30.

Sometimes armed authorities confiscate the wealth of the rich, or at least contrive to keep their property rights highly unstable. But sometimes they do not do this. When not, why not? A Machiavellian hypothesis would be that confiscatory politics, if taken to an extreme, is self-defeating, and people with guns know it. Not all extortionists, but at least the shrewder ones, can understand the folly of hacking to pieces the goose that lays golden eggs. They may restrict their "take" from local producers and shopkeepers, to prevent them from going out of business. Mancur Olson's (1993) famous distinction between "roving bandits" and "stationary bandits" is based on a similar assumption. Public predators, too, are potentially rational, and can therefore willingly restrict themselves. Tax collectors, scheming to increase their annual harvest, have a palpable interest in a thriving commerce.[25] Their legislative colleagues have the same motive to stay their hand and refrain from constantly rewriting the commercial code, for "What prudent merchant will hazard his fortunes in any new branch of commerce when he knows not but that his plans may be rendered unlawful before they can be executed?"[26]

An earlier version of this argument was advanced by David Hume in "On Commerce." If the Spanish fleet were destroyed, Hume begins, it would take decades to rebuild, whereas the Dutch fleet could be rebuilt and set afloat within months. Military resilience, in other words, depends to some extent upon the way the economy is governed. The Spanish government is arbitrary and autocratic, which means that its behavior is erratic, that it easily breaks its promises, and that all shipbuilding is under state control. The Dutch government is liberal, which means that its behavior is basically predictable, at least to the business community, and that it has granted legal certainty to private entrepreneurs who, confident in the security of their property rights, freely engage in all manner of industry and commerce, including shipbuilding and long-distance trade. Commercial shipbuilding is a vibrant part of the Dutch economy, as a result, and one that the government can temporarily commandeer in times of emergency and divert to military ends. Commercial seamen can also be drafted into the navy, at a moment's notice, and without damaging the life-sustaining productivity of domestic agriculture.

Although they can be extracted by force, taxes flow more easily if perceived to be legitimate. The business community accepts high

---

[25] *Federalist Papers* 60.
[26] *Federalist Papers* 62.

wartime contribution to national defense because it knows that its wealth was accumulated under the protection of the public power. Without the state, a rich man can own his property only the way a dog "owns" his bone, which means insecurely, and without any capacity to sell, lease, mortgage, or bequeath it. Because wealthy individuals also understand that a military victory by a foreign army may destroy or diminish their own personal wealth, they will ante up taxes to prevent it. By making its own behavior predictable, in short, the Dutch government conjured out of a previously sluggish economy a suddenly wealthy and grateful group of "partisan friends." The self-restraint of "those with guns" balloons the resources available to the government to achieve its most vital ends.

This analytical fable suggests that political rulers choose liberalism when they see the growth of private commercial fortunes as an asset rather than a threat. Hume's recounting of the Dutch case also brings us close to the idea of special interests as we now conceive them. Special interests play a central role in every liberal-democratic regime. Whatever autonomy we attribute to the American law, we would not want to claim that it is untouched by the corporate or class interests of American business. Nor have laws affecting, say, the legal or medical professions developed without any sensitivity to the perceived self-interest of lawyers and physicians. Law begins as an instrument of political rulers but at some point begins to serve them by protecting the interests of organized social interests on whose voluntary cooperation rulers acutely depend.

The question is, What do we want to make of the influence of special interests on the laws before which all citizens are supposed to be treated equally? To assert that "the rule of law" has nothing to do with special-interest legislation is to admit, implicitly, that the rule of law has never existed anywhere at any time. This may not be the most useful approach to the rule of law, although it admittedly registers an appropriate moral disquiet with unequal access to law-making power.

A slight detour may help us make some progress on this front. In the early 1990s, a good deal of Russian legislation was being drafted by foreign experts and, surprisingly often, was quickly elevated into valid law, by either legislative action or presidential decree. Enigmatic, however, was the seemingly universal acceptance of domination of the domestic law-making process by sketchily informed foreigners. Even more curious, and closely related, was the virtual absence of special-interest legislation. Why was there so little special-interest legislation in early 1990s Russia? Had Russian law attained overnight a degree of impartiality or neutrality of which Western countries could only dream? The correct answer is revealing. It turned out, upon inspection, that almost no important domestic Russian actor expected laws or decrees to be reliably implemented. Parties whose conduct was presumably being regulated were therefore not very interested in shaping the law at the level of parliament. Instead, they focused on finding a low price for one-go export permits at the ministerial level and ad hoc immunities at the level of enforcement. Russians with clout serenely consigned the law-making process to foreign consultants, while keeping the buying and selling of de facto exemptions to themselves.

The Russian case suggests that special-interest legislation has an ambivalent relation to the rule of law and is not a purely sinister development. The rule of law, as we commonly understand it, is likely to emerge when two conditions are present simultaneously: when the political ruler has a good reason to make his own behavior predictable and when profit seekers start asking for rules. We have discussed the first condition, so what about the second? To examine when profit seekers start asking for rules is to examine the origins of the rule of law in special-interest legislation.

As a society becomes politically freer, it is perfectly natural for organized interests increasingly to voice their special concerns and press for modifications of overly general legal rules to suit their particular circumstances. Well-organized groups press for special dispensations, tailor-made laws, to be woven into the regulatory framework. Freedom, therefore, naturally stimulates the "growth of the state." Such a development is driven not by the ambitions of bureaucrats, as some conservatives argue, but by the capacity of private groups to press their demands effectively. States swell in size along with irrepressible social demands. This is why it has proved virtually impossible to "shrink the state" in advanced capitalist democracies where the population is steadily graying and retired cohorts are disproportionately likely to vote. On the other hand, it *has* proved possible to shrink the state and cut back on cradle-to-grave benefits in postcommunist countries. This is because the burdens of eldercare, jettisoned by the state, have been transferred onto the shoulders of women, who have no "voice" or capacity to refuse. Universal suffrage provides seemingly little leverage, perhaps because swing votes can be easily purchased or perhaps because apparently competing parties are secretly in league. In any case, elites know how to funnel resources to themselves while making the public coffers look empty, thereby deflecting redistributive demands. The elderly citizens who continue to vote in high proportions have no special political access.

**45**

And none of the groups with clout has the slightest interest in pressuring the government to improve health care for the elderly and the sick.

We are used to thinking of special-interest legislation as devoid of normative content. Indeed, it is sometimes described as a form of "corruption," where private interests colonize public institutions, where rules that ought to serve all citizens equally are warped to the advantage of a few. Back-room manipulation of the law-making process seems the most commonplace way in which norms of fairness are violated and democratic accountability breaks down. Individuals and groups are partial to themselves. They should not therefore (from the standpoint of impartial justice) be judges in their own cases. When self-interested groups become judges in their own cases, as they do in every functioning democracy, laws become "the unjust envoys of the unjust passions of lawmakers."[27]

But the Russian experience suggests that we abstain for a moment from moral disapproval. It helps us see special-interest legislation somewhat differently, if not as an ideal, at least as an accomplishment, and not necessarily a negligible or costless one. Looked at from the postcommunist perspective, in fact, special-interest legislation appears not as a deviation from but as a step toward democracy and the rule of law. The dissolution of an autocratic government that labored to silence private voices naturally releases the self-seeking of the few groups that are well-organized enough to become judges in their own cases. The vast majority cannot organize to exert political leverage and is therefore a great loser in such a system. But if the few winners begin to codify their partiality in written legislation that is reliably enforced, the system they create begins to resemble not anarchy but an inchoate form of democracy and the rule of law.

The pressure exerted by special interests to incorporate into generally applicable legislation regulations designed to promote their private advantage can, as mentioned, be viewed as a form of corruption. But this is not a completely satisfying label, because the rise of special-interest legislation is also the beginning of a process whereby political authorities, with the means of repression in their hands, are drawn into consultative relations with nonpolitical actors. The ruler who starts down this road accepts limits on his own discretion, in the name of the reliance interest of property owners, despite the challenge to his own rule that this may pose, for the sake of the long-term benefits of cooperation. The liberal project is not to wipe out this kind of corruption but rather to extend it

---

[27] Rousseau, *The Social Contract*, II.7.

to include those it originally locks out. To pursue this theme, we turn from Machiavelli to Rousseau.

## Lineages of Equality before the Law

According to Rousseau, special-interest legislation is the quintessence of corruption: "[W]hen particular interests begin to make themselves felt and sectional societies [*les petites sociétés*] begin to exert an influence over the greater society, the common interest becomes corrupt." If the fairness of a criminal trial depends on the social group to which the defendant belongs, we should cry "corruption" and complain about the violation of the rule of law. Because the wealthy routinely dominate the legislative process, Rousseau also informs us, "laws are invariably useful to those who own property and harmful to those who do not."[28] In every known society, he continues, "iniquitous decrees that aim to protect only particular interests are passed under the false name of 'Laws.' "[29] The only way to abolish such special-interest legislation would be to make sure that "there should be no sectional associations in the state."[30] But this cannot be done.

Corruption is inevitable, Rousseau insists, because organized interests, with varying degrees of power, irrepressibly emerge in every society. A few powerful groups naturally sprout forth and cannot be prevented from manipulating law for their private advantage. Special-interest legislation, however unjust, is therefore not the exception but the rule: "The universal spirit of the Laws of all countries is always to favor the strong against the weak, and the one who has against the one who has nothing. This inconvenience is inevitable, and it is without exception."[31] The poor man initially delights in the social contract, believing it to be a league for mutual relief and benefit; but he soon discovers that it is a swindle designed to benefit the rich. The rich man will always use his influence to make, interpret, and apply laws to serve his narrow class interests, disregarding the needs and fears of most of his fellow citizens.

In behaving this way, the rich disclose the darkest truth about human nature. Whenever they can, people will avoid an equal sharing of burdens. If they can get away with it, they will engross sweet pleasures

[28] Ibid., I.9.
[29] Ibid., IV.1; "on fait passer faussement sous le nom des Loix des décrets iniques qui n'ont pour but que l'intérêt particulier."
[30] Ibid., II.3.
[31] Rousseau, *Émile* (1969: 524).

and gratifications for themselves and their immediate circle and offload thankless tasks and noxious living conditions upon others. They are programmed by nature to dislike justice. They want rights without responsibilities and are eager to exempt themselves from generally applicable rules. Because such partiality and favoritism cannot be eradicated from the human heart, a would-be polluter will reason as follows: the good I personally derive by polluting far outweighs the bad it will cause me, even though I would benefit if no one was ever allowed to pollute. The best outcome, of course, is for all others to obey the rules, while I exempt myself. Rational choice theory has made us all familiar with this ostensibly iron logic. Rousseau introduced it to illustrate that human beings cannot escape from Original Sin.[32] Because human beings often think in this sinful way, man-made laws will always reflect special interests and will therefore never be truly legitimate. To be ruled impartially – that is, "by laws not men" – would be possible only for a population of gods.

Rousseau echoes the liberal claim that the unity of legislative and executive power is the very definition of tyranny. Such a unity is pernicious precisely because it permits special-interest legislation. In particular, it allows lawmakers to make draconian laws with the certainty that these laws will never be applied to themselves or their families. A clean separation between legislative and executive powers, by contrast, would compel lawmakers, while making laws, to adopt the standpoint of average citizens, that is, to sympathize with those who will be punished if they disobey the law. This ideal is never realized in practice. In the United States, for instance, the kind of separation of powers Rousseau describes does not exist. When white legislators attach harsh penalties to the consumption of drugs consumed by blacks and lenient penalties to the consumption of drugs consumed by whites, they are promoting special-interest legislation, in Rousseau's sense. This is made possible by the fact that executive and legislative and judicial power alike all lie in the hands of a single dominant group. White legislators know that those who belong to their own privileged social network will not have to live under the tough-on-crime bills that predominantly affect blacks. Those who make, interpret, and apply America's laws would not be so easily reconciled to America's high per capita incarceration rate, for example, were their own children being so frequently locked up. Formulated in Rousseau's language, they are judges in their own case, as if they were still living in the state of nature.

---

[32] Rousseau, *The Social Contract*, IV.1.

Although low expectations are in order, abandoning all hope is not. The malady of special-interest legislation cannot be cured; but its symptoms can be periodically and temporarily assuaged. Law can never serve all members of a community equally, but it can serve a relatively large proportion of ordinary citizens, rather than the rich alone. Inequality cannot be abolished; but if it is somewhat reduced, then the predatory violence, humiliation, dependency, and unpredictability inflicted on the weak can be kept under control.[33] With this in mind, Rousseau delivers the following piece of sage advice: "[I]f there are sectional associations, it is wise to multiply their number and to prevent inequality among them."[34] Here, the great scourge of interest-group liberalism suggests a strategy usually associated with James Madison and Robert Dahl. Instead of trying to repress organized interests, we should strive to multiply them.

In a perfectly just society, legislation would be perfectly neutral and impartial. Laws would embody the perfect fairness, untainted by partiality or favoritism, that Rousseau associated with the General Will. Such laws would not prove more useful to well-organized groups than to poorly organized groups. Given the deep roots of human partiality, however, such an ideal society cannot exist. In real as opposed to imaginary societies, Rousseau argues, law is always an instrument of partial interests. This is not to say that law is *nothing but* a stick with which the strong beat the weak. Recognizing the connection between law and group interest does not require us to abandon the important distinction between *rule of law* and *rule by law*. We simply need to reformulate the distinction to make it compatible with observable behavior. We can do this along the lines laid down by Rousseau.

Although he did not employ these particular phrases, Rousseau's principal contribution to legal theory is his idea that, in existing societies, rule of law and rule by law occupy a single continuum and do not present mutually exclusive options. The contrast signals a difference of degree, not of kind. All states rule through law to some extent. This tool, like every other, inevitably imposes certain restrictions on its user. How confining are these restrictions? How is the government's residual discretion disciplined? In whose interest is it called to account? How predictable do these restrictions make the government's behavior to which groups?

---

[33] Ibid., II.11.
[34] Ibid.

According to Rousseau, law is always a tool of the rich as well as the powerful. It codifies an agreement between political rulers and the most wealthy citizens for their joint advantage. But power and wealth are distributed differently in different societies and in the same society at different times. Sometimes power and wealth are monopolized by a few; at other times, they are more widely dispersed. A crude kind of rule by law is predominant in the first case, whereas a more equitable rule of law emerges in the second. Law is equally instrumental in both cases. Even when we get as close as is humanly possible to ideal justice, the legal system will still respond favorably to influential groups trying to shape and apply law in pursuit of their partial interests. The difference between systems that approximate the rule of law and systems that rely on rule by law lies not in the nature of law, therefore. The difference lies in polyarchy, the multiplication of influential groups, the pluralistic organization of power. When power and wealth become widely dispersed, law becomes not a stick used by the few against the many but a two-edged sword.

Extrapolating from Rousseau's analysis, we can draw the following conclusion. Societies may approximate the rule of law if they consist of a large number of power-wielding groups, comprising a majority of the population, and if none of them becomes so strong as to be able thoroughly to dominate the others. All justice is victor's justice. But the more democratic a society becomes, the more victors there are, the larger the proportion of citizens who are strong enough to wield effectively the "stick" of law. We cannot replace special-interest law making and law enforcement with general-interest law making and law enforcement. But Rousseau's framework, while mocking utopian hopes, does not condemn us to misanthropy. For we may be able to loosen the grip of a few organized interests on power by forcing them to share political leverage with a variety of other groups. This is polyarchy; it is also rough justice, the only kind human beings will ever experience. Formulated differently, the balancing of many partialities is the closest we can come to impartiality. This may not sound particularly ideal, but it is nevertheless historically quite rare and very difficult to achieve.

It is much more common, in fact, for legal instruments to be employed, with various degrees of injustice, to serve the joint and several interests of the government and the wealthy. A government's use of legal instruments to silence its critics and a slaveholder's use of legal instruments to retrieve a fugitive slave are two examples of this kind of rule by law. On the more liberal pole of Rousseau's spectrum, law can be used, with varying degrees of justice, to serve the interests of a broad swath of society, including some of the uneducated and the poor. A realistic example of rule of law would therefore be a criminal suspect's use of legal instruments to reveal that the police fabricated evidence in his case. We associate the rights of due process, including timely "notice" and the right to confront adverse witnesses, with the rule of law because they are tools that can help relatively weak parties protect themselves against those who otherwise wield considerably more power.

Rule by law is dominant when a few privileged groups – say, landlords, employers, producers, and creditors – control the use of discretion in legislative, adjudicative, and law enforcement processes. The rule of law, by contrast, is ascendant when tenants as well as landlords, employees as well as employers, debtors as well as creditors, wives as well as husbands, and consumers as well as producers can use the law to protect their interests. The moral dimension of this arrangement can be brought to light by the following consideration. If all organized interests renounce violence and resort to the same body of law and the same legal system to protect their interests and carry out their purposes, they are implicitly *relativizing* their personal claims on collective assets, admitting that their perspective is partial and that they do not deserve to prevail in every case. To paraphrase Rousseau again, justice cannot be achieved on this earth, but it can be approximated if corruption (influence by groups with special objectives on laws binding equally on all members of the community), instead of being monopolized by a few, is spread widely through a society that accepts the legitimacy of its own pluralism.

To say that "law is a tool of the powerful" is not to embrace or promote cynicism. Rather, it is to offer advice to anyone who wants to come to the help of the oppressed. If you aim to protect the rights of women, organize a women's movement. If you want to protect the civil rights of black Americans, organize a civil rights movement. Law is not contaminated simply because it is an instrument of power. The degree of justice or injustice depends on who wields power and for what ends.

To Rousseau's pluralistic theory of the rule of law, we can add the idea of elite competition as another condition for approximating liberal justice. Imagine a society in which the laws governing the health system were, at first, essentially written by doctors to serve the interests of doctors. Patients themselves, we can stipulate, do not have enough political clout to revise legislation in their own interests. At some point, another corporate group (call them lawyers) may sit up and take notice of the enormous profits being earned by doctors and contrive to take a cut. Such a rechanneling of income streams is very difficult to achieve, however, without alleging some overriding public interest. Thus, lawyers help rewrite legislation governing the health system to take patients' rights into account. They are happy to do this because, alongside whatever benevolent motives they may have, they can insinuate themselves as for-profit managers of the just interests of patients. The public interest is served indirectly, as the by-product of competition for scarce resources among competing elites. Norms of justice and ideas of the common good are not politically powerless, therefore; but they can be asserted most effectively when rival unjust interests are relatively well balanced. By and large, in the struggle among organized interests that we call politics, the power of norms is a tipping power. If other forces are correctly aligned, the common good can occasionally prevail. But, as Rousseau endlessly reminds us, this seldom occurs.

Unlike a tort, a crime is allegedly an injury to the community as a whole. But societies do not ordinarily determine the relative heinousness of felonies and misdemeanors by considering the interests and aspirations of all citizens equally. Put crudely, we usually label as "crimes" those transgressions that harm the interests of "the ruling class." As Rousseau would be quick to add, this ruling class can be large or small. In the United States, it is fairly large, which does not always make its special-interest legislation morally appealing. Because whites have more influence over law than blacks, possession of powder cocaine is treated more leniently than possession of crack cocaine. To the extent that men have more influence on law than women, legislation affecting forms of assault that affect women only may bear traces of a peculiarly male point of view. All legal systems are unjust to some degree. But the greater the percentage of citizens trapped among the permanent losers, who are never able to use the law to protect their interests, the more we can say, following Rousseau's analysis, that the system resembles rule by law and deviates egregiously from liberal justice.

According to Rousseau, when the rich and the powerful league together to shape laws in their joint interest, disregarding the concerns of ordinary citizens, they in effect secede from the larger society. They create a tiny republican enclave for themselves, based on consent, and treat the remaining inhabitants of the territory more or less as livestock. Elite separatism can be either stable or unstable. Rousseau insists that such a move, implying that the excluded can be ruled by force, *justifies* rebellion. But this does not imply that rebellion is necessarily feasible. A two-track legal system, or a dual state, giving predictability to a few and unpredictability to many, will not look legitimate in the eyes of ordinary citizens. But ruling groups are not always worried about a generalized perception of the illegitimacy of the current distribution of power and privilege. What matters to them is that lethally armed Interior Ministry troops and other groups whose cooperation they need believe that the regime is legitimate. True, unequal treatment undermines the willingness to cooperate. And the poor will not comply voluntarily with law if they observe the rich obeying laws that suit their special interests and disregarding laws that thwart their special interests. But those on top do not necessarily care that those on the bottom view the whole system as morally rotten. They care only about the perceptions of those whose cooperation they need. The others, presumably, can be walled in or walled out.

## Rules That Rouse a Sleeping Power

Up to this point, I have been assuming, following Machiavelli and Rousseau, that law is a tool of power. Although this assumption is fair, and superior to the notion that law descends upon societies from a Heaven of Higher Norms, it is incomplete, because rules can also create or constitute power or summon power from out the vasty deep. This is especially but not exclusively true of constitutional rules. Machiavelli and Rousseau knew this perfectly well.

The powerful choose to rule through laws when this method of governance magnifies as well as stabilizes their rule. Laws that magnify power, strictly speaking, are not instruments of power but rather tools of the ambition for power. For instance, a ruler can choose to rule through *general* laws because he does not have enough time to make ad hoc decisions on thousands of individual cases scattered throughout a large domain. While increasing the range of the ruler's writ, generality decreases discretion. The ruler may accept this voluntarily, however, because discretion is a burden as well as a benefit. For one thing, it takes too much time.

The most elemental weakness of the powerful, however, is their mortality. Their jewel boxes may be overflowing, but tsars and emperors nevertheless have to die and be entombed. So how can they compensate for this, their most vexing physical debility? For one thing, they can identify emotionally with their biological descendants. Because of the veil of ignorance that separates the future from the present, they cannot know where their descendants will end up in their society's future distribution of power and privilege. Mortality therefore gives the powerful, to the extent that they are in the grip of family feeling, at least some incentive to organize society in a way that protects people out of power from people in power. Admittedly, this real-world analogue to Rawls's hypothetical original position influences political decision making only weakly and episodically. That helps explain why the emergence of liberalism is always slow, fragile, and reversible.

Nevertheless, if certain elements of constitutionalism emerge even in autocratic regimes, the mortality of the ruler is one reason why. Historically, ruling groups seem to accept constitutional or semiconstitutional limits on power before they accept democratic methods for selecting leaders. The ruling groups that surround a monarch, knowing that he will not live forever, organize rules of succession with his consent. He gives his consent presumably because the fantasy of his bloodline continuing to occupy the throne blunts the sting of personal mortality. Rules of success, which limit discretion and provide some predictability, form the core of the constitution of a monarchical regime. A royal constitution is a step beyond personal rule, creating "the king's two bodies." When the old king expires, his successor is elevated immediately to the throne. Admittedly, the rules for identifying a successor are complicated and do not always decide all controversies, so discretion will be exercised, although secretively.

The need to avoid chaos during an interregnum is a lasting problem of all political regimes, democratic as well as monarchical, because elected leaders too can die. So the most basic weakness of mankind, namely mortality, reveals another fundamental sense in which power, including the power of democratic regimes, is dependent on the rule of law. The perceived need to manage destabilizing interregna helps explain why the powerful, whatever the level of foreign threat, sometimes choose to rule through law. Law can be enabling rather than disabling. In the private realm, too, laws of inheritance do not limit merely but actually create the power to bequeath property to an heir. Without probate courts to settle disputes over inheritance (and the legislation governing the decisions of such courts), it would be impossible for the living to impart residual force to their desires after their own deaths. In both cases, the law prolongs the efficacy of will across the border separating the living from the dead. Because it is as much an instrument of will as a restraint on will, it can be and is voluntarily employed by people who wish to consolidate and extend their power.

As a follower of Machiavelli, Hamilton elaborates creatively upon the way rules can create power in *Federalist* 28. Because unforeseeable emergencies, including foreign invasion and domestic insurrection, are bound to occur, government must be granted the right to raise a regular army as well as the discretionary ability to use it in ways not fixed in advance. A foreign or domestic enemy will not act according to rules; and the power to resist such an enemy must therefore remain equally unshackled. But how can the framers of a constitution prevent such a dangerous discretion from being misused? Formulated more generally, what prevents the national representatives of the people, once the power to raise a regular army is placed in their hands, from betraying the people and acting for their own corporate self-interest?

As Napoleon, Hamilton's contemporary, showed, deliberative forums do not present a serious obstacle to a political ruler who controls a standing army. The only effective inhibition, Hamilton therefore writes, is the expectation of rebellion. Here we return to the Przeworski thesis, but with a twist. The threat of armed rebellion is not credible in most republics, for a variety of reasons. First, citizens usually remain unaware of the looming seizure of power until it is too late and a military clampdown has already occurred. Second, even if they become aware of tyranny-in-the-making, citizens are atomized and have a difficult time organizing promptly any kind of effective resistance against a militarily well-equipped central government. Third, even if they become aware and begin to organize, the would-be tyrant will spy their incipient resistance and crush it in the bud.

The solution to this problem, argues Hamilton, is a republic of republics, borrowed from Machiavelli. The *Discourses* was such an important book for the American Framers, because Machiavelli was first and foremost an anticolonial theorist. His greatest aspiration was to identify a founder able to forge a league among the Italian republics and to drive out the foreign powers, Spain and France. If the Italian city-republics did not successfully band together into a union, he reasoned, then the occupying powers would exploit conflicts among them to consolidate their domination. Only a robust union among the republics, based on a sense of common destiny, could lead them to pool their efforts and counteract the colonial policy of divide and rule. This sense of common nationhood could not thrive under a prince but only if all Italy was organized as a republic – indeed, as a republic of republics. Machiavelli conceives this union as a cure for myopia in a very special sense. If the individual republics remained disunited, then foreign powers will use salami tactics to pick them off one at a time. Those who are not being attacked at the moment will delude themselves into thinking their turn will never come. They will be wrong.

This was Hamilton's reasoning exactly. Because they are focused on political events, local leaders at the state level will apprehend usurpation by the federal rulers before the people, who are normally busy with other matters, would notice them. Read in the light of *Federalist* 28, the Second Amendment does not protect the right of an individual gun-slinger to shoot an intruder, for that would be tantamount to providing constitutional cover to every potential assassin who believed he had just conversed with a vengeful divinity. Instead, the Second Amend-ment protects "that original right of self-defense which is paramount to all positive forms of government,"[35] namely the right of state citizens to participate in collective armed resistance against federal usurpation un-der the direction of elected state magistrates in the context of organized state militias.[36]

Elected state governments give the right of rebellion hands and feet. They solve the perennial collective action problem that has usually pre-vented the popular majority from responding effectively to the outrages of a well-organized minority. Hamilton speaks here of "regular measures for defense," to be distinguished from an irregular and impermissible resort to arms by private individuals, unguided by local magistrates.[37] Not only constitutionally but actually as well, citizens can protect them-selves against government exclusively by means of government: "Power being almost always the rival of power."[38] The multitude without leaders is not a political force. It will melt away when confronted, unable to keep a united front under attack. Only recognized political leaders can rally the troops, keep the multitude disciplined and unified enough for supe-rior numbers to prevail over the well-organized few. Local magistrates, presumably bathed in electoral legitimacy, will use state assemblies and horizontal committees of correspondence to marshal resistance and co-ordinate efforts by the several states. Thus will tyranny be deterred. Fearing "an immediate revolt of the great body of the people, headed and directed by the State governments,"[39] the national leadership will be kept in check. Because the republic of republics is large and sub-divided, it will be easier to work up such a resistance into an effective fighting force by stealth, before the federal tyrants have an opportunity to stamp it out. If the people at large, once alerted, agree with their local magistrates that the federal power is acting tyrannically, they will throw their considerable weight into the cause of rebellion, which will then necessarily succeed. Anticipating such a reaction, federal authorities

[35] *Federalist Papers* 28.
[36] Historically, the right of rebellion never belonged to people individually but only to the collected people under the supervision of its local magistrates. See Skinnner (1978).
[37] *Federalist Papers* 28.
[38] Ibid.
[39] *Federalist Papers* 60.

will be very unlikely to embark on such a course. People with guns obey people without guns because the latter, it turns out, have rifles stashed in their closets.

Hamilton's analysis is based on an implicit distinction between dormant power and active power. The people at large have the power to resist tyranny, but that power is merely latent because the people are inattentive or busy and also poorly organized. The federal system, as he describes it in *Federalist* 28, does not create power where none exists, but rather puts in place a series of alarm bells and rallying devices that will be triggered in case the federal authorities visibly move to seize power. In an emergency, constitutional rules will transform dormant power into active power. They do so by giving "select bodies of men,"[40] namely local leaders, an incentive to call up the reserve army of the people, which would otherwise be too dispersed and inattentive to respond in a forceful and timely manner. This arrangement is closely related to the mechanism described by Barry Weingast (1997): a liberal constitution draws a "bright line" beyond which the government is forbidden to go. If the government crosses that line, then all social groups will league together to resist, even those groups whose interests are not immediately affected, on the grounds that only tightly united and coordinated opposition can prevent the strategic use of salami tactics by a shrewd tyrant.

### Dependency Denial as the Opium of the Rich

A final weakness of the strong is their self-destructive arrogance and overconfidence. Western literature is full of colorful illustrations; and this is also Machiavelli's principal concern. The rich and powerful get into trouble because they begin to believe that the world owes them a living. Revolving-door CEOs who parlay their previous public service and associated foreign access into lucrative business contracts claim that they made their money wholly on their own, with no help from their fellow citizens. You sometimes get the impression that the rich never take government-inspected elevators or drive on publicly funded highways. The problem, in brief, is amnesia. The rich and powerful tend to forget their actual dependence on cooperation by the weak and poor, whose pooled resources are managed by our common representative government. Great property owners sometimes seem oblivious to the fact that they would own nothing were not the borders of their country protected

---

[40] *The Federalist Papers* 28.

by the monetary and personal contributions of ordinary citizens. This is why they sometimes act in appallingly brazen ways, as if the rest of society had no right making any demands at all upon them. These outrages may eventually excite a backlash, at least in the form of sabotage and perhaps in the form of revolt.

A Machiavellian constitution maker, faced with such an amnesiac elite, will do his best to counteract his group's tendency to self-defeating arrogance. He will, first and foremost, replace hereditary recruitment to high office with elections.[41] He will do this not because heredity confers power on fools, but because periodic elections help *remind* the elite of what it has a tendency to forget, that it depends on voluntary cooperation by the poor. Machiavelli resorts to the figure of a Great Founder or constitution maker here because he recognizes that a privileged class is unlikely to recognize its own tendency to overconfidence or to arrange, of its own sweet will, to have itself periodically humbled. It should be willing to subject itself to an occasional spanking in order to correct its inane fantasy that the rich do not depend on the poor. It should be willing to do this for the sake of preserving its power over the long term, but it will not. While such a system cannot be put in place by design, however, it can come into being unintentionally, by chance. Afterward, the lucky city will flourish because of its constitution's beneficial effects. Such, says Machiavelli, was the story of Rome.

A political system that guarantees basic liberties for most citizens, allowing them "voice opportunities" in the law-making and policy-making process and redistributing considerable wealth in their direction (in the form of publicly funded education and so forth), is what Machiavelli and his predecessors would have called a "mixed regime."[42] Such a regime is stable, he argues, largely because it is tumultuous. That is to say, the poor never let the rich forget their presence. As a consequence, the rich tend not to go overboard, ultimately provoking a real insurrection, as they would do if they could live in pure acoustical separation from the poor.

---

[41] One of the greatest defects of tyrannical governments is the tendency of tyrants to view all talented associates as potential rivals. This is not paranoia, necessarily; but even if it is realistic, its consequence is to deprive the community of talented contributors to the public weal. Multiparty democracy is a well-designed solution to this problem. Even if Helmut Kohl managed to eliminate all talented individuals – that is to say, potential rivals – from his own entourage, he was not able to eliminate them from the ranks of the other party. This is one way that a democratic constitution can protect a ruling elite from its own myopia.

[42] Machiavelli's predecessors in elaborating this theory include Polybius as well as Aristotle.

This analysis implies that active and even boisterous citizenship is essential for the rule of law. Laws against public-sector corruption, for instance, will remain dormant and ineffective unless ordinary citizens become engaged and alert enough to pressure public officials into disciplining each other, something they are unlikely to do of their own sweet will, whatever the written law. In a democratic society, in other words, a certain degree of initiative from ordinary citizens, beyond a willingness to stand in line on election day, is a precondition for law to function as it should. The right to sue abusive officials on the basis of a statute requires just as much activism on the part of the individual rights holder as the right to vote. This is why Machiavelli insisted that laws have to be "brought to life by the virtue of a citizen who rushes spiritedly to execute them."[43] On-paper rights, however much fanfare they are given, will be worth little without the capacity to use them. This is why the distinction between rights talk and virtue talk rings hollow. If ordinary citizens do not learn how to use the tool of law effectively for their own purposes, public officials and their privileged partners will know what to do.

Machiavelli's concern for the self-defeating arrogance of political rulers is echoed by Juan Linz (1994) in his essays favoring parliamentary over presidential government. His position, basically, is that a popularly elected president may be enticed into omnipotence fantasies and may, as a result, embrace extreme policies, even without the consent of a society's most important forces, whose consent he actually needs. Anyone who deeply believes that he deserves to have his way 100% of the time will "betray strong symptoms of impatience and disgust at the least sign of opposition from any other quarter."[44] A prime minister in a coalition government has a very different perspective on the world. His political style will be more moderate and conciliatory. He knows that he cannot get anything done without constant negotiations with his coalition partners. For this reason he will not be shocked and furious that he cannot fly or accomplish other impossible feats. He adopts a moderate political style because the form of government prevents him from forgetting his dependency on cooperation and therefore compromise.

## What Can (and Cannot) Be Done?

The suggestion that the rich and the powerful will sometimes voluntarily surrender a part of their wealth and power naturally excites a

---

[43] Machiavelli, *Discourses*, III.1.

[44] *Federalist Papers* 71.

skeptical response. Political and economic elites, who are all-too-human in this respect, often fail to be behave justly even when it is in their manifest interest to do so. This is sometimes because they distrust each other too much to cooperate even when they know where their true interests lie. At other times it is simply because they are lazily myopic and fail to think ahead. Intellectuals make a great deal of this failure of the rich and the powerful to look ahead, however. Perhaps they make too much of it because it presents one of the few moments in which intellectuals, who claim to specialize in curing myopia, believe they can play a decisive political role.

But, like Machiavelli, Linz and other constitutional theorists assume that political and economic elites *can* be convinced by argument and evidence to accept limits on their own power. They will do so, it is thought, if they can be convinced that self-restraint is the only way they can overcome or at least manage their own self-defeating impulses. Political scientists tend to agree that the rich and the powerful are not always so far-seeing. At other times, moreover, the rich and the powerful see well enough ahead and correctly conclude that they have nothing to fear from a refusal to share either prosperity or power. They will change their minds only when they begin to believe that they need voluntary cooperation from groups whose interests they currently disregard. An adept ruler, as discussed, can keep his subject population passive and disorganized. By employing various divide-and-rule strategies, a small ruling group can insulate itself from the threat of revolt. This situation can be relatively stable because, without an active citizenry, the incentives facing an entrenched elite are unlikely to change.

In such a situation, only an external shock is likely to provoke an internal transformation. If local elites are suddenly threatened by foreign elites, they will have a very powerful reason to restrain themselves. They may even choose to transfer legal certainty, individual rights, and democratic influence downward, widening the circles of consultation and granting legal access to ordinary citizens. In this way they can hope to transform their subject populations into stakeholders of the domestic regime. On the other hand, if local elites become partners or clients of foreign elites, they will be sorely tempted to create a nonparticipatory, nonredistributive, regulatory, and repressive regime. A caricature of the rule of law may emerge in such a setting; but it will provide predictability and serviceable use of legal instruments only to a very few.

## References

Aristotle. 1992. *The Politics*. Trans. T. A. Sinclair. Rev. Trevor J. Saunders. Harmondsworth: Penguin.

*The Federalist Papers*. 1961. New York: Mentor.

Hume, David. 1985. "Of Commerce." In *Essays Moral, Political, and Literary*. Indianapolis: Liberty Classics.

Linz, Juan. 1994. "Presidential or Parliamentary Democracy: Does it Make a Difference?" In Juan J. Linz and Arturo Valenzuela (eds.), *The Failure of Presidential Democracy: Comparative Perspectives*. Baltimore: Johns Hopkins University Press.

Machiavelli, Niccolò. 1966. *Discourses on Livy*. Trans. Harvey C. Mansfield and Nathan Tarcov. Chicago: University of Chicago Press.

1985. *The Prince*. Trans. Harvey C. Mansfield. Chicago: University of Chicago Press.

Olson, Mancur. 1993. "Dictatorship, Democracy, and Development." *American Political Science Review* 87, 3: 567–76.

Rousseau, Jean-Jacques. 1969. *Émile*. In *Oeuvres complètes*, vol. 4. Paris: Pléiade.

Shakespeare, William. 1966. *The Tragedy of Coriolanus*. Ed. Reuben Brower. New York: Signet.

Skinnner, Quentin. 1978. *The Foundations of Modern Political Thought*. Vol. 2. Cambridge: Cambridge University Press.

Strayer, Joseph R. 1970. *On the Medieval Origins of the Modern State*. Princeton: Princeton University Press.

Tocqueville, Alexis de. 1969. *Democracy in America*. New York: Harper and Row.

Weber, Max. 1994. "Suffrage and Democracy in Germany." In Peter Lassman and Ronald Speirs (eds.), *Political Writings*. Cambridge: Cambridge University Press.

Weingast, Barry. 1997. "The Political Foundations of Democracy and the Rule of Law." In José María Maravall and Adam Przeworski (eds.), *The Rule of Law*. New York: Cambridge University Press.

## Chapter Two

# Power, Rules, and Compliance

General Pinochet warned in October 1989, a few weeks before Chile's first democratic elections after the 1988 referendum, that "if someone touches one of my men, the rule of law is over" (si me tocan a uno de mis hombres, se acabó el Estado de Derecho). There seems to be something profoundly paradoxical about the general's subtle warning. It implies that the existence of the rule of law depends on the will of a single person, but part of the meaning of the rule of law is precisely that the institutional order is something other than the product of a single will.

This is usually misunderstood by those who discuss the rule of law. They often affirm that the point is to institute "a government of laws, not of men." Yet this statement is at best ambiguous. A government cannot consist of laws. A government of laws can only mean that the rulers are bound by what the law establishes, that is, that a government of men complies with the laws. The underlying confusion is also apparent in other, equally misleading phrases that people link to the rule of law, such as "the sovereignty of the law" or "the supremacy of the law." All this is empty rhetoric. The law, being a human creation, must necessarily be subject to human will. In fact, the very term "the rule of law" is in itself rhetorical.[1] The law cannot rule. Ruling is an activity, and laws cannot act.

What all these metaphorical expressions have in common is the assumption that the law somehow stands above men. Because Pinochet,

---

[1] In other languages the term used for the rule of law (e.g., *Rechtsstaat, Estado de Derecho*) is free of these metaphysical implications. I am going to consider that, with respect to the argument I defend in this chapter, there are no significant differences between the doctrine of the rule of the law as it has developed in the Anglo-Saxon world and continental Europe.

I thank Adam Przeworski for his very valuable comments.

when issuing his warning, was showing that he had the power to subvert the law, some consider that this is sufficient to discard the possibility of a rule of law under these circumstances. But this conclusion is unwarranted. It is always possible to think of situations in which the law does not stand above men. Suppose it was not Pinochet who made this statement, but the bourgeoisie, or society as a whole. Obviously, if there is a unanimous opinion in society that the law does not hold, and that opinion is common knowledge, the law does not hold. The law cannot stand above men because, as Jon Elster has emphatically said, *"nothing is external to society"* (1989: 196). Thus, there are always circumstances under which the law can be ignored, discarded, violated, or suspended.

There is another, more reasonable rendering of the rule of law. This is not that the law rules over men, but rather that, *given the laws and the incentives they create, men have no interest in subverting the institutional order*. The ideal behind the rule of law is that of universal compliance with the rules that define the political system and regulate its functioning. Even if nothing is external to society, a society that is well ordered in institutional terms is a society in which the rules are such that no one finds it advantageous to act contrary to them.

From this point of view, what Pinochet's warning reveals is the fragility of the rule of law in Chile at that particular moment. The survival of the rules depended on the will of a single person. This means that the rule of law was precarious. Of course, there is less fragility when subversion of the rules requires the coordination of larger numbers of actors (in the most extreme case, the whole society), but the possibility of breaking the rules is always present. It cannot be eliminated.

One of the main characteristics of institutions is that they are impersonal, in the sense that their functioning does not depend on the idiosyncrasy of individuals. An institution is well designed when it is not affected by the replacement of the individuals who have to act in accord with its rules. Whatever the preferences of individuals who have to act institutionally, the institution survives when the incentives it creates induce individuals to comply with the rules. In this sense, there is rule of law when politics is fully institutional, that is, when every political act is done according to the institutional rules. The challenge posed by the rule of law is the design of a set of rules that guarantee their own survival because the incentives contained in these rules deter everyone from subversion.

The idea of the rule of law can be easily connected with one of the oldest aspirations of political theory, the design of a stable institutional system, an institutional system that could survive indefinitely.[2] A stable institutional system is a system in which there is always compliance with the rules. All conflicts have to be solved according to these rules. This can be understood in at least two ways, one formal and another substantial. In the formal sense, stability is a direct consequence of compliance. The system is stable even if the institutional rules change dramatically from time to time because the rules never break down. A Jeffersonian political system where every generation turns the political rules upside down in a constituent assembly would be stable as long as the rules, whatever they are at each moment, are respected. In the substantial sense, the stability of the rules is something other than compliance insofar as it requires a relative permanence of certain rules that define a particular kind of political system.

The aspiration of an eternal institutional system in the substantial sense is probably as much a chimera as a scientist's bid to design a "perpetual motion machine." Institutions cannot last indefinitely. Unforeseeable social changes that transform the balance of power between existing social forces, or that destroy some old forces and create new ones, may make the existing institutions ineffective.[3] However, to maintain that institutions (except the Roman Catholic Church) do not last forever is hardly a remarkable conclusion. But it does raise an interesting question: what is the aim of institutional stability? This leads to a still more general question: why is compliance with the rules so important? What if the rules are subverted, and the system is not stable?

---

[2] Referring to the constituent period of the United States, Hannah Arendt wrote that "the whole discussion of the distribution and balance of power, the central issue of constitutional debates, was still partly conducted in terms of the age-old notion of a mixed form of government which, combining the monarchic, the aristocratic, and the democratic elements in the same body politic, would be capable of arresting the cycle of sempiternal change, the rise and fall of empires, and establish an immortal city" (Arendt 1990: 231).

[3] The theocratic institutions of the Byzantine Empire lasted for eleven centuries. The empire survived even though it did not have a succession rule for the emperor, which led to all kind of plots, coups, crimes, and civil wars. The instability in the post of emperor was incredibly high for a theocratic autocracy: the mean reign of the emperor for the period 395–1453 was only 9.9 years (calculated from data included in Finer 1997: 636), which is not so different from the average duration of 45 cabinets (minimal winning one-party cabinets) in some parliamentary democracies for the period 1945–96, 8.0 years (Lijphart 1999: 137). Despite the chronic conflict over the succession of the emperor, the empire proved to be extremely stable, but not eternal. Its institutions could not cope with the emergence of the landed class after Leo VI in the tenth century allowed civil servants to own houses and land in the territories where they were sent to work. The clash between the new landed class and the warrior aristocracy led to the final crisis of the system (Finer 1997: 644).

Someone could refuse to answer these questions, arguing that institutions are an irrelevant concern. Compliance with the rules would simply be explained by the fact that these rules reflect the distribution of the bargaining power among the different social forces. If the exercise of power under the rule of law coincides with the power of the relevant social forces, then no one will have incentives to break the law. None of the relevant forces will be able to improve their share by breaking the law. The configuration of the contents of the law is to be determined, therefore, by the distribution of power, so that once the law is enacted, there will be no reason not to comply with it. The Chilean political system at the end of the 1980s could be stable only insofar as the special status of General Pinochet and his men was recognized. Had this special status not been respected, Pinochet would have had an incentive to break the rules.

This argument is a nonstarter. It simply ignores the fact that some institutional rules create new power, power that cannot easily be reduced to the bargaining power of the preinstitutional stage. What is the counterpart in noninstitutional terms of the institutional power a parliament has to pass laws? Of course, some institutional rules produce institutional facts that parallel or mirror noninstitutional realities. However, we do not have to suppose that all rules are just the institutional dressing for the operation of some prior bargaining power that is not institutional in nature.

John Searle's distinction between regulative and constitutive rules is highly relevant at this point and will play an essential role in my argument. Constitutive rules make possible certain actions that could not take place without the rule. Someone cannot vote, cannot speak English, or cannot play chess unless there are rules that define voting, English grammar, or the movements of the pieces on a chess board. Constitutive rules create institutional power, a sort of power that does not necessarily coincide with brute power. Someone exercises institutional power whenever he does something that is authorized or dictated by constitutive rules, that is, whenever he acts according to the rules.

The rule of law refers, perhaps not uniquely but indeed fundamentally, to the principle that every political act has to be the consequence of the distribution of institutional power within the system, so that brute power is never used. But what is the point of avoiding brute power? This question makes sense only if the consequences of exercising institutional and brute power can be different. Generally speaking, it can be said that the point of having institutional rules is to tame brute power.

People may desire certain outcomes that can only be reached institutionally and may want to avert some other outcomes that follow from brute power. In *Mind, Language and Society*, the book in which Searle summarizes and brings together his philosophical ideas, he says that "the whole point, or at least much of the point, of having institutional facts is to gain social control of brute facts" (1998: 131). In an institutional system, everyone understands who is authorized to do what according to which procedures. If this institutional system is a rule of law, that is, if the institutional system is stable because compliance is guaranteed, then individuals are certain that some outcomes will be observed, while some others will be avoided. When this institutional certainty is put at the service of a political system that we consider fair, such as democracy, the rule of law becomes an attractive companion to this political system.[4]

In this chapter, however, I do not analyze the effects of the rule of law. Rather, I examine its foundations. The argument has two parts. First, I explain why the problem of compliance arises in the context of the rule of law. This may seem obvious. Compliance is problematical because someone might be better off breaking rather than following the rules. But when this response is reformulated in more rigorous terms, it turns out that new ideas about the nature of institutional rules emerge. The existence of the problem of compliance forces us to amend substantially Searle's theory of constitutive rules. I argue that political constitutive rules do not always make possible the activity that comes under the rule, or at least that the way in which the activity is made possible is rather different from the way in which rules of games or languages make possible the activity of playing a game or speaking a language. Some political actions that can be carried out in virtue of a constitutive rule can be also carried out with very similar consequences by noninstitutional means. Compliance is problematical when there are institutional and noninstitutional means of doing certain things.

This explanation for compliance implies that, in contrast to what we are told by the orthodox theory of constitutive rules, the "constitutiveness" of these rules, at least in the realm of politics, is a question of degree. This explains, among other things, the existence and resolution of institutional crises in which constitutive rules collapse. In order to illustrate this point, I examine the case of Ecuador in 1997, when

---

[4] There can also be "brute certainty," in the sense that the outcomes produced by the exercise of brute power may be perfectly foreseeable. But if the point of institutional rules is to tame brute power, then only institutional certainty is valuable.

three different individuals simultaneously claimed to be the authentic president of the country.

In the second part of the argument, I describe some mechanisms that might explain how compliance is possible when the distribution of institutional power does not coincide with the distribution of brute power. Institutional rules may achieve some partial autonomy with regard to brute power thanks to the creation of institutional interests that can be satisfied only if there is compliance with the rules. These institutional interests either weaken brute power or compensate brute interests that are not satisfied within the institutional system. In addition, I take up Adam Przeworski's explanation for the stability of democracies in rich countries. As he argues in this volume, democracies may survive if actors are risk-averse and there is much at stake. If subversion of the rules does not pay under some circumstances due to the attitude toward risk, then institutional rules could survive even if they do not match the distribution of brute power.

## The Idea of the Rule of Law

So far, I have been referring to the rule of law as compliance with the institutional rules that define the political system. This usage is too loose. There may be compliance with rules in systems that have little in common with those that possess the rule of law. It is necessary, therefore, to be more precise about the peculiar features of the problem of compliance when we are dealing with the rule of law.

It is not clear what sort of thing the rule of law is. Let me start by saying what, in my opinion, it is not. The rule of law is not a form of government. Democracy and dictatorship are forms of government, but the rule of law is not. Even if the formula "a government of laws, not of men" may suggest the possibility of a "nomocracy" as a distinct form of government, this is just a metaphysical possibility, devoid of any political meaning whatsoever. Nor is the rule of law the juridical articulation of politics. We can conceive political systems that use the technology of law for the exercise of power but in which the rule of law does not apply ("ruling through law" instead of "ruling according to the law"; see Schmitt 1982: ch. 13).

A more positive characterization might be this. The rule of law is a property of the political system. It is not a discrete property: there is no way of identifying a clear threshold that divides political systems into two categories, those that have a rule of law and those that do not. Perhaps those who say that the rule of law is an ideal or an aspiration actually mean that the property can be graduated, with only a few cases coming close to the extreme of the pure rule of law.

The property expressed by the rule of law is compliance with the law in a legal system.[5] The requirement of a legal system already restricts the kind of compliance to be analyzed. An analogy with Robert Dahl's definition of polyarchy might be in order at this point. Dahl considers that polyarchy is a system in which governments are selected through elections and where elections are held under certain conditions. Dahl's eight conditions for polyarchy have become canonical in the literature on democracy: freedom of association, freedom of expression, free elections, and so on (Dahl 1971: ch. 1). In order to simplify as much as possible, I follow Dahl's strategy: the rule of law exists when there is compliance with the law and the law satisfies some minimal conditions. Curiously enough, one classical treatment of the features of the law also identified eight conditions. Because matters of clarification are only instrumental to the general argument I defend here, I am happy to adopt Lon Fuller's conditions with one caveat (Fuller 1969: ch. 2; for similar lists, see, e.g., Raz 1979, 1990b; Solum 1994). The eight conditions are: (1) laws must be general; (2) laws have to be promulgated (publicity of the law); (3) retroactivity is to be avoided, except when necessary for the correction of the legal system; (4) laws have to be clear and understandable; (5) the legal system must be free of contradictions; (6) laws cannot demand the impossible; (7) the law must be constant through time; and (8) congruence must be maintained between official action and declared rules.

The first seven conditions seem beyond dispute. Obviously, many doubts could be expressed, for example, about the elusive meaning of generality applied to the law or, more broadly, about the need to interpret the law. On the other hand, the seven conditions are not clear-cut and admit different degrees of realization (this is one of the reasons why the rule of law is not a discrete property): for instance, it is impossible to have a complex legal system that is fully consistent, with no internal contradiction whatsoever. Finally, the seven conditions do not mention one further necessary condition for the existence of a legal system, namely that judges adjudicate according to norms and not according to their own views and opinions. But apart from these qualifications, and many others that could be mentioned, I just want to convey the sort of ideals that articulate the law in the rule of law. The fact that these ideals are not easily translated into practice is not an insurmountable problem as

---

[5] On the concept of legal system, see Raz (1990a: ch. 4).

long as their meaning is quite clear. Here I am less concerned with exploring the law as with the phenomenon of compliance when there is a legal system.

The eighth condition is of a different type. It is not a condition that the law must satisfy. In fact, it refers not to the law itself but to compliance with the law. Yet compliance with the law is not one of the features that the law must have in order to constitute a legal system. The problem of compliance only arises once the legal system is established. It is not by chance that in his reply to critics, Fuller defines the rule of law in terms of his eighth condition, showing that this condition is not on the same footing as the other seven. He says that the basic principle of the rule of law is "that the acts of a legal authority toward the citizen must be legitimated by being brought within the terms of a previous declaration of general rules" (1969: 214).

Fuller's definition is in a sense too narrow. There is no need to restrict the issue of compliance to acts performed by the government with respect to citizens as individuals. When the rule of law is limited to the relationship between the state and its subjects, it becomes a matter of guaranteeing the basic rights of citizens against arbitrary interference by the state.[6] But suppose that a government makes economic policy by decree when it is not authorized to do so; or that a president breaks the rule of limited mandate and competes for a third term in the new presidential elections even though he is not allowed to do so. These are acts by the government that conflict with declared rules. However, they are not necessarily acts toward the citizen. They do not have to affect the basic rights of individuals. Why should such violations of the rules by the government not count as a breakdown of the rule of law?

I propose to define the rule of law as compliance with the law, when the law is general, public, prospective, clear, consistent, performable, and stable. This definition includes under the problem of compliance both interference with the basic rights of individuals and obedience to the rules that establish who has the authority to rule and how this authority is to be exercised.

When the seven conditions do not hold, the problem of compliance is of much less interest. If the state can make the law without publicizing it, if the law can be retrospective, if the law cannot be followed, then the state is free to do whatever it wants to. Under these circumstances, discussion of compliance would appear pointless.

---

[6] Other definitions that also make this mistake of arbitrary domain restriction of the rule of law are those of Hayek (1959), Dworkin (1985), and O'Donnell (1999).

It can be argued that the preceding definition is still too vague. I have yet to touch the question of rulers' discretion. The very misleading formula of "a government of laws, not of men" could be understood as a restriction of rulers' discretion. If rulers are bound by the law, they cannot but comply with the law. The rulers, obviously enough, have the legal obligation to comply with the law, but nothing follows from this about the degree of discretion politicians will enjoy in government. We are no closer to the ideal of the rule of law if there are constitutional rules that tie politicians' hands (e.g., rules that fix monetary policy, rules that forbid fiscal deficits) than if politicians are free to implement their preferred economic policies. The rule of law has no bearing on the debate rules versus discretion.

The rule of law, however, has something to say on the kinds of constraints rulers have with regard to law making. In matters of policy the discretion of the ruler is irrelevant for the rule of law, but when it comes to defining and changing the rules, things are more complex. Suppose that someone in the system has sole authority to change the law subject to the previous seven conditions. This person always complies with the law. He has no reasons not to obey the law, because the existing law is the consequence of his will. Whenever the law dictates something he dislikes, he is free to change the law.[7] According to the definition of the rule of law I have already advanced, we seem compelled to accept this political system as a rule of law. We have compliance with a legal system. On what grounds could we object to this use of the rule of law?

If we accept that this system is a rule of law, we are bound to accept that a dictatorship with a legal system could be a rule of law. For some, this is almost a heresy. For others, there is nothing wrong or absurd about this conclusion: some doctrines of the rule of law (notably in Germany) were born without any democratic pedigree. It would be rather arbitrary to try to settle the issue by a sort of linguistic decree on the use of this expression. It is more sensible to draw a distinction between two senses of the rule of law, the weak or static sense and the strong or dynamic one. The problem of compliance is particularly interesting with respect to the second sense.

The element that differentiates the weak from the strong sense is the distinction between obeying the law and being subject to the law (or

---

[7] Following the example of Byzantium mentioned in note 3, Emperor Basil I approved a law in his name and the name of his two sons, Leo and Constantine, forbidding fourth marriages and restricting the possibility of a third one. Once Leo became Emperor Leo VI, he changed the law and married four times (Runciman 1977: 97–100).

being constrained by the law).[8] The idea of obeying the law does not presuppose anything regarding the reasons that explain compliance. As I have just pointed out, someone could obey the law simply because he makes the law at will. The idea of being subject to the law is more demanding: now, rulers face constraints that limit their capacity to change the law. If these constraints cannot be lifted, the only alternative to obeying the law is breaking it. Subjection to the law is a matter of degree, depending on the force of the constraints.

The weak sense of the rule of law has nothing to say about changes in the rules. It can be called static because it does not make any assumptions about the fate of the rules. The strong sense is dynamic insofar as it assumes that rulers face, to different extents, constraints with respect to changing the law. Questions about the feasibility of the rule of law become truly interesting when they involve the strong, dynamic sense, that is, when the real issue of compliance is at stake.

## Political Constitutive Rules

The rule of law requires compliance with the rules. The point of the rule of law is that the rules are always respected. The political system is closed or self-contained, in the sense that the system never resorts to extralegal resources to settle an issue. When a revolution or a coup destroys the system, that is, when conflicts are not solved according to the rules, the rule of law vanishes.

But why is compliance a problem? What reasons could individuals have not to follow the prevailing rules? In order to understand why compliance is a problem at all, we have to analyze the nature of rules. Rules are the basic tool of political life. I say "tool" in a very literal sense. Rules are the most important technological invention in the political realm. Thanks to political technology we can create institutions, sign contracts, choose governments, buy goods. Rules make possible all kinds of actions that would be simply unthinkable without them. H. L. A. Hart notes in passing that the discovery of enabling rules is as important for society as the invention of the wheel (1961: 41). The analogy can be taken further. Perhaps the similarity between rules and the wheel goes beyond their consequential nature for society: both wheels and rules broaden the space of feasible actions.

---

[8] By distinguishing between these two senses of the rule of law, I am not implying that political systems can be classified according to the type of rule of law they posses. Within a political system, the authority may be subject to the law in some areas but not in others, even if in all of them the authority has to comply with the law.

Not all rules are enabling. Here, it is essential to remember Searle's distinction between regulative and constitutive rules (1969, 1995, 1998).[9] Regulative rules regulate behavior that is independent of the rules. Such behavior may exist before the rule is introduced. The rule prohibiting walking on the grass regulates the exercise of walking but does not define what counts as walking. By contrast, constitutive rules make possible certain activities that cannot be carried out without the existence of the rule. Chess cannot be played without the rules that define the game of chess. A language cannot be spoken without the grammar rules that define what counts as valid language. Someone cannot vote for the presidency without the rules that establish the institutions of voting and the presidency. Constitutive rules generally take the form of "$X$ counts as $Y$ in certain contexts." Searle admits that constitutive rules, as well as constituting an activity that would otherwise be impossible, can also regulate the activity being constituted.

Constitutive rules cover a variety of rules that have been examined under different names by students of the law: norms of competence, Hart's secondary rules (rules of recognition, rules of change, rules of adjudication), power-conferring norms. The common characteristic of all these rules is that the activity somehow depends on the rule. But the nature of this dependence is not always clear. It is not clear whether this dependence is merely definitional (by construction), or whether it tells us something more fundamental about the nature of institutions. I am going to analyze the dependence of the action on the rule in some detail. My point here is that political constitutive rules have some features of their own that are not shared with other constitutive rules, such as those employed in games or languages. The reason why political constitutive rules are different from other constitutive rules sheds some light on the peculiarity of political activity.[10]

The first examples of constitutive rules provided by Searle were all borrowed from languages or games. Let us start with games. Games are fairly isolated activities in the life of individuals (Raz 1990a: 123). They create activities that are fully autonomous. These activities do not have any counterpart in the real world. Games create spheres of action that cannot be connected in any meaningful sense with actions or facts outside the game. Once someone starts to play the game, his actions are entirely dependent on the rules. His actions are meaningless unless

---

[9] For critical discussions of Searle's distinction, see Raz (1990a: 109–10) and Schauer (1991: 7).

[10] I am developing here some points I made in previous work (Sánchez-Cuenca 1998).

connected with the rules. Moreover, when someone is playing a game, he always has an outside option, the option of abandoning the game. An individual can be obliged to play a game, not because he is bound by its rules, but simply because someone else is coercing him to play the game. The player does not need a constitutive rule to leave the game. His will to do so suffices. In the absence of external pressures, exit is always an option when playing a game.

The isolation and self-containment of games make the violation of constitutive rules logically impossible. A player cannot move the castle across diagonals in the chess table. Obviously he can make some equivalent physical movements, but these are unrelated to chess. The castle cannot be moved diagonally because there is a constitutive rule that establishes that a piece counts as the castle only when it is moved either horizontally or vertically. But even if someone disagrees with this argument, it is still true that the issue of compliance does not arise insofar as playing games is optional and the player can abandon the game whenever he considers he is better off not playing than playing.

Note that the possibility of cheating does not invalidate my point. First, cheating is not always an option. I do not see what cheating could mean with respect to chess (leaving aside the problem of the clocks that measure the time available to move the pieces). Second, cheating is not really a violation of the rules. The person who cheats does not follow the rules, but he does not break them either. Breaking a rule is something visible, whereas cheating is always done secretly (there is no possibility of cheating at chess because everything is public). The cheat deceives other players, who do not notice that they are being cheated. Apparently, the rules of the game are applied by all the players, so that the game can go on.

Due to the self-containment of games, their constitutive rules may last forever. The stability of the rules that define a game can be eternal because the activity of playing the game is entirely dependent on the rules of the game. Compliance not being an issue, the game survives. The chimerical ideal of the rule of law, the creation of an eternal institutional system, is not so chimerical with respect to games.

Similar considerations can be made with regard to languages. Languages are also self-contained systems of rules that create an autonomous sphere of action. The main difference between games and languages is that the former is a more competitive activity, because there are winners and losers, whereas the latter has more to do with a coordination scheme. This is why, apart from the argument about the logical impossibility of violating the constitutive rules of grammar, in the case of language the possibility of a unilateral deviation is absurd: it prevents communication among the speakers, which is precisely the point of having a common language. The person who unilaterally deviates from the rules of grammar cannot talk with anyone else.

Politics represents a much more complex activity than either playing games or speaking languages. What holds for games or languages is not necessarily true of politics. First, unlike with languages, a unilateral deviation may make sense. The president of a republic may decide to break unilaterally the constitutional rule that establishes a limit on the number of presidential mandates. Second, unlike with games, playing politics is not optional. In most cases there is no outside option. If a person does not like the rules of politics, he cannot decide to abandon the political game. Either he complies with the rules or he breaks them (assuming he does not have enough power to change them). Sometimes, there is an exit option and the person can leave the country. However, this is not always feasible and tends to be costly.[11]

Despite these differences, it is possible to find areas of politics where constitutive rules work almost in the same way as in games. Let us take an electoral system with districts of varying magnitude. There is a district of magnitude four, for example. In this district, a party claims that it has obtained five representatives. What can this claim possibly mean? If only four representatives can be chosen, how can one party win five? There seems to be some logical impossibility here. The rule that establishes that four representatives are chosen in this district cannot be violated within the system. There is no action that could count as a violation of the rule. The action made possible by the rule (the choice of four representatives) is entirely dependent on the rule.

Electoral systems present some other similarities with games. For example, there is the possibility of cheating. Electoral fraud is a form of cheating. It is done in secret and the constitutive rules are apparently followed. After electoral fraud it is still the case that the candidates who win seats are those who obtain more votes. The fraud comes not in the application of the rule but in the counting of votes, and counting is an activity that is not dependent in any meaningful sense on the rule that establishes how seats are allocated. Hence the possibility of cheating.

Electoral systems are peculiar political entities. They create an institutional sphere of action that has no counterpart in the noninstitutional reality. There cannot be voting unless there are some constitutive rules

---

[11] The exit option can nonetheless be crucial in understanding the survival of some dictatorships. See Hirschman (1993).

that define what counts as voting. In this sense, the activity of voting may be considered to be as isolated and self-contained as a game. However, this institutional autonomy is relatively exceptional in politics. In fact, it is easy to understand that although voting is completely dependent on electoral constitutive rules, acceptance of the results of the ballot has no obvious parallel in games. Given that in politics there are few, if any, outside options, the loser of the elections cannot say that he is abandoning the game. Either he complies with the outcomes of the election or he organizes a coup or a revolution. The set of rules that constitutes the electoral system can then be broken down. The losing candidate in a presidential contest may decide that the elections must be annulled. If he has the support of the army, he will break the constitutive rules. He will become the new president despite having lost the elections. He becomes president by sheer force. Obviously, someone could refuse to call him president, because he has not been chosen according to the procedure established by the constitutive rule, but the new ruler, no matter what we call him, will do the kinds of things that the last authentic president did.

Even if from a logical point of view the possibility of a person's becoming president regardless of the constitutive rule that defines the presidency is an absurdity, it must be admitted that there is a long record of such absurdities in history. The rebuttal of a philosopher to the effect that the person who has the executive power is no longer the president as defined by the constitutive rule, so that in the last instance the constitutive rule has not been broken, serves for little. What we need to understand is why this sort of absurdity arises in politics but not in language and games.

We can now introduce Searle's distinction between brute and institutional facts. Brute facts are those that can be described without reference to constitutive rules. Institutional facts can only be described in terms of the constitutive rules that create the institutional reality. That person $X$ killed person $Y$ is a brute fact, but that candidate $W$ won more votes than candidate $Z$ is an institutional fact. In games and languages, institutional facts are fully autonomous with respect to brute facts. There cannot be any correspondence between the two types of facts. There is no equivalent in brute terms to the movement of the castle in chess. Thus, we can safely say that these institutional facts are fully dependent on the constitutive rules that create them.

Politics is different from languages and games because in certain cases it is possible to establish relationships between institutional and brute facts. A person may become president in virtue of the constitutive rule that defines the presidency, but he may also become president through the use of violence. In the first case we have an institutional president, in the second one a brute president. The possibility of becoming a brute president for a politician who does not enjoy sufficient popular support to become an institutional president is what creates the problem of compliance in politics. Insofar as there are noninstitutional paths to become president, I claim that the presidency has only a relative dependence on institutional rules. *The problem of compliance emerges when institutional facts are not entirely independent of brute facts.*

Compare this with chess. There is no noninstitutional way to take the king of your opponent. Even if someone physically removes the piece that counts as the king, this person has not won the game. We cannot distinguish between an institutional winner of the game and a brute winner. The reason is that in chess the whole point of the game is to win according to the rules, whereas in politics the point of winning elections is not to be the winner, or to show that one has more popular support than other candidates, but to exercise power. And some people may want to exercise power regardless of what the votes say.

Just as the example of the electoral system represents one extreme possibility, that of a political activity almost fully dependent on constitutive rules, there are other cases that represent the opposite situation, a constitutive rule that simply makes institutional some brute facts that can exist regardless of the rule. Let me take here one of Searle's own illustrations of constitutive rules (1995: 89). Suppose that country *A* attacks country *B*. Constitutionally, *A* goes to war with another country when the congress formally declares war. Without a declaration, there is no war from the legal point of view. How are we to understand *A*'s attack against *B* when the congress does not issue such a declaration? In this case, it is quite obvious that the activity is possible without the rule. We do not have any trouble imagining how country *A* could go to war against *B* without the constitutive rule that establishes what counts as war. According to Searle, in this case the constitutive rule is still relevant if the declaration of war implies some consequences that are absent when there is no declaration. Although he does not expand on this point, it is easy to imagine, for instance, that when there is a formal declaration of war the government is bound to accept some international conventions on the exchange of war prisoners, or that the government can suspend some constitutional guarantees. But suppose for a moment that the declaration of war has no consequence at all. It is a mere formality. In this case, we may wonder whether the rule "There is war when Congress issues a declaration of war against another country" is constitutive or not. Apparently, the rule is easily reducible to the formula "$X$ counts as $Y$ in certain contexts": "An attack against a country counts as war when the attack is preceded by a declaration of war by the Congress." However, this implies moving a long way away from the original criterion that distinguished between regulative and constitutive rules on the basis of the activity being possible prior to the existence of the rule.

Searle could argue that the activity of waging a war is made possible by the constitutive rule because, as we have seen in the case of presidents, the constitutive rule draws the distinction between attacks that are wars and attacks that are not (institutional and brute attacks). Even if the attack is physically the same event in both cases, only when it is preceded by the declaration of war do we have a case of war. However, the way in which the activity is made possible in the case of the war is rather different from the way in which the activity of choosing four representatives in an electoral district is made possible by the rule. In the electoral example, the rule makes possible the activity in a much stronger sense, as revealed by the fact that the claim of having won five representatives is simply meaningless given the rule. In the example of going to war, an attack against another country without prior declaration is not logically senseless. On the contrary, it is something we all understand. The rule is not needed to attack another country, while the rule is necessary to make it possible to select the four representatives of the district. It seems that even if there is a constitutive rule that defines what counts as war, the occurrence of war is not very dependent on that rule.

If someone were to say that the original definition of constitutive rules still holds on the grounds that every constitutive rule creates, merely by virtue of its existence, an activity otherwise impossible, namely the activity as described by the rule, there would be no criterion to distinguish between political constitutive rules and the constitutive rules of games and languages. The rule that defines how the castle can be moved and the rule that defines what counts as war would be equally "constitutive." It would not be possible to draw any distinction according to the degree to which actions depend on rules because in both cases the activity as described by the rule depends on the rule. However, it seems clear to me that the mode of dependence is very different in each case.

The strange thing about the war example is that the constitutive rule is simply institutional dressing for an activity that can be carried out without this dressing. Here the relationship between the institutional

**77**

and the brute fact is one of identity. The dependence of the activity with respect to the rule is now null. There is no difference between the institutional reality (an attack is produced after a declaration of war has been issued) and the factual reality (an attack takes place): in both cases, the attack occurs. Even if the rule fits the generic formula of constitutive rules, the action constituted by the rule is no different from the action carried out regardless of the rule.

Most politics lies in the area in between the example of war and that of electoral law. Most political activity can be distinguished in terms of its partial or relative dependence on constitutive rules. An equivalent formulation of this idea is that in politics many institutional facts can be put into some correspondence with brute facts. The distinction between institutional and brute facts can also be applied to power. Brute power is independent of constitutive rules. Institutional power is created by constitutive rules (more concretely by power-conferring norms). Parliament's power to remove the government by means of a vote of no confidence is clearly institutional: it depends on some rule that authorizes the parliament to use this procedure. In terms of power, then, *there is a problem of compliance in politics when some outcomes that are produced institutionally can also be achieved through brute power*. This is why in politics the collapse of constitutive rules is not always an impossibility. Politics goes on even if the rules are not respected because in politics there is brute power as well as institutional power. The case of Ecuador in 1997 may be useful to illustrate this whole point.[12]

In June 1996 Abdalá Bucaram won the presidential elections with 52% of the vote. At the start of 1997, Bucaram applied a shock adjustment program (following the advice of Domingo Cavallo, the former minister of finance of Argentina who was then advising Bucaram), which provoked a sudden increase of about 1000% in the prices of basic utilities. People reacted very angrily to this policy. The opposition organized a two-day general strike. The president tried to minimize the impact of the strike, first, by declaring one of the strike days a national holiday and, second, by coming out in support of some of the protests that were actually directed against him. The strike, nonetheless, was a great success. It was clear that support for Bucaram was waning fast. The vice-president, Rosalía Arteaga, tried to distance herself from the president: just before the strike, she proposed that a national

---

[12] There is not much written about this event. For a journalistic view, see the chapters included in Cornejo 1997.

referendum should be held to decide whether the president should remain in office.

After the strike, the president of the unicameral Congress of Ecuador, Fabián Alarcón, headed a political maneuver to depose Bucaram on grounds of mental incapacity. In fact, Bucaram was proud of his popular nickname, El Loco. He had won a deserved reputation as a "crazy person" for his unusual and unpredictable behavior.[13] Alarcón used this reputation to resort to Article 100 of the Constitution, whereby the president can be deposed by a majority of the Congress if there is evidence of insanity. No evidence was disclosed before the vote was held on 7 February. Without medical reports, the decision was clearly outside the law. Alarcón did not try to impeach the president because he always knew that he would not be able to obtain the two-thirds majority required by the Constitution. But he easily collected the majority of votes required to depose the president on grounds of insanity. The Congress went on to name Alarcón Bucaram's successor.

The resulting situation was indeed extraordinary. Three people simultaneously claimed to be the president of Ecuador. Bucaram argued that he had been deposed illegally. Arteaga, the vice-president, said that according to the Constitution she was the new president (if the president does not complete his mandate, he is replaced by the vice-president). Finally, Alarcón said that the Congress had appointed him president. This situation gave rise to various absurd episodes. The minister of defense, for instance, declared a state of emergency, but Alarcón replied that he could not declare anything because he was no longer a minister. The Supreme Court of Justice refused to arbitrate in this conflict, and at the beginning of the crisis the military did not express a preference for any of the three presidents.

The conflict over the presidency reveals the peculiar functioning of constitutive rules in the political competition for power when there are no outside options. While in chess it makes no sense to figure out what would follow if a player announces that he has three kings instead of one, in politics we have to contemplate the possibility of three different people claiming simultaneously to be the president of a country. Unlike games, politics is subject to the risk of institutional crises. In such crises, constitutive rules are suspended, but not entirely. The institution of the

---

[13] Perhaps the most bizarre act to occur during Bucaram's mandate, apart from recording a CD with the group "Los Iracundos," was some sort of state reception in the president's house (Carondelet) given to Lorena Bobbit, the Ecuadorian women who had cut off her husband's penis in the United States, alleging that he used to abuse her.

presidency does not disappear during the crisis, nor does it operate according to the rules of the Constitution. The crisis is overcome when brute power intervenes to fix the institutional breakdown.

Bucaram had some institutional grounds for claiming the presidency because the Congress had misused Article 100. But no one wanted to recognize Bucaram's institutional power. Public opinion, the military, and the opposition forces were all against him. Arteaga, the vice-president, had some grounds for demanding the presidency but, again, she had no support within the system. The military, finally, was inclined to back Alarcón, the president of Congress. The Congress first chose Arteaga as the provisional president of Ecuador on 9 February, on the understanding that in a few days she would transfer the power to Alarcón. Once in power, she tried to resist doing so, arguing that for this transfer to be legal the Constitution should be amended first. However, the pressure of the army finally forced her to accept the transfer on 12 February. Institutional normality was restored.

Bucaram's loss of support due to his attempted shock therapy left him completely isolated: he had no political resources other than those conferred by the institutional rules. The economic crisis gave Congress the opportunity to "expropriate" the president's institutional power. The institutional conflict was solved only when the army decided to side with the majority in Congress. Obviously, brute power intervened: according to the Constitution of Ecuador, the army does not have the authority to decide who the president is. But it is also true that the new president was chosen because of his institutional power as president of Congress.

It could be argued that the army is not brute power. Obviously, the army is an institutional creation. Being a general or a captain is not a brute fact. But even if the army has an institutional structure, it may act contrary to the constitutive rules that define its competencies. When it does so, it acts out of its brute power. The army can act regardless of constitutive rules because, in the last instance, guns are not institutional. The army faces a problem of compliance because its institutional competencies are not independent of its brute power. This is completely different from the judiciary, whose power is exclusively institutional, as Hamilton realized long ago when he described the judiciary as "the least dangerous" branch of government.[14] Due to its lack of brute power, the

---

[14] The judiciary may become more dangerous when the executive is very weak or when judges find allies in their struggle with other powers (see Maravall, Chapter 11 in this volume). According to Burnett and Mantovani (1998), the destruction of the First Italian Republic by the judges was possible only thanks to the contingent alliance of judges, the media, and the major economic groups that owned the media. Before 1992 judges had

dilemma of compliance does not arise so clearly in the case of the judiciary. In the realm of the judiciary, institutional facts are independent of brute facts.

The case of Ecuador reveals several things: first, the fragility of institutional power when it clashes with brute power. Even if Bucaram was not deposed according to the procedures established by the law, he could not make his institutional power prevail once the Congress, public opinion, and the military had withdrawn all support from him. Second, and more important, it confirms the possibility of a crisis of constitutive rules. The coexistence of brute and institutional presidents makes possible the occurrence of situations that, from a purely analytical point of view, make no sense.[15]

In Ecuador the rule of law was suspended during the institutional crisis. The rule of law implies that brute power is never employed and hence that political action has to be the consequence of the exercise of institutional power. Compliance with the law is tantamount to avoidance of brute power. This does not mean that brute power disappears. Brute power obviously affects both the contents of constitutive rules and compliance with these rules, but the rule of law implies that brute power does not directly intervene in the political process. This condition makes sense only if institutional facts have some autonomy with regard to

information about the extent of corruption in politics, but they launched their legal battle against it only when they had won the support of the media.

[15] An even more intriguing case than that of Ecuador is the history of antipopes in the Roman Catholic Church (I am indebted to Pablo Lledó, who called my attention to this fascinating case). The church admits the existence of almost forty antipopes in its long history. The *Encyclopaedia Britannica*, in its fifteenth edition, defines an antipope as "one who opposes the legitimately elected bishop of Rome, endeavors to secure the papal throne, and to some degree succeeds *materially* in the attempt" (emphasis added). The possibility of becoming pope not in accordance with the constitutive rules that define who counts as pope, but through noninstitutional means (*materially*, as the encyclopedia so aptly puts it), by gaining the recognition of other church authorities, implies that the church also faces a problem of compliance. The most explosive phase of this problem was between 1378 and 1417 (see Schatz 1999: ch. 5). This period, known as the Great Western Schism, was initially characterized by the coexistence of two persons each claiming to be the genuine pope and excommunicating each other (one in Avignon, the other in Rome). The situation deteriorated still further when a council convened in 1409 to solve the conflict chose a new pope in place of the other two. Because the two popes affected by the decision refused to resign, for a number of years there were three popes. The crisis was resolved only when the Council of Constance decided that the church's Ecumenical Council, a sort of legislative assembly with constituent powers, had more authority than the pope. Although brute power did not play as important a role as it did in Ecuador, it is interesting to see how the recognition of the authority of the different popes was linked to the support that the different monarchies gave to the various popes.

brute facts – that is, if the outcomes produced by the distribution of institutional power are not identical to the outcomes that would have been produced by the distribution of brute power. If the law is merely the institutional dressing for the distribution of brute power, the rule of law adds little to our understanding of politics. How this autonomy is possible at all is the question that remains to be answered.

## The Partial Autonomy of Political Constitutive Rules

It is important to remember that not everyone would agree as to the existence of the autonomy of institutional facts with regard to brute facts. Some maintain that all constitutive rules are like those in the example of the declaration of war, when the degree of "constitutiveness" is zero or almost zero. Ferdinand Lasalle, in his 1862 lecture on the meaning of the constitution, strongly defended the view that the rules contained in a constitution are determined entirely by brute power. The juridical constitution is only the written expression of this brute power.[16] In fact, Lasalle distinguished between two types of constitution: the sheet of paper and the real constitution, formed by the power structures of society. The elements of the real constitution are not the written rules, but the king, the bankers, the nobility, the great bourgeoisie, the workers, and even the political culture of the country. He argued that if the Chinese law that established that parents are punished for the acts of robbery committed by their children were applied to Germany, the people and the administration would not comply with a rule so alien to German mores. Therefore, a lasting constitution exists "when the written constitution *matches* the *real* constitution, the constitution rooted in the power structures that rule the country" (Lasalle 1984: 109).

For all its analytical sophistication, this is almost the same thesis that Gerald Cohen (1978) presented a century later in his reconstruction of historical materialism. He makes the fantastic claim that all rights of ownership are "superstructural," meaning that for each ownership right it is possible to find a "matching power" that is not institutional in nature. Behind a legal right there is always a brute power. His examples are provided at this level of abstraction: the right to use means of production is matched by the power to use means of production; the right to withhold means of production is matched by the power to

---

[16] This approach to the study of constitutions is developed more extensively in Beard's interpretation of the United States Constitution (Beard 1986). For a rational choice version of this approach, see Knight (1992).

withhold means of production; and so on (p. 220). According to Cohen, compliance with rules would simply be the consequence of the congruence between rights (institutional power) and powers (brute power): "In law-abiding society, men's economic powers match the rights they have with respect to productive forces" (p. 232). Here, constitutive rules are merely superstructural; they are mere institutional dressing for brute power.

This is Marxism at its worst. It overlooks the enabling dimension of rules.[17] As this is not the place to enter into a detailed discussion of Cohen's work, it is enough to show through just one example why his thesis makes sense only at the most abstract, least interesting level. Let us take an essential aspect of ownership, inheritance laws. There cannot be inheritance unless there is some constitutive rule that creates the right to transfer property from the dead to the living. Inheritance laws amount to more than a mere dressing for brute power. The state may decide whether inheritance exists, how the inherited property is to be taxed, whether property can be transferred freely or whether there are some fixed obligations, and so on.[18] As soon as one descends to these more detailed issues, the identification of the "matching powers" becomes harder, to say the least. What sort of thing might the matching powers behind these different aspects of inheritance law be?

If the ludicrous project of identifying a matching brute power for each form of institutional power is abandoned, then the question of how to explain compliance with constitutive rules that are not reducible to brute power requires some answer. I say that political constitutive rules have partial or relative autonomy with regard to brute power when compliance occurs and there is no perfect correspondence between institutional and brute power. An explanation of the relative autonomy of constitutive rules is therefore an explanation of how compliance with political constitutive rules is possible.

Now, some clarification on the kind of question that I want to analyze is necessary. Two different questions arise with respect to political

---

[17] Curiously enough, some Hegelian interpretations of Marx are more sympathetic to the idea of constitutive rules. In his criticism of Cohen, Derek Sayer writes that "state and law are intrinsic to the totality of social relations which actually make up the seemingly 'impersonal' power of bourgeois property, which maintain a social order in which domination can appear to take purely 'economic' forms. They are *constitutive* of bourgeois class rule: *it could not exist otherwise*" (1987: 100, emphasis added).

[18] Elster (1985: 403) makes a similar point. Although he does not talk of constitutive rules, he uses the example of patentable knowledge against Cohen: knowledge cannot be patented unless there is a law (a constitutive rule) that defines the right of patenting something.

constitutive rules. The first concerns how it is that people with brute power accept some constitutive rules that create institutional power not reducible to brute power. How does their brute bargaining power affect the agreement on the adoption of certain constitutive rules? The second question takes as a given the existence of some constitutive rules that create institutional power. Once these constitutive rules are functioning, what guarantees compliance with these rules? The first question, therefore, has to do with the possibility of agreeing on institutional rules in a situation that is not constituted by these rules (it may be a "state of nature," or a previous, different institutional order). The second question refers to the conditions that guarantee compliance with the rules once there has been an agreement on adopting these rules. Note that both questions make sense only if institutional power cannot be reduced entirely to brute power.

It may seem that the questions are not separable. Compliance with a rule occurs when the rule is a self-enforcing equilibrium. But if the rule is self-enforcing, then an explanation of why there is agreement on the rule already counts as an explanation of why there is compliance with the rule. Yet, this is not always so. An individual may comply with the existing constitutive rules, but had he had the power to influence the adoption of some rule or another, he would not have supported the existing rule. That is, the reasons the individual has for agreeing or disagreeing with the adoption of a constitutive rule are not necessarily the same reasons for complying or not complying with the rule once the agreement has been reached.

When the constitutive rule creates an institutional equilibrium that does not alter the underlying game, the reasons to agree on the rule are the same reasons that produce compliance with the rule.[19] This is what we find, for instance, in Calvert's model (1995a,b). Calvert analyzes a prisoner's dilemma (PD). There is a group of players who interact pairwise and where each interaction represents a PD. This game has several noninstitutional equilibria. But there is also a superior institutional equilibrium based on a constitutive rule (although Calvert does not use this

---

[19] The only possible exception occurs when the rule does not produce the results expected by the parties that had agreed to it. This may occur if the rule is so complex that its consequences cannot be determined in advance, or if the rule incorporates some random mechanism. Democracy is based on one such rule with unpredictable results. It is impossible to know beforehand who is going to win elections. As Przeworski shows in this volume, this explains why in democracy someone may agree to democratic rules but not comply with election results.

vocabulary). A director who centralizes all information about the history of interactions among the players is created in virtue of the constitutive rule. Players, at some price, can ask the director for information about whether other players have cooperated or not in the past. This information sustains an equilibrium of conditional cooperation. When there is no director, the costs of gathering information about all the other players are too high, so this equilibrium is not feasible. The constitutive rule, therefore, permits a new equilibrium, an institutional equilibrium that widens the space of equilibria. In this model, the creation of the director does not alter the underlying game. With or without a director, each pairwise interaction is still a PD.

Compare this with the classical Hobbesian contractual story. There is again a PD in the state of nature, but the social contract, understood as a set of constitutive rules that create a political order, changes the nature of the game entirely. The Leviathan goes somewhat further than Calvert's director. The brute power of the players is institutionally centralized in the hands of the Leviathan. Everyone is coerced by the Leviathan to cooperate in social interactions. Punishment (i.e., defection) cannot be applied unless authorized by the Leviathan, whereas in Calvert's model punishment is still decentralized, and each player can decide to defect if he knows that the other player has defected in the previous round of the PD. In Calvert's model, punishment is the exercise of brute power, whereas in Hobbes's it is an exercise of institutional power. Once the Leviathan has been created, the decision to obey commands cannot be modeled after the PD (Hampton 1986). Thus, the game has been altered by the introduction of constitutive rules.

In this case, where the underlying game has been transformed, the reasons for complying with the rules in the new game do not have to coincide with the reasons for agreeing to the adoption of the constitutive rules given the previous, underlying game. More specifically, the reasons for creating the Leviathan may be different from the reasons for complying with the Leviathan once the Leviathan exists.

I am interested in the problem of compliance only when there are already some constitutive rules that cannot be reduced to brute power. Why is compliance with these rules observed if they do not match brute power? At least two possible answers are worth considering. The first refers to the creation of new interests, interests dependent on the existing institutions, that may induce actors to comply even if their brute interests are not satisfied. The second involves the inertia of constitutive rules. The destruction and creation of new constitutive rules may be a costly process, so that if this cost is greater than the benefit of a different set of constitutive rules closer to brute power, then the original rules survive.

With respect to the first answer, it is necessary to introduce a new distinction. Just as the distinction institutional or brute has been applied before to facts and power, it is now possible to speak in terms of brute and institutional interests. Constitutive rules not only create institutional facts or institutional power: they also create institutional interests.[20] If someone wishes to be the president of the constitutional court in a country, the pursuit of this interest cannot be detached from the constitutive rules that create the constitutional court. This is a purely institutional interest. The interest cannot be formed until a constitutive rule creates the constitutional court. I define it as a pure institutional interest because there is no corresponding brute interest. Obviously, if the degree of "constitutiveness" of the constitutive rule is lower, there may be some correspondence between brute and institutional interests. Redistributive interests can be realized both institutionally (e.g., by taxing the rich) and by noninstitutional means (e.g., by robbing the rich).

One very simple explanation for compliance with constitutive rules is that institutional interests may compensate for brute ones. Thus, some people could comply with constitutive rules because the satisfaction of institutional preferences offsets other incentives to break the law. A revolutionary leader may be bought off by the system with some institutional post. The existence of rewards that are dependent on the maintenance of constitutive rules (power, information, influence, honor, etc.) allows the institutional system to produce some institutional selective incentives that reinforce the rules. There are politicians who survive in power thanks to their skill at delivering these incentives. Giolitti

---

[20] Now it is possible to be more systematic about the enabling nature of constitutive rules. They can create new power, new facts, and/or new interests. This can be translated into Savage's ontology: constitutive rules may affect the acts that the agent can make (power), the consequences that may happen to the agent (facts), and the preferences of the agent over the consequences (interests). How much a constitutive rule enables is a matter of degree. For example, Calvert's rule about the director affects only the acts (now the agent may ask the director about the cooperation state of another agent), not the consequences or the preferences, which are still those of the original PD. This is therefore a rule with low enabling capacity. Compare this with the rule that creates the role of the president in a democracy. This rule affects acts (the people have the institutional power to vote for the president), consequences (there is no president without the rule), and preferences (the people have to order the different candidates for president). This rule has high enabling capacity.

was apparently a supreme master at absorbing or co-opting those who opposed the system (Clark 1984: ch. 7): radicals were incorporated into government and one of them became the president of the Chamber of Deputies, while socialist deputies were invited to participate in government and, though they refused, they (and the unions controlled by these deputies) were neutralized through the concession of all kinds of state favors. Only the nationalists could not be absorbed.

But the relationship between institutional and brute interests may become much more complex. For example, the pursuit of institutional interests could weaken brute power, thereby making compliance more likely. To a certain extent, this is the dilemma that socialist parties faced in the first half of twentieth century. Przeworski and Sprague's (1986) description of this dilemma can be translated into brute or institutional terms. Once socialist parties entered into electoral competition, they developed institutional interests (the achievement of a majority of votes) that conflicted with the source of their brute power, their class support. Because workers never constituted a majority of the electorate, a majority was feasible only at the cost of broadening their electoral support, but this implied a weakening of their class profile. And the brute power of socialist parties came from their capacity to organize and mobilize class collective action.[21]

Albeit in a very different context, we find something similar in the debate on the American constitution. The federalists understood that institutional interests may have the effect of making the organization and mobilization of brute power less likely. In fact, this is a recurrent theme in the *Federalist Papers*. Fearing that in a purely majoritarian republic the poor would expropriate from the rich, Madison came up with institutional devices that could minimize this danger.[22] Thus, he considered that in an extensive republic the majority of the poor would find it harder to use their main source of brute power, their sheer number. Referring to the size of the country, he makes this recommendation: "Extend the sphere and you take in a greater variety of parties and interests: you make it less probable that a majority of the whole

---

[21] Social movements often face this kind of dilemma. When a movement decides to participate in institutional politics, it loses its mobilization capacity. There is a trade-off here between institutional and brute power.

[22] As he said at the Philadelphia Convention: "An increase of population will of necessity increase the proportion of those who will labour under all the hardships of life, & secretly sigh for a more equal distribution of its blessings. These may in time outnumber those who are placed above the feelings of indigence.... How is this danger to be guarded against on republican principles?" (Madison 1987: 194).

will have a common motive to invade the rights of other citizens; or if such a common motive exists, it will be more difficult for all who feel it to discover *their own strength* and *to act in unison with each other"* (*Federalist* 10; emphasis added). The institutional system would not reflect the brute interests of the poor, but even so the system could survive because the mere exercise of the rules would run against the poor as a collective agent. The poor would not be able "to act in unison" given the institutional interests created by the system.

A similar logic was applied to the issue of separation of powers and checks and balances. Here the danger is not that the majority acts against the minority, but rather that rulers use the institutional power that is conferred on them against the ruled. In order to avoid this danger, it is necessary to divide power into several branches, so that these branches develop their own institutional interests. Otherwise, collusion among the rulers could lead to a tyrannical government. The essential point is that the different branches of power, due to their different modes of election and their different functions and capabilities, have different institutional interests. As Madison says in *Federalist* 51, "each department should have *a will of its own*" (emphasis added). According to this idea, institutional rules should render these branches "by different modes of election and different principles of action, as little connected with each other as the nature of their common functions and their common dependence on the society will admit."

Federalists thought that the separation of powers could work only if the mechanism of checks and balances was introduced. Without checks and balances, the more powerful branches would try to encroach on the weaker ones. To keep each branch within its boundaries, it was necessary to make them mutually dependent, by giving to each some veto capacity in the decision-making process.

The fragmentation of the political system, due both to the extension of the republic and to separation of powers with checks and balances, was supposed to create institutional interests powerful enough to repress the brute interests of the majority of the poor. Insofar as the poor faced such obstacles to organizing and using their brute power, compliance with institutional rules that did not reflect the brute power of the social groups was possible.

The first answer, therefore, would be that the creation of institutional interests not entirely reducible to brute interests helps explain the autonomy of constitutive rules, either because the pursuit of institutional interests weakens brute power, or because institutional interests offset the brute ones. The second answer is of a different kind.

It focuses on the costs of breaking the rules. The greater these costs, the more autonomous the institutional rules will be with respect to brute power. Russell Hardin (1989) has argued, for instance, that people abide by a constitution due to the costs involved in coordinating to rebel against it. In his view, it is a question of collective action. Moreover, he suggests that the longer constitutive rules have been working in the past, the stronger the expectations that the constitution will continue to hold and therefore the more difficult it will be to coordinate people to rebel against the rules. It seems to follow from this that in countries with a record of frequent coups or rebellions against the prevailing constitutive rules, institutional stability cannot be attained, because no matter what constitutive rules are approved, no one will expect them to last. How countries get out of this trap is an interesting question.

Przeworski, in this volume, proposes a different mechanism. He analyzes a narrower issue, the survival of democracies. It turns out that democracies survive indefinitely above some level of income. The explanation runs as follows: when actors are risk-averse, the richer the country, the greater the risk entailed by noncompliance with the constitutive rules that establish democracy. If the losers of an election attempt to impose a dictatorship but fail, the income loss may be sufficiently great to dissuade them from considering rebellion. The consequence is that even permanent losers in the democratic contest may be better off complying with the rules than rebelling against them. The point is that the richer the country, the greater the inertia of constitutive rules. Inertia is explained by the fact that the risks associated with noncompliance increase with wealth. The partial autonomy of political constitutive rules is produced by the risks entailed by any noninstitutional attempt to change the status quo.

This kind of inertia is rather different from institutional inertia. Institutional inertia has to do with the difficulty of changing constitutive rules according to established procedures. Following George Tsebelis's (1995) theory of policy stability, it can be argued that the greater the number of veto players required to change rules, the greater the institutional stability of the rules. A constitution usually has more institutional inertia than an ordinary law because the number of veto players involved in constitutional reform is higher than in the case of an ordinary law (qualified majorities, the concurrence of several branches of power, popular referenda, etc.). There is no obvious relationship between institutional inertia and Przeworski's income inertia. If institutional inertia is maximized but a substantial part of the society wants to change the rules,

**89**

institutional inertia may trigger a noninstitutional change of the rules.[23] Institutional inertia could be reinforced by income inertia, although this is not a hypothesis I pursue here.

Now, it would be illegitimate to conclude from these two answers that constitutive rules are always independent of brute facts: all I have tried to argue is that there is no reason to assume that under every circumstance constitutive rules are merely expressions of the distribution of brute power. Nor have I defended the view that the role or function of constitutive rules is always to neutralize brute power. In fact, many constitutive rules are unrelated to brute power because they have no distributive implications: Calvert's constitutive rule on the figure of the director, for instance, is simply an institutional device to achieve a Pareto-superior equilibrium in the underlying game. Rather, the point is that constitutive rules may become relatively autonomous with respect to brute power due to (1) the incentives and power that these rules create, and (2) their mere existence, which introduces some inertia or resistance to change.

This conclusion, ultimately, is only the starting point for a theory capable of explaining how brute and institutional powers interact in concrete cases. Here, I have simply attempted to identify the roots of a problem that has not received the attention it deserves. The analysis of institutional rules must explain how the constraints imposed by brute power affect compliance with these rules, and to what extent these rules can neutralize such constraints.

## Conclusions

There are two equally extreme conceptions of politics. Both misrepresent the nature of institutions. One considers that politics can be modeled along the lines of games or languages, as sets of institutional rules that create some rights and obligations in virtue of which individuals make decisions. The other treats politics as a manifestation or reflection of a deeper, more basic prepolitical reality. Neither conception has

---

[23] In his analysis of constitutional changes in the United States, Bruce Ackerman (1998) shows that some of the most important transformations were not made according to the Constitution precisely because of the enormous institutional inertia of the U.S. Constitution. On the other hand, Ackerman's analysis challenges the sharp distinction between brute and institutional means I am using here. He thinks that American constitutional transformations were neither institutional nor brute: "For Americans, law-breaking does not necessarily imply lawlessness"; "By breaking the law we will find higher law" (p. 14). I cannot enter here into a discussion of Ackerman's interpretation of constitutional breakdowns, which is of direct concern to any theory on the rule of law.

much to say about the interplay between the institutional and non-institutional reality. The first considers institutional rules in isolation, detached from the surrounding reality. The second denies any autonomy to the institutional.

With regard to the rule of law, the first conception entertains the absurd view that institutional rules, and not men, rule, that there is supremacy or sovereignty of the law. The second conception regards the very idea of the rule of law as an ideological abstraction.

I have tried to provide a more sensible rendering of the nature of institutional rules. Constitutive rules construct an institutional reality, but at least in politics, as compared with games or languages, this reality is not independent from the rest of the world. Political constitutive rules create a political reality against the background of preexisting powers and interests. Precisely because politics is not fully autonomous, the problem of compliance arises. Compliance with political constitutive rules becomes problematical when rules conflict with the surrounding reality. When similar results can be achieved institutionally and noninstitutionally, the "constitutiveness" of political constitutive rules is a matter of degree. Compliance is more problematical in these mixed cases.

The rule of law stands for a very unlikely aspiration: the creation of a stable political system in which compliance with the rules is guaranteed, these rules being subject to certain conditions I have examined in the second section of this chapter. Under the rule of law, all political activity is lawful. The political system is self-contained, because brute power never enters directly into it. However, it is not independent of brute power, given that its feasibility and endurance depend on the distribution of brute power and the costs of subversion. Whether democracy is the political system that, combined with development, will achieve this aspiration cannot be said.

## References

Ackerman, Bruce. 1998. *We the People. Transformations.* Cambridge, Mass: Harvard University Press.

Arendt, Hannah. 1990. *On Revolution.* 1965. Reprint, London: Penguin.

Beard, Charles A. 1986. *An Economic Interpretation of the United States Constitution.* 1935. Reprint, New York: Free Press.

Burnett, Stanton H., and Luca Mantovani. 1998. *The Italian Guillotine: Operation Clean Hands and the Overthrow of Italy's First Republic.* Lanham: Rowman & Littlefield.

Calvert, Randall L. 1995a. "Rational Actors, Equilibrium, and Social Institutions." In Jeffrey S. Banks and Eric A. Hanushek (eds.), *Modern Political Economy*, 216–67. Cambridge: Cambridge University Press.

1995b. "The Rational Choice Theory of Social Institutions: Cooperation, Coordination and Communication." In Jack Knight and Itai Sened (eds.), *Explaining Social Institutions*, 57–94. Ann Arbor: University of Michigan Press.

Clark, Martin. 1984. *Modern Italy, 1872–1982*. London: Longman.

Cohen, Gerald A. 1978. *Karl Marx's Theory of History: A Defence*. Princeton: Princeton University Press.

Cornejo, Diego (ed.). 1997. *¡Qué se Vaya! Crónica del Bucaramato*. Quito: Edimpres.

Dahl, Robert A. 1971. *Polyarchy*. New Haven: Yale University Press.

Dworkin, Ronald. 1985. "Political Judges and the Rule of Law." In *A Matter of Principle*, 9–32. Oxford: Clarendon Press.

Elster, Jon. 1985. *Making Sense of Marx*. Cambridge: Cambridge University Press.

1989. *Solomonic Judgements*. Cambridge: Cambridge University Press.

Finer, S. E. 1997. *The History of Government*. Vol. 2, *The Intermediate Ages*. Oxford: Oxford University Press.

Fuller, Lon L. 1969. *The Morality of Law*. New Haven: Yale University Press.

Hampton, Jean. 1986. *Hobbes and the Social Contract Tradition*. Cambridge: Cambridge University Press.

Hardin, Russell. 1989. "Why a Constitution?" In Bernard Grofman and Donald Wittman (eds.), *The Federalist Papers and the New Institutionalism*. New York: Agathon Press.

Hart, H. L. A. 1961. *The Concept of Law*. Oxford: Clarendon Press.

Hayek, Friedrich A. 1959. *The Constitution of Liberty*. Chicago: University of Chicago Press.

Hirschman, Albert O. 1993. "Exit, Voice, and the Fate of the German Democratic Republic. An Essay in Conceptual History." *World Politics* 45: 173–202.

Knight, Jack. 1992. *Institutions and Social Conflict*. Cambridge: Cambridge University Press.

Lasalle, Ferdinand. 1984. *¿Qué es la Constitución?* Barcelona: Ariel.

Lijphart, Arend. 1999. *Patterns of Democracy. Government Forms and Performance in Thirty-Six Countries*. New Haven: Yale University Press.

Madison, James. 1987. *Notes on the Debates in the Federal Convention of 1787*. New York: Norton.

O'Donnell, Guillermo. 1999. "Polyarchies and the (Un)Rule of Law in Latin America." In Juan E. Méndez, Guillermo O'Donnell, and Paulo Sérgio Pinheiro (eds.), *The (Un)Rule of Law and the Underprivileged in Latin America*, 303–37. Notre Dame: University of Notre Dame Press.

Przeworski, Adam, and John Sprague. 1986. *Paper Stones: A History of Electoral Socialism*. Chicago: University of Chicago Press.

Raz, Joseph. 1979. "The Rule of Law and Its Virtues." In *The Authority of Law*, 210–29. Oxford: Clarendon Press.

1990a. *Practical Reasons and Norms*. Princeton: Princeton University Press.

1990b. "The Politics of the Rule of Law." In *Ethics in the Public Domain*, 370–8. Oxford: Clarendon Press.

Runciman, Steven. 1977. *The Byzantine Theocracy*. Cambridge: Cambridge University Press.

Sánchez-Cuenca, Ignacio. 1998. "Institutional Commitments and Democracy." *Archives Européennes de Sociologie* 39: 78–109.

Sayer, Derek. 1987. *The Violence of Abstraction: The Analytic Foundations of Historical Materialism*. Oxford: Blackwell.

Schatz, Klaus. 1999. *Los Concilios Ecuménicos*. Madrid: Trotta. Spanish translation of *Allgemeine Konzilien* (1997).

Schauer, Frederick. 1991. *Playing by the Rules: A Philosophical Examination of Rule-Based Decision-Making in Law and in Life*. Oxford: Clarendon Press.

Schmitt, Karl. 1982. *Teoría de la Constitución*. Madrid: Alianza. Spanish translation of *Verfassunglehre* (1927).

Searle, John R. 1969. *Speech Acts: An Essay in the Philosophy of Language*. Cambridge: Cambridge University Press.

  1995. *The Construction of Social Reality*. New York: Free Press.

  1998. *Mind, Language and Society: Philosophy in the Real World*. New York: Basic Books.

Solum, Lawrence. 1994. "Equity and the Rule of Law." In Ian Shapiro (ed.), *The Rule of Law*. Nomos XXXVI. New York: New York University Press.

Tsebelis, George. 1995. "Decision Making in Political Systems: Veto Players in Presidentialism, Parliamentarism, Multicameralism and Multipartyism." *British Journal of Political Science* 25: 289–325.

## Chapter Three

# Obedience and Obligation
# in the *Rechtsstaat*

The problem of obedience may look strange to a legal scholar. Lawyers deal not with obedience but with obligation. The question they ask is not, What behavior does effectively take place? but What behavior ought to take place? According to leading theories, actual behavior has no effect on the validity of a rule. In other words, a rule is binding or not binding independently of the fact that it is being obeyed (or disobeyed). This is just another way of expressing the difference between *is* and *ought* and the law deals only with what ought to be, not with what actually is or will be. Moreover, it is generally agreed that there can be no causal relation between what is and what will be. The fact that something ought to happen does not cause it to happen and the fact that something actually happens has no influence on its being mandatory or forbidden. In other words, the validity of a rule does not depend on its efficacy. Indeed it can be said that the specificity of a rule, as distinguished from a law of nature, lies in its capacity to be violated.

Lawyers and legal scholars therefore leave to sociologists and psychologists the question why men obey the law. True, those who make the rules must have some idea of what makes men obey. If they make and publish those rules, they must assume that knowing the existence of a rule will have some sort of psychological effect on actual behavior and they draft them according to the behavior they expect. Most lawmakers mainly rely on sanctions, in the general sense of both punishment and reward. Yet, whether this is the real reason that explains obedience is something that lawyers cannot tell. They can tell if, according to the law, this or that behavior ought to take place and what, still according to the law, ought to happen if the prescribed behavior does not actually take place, but he is not concerned by the psychological question why it does or does not take place. Furthermore, for lawyers the question is absolutely irrelevant. If I obey the order from a state official to pay taxes, I may be doing this for many different reasons – because I think it is a moral duty, because I fear the sanction, because I expect to gain social prestige by letting the public learn about the large amount I pay, or because I had a dream telling me that I will win at the lottery a hundred times the amount of the taxes. From the point of view of a lawyer, all these reasons are irrelevant, the only question being that of the obligation to pay.

Yet, one can find a connection between the question of obedience and the question of obligation within the specific framework of the doctrine of the *Rechtsstaat*. If a citizen asks why he ought to pay taxes, the legal answer is that he has been the subject of a command by a state official, that this officer did not act on his own will and for his own benefit, but that, by issuing the command, he has himself obeyed a statute. The citizen's direct obligation to obey the officer is an indirect obligation to obey the statute. But it depends on the actual obedience by the officer. Actual obedience by state officials is the justification for my obligation to obey them. Similarly, the obligation to obey statutes stems from the fact that lawmakers have actually obeyed the constitution, which prescribes rules with certain characteristics – namely, that they be general and that they do not infringe on fundamental rights.

This is the reason why the *Rechtsstaat* is defined as a government not of men but of laws only. There is a double advantage to this situation. First of all, laws are general and stable. If they cannot be changed to suit the whims of those who apply them, I can be said to be free, even if they are severe and unjust, because I am able to predict the consequences of my actions. This is precisely the definition of political liberty given by the philosophers of the Enlightenment.[1] On the other hand, if the laws have been made by the citizens themselves, as is the case in a democracy, these citizens are free in another sense, because they are submitted to their own will. Thus, Rousseau is able to write that when a citizen is in prison, he is just forced to be free.

In this classic presentation of the legal system, the hierarchy of norms is a justification of the duty to obey. But, this duty does not simply derive from another duty. It derives from the fact that another duty has been effectively obeyed. My duty to obey the tax officer's command derives from the fact that he himself has obeyed the statute. I have an obligation

---

[1] Montesquieu, *De l'esprit des lois*, XI.3: "La liberté politique ne consiste point à faire ce que l'on veut. Dans un Etat, c'est-à-dire dans une société où il y a des lois, la liberté ne peut consister qu'à pouvoir faire ce que l'on doit vouloir et à n'être point contraint de faire ce que l'on ne doit pas vouloir. . . .[c'est] le droit de faire tout ce que les lois permettent."

if – and only if – it is a fact that the officer has acted according to the statute. The *Rechtsstaat* is a justification to the extent that it is the exact description at each level of the hierarchy of actual obedience by the individual who enacts a norm to a norm of a higher level. It may be considered not only a justification of legal obligations but also a moral obligation: if there is a moral obligation to obey just laws and if the lower officer's command has been derived from just laws, I have a moral obligation to obey the officer's command.

It should be stressed that the theory of the *Rechtsstaat* is significantly different from that of the rule of law. Let us consider a classical definition of the rule of law, such as that given by Finnis. According to Finnis:

> A legal system exemplifies the Rule of Law to the extent . . . that I rules are prospective not retroactive and II, are not in any way impossible to comply with; that III, its rules are promulgated, IV, clear, and V, coherent one with another; that VI, its rules are sufficiently stable to allow people to be guided by their knowledge of the content of the rules; that VII, the making of decrees and orders applicable to limited situations is guided by rules that are promulgated, clear, stable, and relatively general; and that VIII, those people who have authority to make, administer, and apply the rules in an official capacity a) are accountable for their compliance with rules applicable to their performance and b) do actually administer the law consistently and in accordance with its tenor. (1980: 270)

Thus, the rule of law is the description of a situation to be wished for, not of the means to reach that situation. There is no guarantee that I, II, III, IV, V, VI, VII will effectively obtain, even if VIII does. The theory of the *Rechtsstaat* therefore appears to be more ambitious because it pretends to be a means for the establishment of such a situation: all the conditions set forth by the theory of the rule of law, that they be prospective, clear, coherent, and so on, will obtain if every rule is the exact application of a superior rule – for example, the constitution that prescribes that statutes be prospective, clear, promulgated, coherent, and so on. Why the law is exactly applied seems therefore to be an important question not only from the point of view of sociology or psychology, but also from that of legal theory. If political liberty or the duty to obey the law depends on actual obedience by state officials, it becomes necessary to examine if it is true that obedience to the superior rules by state officials is a guarantee of political liberty, and if it is true that state officials obey the law rather than basing their decisions on their own personal preferences.

The traditional doctrine of the *Rechtsstaat* does not address these issues but merely assumes that the organs of the state actually apply superior rules, thus failing to explain why. I first examine the failures of the traditional doctrine of the *Rechtsstaat* and attempt to show that it does not offer the promised guaranties, because strictly speaking there is not even a duty of state authorities to obey superior rules, much less actual obedience. Nevertheless, it does not follow that these authorities exercise their discretion according to their whims. The second part of this chapter deals with constraints, different from obligations, that are produced by the legal system.

## The Theory of the *Rechtsstaat*

There is a fundamental ambiguity in the expression *Rechtsstaat*, and the corresponding expressions in continental Europe that are translations from the German, such as *etat de droit, stato di diritto, estado de derecho*. They are used in two different ways, sometimes to refer to a state that is submitted to the law, sometimes to a state whose organs act according to laws made by other organs.

### *The* Rechtsstaat *as a State Submitted to the Law*

The theory that the state can be submitted to the law presupposes that there is a law that has not been created or posited by the state, and it comes in two different versions. According to the first, this law is external and superior to the state because it is natural law. Without entering the classic discussion as to whether there is a natural law, it can be stressed that if citizens obey a state that is limited by natural law, they cannot be said to be autonomous, because autonomy in this case means the absence of any limitations and therefore amounts to sovereignty. In Rousseau's words, "it is the essence of a sovereign power, that it cannot be limited; it can do everything or it is nothing."[2]

The usual objection to the idea that submission of the state to natural law is incompatible with democracy is that the sovereignty of the people is precisely based on natural law. It follows that if the state – or the people – acts in a way contrary to natural law, it cannot be considered the sovereign. The weakness of this objection is that even if there was such a thing as natural law – and the burden of proof is on those who claim that it exists – and if it was the basis for the sovereignty of the

---

[2] Rousseau, *Lettres écrites de la Montagne*, 2ème partie, lettre 7; see also Neumann (1986).

people, this would be only because of rules that are formal and procedural, rules whose function it is to determine the bearer of sovereignty, and not because of substantive rules. It would be self-contradictory to point to a sovereign and to assign limits to that sovereign. A sovereign people is one that is submitted only to its own norms, and therefore a state submitted to law that it has not posited, such as natural law, is one that is not the realization of autonomy, but the contrary of autonomy. Furthermore, in such a system, even if every particular command were a strict deduction from natural laws, it would still not be true that citizens would be subject not of men but of laws only, because natural laws, even for those who view them as existing objectively, have no clear and unambiguous meaning. They must be interpreted, and this task can be performed only by men.

According to a second version, sometimes called "positivist," the state is subordinate not to natural law, but to positive law, a law made by men, but prior to its own foundation. The usual example is that of Solon or Lycurgus, laying down rules that will bind future lawmakers, or that of a bill of rights.

The most serious difficulty with this theory is that the laws, to which state authorities are submitted, are not at all external to the state. A bill of rights is an act of the state. Thus, in such a system the state is really limited only by its own will. Even if one speaks not of the state as a whole, but of state authorities, they are not really submitted to these old laws, for a reason similar to the one mentioned about natural law. Old rules, such as those laid down in a bill of rights, are spelled out in a language that is necessarily vague. They have to be interpreted, and the interpreter, who often is the controlling authority, enjoys enormous discretion, so that the other state authorities are submitted not so much to prior laws, as to the controller.

On the other hand, one could only say that state authorities are submitted to a bill of rights if it was impossible for them to change it or allow for exceptions. But even if changes or exceptions to a bill of rights are sometimes difficult, they are never impossible in principle, and it often happens in European countries that a rule, which one cannot adopt in the form of a statute, because the constitutional court has declared it to be contrary to the constitution or the bill of rights, is nevertheless enacted after a constitutional amendment has been passed.

One might object that even if the state as a whole is not submitted to a higher law, each of its organs is necessarily limited, because of the separation of powers that prevents the concentration of all powers in the same hands. Nevertheless, such an objection does not take into account the fact that powers are organized in a hierarchy. The legislative power is above the executive, and the judiciary and the constituent power above the legislative, so that the organ in charge with the highest power is rightly called sovereign and is not bound by law. This is true of course of the English Parliament, which is not limited by a constitution and a constitutional court, but it is also true where there is a written constitution, because it is always possible to bypass any limitation of the legislative power, by means of a constitutional amendment. Thus, there is still a sovereign, which is the constituent power. Sometimes, the constituent power is divided between several authorities; sometimes the amending procedure makes it difficult to revise the constitution. But this division has no more effect on the principle of sovereignty – that is, on the absence of any limitation by law – than does the physical or psychological weakness of the tyrant in a system that does not claim to be a *Rechtsstaat*. It is thus an impossibility to think of a state that would really be submitted to a law that it did not make itself and cannot change. In this sense there is no such thing as a *Rechtsstaat*.

## The Rechtsstaat *as a State Power in the Form of Law*

According to another version of the theory of the *Rechtsstaat*, if the state cannot be limited by a law that it did not make or that it cannot change, liberty will nevertheless be guaranteed if the organs of the state apply superior norms. Unfortunately, this version actually refers to two very different theories, related to two very different meanings of the expression "application of the law" or two conceptions of the hierarchy between two norms. First, a superior norm can prescribe that an organ of the state behave in a specific way – for example, that it issue a command with a specific content and specific subjects. This is the relation between the penal law and the decision of a criminal court, when that court has no discretion as to the punishment. If the decision of the court is called "decision," it is an inappropriate name, because it is nothing but the conclusion of a syllogism. This is the reason why Montesquieu writes that the judge is the mouthpiece of the law and that judiciary power is null.[3] In this case, the court's decision is legally valid, if and only if the deduction from the major premise constituted by the superior norm is logically valid.

But the relation is more often very different. The superior norm may empower an organ to take a particular decision, without prescribing that

---

[3] Montesquieu, *De l'esprit des lois*, XI.6.

**99**

this decision be given any particular content. The decision will then be valid, provided that it has been taken by the competent organ, whatever the content. Or the superior norm may specify the content in very general terms, for example, by prescribing an aim or an end, leaving to the organ the choice of the means, or by setting limits to the power of the organ. In that case, the organ will enjoy discretion. Its decision cannot be logically deducted from the superior norm. The relationship between the decision and the superior general norm is not one of conformity but of mere compatibility.

If all one has in mind, when speaking of the application of the law, is the second type of relation or hierarchy, then a very important consequence follows: one ought to name *Rechtsstaat* not some type of state, the liberal state, but any state with a legal system structured with such a hierarchy.[4] But this Rechtsstaat provides no guarantee either of political liberty, or of democracy, and this is due to several reasons.

First, it may be that statutes are made by elected representatives of the people, but rarely by these representatives alone. In most modern states, statutes are subject to judicial review. In order to exercise their control, courts must interpret the constitution, the bill of rights, and a number of unwritten principles. But legal interpretation, whether an interpretation of statutes or of the constitution, is not a cognitive but a volitive activity. The courts have a wide discretion to interpret the constitution in one sense or another and to decide that statutes are valid or not valid. In short the courts share with elected representatives of the people the legislative power, which in principle is granted to the latter alone.

Second, in the modern state, the executive function implies the power to issue regulations, which, in substance, resemble statutes, because they are very general and may be enacted for policy reasons, so that, although the executive power acts within the limits determined by the lawmaker, it cannot be said to be obeying statutes. One must also stress that the executive power exercises, by various means, an important influence on the legislatures, and thus on the content of statutes.

The second half of the twentieth century has seen the development of the so-called executive agencies. These agencies do not obey the

---

[4] In Kelsen's view, because law and the state are two names with the same reference, and because every legal system has the same hierarchical structure, every state is a *Rechtsstaat*.

head of the executive power and enjoy wide discretion in the application of statutes. In fact, their function often far exceeds mere execution, because many among them are at the same time in charge of designing a policy by drafting general rules, applying them to particular cases, and adjudicating on the violations of their own rules and commands.

Even so, the judicial function cannot be viewed as one of application of statutes. Modern statutes do not order courts to take specific decisions, as was the case in the conception of the Enlightenment. Criminal codes give judges a choice of the punishment at least between a maximum and a minimum sentence and civil courts have a very wide discretion in the allocation of damages. More important is the power to interpret both the texts of the applicable statutes and the facts to be adjudicated. The interpreter is able to determine freely the content of the statute that he is supposed to apply. Furthermore he does this retrospectively because, according to the standard fiction, he discovers the meaning that the statute has had from the day of its enactment. As Bishop Hoadley rightly wrote in the seventeenth century, "Whoever hath an absolute authority to interpret any written or spoken law, it is he who is truly the law-giver to all intent and purposes, and not the person who first wrote or spoke them; *a fortiori*, whoever has an absolute authority not only to interpret the law, but to say what the law is, is truly the law-giver" (quoted in Kelsen 1961: 153).

One could therefore easily be tempted to conclude that the *Rechtsstaat* is a myth: neither the state as a whole nor its organs can be said to obey rules that they have not made themselves and that they cannot change. Yet, a closer examination shows that state authorities, if they are not bound by rules, are nevertheless constrained in several ways, and it remains to be seen if these constraints can produce similar effects and thus be constitutive of a different type of *Rechtsstaat*.

## Factual Constraints in the *Rechtsstaat*

There are several situations in which state organs are constrained to act in a certain way, without really meeting an obligation or obeying the law. Their behavior is therefore predictable and citizens can obtain at least some of the benefits expected of the *Rechtsstaat*. We can briefly examine some examples of such situations. They result from the existence of constitutive rules, from the organization of mechanical constitutions, and from the necessity for courts to act rationally.

## Constitutive Rules

Following a classical theory, we may distinguish two types of legal rules that are followed in very different ways. First, a rule such as "driving over 130 kilometers an hour on French motorways is forbidden." I can choose to obey or not. I know that driving at higher speed, I risk being arrested and punished, but I can still decide to disobey. On the contrary, the rule "land and houses can only be sold by a contract that must be written by a notary and registered by the state" or "marriages must be celebrated by the mayor" cannot be violated. I cannot even think of selling or buying property without going to a notary or have my marriage celebrated by a person other than the mayor. Trying to write a contract to buy property without going to the notary or trying to get married in some way other than having the marriage celebrated at the town hall by a competent officer is not disobedience and I do not risk punishment. The only consequence is that the sale or the marriage will not be valid. I will have bought nothing or I will not be married. Thus, if I want to get married or buy property, I will say not that I ought but that I must follow the rule.

This is true of some of the rules regarding state organs, especially but not exclusively of procedural rules. If the constitution provides that a statute can only be adopted by a simple majority after three readings in parliament, even if an overwhelming majority of members has voted for it twice, the statute has not been passed.

The type of behavior of someone following these constitutive rules cannot be called obedience, because there is no choice not to obey. Nevertheless, if the whole purpose of the *Rechtsstaat* is to justify the obligation of citizens to obey specific commands of state organs, through the idea that these organs apply superior rules, then this purpose is achieved not only if the application takes place because the organs obey the rules, but also if it takes place because the organs act in a way that they cannot avoid.

## The Mechanical Conception of the Constitution

Some political thinkers of the Enlightenment believed that a constitution well designed could give birth to similar situations. In their view, a constitution was not a norm that could be obeyed or violated, but a mechanism capable of producing some specific effects. A good example of such a mechanism is that of the English constitution, or at least the ideal model drawn from that constitution. In that model, the legislative power belongs to a complex authority, composed of three organs, the House of Commons, the House of Lords, and the king; the executive power belongs to the king. The king thus takes part in the exercise of two powers. All three authorities are completely independent and cannot be punished for the decisions they take. The difficulty comes from the special position of the king. As an executive power, he is under an obligation to apply statutory law, which he contributed to making. If he disobeys and gives orders that are not in conformity with the law, he cannot be punished, because he is independent, but if he remains unpunished, everything happens as if he were the sole legislator. Thus, the distribution of powers is self-destructive, because instead of being a part of the legislative power and the sole executive, the king will have both powers in his hands.

The solution is to be found in the institution of ministers, who countersign the acts of the king as an executive and are held liable for those acts. Because they are liable, they are expected to refuse their signature if an act is against the law. The law therefore will always be correctly applied. The king will be unable to exercise both powers. On the other hand, the two houses may be tempted to introduce legislation that would infringe on the executive powers, but the king, as part of the legislative power, will protect his power and oppose that legislation. It is assumed therefore that the distribution of powers – and the distribution of powers is nothing else than the constitution – will be automatically preserved. It will be preserved, not because the various authorities will be virtuous and obey, not even because they will be enticed to obey, but because, whatever they do and even if each one of them tries to violate the constitution, they can never succeed. If the mechanism has been well designed, then it is not the case that the constitution ought not to be violated, but simply that it is in effect inviolable.

The end result again is, if the mechanism works as it should, that citizens will obey orders given by the executive – and, in doing so, indirectly obey higher laws – that are general and that cannot be changed according to the whims of the law-applying organ.

In the minds of its promoters, this piece of constitutional engineering is also supposed to influence some substantial characteristics of statutes. If the three legislative authorities have conflicting interests, the adoption of new statutes will prove difficult. This is viewed as an advantage, because if there are few laws, there will be little interference in the private sphere, and the autonomy of the individual and of the markets will be preserved. On the other hand, the statutes that will be passed will necessarily be the result of compromises, which means that they will be moderate. Thus, instead of prescribing to lawmakers – for example, by means of a bill of rights – to issue moderate legislation and to respect the autonomy of individuals, a prescription that may or may not be obeyed, the constitution will achieve this same result through a clever distribution of power.

Of course, such a perfect design can never really be realized, but what is important is the view that one could hope to rely on such mechanism and replace a duty of obedience with an impossibility not to comply.

### Constraints in the Exercise of Discretion

Another type of constraint arises in situations when, from a legal point of view, authorities have complete discretion – for instance, in the case of constitutional assemblies, legislatures, administrative bodies, or courts when they interpret the law. I take only two examples of such constraints.

The first is taken from the French national Convention of 1795.[5] This assembly had been elected in 1792 to write a new constitution after the abolition of the monarchy. In June 1793 a very democratic constitution was actually approved under the influence of Robespierre. It included male universal suffrage. Nevertheless, because of the war that was going on and the revolutionary situation, its application was postponed and after the fall of Robespierre, the Convention decided to write a new constitution, which would be much more conservative, but would keep the appearance of democracy. One of the notable features of that new constitution was that men who did not pay taxes because of hardship were excluded from the right to vote. Yet, the Convention did not wish to acknowledge that it had abolished universal suffrage. This situation had a very important consequence: the adoption of two new concepts of citizen.

From the beginning of the Revolution, a citizen was nothing but a member of society. Every person, no matter his sex, age, or origin, who was a member of society, was a citizen. This did not mean that all could vote. Obviously, those who were naturally incapable would be excluded from the vote and "naturally incapable" referred to an incapacity considered natural at the time. Thus, infants, idiots, and also women were considered naturally incapable of voting. According to the 1793 constitution, they had the rights of citizens but could not exercise them.

[5] The concept of citizenship in the period of the French Revolution in La Torre (1998).

But in 1795 the Convention could not carry on with this distinction between a right and the exercise of a right, because poverty could hardly be considered a "natural" incapacity. The only way out, if the Convention was to keep the fiction of universal suffrage, a system where all citizens have a right to vote, was to change the definition of the citizen: a citizen for the Convention is a man over twenty-one who has been living in the same town for more than a year and pays a minimum amount of tax. These men have at the same time the right and the exercise of the right. All those who meet those conditions are citizens and all citizens may vote. One can say that the new definition of "citizen" is a result of constraints bearing on the constituent power.

But this was not the end of the story, for women, children, idiots, and poor men, who had been citizens until then, had lost this quality. If they had ceased to be citizens, what were they? That was the question asked by Thomas Paine, who had been a member of the Convention from the beginning and close to the more progressive groups of this assembly. Again, the solution to this difficulty was to create a new concept: that of citizen *lato sensu*. In that sense a citizen is any person, whether a citizen in the strict sense or not, living in France who is not a foreigner. Thus, the Convention writes at the end of the new Constitution that foreigners have the right to buy or inherit property in France, "in the same way as French citizens." These citizens evidently included women and children. The insertion of that special provision was hardly necessary to protect the rights of foreigners. Actually foreigners were not even a legal category. From the beginning of the Revolution, all those who lived in France were citizens and had equal rights, and this was still true in 1795. The word "nationality" was not used until the nineteenth century. But, if the Convention wanted to proclaim once more the principle that all have equal rights, it had to find a new formulation. Equality between all citizens was impossible, because foreigners were not citizens. Thus, it had to be equality between foreigners and all those who have the right to own and inherit property in France. This category exceeds that of citizens strictly speaking, because women and children can of course also own property. One is therefore constrained to create this category and give it a name. For lack of a distinct name, the category is called that of "citizens." Citizens, *lato sensu*, are all those who live in France and are not foreigners, that is, they have French nationality. The new concept therefore means "national." It is striking that it had been produced originally not from the necessity of distinguishing between French and foreign, but out of the necessity of distinguishing between French and French.

**105**

It is easy to see that the Convention had complete discretion to grant the right to vote. There was an obligation neither to restrict it to a fraction of the people over twenty-one nor to create concepts like that of citizen or national. But once the decision had been taken to refuse the right to vote to those men who did not pay taxes, the necessity to provide a justification led to the creation of the two new concepts.

The second type of situation is that of a supreme court, that is, a court whose decisions are not controlled by a superior court. If it is agreed that such a court can freely interpret the laws that it is supposed to apply and thus remake them, the question arises of the reasons for the relative stability of its jurisprudence. After all, if it can freely remake the law, why not remake it according to changing political moods among its members? The classical answer to that question would be: even without sanctions, the court is under an obligation to apply the law. But such an answer would be unsatisfactory for two reasons: first, because we want to know why the court does conform to that obligation; second, because the law that the court ought to apply is not an objective standard, but the meaning of a text, which it has itself interpreted.

Another answer is to be found in the situation of members of the court and of the court as a whole vis-à-vis other institutions. Courts are collegiate bodies and their members tend to disagree on most issues. In the course of their internal discussions, some type of arguments will never be used, not primarily because they are not permissible but above all because they could never persuade others. It would be impossible, for instance, to justify one's position by saying that it corresponds to one's personal values. In order to persuade it is necessary to show that the proposed decision is consistent with some ideas that have been previously agreed upon and thus can be considered "objective." Second, even though a court is supreme, it is supreme only within a court system, not in the greater legal system. It follows that its decisions can be overridden by political organs: the decisions of a court of cassation, by a legislature; those of a constitutional court, by the constituent power. Even without such checks, the court might still be constrained by its own supremacy. Its decisions concern concrete cases and are specific rulings regarding those cases, but they are justified by the statement of general propositions, rules, principles, and the like. A supreme court can influence the lower courts and, beyond the courts, influence the behavior of individuals only if these individuals make decisions by taking into consideration the consequences of their actions – that is, if they are able to predict that the courts will react to their actions in a particular way. This will happen only if the jurisprudence of the court is not subject to frequent changes. The court therefore faces the following paradox: its power is greater (in the sense that it exerts a greater influence on actual behaviors) if it is more constrained by past decisions.

These constraints are different from legal obligations and taking them into account is different from obedience. Nevertheless, one could claim that the result is similar to that which is expected of the *Rechtsstaat*: in the *Rechtsstaat*, the duty of citizens to obey is justified by the obedience of political authorities to general rules, because it means that they themselves will obey indirectly the general rules. But the same benefit can be expected if, instead of applying general and superior rules, political and court authorities cannot base their decisions on personal preferences and are forced to act with regularity. Just like in the *Rechtsstaat*, these authorities are limited. True, they do not apply superior rules and they are not exactly limited by them, but they are still constrained by their situation in the legal system or by the structure of legal argumentation, so that citizens are politically free, because they can predict the consequences of their actions.

Nevertheless, the theory of legal constraints could not be used as a new version of the theory of the *Rechtsstaat* because of several reasons. The first and most important reason is that some decisions can be explained by the existence of legal constraints, but not all decisions. As a matter of fact the majority of decisions can be explained only by the ideology of the law-making body, whether a legislature or a supreme court. If a supreme court can make decisions by a 5-4 majority, this shows that the constraints produced nothing but a possibility of choice, but the choice is not the result of a constraint and could actually have been different. Second, even when the authorities who make the rules and issue commands are not free to act as they please and are constrained to decide in a certain way, they do not apply higher rules, so that ordinary citizens, when they obey these rules and commands, do not indirectly obey superior law. Third, the strength of the theory of the *Rechtsstaat* comes from its relation with democratic theory. If the people have made the higher law and if particular commands are derived from that higher law, then one is always indirectly submitted to the presumed will of the people. This does not obtain if the executive and the courts enjoy discretion, because it is to their will that citizens will be submitted to their will. But it does not obtain either if the executive and the courts are constrained because citizens will be submitted neither to the will of the people, nor to superior law, but to the blind necessity created by the system.

## References

Finnis, J. 1980. *Natural Law and Natural Rights*. Oxford: Clarendon Press.
Kelsen, Hans. 1961. *General Theory of Law and State*. New York: Russell & Russell.
La Torre, M. (ed.). 1998. *European Citizenship: An Institutional Challenge, The Hague*. London: Kluwer.
Neumann, Franz L. 1986. *Political Theory and the Legal System in Modern Society*. Heidelberg: Leamington Spa.

## Chapter Four

# A Postscript to "Political Foundations of Democracy and the Rule of Law"

Maravall and Przeworski open this book with a difficult question: why do governments act according to laws? The fact that so many governments, both contemporary and historical, have difficulty doing just this indicates that the answer is not obvious. The principal argument of this book is that the force of law is not normative – citizens and political officials do not obey law because of a duty to obey law. Instead, political officials obey the law because they have incentives to do so.

Maravall and Przeworski fill out this logic. For example, they suggest that the constitution is important for the rule of law. "But the constitution matters not because governments feel a duty to obey it. Rather, it serves as a focal device, enabling particular individuals to guess what others will consider as major transgressions and thus to agree when to act." To police the behavior of government officials, "Actions of groups with different interests must be coordinated."

Maravall and Przeworski emphasize another important aspect of the rule of law, that "laws inform people what to expect of others.... At the same time, [laws] facilitate coordination of sanctions against a government that deviates from its own announcements. In this sense, publicly promulgated rules provide an equilibrium manual." They note that "laws indicate to citizens when to act against the government. By coordinating expectations, they facilitate collection actions that impose sanctions on governments."

In short, one answer to Maravall and Przeworski's question is that political officials obey the law because not doing so puts their political future at risk. How does this work?

The approach developed in my 1997 article suggests one way to develop the logic underlying this argument (Przeworski suggests another). Although its main application is to democracy, the model in this article applies more generally (as the title suggests) to the rule of law. As with

**109**

other works in the "equilibrium institution" perspective, this article argues that institutions – such as constitutions, democracy, independent judiciary, free markets – must be supported by political officials who have incentives to honor these institutions. Democracy survives only if political officials have incentives to honor the rights of citizens, respect the outcome of elections, and refrain from using force to settle conflicts. Free markets exist only so long as political officials refrain from intervention and regulation. An independent judiciary holds only when elected officials and bureaucrats abide by judicial rulings.

As Maravall and Przeworski suggest, political officials must have the incentives to honor law. Diamond (1999: 70) puts it this way with respect to democracy: "Only when [citizen] commitment to police the behavior of the state is powerfully credible ... does a ruling party, president, or sovereign develop a self-interest in adhering to the rules of the game, which makes those constitutional rules self-enforcing." Citizens must have the ability to defend principal institutions of the rule of law.

## The Logic of the Equilibrium Approach to the Rule of Law

In parallel with Holmes and Przeworski (Chapters 1 and 5 in this volume), the ruler or sovereign obeys restrictions on his power only when it is in his interest to do so. In my approach, the fundamental problem of the rule of law is one of citizens policing the state. When citizens possess the ability to react in concert to potential transgressions by the state, they can deter the state: because leaders risk being deposed when transgressing citizen rights, they will avoid doing so. Paralleling Holmes' argument, rulers obey restrictions on their behavior only when it is in their interests to do so.

Policing the state is therefore a form of coordination problem: when citizens have the ability to coordinate against transgression by the sovereign or ruler, the ruler is deterred from transgressing citizens' rights. As Holmes (Chapter 1 in this volume) observes, "The threat to withdraw cooperation, in fact, provides a more enduring motivation for the regularization of government power than the threat to inflict physical harm noted by Machiavelli and stressed by Przeworski." Yet acting in concert to police the state is problematic in large part because citizens naturally disagree about what is good and bad, that is, what constitutes a transgression. These differences lead naturally to profound differences in opinion about the appropriate role of the state, political structure, and rights of citizens. These profound differences, in turn, hinder citizen coordination against the state.

The first result of my model is to demonstrate that when citizens differ about the appropriate role of the state and the rights of citizens, sovereigns can take advantage of them through the well-known mechanism of divide and conquer. The sovereign transgresses the rights of some citizens while retaining the support of other citizens sufficient in number to keep the sovereign in power. This scenario is repeated endlessly across time and place: in seventeenth-century England, the group who became known as the Tories by century's end supported the Stuart kings who transgressed the rights of groups later known as Whigs. Similarly, conservative landowners supported Pinochet and the military in the 1973 Chilean coup against the democratically elected president, Salvadore Allende.

The model shows that this pattern is an equilibrium and is thus stable. Because of the difficulties in solving the citizen coordination problem, I argue that it is the most natural equilibrium. Of course, it is not possible for a complete rule of law to be observed in this setting (although, as Barros, Chapter 8 in this volume, suggests, elements of the rule of law can emerge even in dictatorships).

For the rule of law to emerge, citizens must somehow solve their coordination problem so that they can act in concert against potential transgression. Their fundamental differences about the state make this coordination problematic.

Solving this coordination dilemma requires constructing a coordination device – often a constitution but generally a pact. The essence of the new device is that it coordinates citizens in their reaction to the state. Thus, the constitutions and pacts qua coordination devices typically create new procedures for governmental decision making and the rights of citizens. These specifications define the meaning of a transgression, thus helping citizens to coordinate: a government that violates these procedures or rights is, by definition, transgressing.

In more recent work, I argue that pacts become self-enforcing when they meet four conditions (Weingast 2002 and forthcoming). First, the pact must create (or be imbedded in a context that has already been created) structure and process – citizens' rights and a set of rules governing public decision making – defining a series of limits on the state. Second, the parties agreeing to the pact must believe that they are better off under the pact than without it. If this condition fails for one of the parties, that party will be better off without the pact, so the pact will fail. In particular, the parties must believe that the structural and procedural limits on average lead the government to make them better off. Third, each party agrees to change its behavior in exchange for the others simultaneously doing so. Fourth, the parties to the pact must be willing to defend it against transgressions by political leaders. That is, they must be willing to defend not only the parts of the pact benefiting themselves but also the parts benefiting the others against transgressions by political leaders. This fourth condition occurs when each party anticipates that its rights will be defended by the others; that each party is better off under the agreement than not; and that, if ever one party fails to protect the rights of others, the others will fail to come to its rescue. Put another way, the pact becomes self-enforcing when all parties are better off under the pact and when all realize that unilateral defection implies that the others will also defect, destroying the pact.

In short, a critical element of the rule of law is that constitutions and pacts solve the citizens' coordination problems so that they can react in concert against potential transgressions. When citizens have this ability, they can deter rulers from contemplating transgressions.

## Implications for Consensus

Perhaps consensus was a poor choice of words, although I did so because the previous literature had done so, and I sought to apply my model to the problem previously studied. There is a profound difference between the use of this concept in my work and in the earlier literature on democracy. The earlier literature had consensus as an independent variable. Some political cultures had consensus and hence democracy, whereas others did not. The degree of consensus – and, more generally, political culture – was the independent variable.

In parallel with Holmes and Przeworski (both in this volume), my model denies this logic. In this model, consensus is not an independent or a causal variable. Rather, the causal mechanism involves the coordination problem. Do citizens in a society possess a mechanism for coordinating against the government?

Consider a society with a constitutional mechanism that constructs the relevant focal points allowing citizens to police their government. I observed that this endogenous behavior – the ability to coordinate – would appear to political scientists working within the behavioral tradition as a consensus. That approach assumed that culture as an independent variable.

The new equilibrium approach to culture (Chwe 2001; Fearon and Laitin 1998; Ferejohn 1991; Przeworski, Chapter 5 in this volume) holds that political culture emerges from the equilibrium behavior of a group: culture arises when all citizens behave in a given manner in a particular circumstance and, further, that they behave in that manner because of the incentives they face.

My equilibrium argument suggests that societies that have solved their coordination problems behave as if they have a consensus. However, this is not because citizens agree but rather because they have been able to move beyond their disagreements to agree on a coordination device from which to police the government.

To put this another way, the political-culture-based approach about consensus and my approach are "observationally equivalent" along the dimension of behavior within an equilibrium. But the mechanisms are diametrically opposed.

## Conclusions

The essays in this volume advance our understanding of the mechanisms underlying the rule of law. A common theme, taken in my chapter and the one that follows, is that sovereigns and governments obey restrictions on their behavior when it is in their interests to do so. My chapter reveals one of the mechanisms supporting this logic.

## References

Almond, Gabriel A., and Sidney Verba. 1989. *The Civic Culture: Political Attitudes and Democracy in Five Nations*. 1963. Reprint, Newbury Park: Sage Publications.

Chwe, Michael. 2001. *Rational Ritual: Culture, Coordination, and Common Knowledge*. Princeton: Princeton University Press.

Diamond, Larry. 1999. *Developing Democracy*. Baltimore: Johns Hopkins University Press.

Fearon, James, and David Laitin. 1996. "Explaining Interethnic Cooperation." *American Political Science Review* 90: 715–35.

Ferejohn, John. 1991. "Rationality and Interpretation: Parliamentary Elections in Early Stuart England." In Kristen Renwick Monroe (ed.), *The Economic Approach to Politics*. New York: HarperCollins.

Lipset, Seymour Martin. 1960. *Political Man*. Garden City, N.Y.: Anchor Books.

Weingast, Barry R. 2002. "Self-Enforcing Constitutions: With an Application to American Democratic Stability." Hoover Institutions, Stanford University. Unpublished manuscript.

Weingast, Barry R. Forthcoming. "Constructing Self-Enforcing Democracy in Spain." In Joe Oppenheimer and Irwin Morris, eds., *From Anarchy to Democracy*. Stanford: Stanford University Press.

**Chapter Five**

# Why Do Political Parties Obey Results of Elections?

If democracy is to exist, at least one rule must be observed, namely the rule that specifies which of the political parties should occupy the office of government. My purpose is to investigate under what conditions political parties competing in elections obey their results.

According to one view, people obey laws when they share a particular kind of culture. This culture may value the rule of law per se, regardless of the outcomes it generates. It may impose on people the duty to obey outcomes resulting from rules to which they agreed. Or it may foster temperamental characteristics predisposing them to obey laws. But whatever the specific features, rule of law can be sustained if and only if a society is characterized by a particular culture.

An alternative theory sees the emergence of a rule of law as an outcome of conflicts of interests. While situations in which everyone acts according to law can be described in cultural terms, this theory claims that such situations arise when the conflicting political forces find it in their best interest to act in conformity with some laws, given what everyone else is doing.

The controversy concerns the causal mechanisms that generate these situations: are they an expression of some antecedent cultural patterns or are they an effect of pursuit of interests? Both views arrive at the same conclusion – namely, that there are some situations in which political actors act in conformity with laws. Hence, observing situations in which the law rules is not sufficient to identify the mechanisms that generate them. If we are to adjudicate between these explanations, we must observe historical patterns under which such situations emerge and then examine whether these explanations can make sense of history. Here, then, are some facts.

No democracy ever fell in a country with a per capita income higher than that of Argentina in 1975, $6,055.[1] This is a startling fact, given that just between 1951 and 1990 thirty-nine democracies collapsed in poorer countries, whereas thirty-one democracies spent 762 years in wealthier countries and not one died. Affluent democracies survived wars, riots, scandals, economic and governmental crises, hell or high water.

The probability that democracy survives increases monotonically with per capita income. In countries with per capita income under $1,000, the probability that a democracy would die during a particular year was 0.1636, which implies that its expected life was about six years. Between $1,001 and $3,000, this probability was 0.0561, for an expected duration of about eighteen years. Between $3,001 and $6,055, the probability was 0.0216, which translates into about forty-six years of expected life. And what happens above $6,055 we already know: democracy lasts forever.

Moreover, dictatorships established by electoral incumbents occurred at lower incomes than those founded by the forces out of office. In very poor countries, the probabilities are exactly equal that a dictatorship would be established by the electoral winners or losers. In countries with intermediate income levels, between $1,001 and $6,055, the electoral losers are much more likely to do so. Above $6,055 neither side does.

Other factors pale in importance in comparison to per capita income, but one is nonetheless telling. Democracies are more likely to fall when one party controls a large share of seats in the lower house of the legislature, more than two-thirds. Moreover, democracies are most stable when the heads of governments change every so often, more often than once in five years (but not as often as once in two years). These observations indicate that democracy is more likely to survive when no political force dominates completely and permanently.

In the remainder of this chapter, I examine whether either cultural or rational choice explanations can explain these patterns. I first investigate the structure of cultural explanations, arguing that none of the extant cultural theories is sufficiently systematic to offer a plausible explanation. Because these ambiguities seem to be inherent in cultural views, I begin with a brief recapitulation of their history and only then analyze their logical structure. I also summarize some statistical findings that show that at least the observable patterns of culture play no role in explaining the stability of democracy. Having arrived at a negative

---

[1] These are 1985 purchasing power parity dollars, from Penn World Tables, release 5.6.

conclusion with regard to cultural explanations, I summarize a rational choice model, developed elsewhere (Przeworski 2002), and show that this model not only makes perfect sense of the observed patterns but also explains why democratic government is limited even when the incumbents have full discretion in law making.

## Culture and Democracy[2]

### Rival and Nonrival Explanations

Cultural explanations claim that some definite cultural patterns, something that could be termed "the democratic culture," are necessary for democracy to be sustained. This is a twofold claim: (1) democracy endures only if it is supported by the cultural patterns of a society, and (2) specific cultures may or may not be democratic. This claim, however, is not yet sufficient to constitute an explanation rival to the one based on pursuit of interests. Cultural explanations are rival only if they assert that the democratic culture necessary for democracy to endure arises independently of development and is not an effect of democracy. If this culture is a lawful consequence of economic development, then the two explanations cannot be empirically distinguished. If this culture is an effect of democracy, then it plays no causal role. To distinguish rival from complementary explanations, I first briefly sketch a history of cultural views and then analyze their structure.

### A History of Cultural Views

Montesquieu, in *Lettres persanes* (1993 [1721]) and then in *De l'esprit des lois* (1995 [1748]), was the first to argue that each form of government requires definite cultural patterns to be present if it is to endure.[3] Each form has a ruling principle: despotism rests on fear, monarchy on honor, and republic on virtue. These principles are what makes each form of government function – "ce qui le fait agir" (III.1). They

---

[2] This section is a summary of Przeworski, Cheibub, and Limongi (1998).

[3] Rousseau (1985 [1771]) carried this view even further, arguing that each specific type of democratic institution can prosper only if it is compatible with the mores of a particular society. Even if his view of Poland was quite folkloric, his claim was general: "One must know thoroughly the nation for which one is building; otherwise the final product, however excellent it may be in itself, will prove imperfect when it is acted upon – the more certainly if the nation is already formed, with its tastes, customs, prejudices, and failings too deeply rooted to be stifled by new plantings" (1985: 1).

have to be in turn consistent with other elements of culture. According to Versini (1995: 24–5), Montesquieu's list evolved gradually as he was learning about experiences of different countries: in *Pensées* no. 645 of 1737–8, the cultural elements included "la religion, les moeurs et les manières"; in *l'Esprit*, these first (XIX.4) became "la religion, les exemples des choses passées, les moeurs, les manières," and later on "la religion des habitants, leurs inclinations, leurs moeurs, leurs manières and des rapports entre elles." This is an open-ended list: ultimately everything seems to matter, from marital institutions, to celibacy of priests, to religious toleration.

Moreover, cultural causes are not the only ones: climate is crucial, as is the quality of land, size of the territory, and "commerce" (the economy). What, then, causes what? Versini (1995: 38) claims that "les causes morales sont finalement 'dominantes' dans De l'Esprit des lois." But he infers this conclusion only from the final order of topics discussed by Montesquieu, not from any explicit statements to this effect. Montesquieu sometimes used only the language of compatibility, not of causality, as in "Quel est le législateur qui purrait proposer le gouvernement populaire a des peuples pareils?" (XIX.2). Yet, he was looking for "l'ordre des choses" (XIX.1). Then, a little later, he observed that "Plusieurs choses governent les hommes ..." and "A mesure que, dans chaque nation, une de ces causes agit avec plus de force, les autres lui cédent d'autant" (XIX.4). And all throughout he emphasized that laws educate; they are not just an effect. Hence, neither the causal relation between principles and cultures nor that between laws and principles is obvious.

Montesquieu's comparative study of forms of governments presages the difficulties culturalist views were to face ever since. The first one is to identify those features of culture that matter for the form of government. The second is to determine the causal links among the economy, political institutions, and culture.

Montesquieu's general hypothesis acquired a developmentalist perspective in the writings of Scottish moral philosophers, who "transformed Montesquieu's states of society into an elaborate sequence of stages in the historical development of civil society in order to account for the process for which a new word had to be coined, namely, 'civil-isation'" (Collini, Winch, and Burrow 1983: 18). The twist they gave was to think of cultures as progressing from primitive to civilized and to claim that some forms of political life can be sustained only among the latter. Political institutions, in their view, could not be simply invented *ab ovo*, introduced by design, but had to correspond to feelings

**117**

of sympathy, habits of sociability and deference, and a learned sense of public utility.

This issue – "To What Extent Forms of Government Are a Matter of Choice" – gave the title to the first chapter of J. S. Mill's *Considerations on Representative Government* (1991 [1861]). Mill did believe that some cultural patterns are incompatible with democracy: "[A] rude people, though in some degree alive to the benefits of civilized society, may be unable to practice the forbearances which it demands; their passions may be too violent, or their personal pride too exacting, to forego private conflict, and leave to the laws the avenging of their real or supposed wrongs" (p. 15). People may find the representative form of government repugnant, they may desire it but be unwilling or unable to fulfill its conditions, or they may be technologically unprepared to exercise it. Yet Mill (pp. 18–19) insisted that these conditions are malleable: "[T]hese alleged requisites of political institutions are merely facilities for realizing the three conditions.... it is an exaggeration to elevate these mere aids and facilities into necessary conditions. People are more easily induced to do, and do more easily, what they are already used to; but people also learn to do things new to them." People may be unprepared for democracy, but they can be taught to behave as democrats.

The complicated issue is the direction and the chain of causality. To the extent to which they distinguished technology, wealth, culture understood as beliefs and habits, and culture understood as appreciation of ideas and symbols, most developmentalist views, from the Adam Smith (Winch 1978: ch. 3), through most stage theories (Comte, Maine, Cambridge "comparative politics" school, Toennies, Durkheim, to cite just some), to the contemporary modernization theory, were ambivalent about the chain of causality that moved civilizations from one stage to the next one. Was it material progress that drove culture and political institutions or cultural transformations that advanced material progress and forms of government?

The modern attempt to resolve these issues was the book of Almond and Verba (1965), which also ushered in a new methodology. Almond and Verba began by observing that while technological aspects of the Western culture were easy to diffuse to the new nations, Western political culture was less apparently transmittable. And there is a causal relation between culture and democracy: "If the democratic model of the participatory state is to develop in these new nations, it will require more than the formal institutions of democracy.... A democratic form of participatory political system requires as well a political culture consistent with it" (p. 3). Although Almond and Verba accepted that, in the general vein of modernization theory, economic development is necessary for democracy, they claimed it was not sufficient, as evidenced by the fact that the correlations found by Lipset (1959) were far from perfect.

For Almond and Verba culture furnishes the "psychological basis" of democracy. Moreover, as distinct from Laswell (1946) and other studies in the psychoanalytic vein, theirs was a mentalistic psychology. Culture is the "psychological orientation toward social objects" (p. 13). "When we speak of the political culture," Almond and Verba explain, "we refer to the political system as internalized in the cognition, feelings, and evaluations of its population." And, finally, "The political culture of a nation is the particular distribution of patterns of orientation toward political objects among the members of the nation."

Given this conceptualization, culture can be studied by asking questions of individuals, and the culture of a nation is nothing but a distribution of the answers. The methodological innovation was to characterize what used to be studied as "the national character" by examining history or, as "the modal personality," by inquiring into patterns of childrearing, by asking people what they knew, liked, and valued. Thus, even if Almond and Verba's study was criticized on conceptual and methodological ground (Barry 1978; Wiatr 1979), it gave rise to a new industry.

Asking people questions about their knowledge of political institutions, their preferences for systems of government, and their evaluations of political processes, actors, and outcomes is now a routine activity all around the world. Answers to these questions are interpreted as harbingers of democratic stability and are often read nervously: Brazil, for example, seemed to verge on the brink in 1991 when only 39% of the respondents thought that democracy is always the best system of government, as contrasted with, say, Chile, where in 1990 76% did. Almond and Verba, Inglehart (1990), and Granato, Inglehart, and Leblang (1996) attempted to show that answers to such questions can predict whether democracy survives or falls. But their analyses suffer from serious methodological pitfalls. The fact is that surveys of "democratic attitudes" are conducted repeatedly in old and new democracies; pages of academic journals are filled with percentages of Americans, Spaniards, Chileans, Poles, or Kazakhs saying that they like or do not like democracy (for a taste, see *Journal of Democracy* 53 [2001]), and there is not a shred of evidence that these answers have anything to do with the actual survival of democracy.

## What Is It about Culture That Matters and How?

As this brief historical sketch indicates, the view that democracy requires a definite cultural basis has many lives. Something about culture seems necessary for democracy to emerge or endure. But what? Montesquieu thought it was an irrational motive force ("les passions humaines qui le font mouvoir," III.1) – fear, honor, virtue – which, in turn, reflect religions, mores, and manners. Stage theorists looked for feelings and habits, as well as for a rational sense of public utility. Mill was more systematic, distinguishing among a preference for democracy, the temperamental characteristics necessary to sustain it, and a sense of community. Almond and Verba looked at beliefs, effects, and evaluations of the political process and political outcomes. Inglehart wanted to know whether people are satisfied with their lives, whether they trust each other, and whether they like revolutionary changes. Other survey researchers inquired whether people value democracy per se, regardless of the conditions with which it has to cope and the outcomes it generates.

Yet if culturalist views are to furnish a compelling explanation of the origins and the life of democracy, they must specify what it is about culture that matters and how. Let us first distinguish different aspects of culture that may matter:

First, people value democracy per se, regardless of the outcomes it generates. They want to bring it about and they defend it against threats because democracy is based on political equality (Tocqueville), because it is an expression of liberty (Dunn 1992), or for whatever noninstrumental reason. They believe that democracy is unconditionally the best (or the least bad) system of government, say so when asked, or act as if they did so believe.

Second, people see it as their duty to obey outcomes resulting from rules to which they "agreed."[4] I put "agree" in quotation marks, because the agreement in question can be putative: people would have chosen these rules had they been consulted. Democracy is then legitimate in the sense that people are ready to accept decisions of as yet undetermined content, as long as these decisions result from applying the rules. Even if they do not like them, people comply with the outcomes of the

---

[4] On the difficulties of this conception as a positive theory of action, see Dunn (1996: ch. 4). Note as well Kelsen's (1988 [1929]: 21) observation that "The purely negative assumption that no individual counts more than any other does not permit to deduce the positive principle that the will of the majority should prevail."

democratic interplay because they result from applying rules they accept. Neubauer (1967: 225) claimed that "socialization into the 'rules of the game' " is a precondition for democracy.

The theory of political obligation has a second variant, one that emphasizes participation rather than implied consent. In this version, people see it as their duty to obey outcomes in the making of which they had a chance to participate. Equally with all others, they had an opportunity to make public their reasons (Cohen 1998) or at least to vote, and having had this opportunity makes the outcomes normatively binding. "Participatory culture" is then the key to democratic stability.

Third, people have values and perhaps temperamental characteristics ("democratic personality," in the language of the 1950s) that support it. Lipset (1960: 153) maintained that "if a political system is not characterized by a value system allowing the peaceful 'play' of power ... there can be no stable democracy." These characteristics may include "republican virtue," trust,[5] empathy, tolerance, moderation, or patience. People may love the collectivity above themselves; they may trust that the government will not take an unfair advantage of them even if it is in the hands of their adversaries; they may be ready to respect the validity of views and interests different from theirs; they may be willing to accept that others should also have rights; or they may be willing to wait for their turn.

Finally, what may matter for democracy to be possible is not so much what people share but that they do share something: "consensus."[6] J. S. Mill (1991: 230) presented perhaps the first in the long line of arguments to the effect that "Free institutions are next to impossible in a country made up of different nationalities. Among a people without fellow-feeling, especially if they read and speak different languages, the united public opinion necessary to the working of representative government cannot exist." Unless people share basic characteristics, such as language, religion, or ethnicity, they do not have enough in common to sustain democracy. But homogeneity with regard to such basic characteristics is not sufficient: "agreement" about some basic values, rules of the game, or what is not required for democracy to function (Dahl

---

[5] Trust is the recent fashion of democratic theorists. But one might wonder if democratic citizens should trust their governments too much: should not they, instead, monitor what governments are doing and sanction them appropriately?

[6] Such consensus may be "overlapping" (Rawls 1993), in the sense that the reasons people accept the particular institutional framework may be different among groups holding different "fundamental" values.

1956; Lipset 1959; Eckstein 1961).[7] Thus, Weingast (1997: 254) thinks that democracy is unstable in Latin America because "Latin American states are not characterized by a common set of citizen values about the appropriate role of government."

Clearly, these cultural underpinnings of democracy need not be mutually exclusive. But if culturalist views are to have an explanatory power, they must distinguish and specify. Otherwise, it will never be possible to conclude that culture does not matter.

The second issue concerns causality. For even if all the enduring democracies were found to share a definite "democratic culture," this observation would not be sufficient to determine which, if either, comes first: democratic culture or democratic institutions. At the risk of being pedantic, we need to distinguish causal chains that may connect economic development, cultural transformations, and political institutions:

First, culture causes both development and democracy, whatever the causal connection between the latter two. This is a "strongly culturalist" view.

Protestantism is one candidate for a culture that promotes both development and democracy – at least this was the view of Lipset (1959, 1994). In turn, Catholicism, in the view of Wiarda (1981), impedes both development and democracy in Latin America.[8] Confucianism was seen not so long ago as an obstacle to both, but now it appears to be good for development while being considered by some, notably President Lee Kuan Yew of Singapore, as antithetical to democracy.

Second, both development and culture are needed independently for democracy to be possible. Even if development generates some cultural transformations, these transformations are not sufficient to generate the democratic culture, which is, in turn, necessary for democracy to survive. This was the view of Almond and Verba, discussed earlier, still a strongly culturalist view.

---

[7] Eckstein (as well as Eckstein and Gurr 1975) is among those who claim that democratic politics requires that democratic values also permeate less inclusive social units, such as families, communities, or workplaces.

[8] According to Wiarda (1981) the political systems of contemporary Latin America are the product of a political culture that is unique to the region and incompatible with democracy. This culture, which he calls the "corporative model," follows directly from "the Spanish colonial system of organicism, patrimonialism, manorialism, corporatism, and feudalism" (p. 39). When applied to particular countries, this approach leads to observations such as "Dominican political culture historically has not been conducive to democratic rule. We consider this a very important factor. Dominican political culture, inherited from Spain, has been absolutist, elitist, hierarchical, corporatist, and authoritarian" (Wiarda 1989: 450).

Third, a particular culture is necessary for democracy to be possible but this culture is automatically generated by economic development. Lipset (1959, 1960) described several ways in which development generates cultural preconditions for democracy: by promoting moderation and tolerance, and allowing the lower strata to "adopt longer time perspectives and more complex and gradualist views of politics" (1959: 83). Clearly, in this view cultures, in plural, are sufficiently malleable to become "modernized" as an effect of economic development. Thus, the causal chain goes from development, through culture, to democracy. This view is "weakly culturalist."

Fourth, a particular culture is necessary for democracy to endure but this culture emerges as an effect of democratic institutions once they are in place. This was the view of J. S. Mill, who thought that while people prefer to do what they know how to do, they can be taught to do new things. The educational impact of laws was the persistent theme of Montesquieu as well as of Tocqueville. In this view, we should expect that all enduring democracies should have the same political culture and that this culture would emerge as a consequence of democratic institutions being in place.

Only the two "strongly culturalist" views constitute rivals to the economic explanation. Cultural explanations are rival only if they assert that the relevant culture arises independently of economic development and has a causal efficacy independent of development. If "culture" is just a description of what people believe and do in an interest-supported democratic equilibrium, then it just elaborates, rather than rivals, the economic explanation.

## Cultures and the Democratic Culture

Are particular, otherwise identifiable cultures conducive or detrimental to the rise and durability of democratic institutions? The issue is the following. Suppose we were to observe that, independently of their wealth, most countries with a particular cultural trait are democracies and few countries without it are. We would then have prima facie evidence that, whatever the "democratic culture" is, this trait furnishes its necessary ingredients. But note that if we fail to find such patterns, it may be for two distinct reasons: either because the rise and durability of democracy need not call for a particular set of cultural patterns or because, while democracy does have cultural requisites and cultural barriers, all cultures are, or at least can be made, compatible with these patterns.

Historically, the discussion of this topic revolved mainly around cultures identified by dominant religions. The idea of the primary causal force of religion is due to Max Weber's (1958 [1904–5]) argument that religiously motivated, ascetic "calling" for accumulation of wealth was the key to the economic success of capitalism. Weber (p. 180) claimed that "One of the fundamental elements of the spirit of modern capitalism, and not only of that but of all modern culture: rational conduct on the basis of the idea of the calling, was born ... from the spirit of Christian asceticism." This "spirit of capitalism, in the sense of a definite standard of life claiming ethical sanction" (p. 58) was the principal explanation of the difference between Protestants (or at least the ascetics among them) and followers of other religions with regard to economic conduct (p. 40).

Weber had next to nothing to say about the consequences of this spirit of capitalism for politics in general and democracy (about which he had ambivalent and changing beliefs) in particular. There is one passage (p. 45) in *The Protestant Ethic and the Spirit of Capitalism* in which Weber cited Montesquieu to the effect that the English "had progressed the farthest of all peoples of the world in three important things: in piety, in commerce, and in freedom" and then asked, perhaps rhetorically, "Is it not possible that this commercial superiority and their adaptation to free political institutions are connected in some way with that record of piety which Montesquieu ascribes to them?" Yet he did not follow this thought and, at the end of the text (p. 182), just announced that "The next task would be rather to show the significance of ascetic rationalism ... for the content of practical social ethics, thus for types of organization and the functions of social groups from the conventicle to the State." Here he stopped.

Yet the idea that Weber saw in Protestantism the wellspring of modern democracy is widespread among contemporary political scientists. In the most influential article on the conditions for democratic stability, Lipset (1960: 165) claimed that "It has been argued by Max Weber among others that the factors making for democracy in this area [northwest Europe and their English-speaking offsprings in America and Australasia] are a historically unique concatenation of elements, part of the complex which also produced capitalism in this area," because "The emphasis within Protestantism on individual responsibility furthered the emergence of democratic values."[9] In turn, Catholicism,

---

[9] Lipset does not point to any specific text of Weber. Neither do Almond and Verba (1965: 8), who assert that "the development of Protestantism, and in particular the nonconformist

in Lipset's (1960: 72–3) view, was antithetical to democracy in pre–Second World War Europe and Latin America.

In his presidential address to the American Sociological Association, Lipset (1994: 5) attributed the origins of these views not to Weber but to Toqueville, again without indicating a specific text. Yet, Toqueville (1961: 1:427), referring to Irish immigrants, not only observed that "Ces catholiques ... forment la classe la plus républicaine et la plus démocratique qui soit aux Etats Unis," but went on to conclude that "on a tort de regarder la religion catholique comme un ennemi naturel de la démocratie," pointing in particular to the egalitarian features of Catholicism.

Catholicism is not the worst enemy of democracy: Islam and Confucianism hold the palm (Eisenstadt 1968: 25–7). Huntington (1993b: 15) reported that "No scholarly disagreement exists regarding the proposition that traditional Confucianism was either undemocratic or antidemocratic." Similar views about Islam abound (Gellner 1991: 506; Lewis 1993: 96–8).

Yet Lee Teng Hui (1997), the former president of Taiwan, found in traditional Confucianism an emphasis on limited government that is essential to democracy. And in a systematic review of writings on Confucianism and democracy, Im (1997) found a very mixed picture: on the one hand, Confucianism has no concept of civil society and no concept of individual rights (but instead of roles people should perform) or of the rule of law but, on the other hand, it has deep traditions of limited government, recognizes the right of rebellion against rulers who deviate from the prescribed "Way," is religiously tolerant, and is antimilitaristic. Moreover, at least in Korea, a plurality of opinion, a public sphere, existed during the six centuries of the Chosun dynasty.

The discussion within and about Islam is equally complex. According to Esposito and Voll (1996), the three basic tenets of Islam lend themselves and have been subject to more or less antidemocratic interpretations. Thus, the principle of the Unity of God (tawhid), while requiring consistency with God's laws, can leave interpretation of them to every capable and qualified Muslim and need not be inconsistent with a system of government in which the executive "is constituted by the general will of the Moslems who have also the right to depose it" (p. 24) or with "an assembly whose members are the real representatives of the people" (p. 27). Similarly, the principle of God's representative on

sects, have been considered vital to the development of stable political institutions in Britain, the Old Commonwealth, and the United States."

earth (*khilafah*) need not be interpreted in individual terms but can be extended to all men and women. Finally, the traditions of consultation, consensus, and independent interpretative judgment can be used as arguments for or against democracy. And, in fact, Eickelman and Piscatori (1996) show that such doctrinal interpretations have in the past served and now serve to justify quite different political arrangements.

There are several reasons to doubt that cultures, or civilizations, as Mazrui (1997: 118) prefers to think of Islam, furnish requisites for or constitute irremovable barriers to democracy:

First, the arguments relating civilizations to democracy appear terribly ex post: if many countries dominated by Protestants are democratic, we look for features of Protestantism that promote democracy; if no Muslim countries are democratic, obviously there must be something about Islam that is antidemocratic. Eisenstadt (1968), for example, finds that the Indian civilization has what it takes but Confucianism and Islam do not, and one wonders what he would have found if China were democratic and India not.[10]

Second, one can find elements in every culture, Protestantism included, that appear compatible and elements that seem incompatible with democracy. Protestant legitimation of economic inequality, not to speak of the very ethic of self-interest, offers a poor moral basis for living together and resolving conflicts in a peaceful way. Other cultures are authoritarian but egalitarian, hierarchical but respectful of the right of rebellion, communal but tolerant of diversity. So one can pick and choose.[11]

Third, each of the religious traditions has been historically compatible with a broad range of practical political arrangements. Tunisia is not Afghanistan, South Korea is not North Korea, Costa Rica is not El Salvador; postwar Germany is not Hitler's Germany. This range is not the same for different religious traditions but is broad enough in each case to demonstrate that these traditions are quite flexible with regard to the political arrangements with which they can be made compatible.

Finally, and most important, traditions are not given once and for all: they are continually invented and reinvented (Hobsbawm and Ranger 1983), a point stressed by Eickelman and Piscatori (1996) in their analysis of Islam. In fact, the very analyses of the Confucian tradition just

[10] The ex-post method is even more apparent in cultural analyses of economic growth. See Sen (1997).
[11] Thus Nathan and Shi (1993) find elements of democratic culture in China, while Gibson, Duch, and Tedin (1992) discover them in Russia.

cited are best seen as attempts to invent a democratic Confucianism. Cultures are made of cloth, but the fabric of culture drapes differently in the hands of different tailors.

This view has been recently vigorously contested by Huntington (1993a: 40). He began by observing that "Western concepts differ fundamentally from those prevalent in other civilizations. Western ideas of individualism, liberalism, constitutionalism, human rights, equality, liberty, the rule of law, democracy, free markets, the separation of church and state, often have little resonance in Islamic, Confucian, Japanese, Hindu, Buddhist or Orthodox cultures." And, he continued, "Western efforts to propagate such ideas produce instead a reaction against 'human rights imperialism' and a reaffirmation of indigenous values, as can be seen in the support for religious fundamentalism by the younger generation of non-Western cultures." It is difficult to guess on what bases can one arrive at this assertion: most students of Islamic religious fundamentalism attribute its rise to the deteriorating economic conditions of the urban masses, not to 'human rights imperialism'; the rise of religious fundamentalism is limited to some countries within some cultural areas and is prominent in the most "Western" country of them all, the United States. But, more important, the Cassandras of the impending *Kulturkampf* (also Fukuyama 1995) would be well advised to look back before they plunge forward.[12]

Contrary to Lipset or Almond and Verba, Weber himself (in Gerth and Mills 1958: 337–8) thought that the political role of organized religions depends on their interests, not their content: "The widely varying empirical stands which historical religions have taken in the face of political action have been determined by the entanglement of religious organizations in power interests and in struggles for power, ... by the usefulness and the use of religious organizations for the political taming of the masses and, especially, by the need of the powers-that-be for the religious consecration of their legitimacy." In a study of the rise of European Christian Democracy, Kalyvas (1996) showed that the relation between Catholicism and democracy followed strategic considerations of the Catholic Church. And in a daring comparison of nineteenth-century Belgian ultramontane Catholic fundamentalism and the contemporary Algerian Islamic fundamentalism, Kalyvas (1997) concluded that the different outcomes in these two countries were due to the organizational structure of the respective religions rather than to their cultural content. Linz and Stepan (1996: 453) came to the same

---

[12] For a critique dispelling the myths perpetuated by Huntington, see Holmes (1997).

conclusion with regard to the recent cases of democratization. Finally, Laitin (for a recent summary, see 1995) examined in several contexts the role played by "cultural entrepreneurs" in the dynamic of cultural change, providing extensive evidence that, while conflicts over culture can end in different outcomes, they are a matter of interests and strategies, not of any primordially given cultural contents. Thus, the claim that the antidemocratic proclivities of "civilizations" are given once and for all hurls itself against historical experience. To go back to Mill, "People are more easily induced to do, and do more easily, what they are already used to; but people also learn to do things new to them."

### Empirical Evidence

Testing the importance of cultures for the survival of democracies is next to impossible. Yet the predictive power of wealth is so overwhelming that little room is left for cultures, whatever they may be. When one analyzes political regimes between 1950 and 1990 on the basis of per capita income alone, one will correctly classify 3,199 out of 4,126 (77.5%) of all annual observations (Przeworski at al. 2000). Hence, economic explanation alone goes a long way.

When added to economic variables, specifically per capita income, the frequency of the three religions for which we have data – Catholicism, Protestantism, and Islam – has no impact whatever on the durability of democracy. Only when past political instability, measured as the number of transitions to authoritarianism during the country's history, is taken into consideration is the frequency of one religion positively related to the probability that democracy would survive in this country. And this religion is Catholicism.

To test the hypothesis about the impact of cultural heterogeneity, one can use indexes of ethnolinguistic and religious fractionalization.[13] Heterogeneity makes democracies less likely to survive: this much confirms common wisdom. But it makes dictatorships less likely to survive as well: heterogeneity just makes political regimes less stable.[14] Thus, the claim that common values are needed to support democracy reduces to the

---

[13] Fractionalization indexes measure the probability that two randomly chosen individuals do not belong to the same group. The index of ethnolinguistic fractionalization is taken from the Web (and due to Easterly and Levine). Their data set also contains indexes measuring the percentage of the population not speaking the official and the most widely used language. These two indexes have no effect on regime stability.

[14] Indeed, the effect of ethnolinguistic, but not religious, fractionalization vanishes once past political instability is controlled for.

observation that all political regimes are less stable in heterogeneous countries.

This is scant evidence, but cultures just do not lend themselves to classifications. Hence, the opportunity for statistical analyses is limited. One would have obviously liked to be able to classify cultures as hierarchical or egalitarian, universalistic or particularistic, religious or secular, consensual or conflictive, and so on. But the evidence we do have does not support the claim that some cultures are incompatible with democracy. They seem to have no effect on whether democracy endures.

## Interests and Democracy

### A Model

The prototype of democratic politics that underlies this analysis reflects two modern understandings of democracy: Schumpeter's (1942) focus on filling governmental offices by elections and Montesquieu's (1995 [1748]) emphasis on limiting governmental actions to those enabled by law.

There is a society in which per capita income is $y$. The society consists of three types of income earners: poor, middle, and rich. Incomes of the poor and the middle are lower than the average; incomes of the rich are higher than the average.

There are two political parties (or coalitions thereof): a left party represents the poor and a right party the rich. When an election comes, the two parties propose to redistribute incomes. They have two sets of instruments. They can either alter market incomes by instruments such as minimum wage, union legislation, labor-market regulation, monetary policy, or trade policy, or they can transform post-fisc incomes by taxes and transfers. The left party proposes to tax the rich and to transfer the revenue to the poor and perhaps the middle. The right party proposes to reduce the income of the poor, redistributing to the rich and perhaps the middle. Each party can tax its own supporters. Note that, contrary to standard models, redistribution from the poor to the rich is possible.

Some rule defines what constitutes electoral victory: for example, the rule may be that whoever happens to win a majority of votes is the winner. The probability that either party would win is known ex ante but, even when the electoral platforms are announced, the exact result of an election remains uncertain. Once votes are counted, someone is declared the winner according to this rule.

**129**

The designation of "winners" and "losers" is an instruction to the parties as to what they should and should not do. The winners should move into a White, Pink, or Blue House or perhaps even a *palais* and, while there, should not redistribute more than what they proposed and should hold elections again. The losers should not move into the house, but should accept what they are given and participate in elections again.

Parties decide whether to obey these instructions or to rebel against them. The reason compliance is problematic is that voting is an imposition of a will over a will (Schmitt 1988). Elections authorize compulsion: they empower governments, the rulers, to seize money from some and give it to others, to put people in jail, and sometimes even to take their life. This is what "ruling" is (Kelsen 1988; Bobbio 1984). Authorized to coerce, the electoral winners promote their values and interests against those of electoral losers. Hence losers lose. As Condorcet (1986: 22) pointed out, "what is entailed in a law that was not adopted unanimously is submitting people to an opinion which is not theirs or to a decision which they believe to be contrary to their interest."[15] And though winners win, they still suffer limitations on their power. Rather than exercise moderation and risk losing office by holding elections, they can extract more or not hold elections.

If both the winners and the losers obey, production occurs, incomes are redistributed according to the winning platform, and a new election is called. If either party rebels, a conflict ensues. What happens depends on the balance of military force: the political posture of the military or the actual physical force of supporters. The result may be that democracy survives, but this state of affairs will be ephemeral, because repeated attempts to subvert it are likely to bring democracy down sooner or later. If the rebelling party wins or if both parties turn against democracy, a dictatorship is established.

Under dictatorship, the victorious party redistributes incomes by giving subsistence income to those defeated and distributing the rest among its supporters.[16] But dictatorships not only redistribute income: they use force to repress their opponents. Concentration camps, gulags,

---

[15] "[I]l s'agit, dans une loi qui n'a pas été votée unanimement, de soumettre des hommes à une opinion qui n'est pas la leur, ou à une décision qu'ils croient contraire à leur intérêt...."

[16] Dictatorships can be narrow, self-selective, or broad. A narrow dictatorship treats as enemies everyone other than its own types, that is, the poor for the left party and the rich for the right party. A self-selective one treats as enemies all those who voted for the other party. A broad dictatorship, finally, includes the middle types in the addition to the core supporters of the victorious party. For reasons spelled out later, I assume for the moment that dictatorships are narrow.

internment camps (Buru Island in Indonesia after 1964, Dawson Island in Chile after 1973, Robben Island in South Africa), the Cambodian "killing fields," and the Argentine "disappearances" are a standard repertory of dictatorial rule. And even where such barbarism is less rampant, the threat of imprisonment, torture, or death is sufficiently foreboding that, even if those dominated by a dictatorship would receive the same income as the electoral losers, their expected utility does not increase homogeneously. The same income generates lower utility when one's physical integrity is threatened.

Any model contains some assumptions that are innocuous, in the sense that qualitative conclusions would not change if they were relaxed. All the assumptions about income belong to this category. But the reader should stand warned that the assumption that the same income gives lower utility to those who suffer from dictatorship is crucial for the central result. If you believe it, you will have to believe the rest, so that the time to doubt is now.

To recapitulate, two parties compete in elections proposing to redistribute incomes. Once the platforms are announced, voting takes place. One of the parties is declared winner. Both the winner and the loser decide whether to obey the election result or to turn against democracy. If both obey, incomes are redistributed and another election takes place. If at least one rebels, either democracy survives for some time or a dictatorship is established.

I first present consequences of these assumptions for the survival of democracy, then for distributions of income feasible under democracy, and finally some extensions and interpretations.

### Affluence and the Survival of Democracy

For each country, characterized by a distribution of market incomes, electoral institutions, and relations of military force, there is some threshold of per capita income, $y^H$, above which both the electoral winners and the electoral losers unconditionally accept the results of elections, with the redistributive consequences they entail. Hence, democracy survives at all $y \geq y^H$.

The intuition behind this conclusion is that in affluent countries even the electoral losers have too much at stake to risk being defeated in a struggle over dictatorship. In poor societies there is little to distribute, so that a party that moves against democracy and is defeated has relatively little to lose. But in affluent societies, the gap between the well-being of electoral losers and of people oppressed by a dictatorship is large. Thus, even if the income a particular group expects when it rebels is higher than the income it expects under democracy, the possibility of losing the struggle over dictatorship is foreboding in affluent societies. As per capita income increases, the dictatorial lottery becomes more uncertain relative to the democratic lottery. Hence, at some level of income, democracy is better than dictatorship. It is risk aversion that motivates everyone in affluent societies to obey the results of electoral competition.

To see this argument, examine Figure 1A, which portrays as a function of per capita income the instantaneous utilities of being a dictator, of having won an election, of having lost an election, and of being dominated by a dictatorship, all for the poor. As per capita income increases, so do the stakes in attempts to subvert democracy, where by "stakes" I mean the difference between losing an election and losing a conflict over dictatorships. As a result, you see in Figure 1B that the value of democracy increases faster in average income than the value of dictatorship, both for the electoral winners and for the losers. All this is also true for the rich.

This result also sheds light on the role of economic crises in threatening democratic regimes. What matters is not the rate of growth per se but the impact of economic crises on the level of per capita income. Each country has some threshold of income above which democracy survives independently of election results, $y^H$. Economic crises matter if they result in income's declining from above to below this threshold but not when they occur at income levels below or well above this threshold. In Trinidad and Tobago, per capita income fell by 34% between 1981 and 1990 but the 1990 income was still $7,769 and democracy survived. In New Zealand, income fell by 9.7% between 1974 and 1978, but the 1978 income was $10,035. Yet in Venezuela, which enjoyed democracy during forty-one years, per capita income declined by 28% from 1978 to 1989, when it reached $5,919, and has continued to fall since then. Hence, this decline may be responsible for the emergence of antidemocratic forces in that country.

Democracy can survive in poor countries but only if everyone is at least moderately risk-averse, no one has overwhelming military power, and patterns of redistribution reflect military force. Income distribution also plays a role: in equal societies democracy survives under a broader range of conditions. In a country with a highly egalitarian income distribution, such as India, the left party opts for democracy when its odds of establishing dictatorship are lower than 4 to 1; in a highly unequal society, such as the Philippines or Brazil, only when they are lower than 2 to 1.

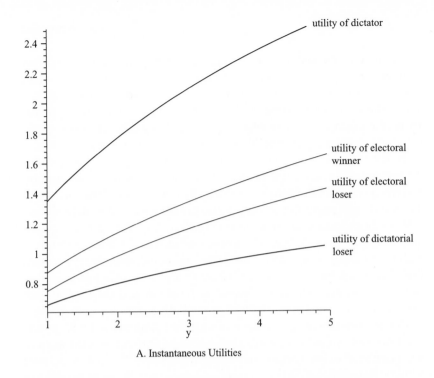

A. Instantaneous Utilities

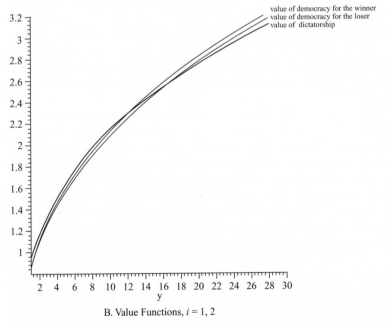

B. Value Functions, $i = 1, 2$

Figure 5.1. Illustrative values for the poor of being the dictator, winning and losing elections, and being dominated by dictatorship, as a function of per capita income.

When one side has an overwhelming military power, it turns against democracy even when everyone is highly risk-averse. But even when military power is more balanced, democracy survives in poor countries only if the expected redistribution reflects the balance of military force. Thus, for example, in a society with a highly egalitarian income distribution, democracy is possible even when the right party has 16 to 1 odds of winning a conflict over dictatorship. But it is possible only under the condition that the left party has almost no chance to win an election and the incomes of the poor are reduced by the policies of the electorally dominant right party. Democracy is also possible when the left party has 4 to 1 odds of establishing dictatorship. But then democracy survives only if the left is almost certain to win elections and taxes the rich at a high rate. Finally, when the military odds are equal, democracy survives under a broad range of electoral chances and redistributive schemes. Nevertheless, the rich cannot expect to be taxed and the poor cannot expect their incomes to be reduced at too high a rate.

Hence, if democracy is to survive in poor countries, political power must correspond to the military strength. Note that this was the ancient justification of majority rule. According to Bryce (1921: 25–6, emphasis added), Herodotus used the concept of democracy "in its old and strict sense, as denoting a government in which the will of the majority of qualified citizens rules, ... *so that physical force of the citizens coincides (broadly speaking) with their voting power.*" Condorcet as well, while interpreting voting in modern times as a reading of reason, observed that in the ancient, brutal times, authority had to be placed where the force was.[17]

Established in 1947, when the country had a per capita income of $556, democracy survived in India. An explanation in terms of the model might be the following. Per capita income in India was very low in 1947 and has grown only slowly since then. But income distribution was highly egalitarian in India – as of 1951, the ratio of the top to the bottom quintile was 6:14 – and it became even more egalitarian by 1990, when this ratio was 4:30. Hence, the model implies that the poor supported democracy even if per capita income was low because their share of this income was very high. The military was apolitical, so that

---

[17] "Lorsque l'usage de soumettre tous les individus à la volonté du plus grand nombre, s'introduisit dans les sociétes, et que les hommes convinrent de regarder la décision de la pluralité comme la volonté de tous, ils n'adoptérent pas cette méthode comme un moyen d'éviter l'erreur et de se conduire d'aprés des décisions fondées sur la vérité: mais ils trouvèrent que, pour le bien de la paix et l'utilité générale, *il falloit placer l'autorit é où etoit la force*" (Condorcet 1986: 11, emphasis added).

neither side could not rely on its support. Electoral chances are more difficult to assess: while the Congress Party won several elections after independence with an overwhelming share of seats, it never won more than 50% of the votes.

The value of democracy for the electoral winners is higher than for the losers. Hence, it is possible that a party would prefer democracy when it wins the election but not when it loses. Examine again Figure 1B. At low income levels, the left party rebels against democracy whether it wins or loses the election. At intermediate income levels, electoral winners accept the result but electoral losers turn against democracy. Then, above some income level, the party obeys the results even if it lost. Note that this result reproduces the empirical patterns with which we began. If the other party accepts when it loses, results of elections are obeyed, but only because they turned out in a particular way. One should thus expect to observe countries in which the same party repeatedly wins elections and both the winners and the losers obey the electoral decisions, but in which the winners would not accept the verdict of the polls had it turned differently – situations to which Alvarez et al. (1996) refer as the "Botswana" case.

## Redistribution of Income

Any electoral incumbent faces two constraints to redistribution. One stems from the fear that if redistribution is large, the electoral losers would turn against democracy. I call this the "rebellion constraint." Say the left party wins an election. If the rich are to accept the electoral defeat, the left party can extract at most at the rate such that the value of democracy to the rich when they lost an election and are taxed at this rate is exactly equal to the expected value of their dictatorship. If the left party prefers democracy when the tax is not greater than this rate, then this rate is the rebellion constraint.

The second constraint is purely economic. If redistribution reduces the supply of investment or of labor services or if it causes distortions in some other ways, then the income-maximizing degree of redistribution will be mitigated by these deadweight costs. Because cooperation of the poor is necessary to generate the incomes of the rich, the right party must be concerned that the poor be able to work, which means that they must receive at least subsistence income. In turn, the left party must be concerned that if the postredistribution income of the rich types were to be lower than of the middle, the rich would not utilize a part of their endowment and would generate as little income as the middle types.

Hence, the postdistribution income of the electorally victorious poor may be maximized at some tax rate well below 100%. I refer to this condition as the "incentive constraint."

The maximum rates of redistribution feasible under democracy, that is, the rates compatible with the rebellion constraint, increase with per capita income. Hence, the scope of income redistribution that would not threaten democracy is narrower in poorer countries. The minimum tax rates also decline, so that in more affluent countries democracy survives under a broader range of redistributive schemes. In sufficiently wealthy countries democracy survives whether elections have no consequence for income distribution or each electoral winner redistributes a significant share of incomes.

Because in sufficiently affluent countries democracy is sustained under high tax rates, incentive constraint may bite first. In such situations the incentive constraint moderates the distributional zeal of the left party before the rebellion constraint comes into play.

These conclusions explain why poor countries, even those with highly unequal distribution of incomes, redistribute less income than affluent countries. While the total share of taxes in GDP is far from an ideal measure of redistribution, it is striking that under democracy this share increases steeply. Moreover, while Milanovic (1999) reports that the degree of income redistribution is sizable in the OECD countries and that countries with more unequal distributions of market incomes redistribute more through the fisc, several poor countries that have a much more unequal income distribution redistribute almost no income (Cortés 1997; Deininger and Squire 1996). The fear of rebellion prevents incumbents in poor countries from redistributing incomes.

### Extensions and Interpretations

The Role of Electoral Chances. The explanation in terms of risk aversion must be distinguished from that focusing on the role of electoral chances. Przeworski (1991) argued that democracy is sustained when the losers in a particular round of the electoral competition have sufficient chances to win in the future to make it attractive for them to wait rather than to rebel against the current electoral defeat. The argument was that when the value of electoral victory is greater than the expected value of dictatorship, which, in turn, is greater than the value of electoral defeat, then political actors will accept a temporary electoral defeat if they have reasonable prospects to win in the future. In the light of the model developed here, such prospects are neither sufficient nor necessary for democracy to survive. In poor countries, they are not sufficient. Above some income level, in turn, losers accept an electoral defeat even when they have no chance to win in the future, simply because even permanent losers have too much to risk in turning against democracy. Political forces are "deradicalized" because they are "bourgeoisified."

Yet the distribution of electoral chances has a powerful effect on the income threshold, $y^H$, above which losers accept the verdict of elections. Specifically, poverty is a constraint on feasible electoral institutions. If democracy is to survive in a relatively poor country, electoral institutions must be designed so as to allocate chances in a very specific way. In more affluent countries, in turn, institutional design is much less important for the survival of democracy.

The Role of Voting. What difference does it make that rulers are elected by votes, not by a lottery?[18] To study the impact of vote distribution on the stability of democracy, the basic model must be modified in two ways. First, assume that the probability that a dictatorial attempt is successful depends on the numbers supporting a particular party in the election[19] Second, assume that when a conflict over dictatorship breaks out, anonymity is lifted, so that each party can identify its supporters and its opponents and distribute the spoils of dictatorship appropriately.

With these assumptions, democracy is more fragile when the left party loses overwhelmingly or loses by a narrow margin. When the left party wins by a wide margin, it has a good chance of being successful in an *autogolpe*, while the right party is attracted by the eventuality that its dictatorship would be narrow, so that the payoff per member would be high. Hence, both parties rebel. When the left party loses by a small margin, it has a fair chance of being successful in an insurrection and its dictatorship would be quite narrow. In turn, when the right party wins by a large margin, it has a good chance of establishing its dictatorship but this dictatorship would be broad and thus unattractive to the rich. Finally, when the left party wins by a small margin, it enjoys the spoils of victory, while its chance of establishing a dictatorship is not great. Hence, democracy prevails when the right party wins overwhelmingly or when the left party wins by a small margin. Again, these are the observed patterns.

---

[18] For many differences other than those relevant here, see Manin (1997).

[19] Once anyone starts fighting, nonparticipation is not a feasible option: if you do not fight, you will certainly lose. As Sartre (1960) pointed out, the people who lived along the Faubourg St. Antoine took arms to destroy the Bastille because if they had not taken arms, they would have ended up in the Bastille.

The Role of Constitutions. By "constitutions," I mean only those rules that are difficult to change, because they are protected either by supermajorities or by some other devices. Note that in some countries, such as contemporary Hungary, constitutional rules can be changed by a simple majority, whereas in other countries, such as Germany, some clauses of the constitution cannot be changed at all.

Constitutions are neither sufficient nor necessary for democracy to survive. Constitutions are not sufficient because agreeing to rules does not imply that results of their application will be respected. We have seen that under a variety of conditions, parties obey electoral verdicts only as long as they turn out in a particular way. Hence, the contractarian theorem – "if parties agree to some rules, they will obey them" or "if they do not intend to obey them, parties will not agree to the rules" (Buchanan and Tullock 1962; Calvert 1994)[20] – is false. If one party knows that it will be better off complying with the democratic verdict if it wins but not if it loses, while the other party prefers democracy unconditionally, parties will agree to some rules knowing full well that they may be broken. Under such conditions, a democracy will be established but it will not be self-enforcing.

To see that constitutions are not necessary, note that above some income threshold democracy survives even though the rules of redistribution are chosen by each incumbent. Hence, democratic government is limited not because of some exogenous rules but for endogenous reasons: because of either the rebellion or the incentive constraint, whichever bites first. In equilibrium a democratic government obeys some rules that limit redistribution, but the rules that are self-enforcing are those that satisfy either constraint.

Alternatively, assume that the rule defining what constitutes an electoral victory no longer involves winning a majority of votes but entails some other measure of increasing votes, say a majority of legislative seats. Suppose again that under the current rule the expected value of democracy is so low for the left party that it opts for dictatorship whether it has won or lost the election. Say it won the current election and it manipulates the electoral rules to its advantage. The conditions for a democratic equilibrium to hold then would be that its supporters

---

[20] According to Calvert (1994: 33), "Should players explicitly agree on a particular equilibrium of the underlying game as an institution, and then in some sense end their communication about institutional design, they will have the proper incentives to adhere to the agreement since it is an equilibrium.... Any agreement reached is then automatically enforced (since it is self-enforcing), as required for a bargaining problem."

would prefer democracy under the new rule, which is a rule that makes the right party indifferent between democracy and dictatorship.

Hence, the rules that regulate the functioning of a democratic system need not be immutable or even hard to change. After all, in France successive incumbents changed electoral rules eleven times since 1875. When a society is sufficiently wealthy, the incumbents in their own interest moderate their distributional zeal and tolerate fair electoral chances.

Weingast (1997) may still be correct in claiming that the constitution is a useful device for coordinating actions of electoral losers when the government engages in excessive redistribution or excessive manipulation of future electoral chances. Yet the constitution is not a contract, because there are no third parties to enforce it (Hardin 1989). Democratic rules must be thought of as endogenous (Calvert 1994, 1995).

Laws Constitute Equilibria. Even if fixed exogenous rules are neither sufficient nor necessary for democracies to survive, laws do play a role in constituting democratic equilibria. Calvert (1994) goes too far when he claims that institutions are just descriptions of equilibria in preexisting situations.[21] For democracies to exist, political parties must know at least how to interpret the results of voting; that is, they must be able to read any share of votes (or seats) as a "victory" or "defeat." Hence, the rule that defines victory is "constitutive" in the sense of Searle (1995): it enables behaviors that would not be possible without it, namely, a peaceful alternation in office. This rule plays a twofold role. (1) A democratic equilibrium may exist when under this rule but need not under other rules. For example, an equilibrium may exist when the rule is that a party is the winner if it receives a majority of votes but not if the rule were that it obtains one-third. (2) Given one rule, a different party may be "the winner" than under some other rule under which a democratic equilibrium also exists. Hence, the particular rule both enables a democratic equilibrium and picks one among several equilibria possible.

Conversely, given a society characterized by a level and distribution of income, there is some set of rules that will be obeyed by the electoral winners and losers regardless of the distribution of votes. Some rules are self-enforcing. Moreover, even if the rules are endogenous, it is always a particular law that political forces obey. The normativity of

---

[21] In Calvert's example, the institution that induces a cooperative equilibrium is the "director." This equilibrium would not have occurred in the original situation he describes without the institution of the "director." Hence, it is not an equilibrium of the underlying situation.

law is thus due to the fact that it enables the equilibrium in which the protagonists obey the particular law in their interests. As Kornhauser (1999: 21) puts it, "The legal structure identifies which of many equilibria the players will in fact adopt. The enactment of a law results in the institution of a new equilibrium."

## Conclusions

The conclusions are self-evident, so I just state them. Electoral winners and losers obey the results of democratic competition and thus democracy is sustained merely as a consequence of political forces pursuing their interests. Whether this explanation is sufficient or some cultural patterns are necessary for democracy to endure is just hard to tell, as is whether democracy can survive even when it is not supported by economic self-interest.

One source of confusion, however, still needs to be clarified. Suppose that a democratic equilibrium is supported exclusively by a strategic pursuit of self-interest, economic or other. In equilibrium, the protagonists obey the verdict of the polls and limit their actions to those enabled by law. They participate in a competition that has uncertain outcomes, and they obey the results; they are law-abiding; they act so as to perpetuate democracy. Moreover, governments obey limitations on their power. All this is just a description of the actions that are pursued in equilibrium. But it is just a small step to impute these observable actions to psychological motivations, to say that individuals are motivated by a sense of duty to accept outcomes of competition in which they participate, that they accept the normativity of the law, that they cherish democracy. Equilibrium actions are parceled out to individuals and psychologized as motivations.

This ambiguity, and the confusions it engenders, are most apparent in Weingast's (1997) attempt to reconcile different explanations of democratic stability. Weingast set himself to demonstrate that for democracy to be stable, citizens must adopt a shared view of what constitutes illegitimate actions by the state and must be prepared to act against the transgressions of these limits were they to occur. The first task requires a coordination of beliefs while the second, of actions. The first problem is settled when citizens focus on the limits prescribed by the constitution or specified by explicit political pacts. The second is solved when, fearing that they would suffer in the future from state encroachments, citizens put up a united front against illegitimate actions of the state, even if they currently benefit from them. Thus, in the end, democracy is stable when individuals are prepared to rebel in unison whenever the state transgresses some definite limits.

What, then, is the role of culture in supporting this democratic equilibrium? Weingast (p. 253) is careful to emphasize that his is not a causal story, in which values would make democracy stable, nor the reverse. A particular culture and democratic stability are just different aspects of situations in which a society resolves its coordination dilemmas. But what are exactly the aspects of culture that support these situations? Two are prominent – a "consensus" about the limits of legitimate state actions and a common sense of "duty" to defend it – but to pacify everyone, Weingast also adds "consensus on values and stable democracy" (p. 246), "consensus over the rules" (p. 257), "esteem" for limits to state actions (p. 251), "trust" (p. 257), and "mutual tolerance" (p. 257). Yet what kind of "duty" is it that is driven only by self-interest? This is a purely linguistic operation, and it just muddles the issue.

Psychologizing equilibrium actions seems to be a common practice, not limited to this context. There is nothing wrong with such descriptions, but only as long as they are not infused with causal interpretations. If a democratic equilibrium is sustained by a strategic pursuit of self-interest, then in equilibrium the political actors will be law-abiding. But this does not mean that the equilibrium is supported by the motivation to obey the law. This is why testing the comparative statics of competing theories – propositions relating observable conditions to observable outcomes – is crucial for choosing among them. The challenge for those who espouse cultural views is thus to show that they can make sense of the patterns we observe.

# References

Almond, Gabriel A., and Sydney Verba. 1965. *The Civic Culture: Political Attitudes and Democracy in Five Nations*. Boston: Little, Brown.

Alvarez, Mike, José Antonio Cheibub, Fernando Limongi, and Adam Przeworski. 1996. "Classifying Political Regimes." *Journal of International Comparative Development* 31: 3–36.

Barry, Brian. 1978. *Sociologists, Economists, and Democracy*. Chicago: University of Chicago Press.

Bobbio, Norberto. 1984. *The Future of Democracy*. Minneapolis: University of Minnesota Press.

Bryce, James. 1921. *Modern Democracies*. London.

Buchanan, James, and Gordon Tullock. 1962. *The Calculus of Consent: Logical Foundations of Constitutional Democracy*. Ann Arbor: University of Michigan Press.

**141**

Calvert, Randall. 1994. "Rational Actors, Equilibrium, and Social Institutions." In J. Knight and I. Sened (eds.), *Explaining Social Institutions*. Ann Arbor: University of Michigan Press.

——— 1995. "The Rational Choice Theory of Social Institutions: Cooperation, Coordination, and Communication." In Jeffrey S. Banks and Eric A. Hanushek (eds.), *Modern Political Economy*, 216–68. Cambridge: Cambridge University Press.

Cohen, Joshua. 1998. "Procedure and Substance in Deliberative Democracy." In Jon Elster (ed.), *Democratic Deliberation*. Cambridge: Cambridge University Press.

Collini, Stefan, Donald Winch, and John Burrow. 1983. *That Noble Science of Politics*. Cambridge: Cambridge University Press.

Condorcet. 1986. "Essai sur l'application de l'analyse à la probabilité des décisions rendues à la pluralité des voix." In *Sur les élections et autres textes*. Ed. Olivier de Bernon. Paris: Fayard.

Cortés, Fernando. 1997. *La distribución del ingreso en Mexico en épocas de estabilización y reforma económica*. Guadalajara, Mexico: CIESAS.

Dahl, Robert. 1956. *A Preface to Democratic Theory*. Chicago: University of Chicago Press.

——— 1971. *Polyarchy: Participation and Opposition*. New Haven: Yale University Press.

Deininger, K., and L. Squire. 1996. "A New Data Set Measuring Income Inequality." *World Bank Economic Review* 10: 565–91.

Dunn, John. 1992. Conclusion to John Dunn (ed.), *Democracy: The Unfinished Journey*, 239–66. Oxford: Oxford University Press.

——— 1996. *The History of Political Theory and Other Essays*. Cambridge: Cambridge University Press.

Eckstein, Harry. 1961. *A Theory of Stable Democracy*. Princeton: Princeton University Center for International Studies.

Eckstein, Harry, and Ted R. Gurr. 1975. *Patterns of Inquiry: A Structural Basis for Political Inquiry*. New York: Wiley.

Eickelman, Dale F., and James Piscatori. 1996. *Muslim Politics*. Princeton: Princeton University Press.

Eisenstadt, S. N. 1968. "The Protestant Ethic Theses in the Framework of Sociological Theory and Weber's Work." In S. N. Eisenstadt (ed.), *The Protestant Ethic and Modernization: A Comparative View*, 3–45. New York: Basic Books.

Esposito, John L., and John O. Voll. 1996. *Islam and Democracy*. New York: Oxford University Press.

Fukuyama, Francis. 1995. "The Primacy of Culture." *Journal of Democracy* 6: 7–14.

Gellner, Ernest. 1991. "Civil Society in Historical Context." *International Social Science Journal* 129: 495–510.

Gerth, H. H., and C. Wright Mills (eds.). 1958. *From Max Weber: Essays in Sociology*. New York: Oxford University Press.

Gibson, James L., Raymond M. Duch, and Kent L. Tedin. 1992. "Democratic Values and the Transformation of the Soviet Union." *Journal of Politics* 54: 329–71.

Granato, Jim, Ronald Inglehart, and David Leblang. 1996. "Cultural Values, Stable Democracy, and Economic Development: A Reply." *American Journal of Political Science* 40: 680–96.

Hampton, Jean. 1994. "Democracy and the Rule of Law." In Ian Shapiro (ed.), *The Rule of Law*, 13–45. *Nomos XXXVI*. New York: New York University Press.

Hardin, Russell. 1989. "Why a Constitution?" In Bernard Grofman and Donald Witman (eds.), *The Federalist Papers and the New Institutionalism*, 100–20. New York: Agathon Press.

Hobsbawm, Eric, and Terence Ranger (eds.). 1983. *The Invention of Tradition.* Cambridge: Cambridge University Press.

Holmes, Stephen. 1997. "In Search of New Enemies." *London Review of Books,* 24 April.

Huntington, Samuel P. 1993a. "The Clash of Civilizations?" *Foreign Affairs* 72, 3: 22–49.

1993b. "Democracy's Third Wave." In Larry Diamond and Marc F. Plattner (eds.), *The Global Resurgence of Democracy,* 3–25. Baltimore: Johns Hopkins University Press.

Im, Huyg Baeg. 1997. "The Compatibility of Confucianism and Democratic Civil Society in Korea." Paper presented at the IPSA XVII World Congress, Seoul, Korea, 17–21 August.

Inglehart, Ronald. 1990. *Culture Shift in Advanced Industrial Society.* Princeton: Princeton University Press.

Jackman, Robert W., and Ross A. Miller. 1996. "A Renaissance of Political Culture?" *American Journal of Political Science* 40: 632–59.

Kalyvas, Stathis N. 1996. *The Rise of Christian Democracy in Europe.* Ithaca: Cornell University Press.

1997. "Religion and Democratization: Belgium and Algeria." Paper presented at the annual meeting of the American Political Science Association, Washington, D.C., 28–31 August.

Kelsen, Hans. 1988. *La démocratie. Sa nature-sa valeur.* Paris: Economica.

Kornhauser, Lewis A. 1999. "The Normativity of Law." *American Law and Economics Review* 6: 3–25.

Laitin, David. 1995. "National Revivals and Violence." *Archives Europeénnes de Sociologie* 36: 3–43.

Laswell, Harold D. 1946. *Power and Personality.* New York.

Lee Teng Hui. 1997. Paper presented at the IPSA XVII World Congress, Seoul, Korea, 17–21 August.

Lewis, Bernard. 1993. "Islam and Liberal Democracy." *Atlantic Monthly* 271, 2: 89–98.

Linz, Juan J., and Alfred Stepan. 1996. *Problems of Democratic Transition and Consolidation.* Baltimore: John Hopkins University Press.

Lipset, Seymour M. 1959. "Some Social Requisites of Democracy: Economic Development and Political Legitimacy." *American Political Science Review* 53: 69–105.

1960. *Political Man.* Garden City, N.Y.: Doubleday.

1994. "The Social Requisites of Democracy Revisited." *American Sociological Review* 59: 1–21.

Manin, Bernard. 1997. *Principles of Representative Government.* Cambridge: Cambridge University Press.

Mazrui, Ali A. 1997. "Islamic and Western Values." *Foreign Affairs* 76, 5: 118–32.

Milanovic, Branko. 1999. "Do More Unequal Countries Redistribute More? Does the Median Voter Hypothesis Hold?" World Bank, Washington, D.C. Unpublished manuscript.

Mill, John Stuart. 1991. *Considerations on Representative Government.* Buffalo, N.Y.: Prometheus Books.

Montesquieu. 1993. *Lettres persanes.* Paris: Bookking International.

1995. *De l'esprit des lois.* Paris: Gallimard.

Muller, Edward N., and Mitchell A. Seligson. 1994. "Civil Culture and Democracy: The Question of Causal Relationships." *American Political Science Review* 88: 635–52.

Nathan, Andrew J., and Tianjian Shi. 1993. "Cultural Requisites for Democacy in China: Findings from a Survey." *Deadalus* 122: 95–123.

Neubauer, Deane E. 1967. "Some Conditions of Democracy." *American Political Science Review* 61: 1002–9.

OECD. 1995. *La distribution des revenues dans les pays de l'OCDE.* Paris: OECD.

Przeworski, Adam. 1991. *Democracy and the Market.* Cambridge: Cambridge University Press.

——— 2002. "Why Democracy Survives in Affluent Countries." Department of Politics, New York University. Unpublished manuscript.

Przeworski, Adam, Mike Alvarez, José Antonio Cheibub, and Fernando Limongi. 2000. *Democracy and Development: Political Institutions and Material Well-Being in the World, 1950–1990.* Cambridge: Cambridge University Press.

Przeworski, Adam, José Antonio Cheibub, and Fernando Limongi. 1998. "Culture and Democracy." In *World Culture Report,* 125–46. Paris: UNESCO.

Rawls, John. 1993. "The Domain of the Political and Overlapping Consensus." In David Copp, Jean Hampton, and John E. Roemer (eds.), *The Idea of Democracy.* Cambridge: Cambridge University Press.

Rousseau, Jean-Jacques. 1985. *The Government of Poland.* Indianapolis: Hackett.

Sartre, Jean-Paul. 1960. *Critique de la raison dialectique.* Paris: Gallimard.

Schmitt, Karl. 1988. *The Crisis of Parliamentary Democracy.* Cambridge, Mass.: MIT Press.

Schumpeter, Joseph A. 1942. *Capitalism, Socialism, and Democracy.* New York: Harper & Brothers.

Searle, John R. 1995. *The Construction of Social Reality.* New York: Free Press.

Sen, Amartya. 1997. "Culture and Development: Global Perspectives and Constructive Criticism." Paper prepared for UNESCO's Office of the World Culture Report. Paris.

Tocqueville, Alexis de. 1961. *De la démocratie en Amérique.* Paris: Gallimard.

Versini, Laurent. 1995. Introduction to Montesquieu, *De l'esprit des lois,* 9–64. Paris: Gallimard.

Weber, Max. 1958. *The Protestant Ethic and the Spirit of Capitalism.* New York: Charles Scribner's Sons.

Weingast, Barry R. 1997. "Political Foundations of Democracy and the Rule of Law." *American Political Science Review* 91: 245–63.

Wiarda, Howard J. 1981. *Corporatism and National Development in Latin America.* Boulder: Westview.

——— 1989. "The Dominican Republic: Mirror Legacies of Democracy and Authoritarianism." In Larry Diamond, Juan J. Linz and Seymour Martin Lipset (eds.), *Democracy in Developing Countries: Latin America,* 423–58. Boulder: Lynne Rienner Publishers.

Wiatr, Jerzy J. 1979. "The Civic Culture from a Marxist Sociological Perspective." In Gabriel A. Almond and Sidney Verba (eds.), *The Civic Culture Revisited,* 103–23. Boston: Little, Brown.

Winch, Donald. 1978. *Adam Smith's Politics: An Essay in Historiographic Revision.* Cambridge: Cambridge University Press.

Part Two

**Chapter Six**

# The Majoritarian Reading
# of the Rule of Law

No other Majesty than
that of the People . . . No
other Sovereignty than
that of the Law.

Thomas Paine[1]

In this chapter I challenge one common view of the "rule of law" and, particularly, of what institutional arrangements put the rule of law at risk. According to this perspective, the rule of law is closely connected with (what I call) liberal political systems (which, synthetically, are characterized by a system of checks and balances and entrenched individual rights protected by an independent judiciary). In addition, many among those who defend this view tend to evaluate all moves toward a more majoritarian democracy as threats to the rule of law.[2] Normally, they assume that a majoritarian democracy necessarily results in arbitrary government. This arbitrariness would be the result of basically two features that they associate with majoritarian democracy: its tendency to produce "hasty" decisions and its inherent incapacity

---

[1] "I am a Citizen of a Country which knows no other Majesty than that of the People – no other Government than that of the Representative body – no other Sovereignty than that of the Laws" (Paine 1995: 376).

[2] In what follows, I use the expression "majoritarian systems" in a way similar to that which Thomas Jefferson used when he referred to the idea of "republican government." According to Jefferson, a republican government was "purely and simply . . . a government by its citizens in mass, acting directly and personally, according to rules established by the majority." Taking into account this general definition, Jefferson affirmed that governments were "more or less republican, as they have more or less of the element of popular election and control in their composition." Similarly, I refer to the idea of "majoritarian government" taking into account the Jeffersonian ideal of republican government. In this sense, I say that a government is more or less majoritarian, as it has more or less of the element of popular election and control in its composition. Jefferson (1999).

to establish adequate institutional controls, that is, to establish controls over the will of the majority. Majoritarian democracy, thus, is directly associated with an "unchecked majority," that is, a "populist" regime[3] – in the end, the breakdown of the rule of law.[4]

In what follows, I try to show that it is possible to defend a more majoritarian political system without renouncing, at the same time, the ideal of the rule of law. In this sense, I affirm that there is ample space between the liberal system of government and a "populist" system – enough so to make it possible to defend a reasonable majoritarian system. In the first section of my work, I show how we began to correlate the notion of a majoritarian system with violations of the rule of law. Then, I challenge two of the main arguments that are presented for associating a majoritarian government with arbitrary powers. On the one hand, I affirm that it is possible to have a majoritarian political organization without abandoning the aim of adopting deliberative decisions. On the other hand, I show how this political organization may be compatible with the idea of having controls over the representatives. Finally, I suggest the importance of supplementing this majoritarian reading of the rule of law with a distinct concern about its social preconditions.

## The Rule of Law and Liberal Constitutionalism

Liberal political systems, as I will describe them, are characterized by representative governments organized through a constitution that is considered the "supreme law of the land." The liberal constitutions normally include two parts, one that establishes the organization of government, and the other that establishes certain inviolable rights. The first part usually organizes a system of checks and balances – a system that commonly includes a bicameral legislature (i.e., a directly elected house of representatives, and an indirectly elected senate), executive veto, and a judiciary in charge of preserving the supremacy of the constitution. The second part normally consists of a list of civil and political rights.

Now, for those who associate liberal political organization with one where the rule of law prevails, any deviation from the system of checks and balances appears as a severe threat to the permanence of the rule

---

[3] In what follows, I use the expression "populist regime" (or "populism," in general) in order to refer to a system of "unchecked majorities," that is, a system where the "majority will" finds no significant restraints and where, consequently, minority rights are at serious risk.

[4] One good example of this view may be found in Phillip Pettit's position, as developed in his interesting book *Republicanism* (1997).

of law. Any such deviation seems to open the door to either the concentration of power in the hands of few or the excesses of the "most dangerous" branch of power, namely the legislative branch. Therefore, in these types of situations, one has to expect that some of the characteristics usually associated with the rule of law will be violated (i.e., the stability, generality, and nonretroactivity of the laws, and judicial independence).[5] Along these lines, during the origins of constitutionalism, both in the United States and in Latin America the "Founding Fathers" assumed that the establishment of the rule of law was threatened by two equally undesirable evils, described as "the risk of tyranny" and the "risk of anarchy."

To state it differently, liberals defended their constitutional project against two alternative views about how to organize the institutional structure of society. According to the first alternative, which I call the conservative-authoritarian conception, the constitution had to secure political stability and the respect of certain predefined values (usually associated with the values of one particular conception of the good, typically the Catholic religion). With regard to the organization of powers, the conservatives proposed the concentration of political powers in the hands of one person or a small group of people. They defended, thus, a centralist organization of society and the presence of very strong executives provided with exceptional powers. The strong executives were accompanied by weak legislatures subject to the presidential authority – legislatures with few powers and small numbers, and usually destined to meet for brief periods after long lapses of time. In addition, the conservatives proposed, at least in most cases, the adoption of severe restrictions on the rights of individuals – especially, limitations on citizens' rights to choose their representatives, and limitations on elemental civil rights, such as the ones related to the press, reunion, and association freedom. The respect for such freedoms was usually conditioned upon the respect for the political order and the state's preferred moral values. The conservative model was particularly influential in Latin America during the nineteenth century. The Ecuadorian Constitutions of 1843 and 1869 (both known as the "Letter of Slavery"), the Peruvian Constitution of Huancayo from 1839, the Chilean Constitutions of 1823 and 1833, and the Colombian Constitutions of 1821 and 1886 are all good examples of what I described as conservative constitutions.

The second alternative was (what I call) a populist constitutional conception. According to the populist view, the constitution had to foster

---

[5] See, for example, Raz (1977).

self-government and strengthen the majority will. With regard to the organization of power, those who followed this model proposed the adoption of federalist constitutions, characterized by strong legislatures and, consequently, weak executives, normally subordinated to the will of parliament. Populists were not openly hostile to individual rights but, normally, they assumed that these rights were, in the end, dependent on the will of the majority. In this respect, many liberals argued, the populist constitutions were disrespectful of individual rights and completely unable to ensure the protection of minority groups. The populist conception was particularly influential in the United States, during the origins of constitutionalism. In fact, during the preconstitutional period – a period that is normally characterized as one of "radical constitutionalism" – many states adopted constitutions that appeared to follow what I call the populist pattern. Probably, the best example of this view of the constitution was the very influential Constitution of Pennsylvania, drafted in 1776.[6]

Liberals claimed that they wanted to confront both unacceptable alternatives (the conservative and the populist constitutional models) that, they assumed, provoked either the tyranny of the few, or a situation of anarchy. In both scenarios, they believed, the government tended to be arbitrary, and decisions were made through sudden impulses and momentary passions (Elster 1993). The main features of the liberal constitutions evince their reaction against (what they assumed to be) the main constitutional alternatives to liberalism. First, the *system of checks and balances* may be deemed as the liberal response to both the conservative and the populist conception about the organization of power. Whereas these two alternatives allowed the use of arbitrary powers, the liberals proposed the adoption of a strict system of controls over power. Second, the liberal commitment to a strong idea of *individual rights* may be deemed as a response to the disregard of minority rights that, the liberals assumed, characterized both the conservative and the populist constitutional views.

## Liberalism and Majoritarianism

In the United States, and with the consolidation of independence, the threat of tyranny became less intimidating while, conversely, the

---

[6] In fact, many other states (such as Georgia and Vermont) designed their constitutions, taking that radical document as their preferred example.

threat of majoritarian oppression became more significant. The young American democracies, at the state level, seemed incapable of protecting rights: they were too sensitive to majority claims, and too insensitive to the protection of each individual's most basic interests. As the notable historian Gordon Wood remarked, "the people's will as expressed in their representative legislatures and so much trusted throughout the colonial period suddenly seemed capricious and arbitrary" (Wood 1969: 405–6).

James Madison, the main ideologist of the U.S. Constitution, defended this document as an alternative to the "radical"[7] types of constitutions that had prevailed since independence. In his opinion, the post-Independence period of radical constitutionalism had brought the country to a situation of disorder, led by uncontrolled legislatures. This view became apparent in his work "Vices of the Political System," enormously influential during the U.S. framing period. In that work, Madison asserted that the worst vices of the political system were all related to the activities of the legislature, which produced "multiple," "mutable," and "injust" laws. In Madison's opinion, "there is no maxim ... which is more liable to be misapplied, and which therefore more needs elucidation that the current one that the interest of the majority is the political standard of right and wrong.... [It] would be the interest of the majority in every community to despoil and enslave the minority of individuals; and in a federal community to make a similar sacrifice of the minority of the component of the States."[8]

Later on, these considerations were exposed and developed in *The Federalist Papers* where Madison associated the supremacy of the majority will with the supremacy of factions, and the supremacy of factions with the production of partial or nonneutral laws. In the end, the supremacy of the majority will appeared synonymous with the breakdown of the rule of law: it directly implied the replacement of the "rule of law" with the "rule of men."

The distrust of majority will was even stronger in Latin America, for a variety of reasons. Some based their suspicions on the lack of education that affected the majority of the population;[9] and others, on the lack of

---

[7] I employ this term according to its common use during that period, that is, when the seventeenth century's conservative political thought was compared with the opposite radical political thought.

[8] Letter to James Monroe, 5 October 1786, in Madison (1975: 9: 140–2).

[9] Among many others, Vicente Rocafuerte, who became president of Ecuador, justified his distrust of democracy on the "moral and intellectual backwardness" of most

democratic practice that distinguished these new societies (something that was not similarly true, for instance, in the United States). Most of them, however, distrusted democracy because they (improperly) associated it with some bloody and popular uprisings that had occurred during the Independence period (i.e., the dramatic "black" revolution of Haiti, which decisively marked Simón Bolívar's political views; or the sackings and popular turmoils that followed the victory of Vicente Guerrero in Mexico); or with the actions of some extremely cruel (and not at all democratic) *caudillos* (as happened with the cases of Juan Boves or Ezequiel Zamora in Venezuela, or with J. M. de Rosas in Argentina);[10] or with the irresponsible government of leaders who pursued an authoritarian government, covered with a populist discourse.[11]

In spite of these "internal" differences, the truth is that most of the liberal constitutions adopted in Latin America during the nineteenth century were conceived within a climate unfavorable to majoritarian democracy. Again, majoritarian democracy was associated with the production of "sudden," "immoderate," and finally "irrational" norms that threatened the rights of minority groups.

In sum, both in the United States and in Latin America we find a tendency to identify the rule of law with a particular (liberal) model of constitutionalism, as well as a tendency to evaluate all moves in the direction of a more majoritarian democracy as impermissible departures from the rule of law.

Now, it is not obvious that the only democratic alternative to liberal constitutionalism is that of "populism," that is, a system of unrestrained majority will, disrespectful of minority rights. That does not seem to be true, either as a theoretical claim, or as a description of the legal practice in America. In fact, I argue that there exists quite a bit of space between the liberal and the extreme populist constitutional proposals that the

Ecuadorians. Quoted in Reyes (1931: 143–4). The enormously influential Diego Portales, who also became president of his country, Chile, affirmed that democracy was "an absurdity in the Latin American countries, full of vices, and where citizens lacked any of the virtues required by a genuine Republic." See Portales (1937: 1:177). See also Reyes (1931).

10  See the Venezuelan case, for example, as commented on by Brewer-Carías (1985). Probably the best way to understand how the Argentinean liberal political elite perceived the phenomenon of caudillism is to read Sarmiento's "Civilización y barbarie." See Sarmiento (1977).

11  Normally, this antidemocratic reaction was promoted by some very lucid conservative leaders, such as Lucas Alemán, in Mexico; Juan Egaña, in Chile; or Bartolomé Herrera, in Peru. See Alamán (1997); Basadre (1969).

liberals successfully attacked and defeated. In what follows, I explore the possibility of defending both a majoritarian institutional system and individual rights.

## The Majoritarian Constitution and the Defense of Judicious Public Debate

It may be worth beginning this section by stating the following: liberals proudly defend the scheme of checks and balances by showing the incentives it provides for the adoption of well-reasoned, thoughtful decisions – virtues that, apparently, any alternative system would have problems ensuring. The reasons why the system of checks and balances favors the adoption of these virtuous decisions are diverse. On the one hand, the existence of multiple checks slows down the decision-making process, something that seems very important considering the evils that one reasonably associates with "hasty," "sudden," "impulsive" decisions. On the other hand, the fact that laws have to go "back and forth" (i.e., from one chamber to the other, and back again) seems important in order to force public officers to "think twice" about what they are going to do. Any legislative initiative, we may say, needs to be reflected upon carefully, and the system of checks and balances provides good incentives in this direction. Finally, it is important that all legislative projects be scrutinized by many different "eyes": these different "eyes" may help to "refine" the projects' content, adding or modifying aspects that (for whatever reasons) were not initially considered. This is what Madison defended, for example, when he proposed to "divide the trust between different bodies of men, who might watch and check each other."[12]

Actually, many radicals resisted the liberal position, but not because they ignored the importance of the previous arguments. What they said, instead, was that there were other significant values that the political system had to respect first.[13] Above all, many of them believed that the liberal institutional model was too complex, and that the Constitution had to be clear, simple, and easily understood. Also, and in connection with the previous argument, many affirmed that the system of multiple checks generated confusion regarding what organ fulfilled which task.

---

[12] Farrand (1937: 1: 421–2). See, also, Elster (1993).

[13] In what follows, I do not deal with some problems that were vital at that time but that are less fundamental today, namely, the problems that resulted from disenfranchisement.

In this respect, and according to many radicals, the system of checks and balances appeared to be too risky. Others attacked the liberal proposal, affirming that the establishment of checks fostered a situation of political stalemate or, in the worst cases, a state of "war" between different branches of power.[14] Nathaniel Chipman, for example, foresaw a state of permanent tension between the different interests at stake as a result of the proposed checks and balances. Chipman depicted this situation as one of "perpetual war of each [interest] against the other, or at best, an armed truce, attended with constant negotiations, and shifting combinations, as if to prevent mutual destruction; each party in its turn uniting with its enemy against a more powerful enemy" (Chipman 1833: 171). The radicals could also have said that the importance of establishing checks did not justify the establishment of *any type* of check. We will see, in this sense, that many of them simply proposed adopting *other* types of checks on power.[15] Moreover, they could affirm that it was a defect (and not a virtue of the system) to leave the legislative production in "too many hands": would these laws not be transformed, they could say, into unacceptable patchworks? Although most of these arguments were properly used during the original constitutional debates, I believe that, for many radicals, the main object of concern resided somewhere else: they wanted to preserve their commitment to the majority rule, and considered that the liberal system did not properly honor it.[16]

In order to illustrate the possibility of defending the radicals' ideal of having both a majoritarian system and judicious debates, it may be interesting to make reference to a case like that of the State of Pennsylvania, after the Independence. This case is particularly interesting because Pennsylvania's Constitutional Convention was influenced by a radical way of thinking promoted, among others, by Thomas Paine. Following common radical initiatives, Paine suggested (among other things) establishing a strong unicameral system, something that immediately triggered diverse criticisms. Most of all, many believed that such an initiative would only favor the adoption of "hasty" and "oppressive" measures.

---

[14] In *Federalist* 51, Madison proposed to "counteract" "ambition" with more "ambition," in order to "control the abuses of government." However, it was far from obvious that the "aggregation" of two evils would result in such a desirable and good outcome, rather than in an even greater evil. Hamilton et al. (1988).

[15] An excellent analysis of these issues in Ackerman (2000).

[16] One (not very attractive but common) way to defend this position was based on the Rousseauean assumption according to which the will of the people is only one and, thus, indivisible.

Now, the framers of the Pennsylvania Constitution (the most influential radical constitution after the American Independence) were absolutely conscious of the need to guarantee proper discussion and prevent hasty decisions at the legislative level. They wanted to "cool down" the legislative debates, however, without endangering the majoritarian character of the Constitution. For example, and as a result of these beliefs, they wrote in Section 15 of their constitutional document that

> to the end that laws before they are enacted may be more maturely
> considered, and the inconvenience of hasty determinations as much
> as possible prevented, all bills of public nature shall be printed for the
> consideration of the people, before they are read in general assembly
> the last time for debate and amendment; and, except on occasions of
> sudden necessity, shall not be passed into laws until the next session
> of assembly; and for the more perfect satisfaction of the public, the
> reasons and motives for making such laws shall be fully and clearly
> expressed in the preambles.[17]

Similarly, Thomas Paine recognized the importance of promoting more serene legislative discussions, but affirmed the possibility of achieving that goal without renouncing, at the same time, the majoritarian traits of the Constitution (in this case, particularly, the unicameral legislature). He stated:

> [I]n order to remove the objection against a single house, (that of act-
> ing with too quick an impulse), and at the same time to avoid the
> inconsistencies, in some cases absurdities, arising from two houses,
> the following method has been proposed as an improvement upon
> both. First, To have but one representation. Secondly, To divide that
> representation, by lot, into two or three parts. Thirdly, That every pro-
> posed bill, shall be first debated in those parts by succession, that they
> may become the hearers of each other, but without taking any vote.
> After which the whole representation to assemble for a general debate
> and determination by vote.[18]

---

[17] See "Pennsylvania Constitution of 1776," in Blaustein and Sigler (1988: 29–30). A previous version of the project demanded that each bill be read three times, on three different days, before referral to the next session. In the end, the Pennnsylvanians did not include these later provisions, assuming that they were excessive, given other precautions that they had already adopted. See Shaeffer (1974).

[18] Blaustein and Sigler (1988: 299–300). L'Abbé Sieyès repeated a very similar proposal in his famous opinion on the question of the "royal veto," in 7 September 1789. Sieyés (1990).

The radicals' concern with ensuring a proper exchange of reasons[19] was supplemented by a serious concern with the value of publicity. The radicals wanted legislative debates to be open to the people,[20] legislative projects to be known and discussed by the people, and laws' motivations to be clearly identifiable by the citizenry.[21] In spite of the many criticisms that they received,[22] the radicals made it clear that they did not ignore the importance of having "sedate" and thoughtful debates and demonstrated that they were well prepared to reshape their proposals in order to guarantee those values.

Analogous situations appeared in Latin America, related to some of its most radical constitutions. Typically, that was what happened in Peru, where the Constitution of 1867 – the most radical constitution approved in the country during the nineteenth century – tried both to secure adequate legislative discussions and to honor the majoritarian principle. In effect (and among other things) the Constitution of 1867 extended political rights, established a system of very frequent elections and short mandates, and proposed a unicameral legislature. Then, trying to confront the criticisms according to which the Constitution

[19] This concern with political deliberation should move majoritarians to be more cautious with regard to direct-democracy mechanisms. These mechanisms are not always appropriate for the promotion of political discussions, and many times come to replace or prevent these debates.

[20] The Pennsylvania Constitution established that "the doors of the house in which the representatives of the freemen of this state shall sit in general assembly, shall be and remain open for the admission of all persons who behave decently, except only when the welfare of this state requires the door to be shut."

[21] The noted Federalist Noah Webster, for example, criticized the Pennsylvania Constitution and its concern with publicity. In his opinion, the requirement that "a bill shall be published for the consideration of the people, before it is enacted into a law ... annihilates the legislature, and reduces it to an advisory body." Additionally, he affirmed, this requirement "carries the spirit of discussion into all quarters ... and the warmth of different opinions ... through the state of Pennsylvania." In this way, he judged, the "seeds of dissension are sown in the constitution." Webster (1788: 34 and 47).

[22] See, for example, John Adams's criticism of Thomas Paine's proposals. See, in this respect, Adams (1946: 77–114); Baylin (1992); Walsh (1969: ch. 5). See, also, Benjamin Rush asserting "poor Pennsylvania! ... They call this a democracy – a mobocracy in my opinion would be more proper. All our laws breathe the spirit of town meetings and porter shops." Quoted in Butterfield (1951: 244). In addition, see Fisher Ames's objections to Thomas Paine's work. According to Ames, "Mr. Thomas Paine's writings abound with this sort of specious falsehoods and perverted truths. Of all his doctrines, none perhaps has created more agitation and alarm than that which proclaims to all men that they are free and equal[. The people] believed that by making their own and other men's passions sovereign, they should invest man with immediate perfectibility; and breathe into their regenerated liberty an ethereal spirit that would never die.... With opinions so wild, and passions so fierce, the spirit of democracy has been sublimated to extravagance." Ames (1983: 2: 208–9).

promoted the adoption of "hasty decisions," it established that "the legislative projects or resolutions of general interests will not be open to vote but only after a second legislative discussion, which will take place no sooner than three days after the end of the first one." In this case, as in Pennsylvania's, the radicals made an effort to demonstrate that their initiatives were aimed not at establishing a "populist" regime but, on the contrary, at strengthening the democratic character of society (Paz-Soldán 1954: 263).

The attacks that the radicals traditionally presented against the system of checks and balances do not imply (and historically did not imply) disregarding the importance of having reflective discussions. If the radicals adopted a critical position against the checks and balances during the origins of constitutionalism, this occurred as a result of other reasonable arguments. When we recognize this point, then, it is no longer acceptable to associate majoritarianism with the realm of "folly" or "fury." A majoritarian government may be (and, in many cases, was conceived to be) compatible with a serious concern for judicious debates.

Finally, I would add that the commitment to democratic procedures should not move majoritarians to subject all types of issues to the rule of the many. For example, I think that matters of personal morality should not be subject to majority rule. As Carlos Nino put it, "collective discussion and decision are not substantially more reliable than individual reflection and decision for arriving at morally correct solutions in this regard" (Nino 1996: 203). From a different perspective, but also concerned with the preservation of majority rule, Joshua Cohen (2000) arrives at the same conclusion. I recognize that the idea is not obvious, but I believe that there are very good reasons to defend it.[23]

## The Majoritarian Constitution and Controls over Public Officers

In this section, I challenge a second objection to the majoritarian government, namely, the one that argues that those types of governments

---

[23] My answer would be somehow different with regard to procedural issues. The choice of a particular procedure should not be, in the end, foreign to the majority will. Of course, there is a problem if we leave the control of procedural questions to the same group that wants to violate these political procedures. However, we should remember, first, that "the distinction between substance and democratic procedure is a notoriously difficult one to sustain in politics"; and, second, that "[s]ince there are disagreements about how to settle disagreements (ie disagreements about authority), and since we need those disagreements settled too, we will always be in the uncomfortable position of using the procedures advocated by one or other of the disputants to settle the very dispute to which she is a party." See Waldron (1993: 40). Also, see Waldron (1999). See a different perspective on the relationship between majority rule and procedures in Ely (1980).

disregard the importance of controls over the public officers. Opposing this view, I believe that many radicals, as well as many liberals, have been properly concerned about the importance of controlling power. Both groups have tried to avoid abuses of power, keeping each power within its own limits, and – what is ultimately more important – ensuring the protection of individual rights. However, although both of them feared abuses of power, liberals particularly feared (what they deemed as) the unremitting and very dangerous expansion of the legislative power over the other branches (*legislative encroachments*), whereas radicals seemed to fear most the gradual separation between the people and the representatives (*political alienation*), and the consequent use of public positions for private purposes. Power, the radicals believed, "often convert[s] a good man in private life to a tyrant in office."[24] As a result of these different concerns, liberals and radicals defended and proposed different types of institutional controls. Liberals proposed the adoption of more "internal" or "endogenous" controls, whereas radicals favored more "external" or "exogenous" ones.

It is important to recognize these different views about which *institutional controls are necessary*, because many liberals presented, and still present, their opponents' position as one unconcerned with controlling public officers. Granted, many radicals rejected the liberals' proposal of a system of checks and balances. However, even so it would not be true that most radicals actually had the irresponsible attitude that their opponents attributed to them: most radicals did not believe that majoritarian decisions did not need controls because, for example, the majority decided always correctly. On the contrary, they accepted that all public decisions required controls, and that the best controls were the ones that came from the people at large – something that, in many cases, was accompanied by a strong suspicion of the actual purpose and effect of countermajoritarian mechanisms. Samuel Williams of Vermont, for example, clearly stated this view. He affirmed that "the security of the people is derived not from the nice ideal application of checks and balances, and mechanical powers, among the different parts of the government, but from the responsibility, and dependence of each part of the government, over the people." For the people who shared this view, the basic idea was that "the branches of power should be separate from each other, and each answerable directly to the people, not to the other branches" (Vile 1991: 678).

[24] "Demophilus" (1776: 5).

Those who affirmed this position recommended emphasizing "exogeneous" or external controls, assuming (contrary to their opponents) that the main evil to be remedied was the "tyranny of the minority." "[A]s soon as the delegate power gets too far out of the hands of the constituent power, – they affirmed – a tyranny is in some degree established."[25]

In order to ensure these external controls, they suggested adopting a variety of institutional mechanisms. Most of them defended the principle of annual elections and direct elections for most public positions. However, they also assumed the "insufficiency of election ... to ensure political liberty,"[26] something that moved them to propose the adoption of additional institutional mechanisms. Thus, for example, some proposed the establishment of mandatory rotation for most of the important government officers. Some went even further and claimed the right to instruct representatives, accompanied by a right to recall these representatives in extreme cases.[27] Now, we do not need to support all these measures in order to recognize the importance of the underlying point, which is that their defense of the majority principle does not necessarily require disregarding the importance of establishing controls over power.

Is it possible to say, however, that (in spite of their possible advantages) external controls are unable to prevent legislative encroachments? This, in fact, was Madison's position in *Federalist* 49, where he made reference to the "tendency of republican governments" to an

---

[25] Thomas Young, from Vermont, quoted in Sherman (1991: 190).

[26] Moreover, Taylor deemed that this, the only protection retained by the people, was, in the end, also diluted by the existence of long terms of office. To counteract this, he proposed a return to the old Anglo-Saxon principle according to which "tyranny begins when annual election ends." He stated that "the reversal of this maxim in the tenure of the president and senators of the United States, may possibly be ... mortal to our policy." Taylor (1814: 170 and 226).

[27] It is important to clarify that instruments such as the right to write instructions are not necessarily incompatible with the aim of promoting political deliberation. First, instructions do not prevent deliberations between the people and their representatives, or deliberations among citizens, or, say, deliberations between political parties and interest groups. Second, instructions do not prevent all types of political discussions within the parliament. In the worst case, they prevent the representatives from changing their minds with regard to very specific matters. In this sense, the fact that the representatives of a certain community refused to hear any arguments about legalizing abortion, for example, does not prevent them from discussing freely many other issues. See the radicals' proposals, for example, as they were incorporated in the first constitutions approved during the 1770s, in Lutz (1988). For an interesting analysis of direct-democracy mechanisms, see Cronin (1999); for objections to the right to write instructions, see, for example, Sunstein (1993), and Przeworski, Stokes, and Manin (1999); for distinguishing different types of political deliberation, see, among others, Mansbridge (1995).

"aggrandizement of the legislature, at the expense of the other departments." In that paper, Madison opposed the Jeffersonian initiative to solve all important institutional conflicts by resorting to a popular convention.[28] However, Madison's arguments against this majoritarian initiative were not persuasive. First of all, as Dahl affirmed, it is not obvious that "[p]opular elections (and competing parties)" were insufficient to prevent evils such as encroachments (1956: 13). Also, it is not obvious, as Madison affirmed, that Jefferson's strategy contributed to undermining the respectability of the established government. Finally, I would add that to "disturb the public tranquility" by demanding that the citizenry take part in the resolution of some of the community's public affairs is not necessarily something bad, as Madison suggested. The radicals would consider this possibility as an adequate goal, within a democratic community. Moreover, even if Jefferson's proposal (to call a convention) resulted (somehow) in being "too costly," a defender of the majoritarian government could propose the adoption of other, "less costly" measures, still compatible with the ideal of a majoritarian government and able to prevent the risk of mutual encroachments. Even "endogenous" controls could be welcome, as far as they do not undermine the majoritarian political organization.

In the previous paragraphs, I affirmed that it might be important to strengthen the "exogenous" controls in order to reduce the risks of abuses from the representatives. I also affirmed that this initiative need not impair the desire to avoid legislative engrandizements. However, one could still argue against this preference for "exogenous" over "endogenous" controls, asserting that the former are useless as a means for preventing majoritarian abuses of minority rights.[29] Majorities, one could reasonably say, should not be trusted as guardians of minority rights. Internal, countermajoritarian controls seem to be in order for securing these rights. This is a very common reply against the majoritarian

[28] In *Federalist* 49, Madison highlights Jefferson's proposal, which said that "whenever any two of the three branches of government shall concur in opinion, each by the voices of two thirds of their whole number, that a convention is necessary for altering the constitution or correcting breaches of it, a convention shall be called for the purpose."

[29] It is important to note that, during the origins of American constitutionalism, people like Madison made reference to the need for protecting "natural rights," without clarifying what their conception of "natural rights" was. What is clear, however, is that "natural rights" were defined and (I would add) interpreted without any appeal to the majority will. I believe that majoritarians could and should defend a different notion of rights, which reestablished the links between these basic interests and the most fundamental and reasoned convictions of the people. For a majoritarian view of rights, see, for example, Ackerman (1991).

position but, again, it needs to be much more carefully discussed. First, the fact that we do not want the majorities to be in charge of protecting the same rights that they want to violate (minority rights) says nothing about the virtues of nonmajoritarian institutions as defenders of minority rights.[30] Theoretically, the existence of countermajoritarian checks is totally compatible with violations of the most basic minority interests: the countermajoritarian institution may affirm and provide legitimacy to these violations (i.e., legitimizing the idea that blacks are not equals to whites, as in the infamous *Dred Scott* case).[31] Moreover, it is not even clear that, in the long run, the presence of countermajoritarian institutions helps reduce the violation of minority rights. This intuition seems ratified by contemporary studies of the judiciary's role that show "the courts regularly being more or less in line with what the dominant national political coalition wants."[32] In addition, the final authority of this countermajoritarian institution also puts the rights of the majority at risk. Actually, history has provided us with many examples of reasonable majoritarian demands in defense of basic rights being stopped by unreasonable countermajoritarian decisions (i.e., during the so-called *Lochner* era).

Now, it may be true that "endogenous" controls are not as efficient as they are sometimes presented in protecting minority rights, but is this a reason to just suppress all these controls? I do not think that majoritarians had to adopt such an extreme strategy. Majoritarians have good reasons to reject *many* (very common) "endogenous" controls, for example, as a result of the lack of legitimacy of the controlling agency, or as a result of the scope of these controlling faculties. In particular, I believe, majoritarians have reasons to reject those controls that came to transfer the "last institutional say" to a nonmajoritarian institution (i.e., judicial review). However, a defender of majoritarian government may recognize perfectly (as many of them actually recognized) the importance of having "internal" checks, as far as they are compatible with a proper respect for the majoritarian principle. For example, in order to avoid the countermajoritarian objection to the judiciary, we could prevent it from having the "last (institutional) say" but still preserve an important role for it in the protection of minority rights. Just to imagine one possible solution, the judges could "remand" the challenged law to the

---

[30] See, for example, Waldron (1993).

[31] 60 U.S. (19 How.) 393 (1857). As Mark Tushnet affirmed, "The Supreme Court at its best is clearly a lot better than Congress at its worst. But Congress at its best is better than the Court at its worst." Tushnet (1999: 56).

[32] See Tushnet (1999: 153). Also, see Rosenberg (1991).

parliament, rather than declaring it void in a particular case. In a familiar vein, Senator B. Wheeler, a Democrat who supported the New Deal, favored a constitutional amendment that established the following: "[I]f the Supreme Court held a federal statute unconstitutional, Congress could override it by a 2/3 majority in both Houses, as long an election intervened between the Court decision and the override" (Tushnet 1999). Also, the Canadian "notwithstanding clause" (which allows a simple majority of the political branch of government to pass a law that is immune to judicial scrutiny, with respect to certain parts of the Constitution) represents an interesting contemporary alternative to the U.S. "pure" system of judicial review. By presenting these examples, I simply mean to say that there exist imaginable ways that would permit preserving both the majoritarian features of the political system and a concern for minority rights.

## The Social Requirements of the Institutional System

In the previous pages we concluded that we do not need to associate the establishment of a majoritarian system with the production of "hasty," "passionate," "unreflective," and finally "oppressive" decisions. The adoption of a more clearly majoritarian political system is necessarily incompatible neither with the production of well-reasoned decisions nor with the possibility of having adequate checks over the representatives.[33]

Now, before concluding the chapter, I would like to make a few additional observations. First, I would like to highlight that many radicals assumed that a majoritarian government was not only compatible with the preservation of the rule of law, but also a necessary condition for strengthening it. This claim may be sound if we take into account the importance of having a majoritarian system in order to avert certain threats to the rule of law and, in particular, in order to avert certain

[33] Of course, as it also happens in the countermajoritarian political systems, the majoritarian systems may be unable to prevent the adoption of political decisions that many of us will find intuitively unacceptable. However, this conclusion should not drive us to affirm that, in the end, majoritarian or nonmajoritarian institutions are both equally bad. I believe that a democratic community has stronger reasons for preferring the majority principle, when confronted with such a difficult choice. In the end, as Waldron claims, "[perhaps the defense of] the right to participate has less to do with a certain minimum prospect of decisive impact and more to do with avoiding the insult, dishonour, or denigration that is involved when one person's views are treated as of less account than the views of others on a matter that affects him as well as the others." Waldron (1999: 238).

risks related to the "tyranny of the minority." The radicals had some good arguments in favor of their position. On the one hand, they could affirm that the adoption of a majoritarian system was important in order to make the voice of the people heard. The law, they might reasonably argue, needs to be decisively informed by viewpoints that do not always find a significant place in liberal democracies – given, for example, the weight that countermajoritarian institutions have in these contexts. On the other hand, they could add, the liberals' dismissal of "exogenous," popular controls over the representatives (something that seems implied in the liberals' preference for "endogenous" controls) increases another serious and undesirable risk: the risk that the representatives rule just for themselves (the risk of political alienation). In this sense, they could conclude, the *absence* of a clearly majoritarian government favors the "tyranny of the few."

My second observation would be this: many among those who defended the adoption of a majoritarian government proposed to think about the institutional system in connection with the social organization of their community. In this respect, they differed from their liberal opponents, who proposed a seemingly self-sustaining institutional system. The majoritarians believed, as Robert Dahl put it, that the liberal view "exaggerate[d] the importance, in preventing tyranny, of specified checks to governmental officials by other specified governmental officials," underestimating, thus, the importance of social checks and balances (1956: 22). They wanted to know what economic and social arrangements were most hospitable to self-government, assuming that substantive social and economic inequalities would make the people incapable of exercising the independent judgment citizenship required (Sandal 1996).

Jefferson probably expressed this majoritarian view at its best. On the one hand, Jefferson affirmed his confidence in the adoption of certain (liberal) institutional controls. On the other hand, however, he emphasized the importance of adopting a more majoritarian political system and securing the preconditions of its existence. He detailed this view – and, thus, the basis of his constitutional theory – in a crucial letter to Madison, where he gave his opinion about the new Constitution.[34] In this document, Jefferson agreed with many of the constitutionally adopted

---

[34] Jefferson himself emphasized the importance he attributed to this document as an expression of his constitutional theory. See, for example, his autobiography (Jefferson 1999: 354–5); or his letter to the British radical Joseph Priestley, 19 June, 1802 (Jefferson 1999: 371–3).

"internal" controls; affirmed that the Constitution lacked many important "exogenous" controls (i.e., "the abandonment in every instance of the necessity of rotation in office, and most particularly in the case of the President"); and made reference to the social requirements of the institutional system. In this sense, he accentuated the importance of two initiatives that he deemed necessary conditions for the establishment of any proper institutional system: educating "the common people," and preserving the" agricultural" character of the country using the "vacant lands in any part of America."[35] He stated: "There are two subjects, indeed, which I shall claim a right to further as long as I breathe, the public education, and the sub-division of counties into wards."[36] These two claims reappeared in many other speeches and writings by Jefferson.[37] Obviously, we do not need to agree with his whole project or to defend his particular view of the agrarian society in order to recognize that Jefferson was highlighting something important: namely, that a stable institutional system, capable of producing impartial decisions, required ensuring certain extra-institutional conditions. Again, the radicals could affirm, the *absence* of these social conditions could transform the so-called rule of law into the "rule of a few men."

The idea that the maintenance of the rule of law required ensuring certain material preconditions was also commonly held in many Latin American countries, by many different radical thinkers. A first, though very rudimentary, manifestation of this position appeared in the Rio de la Plata region, with José Artigas, a famous *caudillo* and also a reader of Thomas Paine. Artigas showed concern both with creating a decentralized and more democratic political system and with grounding this new system in a more egalitarian economy.[38] A more articulated expression of this same view appeared, for example, in New Granada, with the radical Murillo Toro, a very active intellectual who even achieved the presidency of his country. Murillo Toro defended a more democratic organization of society, based on the presence of social institutions and on a more egalitarian distribution of property. In his opinion, property had to be distributed in such a way that permitted each person to secure the

---

[35] Jefferson (1999: 360–3).

[36] Letter to Joseph Cabell, 31 January 1814. Jefferson (1999: 197).

[37] See, for example, his letters to Joseph Cabell, February 1816, and to Samuel Kercheval, July 1816 and September 1816. See Jefferson (1999).

[38] See, in particular, Artigas's "Reglamento Provisorio de la Provincia Oriental para el Fomento de la Campaña," where he ordered the redistribution of lands according to the needs and efforts of the lower class. Also, in this respect, see Street (1959); Frega (1998); Sala, de la Torre, and Rodríguez (1978).

conditions of his own existence. One of the clearest expressions of this position in Latin America was that of the Ecuadorian Juan Montalvo, who was probably the most important intellectual figure in Ecuador during the nineteenth century. On the one hand, Montalvo decisively contributed to the creation of grass roots and very influential social organizations in his country (i.e., organizations such as the famous Sociedad de El Quiteño Libre, or the Sociedad Republicana) and represented one of the most important Ecuadorian voices in the defense of democracy. On the other hand, like Thomas Jefferson, he associated the establishment of a democratic system with the diffusion of public education and the egalitarian distribution of lands.[39]

Finally, there is much more to be said with regard to majoritarianism and institutional design. In particular, what particular type of institutional organization would majoritarians advise us to adopt? At this point, I cannot give an appropriate answer to this question, so I only summarize part of what we have mentioned already. I want to emphasize simply that majoritarians have good reasons to object to many contemporary institutional arrangements such as the presidential type of government adopted in most American countries[40] or the system of judicial review as it is exercised in the United States.[41] Also, I believe that they have good reasons to propose substantive reforms to political and nonpolitical institutions, aimed at ensuring a more active popular intervention in the discussion of public affairs. Of course, these considerations need further elaboration, but I leave this task until a future date.

## References

Ackerman, B. 1991. *We the People: Foundations.* Cambridge, Mass.: Harvard University Press.

2000. "The New Separation of Powers." *Harvard Law Review* 113: 633.

Adams, J. 1946. *The Selected Writings of John Adams.* Ed. A. Koch and W. Peden. New York: A. A. Knopf.

Alamán, L. 1997. *Los imprescindibles.* Mexico, D.F.: Cal y Arena.

Ames, S. 1983. *Works of Fisher Ames.* Indianapolis: Liberty Classics.

Basadre, J. 1969. *Historia de la república del Perú, 1822–1933.* Lima: Editorial Universitaria.

Baylin, B. 1992. *The Ideological Origins of the American Revolution.* Cambridge, Mass.: Harvard University Press.

[39] See Murillo Toro (1979); Roig (1984); and Montalvo (1960).
[40] See, in this respect, Nino (1996).
[41] See, for example, Tushnet (1999).

Blaustein, A., and J. Sigler. 1988. *Constitutions That Made History*. New York: Paragon House Publishers.

Brewer Carías, A. 1985. *Instituciones políticas y constitucionales*. Vol. 1. Caracas: San Cristóbal.

Butterfield, L. (ed.). 1951. *Letters of Benjamin Rush*. Princeton: Princeton University Press.

Chipman, N. 1833. *Principles of Government: A Treatise on Free Institutions*. Burlington: Edward Smith.

Cohen, J. 2000. "Privacy, Pluralism, and Democracy." Revised version of a paper presented at the Eastern Division of the American Philosophical Association, Newark, Del., December 1999.

Cronin, T. 1999. *Direct Democracy: The Politics of Initiative, Referendum, and Recall*. Cambridge, Mass.: Harvard University Press.

Dahl, R. 1956. *A Preface to Democratic Theory*. Chicago: University of Chicago Press.

Elster, J. 1993. "Majority Rule and Individual Rights." In S. Hurley and S. Shute (eds.), *On Human Rights*. New York: Basic Books.

Ely, J. 1980. *Democracy and Distrust*. Cambridge, Mass.: Harvard University Press.

Farrand, M. 1937. *The Records of the Federal Convention of 1787*. 4 vols. New Haven: Yale University Press.

Frega, A. 1998. "La virtud y el poder. La soberanía particular de los pueblos en el proyecto artiguista." In N. Goldman and Ricardo Salvatore (comps.), *Caudillismos Rioplatenses. Nuevas miradas a un viejo problema*. Buenos Aires: EUDEBA.

Hamilton, A., J. Madison, and J. Jay. 1988. *The Federalist Papers*. New York: Bantam Books.

Jefferson, T. 1999. *Political Writings*. Cambridge: Cambridge University Press.

Lutz, D. 1988. *The Origins of American Constitutionalism*. Baton Rouge: Lousiana University Press.

Madison, J. 1975. *The Papers of James Madison*. Ed. R. Rutland and W. Rachal. Chicago: University of Chicago Press.

Mansbridge, J. 1995. "A Deliberative Perspective on Neocorporatism." In E. O. Wright (ed.), *Associations and Democracy*, 133–47. London: Verso.

Molina, G. 1973. *Las ideas liberales en Colombia, 1849–1914*. Colección Manuales Universitarios. Bogotá: Tercer Mundo, 1973.

Montalvo, J. 1960. *Juan Montalvo*. Puebla: Editorial J. M. Cajica.

Murillo Toro, M. 1979. *Obras selectas*. Bogotá, D.E.: Camara de Representantes.

Nino, C. 1996. *The Constitution of Deliberative Democracy*. New Haven: Yale University Press.

Paine, T. 1995. "To the Authors of *The Republican*." In *Collected Writings*, ed. Eric Foner. New York: Library of America.

Paz-Soldán, J. 1954. *Las constituciones del Perú*. Madrid: Ediciones Cullena Hispánica.

Pettit, P. 1997. *Republicanism*. Oxford: Clarendon Press.

Portales, D. 1937. *Epistolario de Don Diego Portales*. Santiago de Chile: Ministerio de Justicia.

Przeworski, A., S. Stokes, and B. Manin. 1999. *Democracy, Accountability, and Representation*. Cambridge: Cambridge University Press.

Raz, J. 1977. "The Rule of Law and Its Virtue." *Law Quarterly Review* 93: 196.

Reyes, O. E. 1931. *Historia de la República*. Quito: Imprenta Nacional.

Roig, A. 1984. *El pensamiento social de Montalvo*. Quito: Editorial Tercer Mundo.

Rosenberg, G. 1991. *The Hollow Hope: Can Courts Bring about Social Change?* Chicago: University of Chicago Press.

Sala de Touron, L., N. de la Torre, and J. Rodríguez. 1978. *Artigas y su revolución agraria, 1811–1820*. Mexico: Siglo XXI.

Sandel, M. 1996. *Democracy's Discontent: America in Search of a Public Philosophy.* Cambridge, Mass.: Harvard University Press.

Sarmiento, D. 1977. *Civilización y barbarie*. Mexico: Ed. Porrúa.

Shaeffer, J. 1974. "Public Considerations of the 1776 Pennsylvania Constitution." *Pennsylvania Magazine of History and Biography* 98, 4: 420–1.

Sherman, M. 1991. *A More Perfect Union: Vermont Becomes a State, 1777–1816.* Vermont: Vermont Historical Society.

Sieyés, E. 1990. "Opinión del Abate Sieyés sobre la cuestión del veto real en la sesión del 7 de septiembre de 1789." In R. Màiz (ed.), *Escritos y discursos de la Revolución*. Madrid: Centro de Estudios Constitucionales.

Street, J. 1959. *Artigas and the Emancipation of Uruguay*. Cambridge: Cambridge University Press.

Sunstein, C. 1993. *The Partial Constitution*. Cambridge, Mass.: Harvard University Press.

Taylor, J. 1814. *An Inquiry into the Principles and Policy of the Government of the United States*. Virginia: Green and Cady.

Tushnet, M. 1999. *Taking the Constitution Away from the Courts*. Princeton: Princeton University Press.

Vile, M. 1991. "The Separation of Powers." In J. Greene and J. Pole (eds.), *The Blackwell Encyclopedia of the American Revolution*. Oxford: Basil Blackwell.

Waldron, J. 1993. "A Right-Based Critique of Constitutional Rights." *Oxford Journal of Legal Studies* 13: 18–51.

  1999. *Law and Disagreement*. Oxford: Oxford University Press.

Walsh, C. 1969. *The Political Science of John Adams: A Study in the Theory of Mixed Government and the Bicameral System*. New York: Freeport.

Webster, N. 1788. "Examination of the Constitution of the United States." In P. Ford (ed.), *Pamphlets on the Constitution of the United States*. New York: Burt Franklin.

Wood, G. 1969. *The Creation of the American Republic, 1776–1787*. New York: W. W. Norton.

## Chapter Seven

# How Can the Rule of Law Rule?
# Cost Imposition through
# Decentralized Mechanisms

Let us begin with a definition that is widely agreed upon in the literature: we are in the presence of the "rule of law" when the rules defining permitted and forbidden actions are not discretionary decisions of an individual, but rather take the form of laws that discipline every citizen, regardless of his or her power or status.[1] From this starting definition, it can be inferred that the "rule of law" faces an important political problem. This problem is not related to the difficulties rulers have in imposing and enforcing rules upon individual or collective actors. Indeed, with different degrees of efficiency, rulers have a varied and diverse repertoire of instruments they can use to make subjects obey the law (force, incentives, socialization, etc.). Rather, the central problem with the "rule of law" derives from the difficulties subjects have in making those who rule obey the law. Why should we expect that those who rule – that is, those who control the state resources – will obey the law? Why shouldn't we expect that they would use these resources to disobey the law? Therefore, an analysis of the rule of law implies answering what determines rulers' obedience to the law.

Authors such as Weingast, Przeworski, and Hardin have asserted that the rule of law will rule only if rulers and subjects conclude that it is in their interest to obey the law. That is, the rule of law will be

---

[1] Lawrence Solum considers that the rule of law can be conceived as the conjunction of seven requirements: no extralegal commands are obligatory; actions by government and officials should be subject to regulation by general and public rules; the legal system should meet the requirement of publicity; the legal system should meet the requirement of generality; the legal system should meet the requirement of regularity; the legal system should provide fair and orderly procedures for the determination of cases; and the actions that the rule of law requires and forbids should be of a kind that persons can reasonably be expected to do and to avoid (Solum 1994: 122). For other definitions of the concept, see Burton (1994: 180).

successful if it becomes self-enforcing. If that is the case, however, the preceding questions remain unanswered. What makes the rule of law self-enforcing? In other words, what determines that political leaders find it in their interest to abide by the law? The obvious answer is that they will have an incentive to follow the law if breaking it is costly. Therefore, we need to explore how costs for noncompliance can be imposed on rulers.

What makes the rule of law self-enforcing? What determines that political leaders find it in their interest to obey the law? In "Political Foundations of Democracy and the Rule of Law" (1997), Weingast asserts that the difficulties in establishing the rule of law derive from a massive coordination problem faced by citizens acting in a decentralized manner. The difficulties in coordinating decentralized citizens' actions affect their chances of imposing costs when state leaders do not follow the law. He argues that because state violations of the rule of law have unequal distributional consequences, the sovereign can gain support or acquiescence from those groups that benefit from these transgressions. The different distributional effects of the state transgressions prevent the coordination of citizens' actions and impede, in turn, the imposition of costs to rulers. Because not all actors find it in their benefit to impose costs on a nonobedient ruler, the net result is that the rule of law cannot become self-enforcing.

How, then, can the cost of noncompliance be imposed on rulers? According to Weingast, the rule of law will become self-enforcing if the sovereign's transgression of the rule of law affects all subjects equally and simultaneously. If that is the case, no group will have an interest in colluding with the rulers, and all will be willing to penalize the rulers for their transgressions. The implication is that when a ruler affects all possible allies, they have an incentive to coordinate their actions to restrain the ruler. This situation, in which all subjects can perceive the costs of not enforcing the rules, has a foundational consequence and explains why subjects find an incentive to coordinate actions to punish violations of the rule of law. As Weingast recognized, this situation explains the interest that subjects may have in the establishment of a foundational agreement, but it does not prevent that in future rounds rulers may attempt to collude again with one particular actor, destroying the coordination among subjects that had been achieved. In other words, this situation explains how and why the establishment of the rule of law may be possible, but it is unable to explain how it could be sustained.

How can coordination among subjects be sustained in the long run? Weingast adds that the rule of law becomes a self-enforcing and a sustained situation in those cases in which a *consensus on values* regarding "the *appropriate* limits on state action and the rights of citizens" allows *citizens to react in concert* (emphasis added) (Weingast 1997).[2] The conclusion is surprising because the entire problem of how to make the rule of law self-enforcing started with the acknowledgment of the problems citizens face in acting in concert and achieving consensus on values. Indeed, if acting in concert and consensus on values were present, there would not be a problem with the rule of law.

In the following pages I consider whether these two conditions are needed to warrant the sustained and self-enforcing nature of the rule of law – that is, whether it is necessary that citizens act in concert, and whether it is necessary that consensus on values is achieved.

The literature has informed us of the many factors that interfere with the long-run success of the coordination efforts that subjects pursue in order to punish rulers who transgress the law. Challenges to organizing an effective collective action of the ruled are great and persistent. However, empirical evidence shows that the rule of law has been established and sustained in diverse scenarios. What, then, explains its occurrence? Is it that on rare occasions citizens are able to coordinate their actions? Or are there other paths to sustain the rule of "the rule of law"?

I contend that to punish or deter rulers who transgress the law, concerted action of decentralized subjects is not a necessary condition. Rather, costs can be imposed, precisely because subjects also act in a decentralized manner. This creates uncertainty regarding how and when costs will be imposed and who will impose them, and decreases the chances of collusion. If this is the case, it becomes more difficult, even if there are subjects prone to collusion with the ruler, to be certain whether other subjects will be able to form alternative coalitions to challenge the sovereign's attempt to collude. If costs are imposed in a decentralized and chaotic way, rulers face more difficulties in anticipating with whom to collude and how to bypass possible costs. In other words, they confront greater challenges to foreseeing ways "to survive

---

[2] Weingast, for example, asserts that "in the absence of a consensus about the boundaries of the state, a coalition between the sovereign, and one group of citizens is stable once it is formed. Thus, the most natural equilibrium of the game is coordination failure: Citizens are unlikely to achieve coordination in a wholly decentralized manner. Typically, differential circumstances imply there is no natural focal solution to their problem" (1997: 251).

being accountable" (Maravall 1999). Both situations make nonobedience more costly.

This type of explanation may help in understanding the basic intuition that has affected authors from Tocqueville to Putnam, who have reinforced the importance of an autonomous civil society in guaranteeing the reign of the rule of law. It must be emphasized that I am not arguing, as some have, that an autonomous civil society is important because citizens share values that sustain the benefits of self-restraint. I am arguing that an autonomous civil society is important because it implies the existence of multiple external eyes with interests in the enforcement of law and denunciation of nonobedience. The existence of multiple and decentralized external eyes increases the number of interested "whistle blowers," the number of subjects interested in imposing costs, and the number of subjects who have a stake in law abidance. This multiplicity increases the number of possible alliances as well as the difficulties that rulers face in successfully preempting challenges when they choose to transgress the law. Since the threat decentralized actions involve raises the costs of negotiating and compensating for the acceptance of transgressions, it makes obeying the law more convenient for the sovereign. Lack of coordination of the ruled actions prevents the sovereign from having perfect information regarding what the subjects might do. Thus, the sovereign's ability to anticipate possible "whistle blowers," with whom he needs to collude, becomes more costly and difficult. As Matsuyama, quoted by Weingast, asserts, "the scope of citizen differences makes it difficult for a central authority to discover the appropriate way to coordinate."[3] In other words, because the ruled act in a decentralized manner, the sovereign cannot devise a collusion that may enable him to transgress the law efficiently. Therefore, if costs can also be imposed when subjects act in a decentralized manner, the importance of concerted action as a necessary condition for the reign of the rule of law is diminished.

These statements raise a few questions. First, we should consider whether decentralized actions could actually impose costs. The advanced argument implies that actors can be effective even if they act in a decentralized manner. This assertion appears to go against the argument that suggests that organization of decentralized actions is the weapon weak actors have to confront powerful ones. However, acting in a decentralized manner does not imply that citizens are an inarticulate aggregate of individuals. It is very likely that they will be members

---

[3] Matsuyama in Weingast (1997: 251).

of an association and that they will have some degree of organization. This does not imply, though, that those organizations will act in a homogeneous and unique coalition, or that they will share values or an ideological orientation. The only requirement is that they act as carriers of interests or as carriers of rights that need to be defended. These conditions, carriers of interests and petitioners of rights, *may* enable the activation of demands and actions if they perceive a transgression of the rule of law. Therefore, even if we accept that "people's natural diversity impedes coordination" (Weingast 1997: 251), it does not follow that this diversity will necessarily impede control or attempts to impose costs. Indeed, in the Madisonian and pluralistic arguments, control rests on this decentralized diversity. In my revisited version of those arguments, I am contending that decentralization of actions allows for a "piecemeal approach" to control of transgressions to the rule of law. Paraphrasing McCubbins, it can be said that decentralization allows for a "fire alarm" type of control (McCubbins and Schwartz 1984). Furthermore, it can be argued that given the diversity and multiplicity of interests the sovereign confronts, it can be expected that most transgressions will find someone willing to impose costs.

Two caveats concern the actions of civil society actors. First, it has to be remembered that civil society groups and associations can also act in uncivil and violent ways. Their goals can also include the substitution of the sovereign rather than the imposition of limits to its actions. Thus, although multiple and uncoordinated actions of civil society actors may facilitate the sustainability of the rule of law, they do not warrant its success. Thus, an additional condition for the rule of law to rule is that these multiple and uncoordinated actions should turn on "fire alarms" and "blow the whistle" not only when the sovereign transgress the law but also when societal actors attempt to do it. Second, acknowledging the benefits derived from the decentralized character of the exercise of control does not imply that controllers will avoid the problems involved in organizing a collective action. They will still have to deal with the issue: which collective organization allows them to achieve strength, extension, and efficiency in their claims, without reducing, in the process, the intensity and diversity of the issues they pretend to control?

We must now consider a second question: what type of costs can decentralized actors impose on rulers? The recent literature on accountability has explored different paths through which citizens impose costs on rulers. Two basic mechanisms are highlighted: the system of checks and balances, which performs a horizontal control of governmental actions, and elections, which allow for a vertical control of the rulers' actions. In theory, while the horizontal mechanisms control and oversee the legality of the actions of public officials and governmental agencies,[4] the vertical electoral ones allow citizens to control the actions of their representatives and the orientation of policies. In both cases, it is assumed that the controlled agents will act lawfully or in accordance with the electorate's preferences because they want to avoid the imposition of possible costs.[5] They abide by the law because they anticipate costs that can be imposed and they want to avoid them. In the case of the horizontal mechanisms, the costs that need to be avoided range from penal sanctions to impeachment. In the case of vertical mechanisms, the cost to be avoided is losing elections that will displace rulers from positions of power. However, the literature has mentioned that both horizontal and vertical mechanisms face some difficulties that question their effectiveness (O'Donnell 1993, 1994, 1996, 1999; Shifter 1997; Manin, Przeworski, and Stokes 1999; Zakaria 1997).

What difficulties do horizontal mechanisms of control face? O'Donnell argues that Latin American polyarchies display a notorious deficit of horizontal accountability because the majoritarian principle is considered the defining element of these regimes. Insofar as the horizontal mechanisms imply restrictions on majority decisions, they appear as obstacles to be bypassed or ignored to assure the rule of the majoritarian will. The resulting arrangement erodes a central feature of horizontal accountability: the existence of mechanisms of checks and balances among powers. When this is the case, the chances of imposing costs on rulers are diminished. In O'Donnell's explanation, the effectiveness of horizontal mechanisms in each polity rests on the existing balance found between democratic and liberal values. Shugart, Moreno, and Crisp (2000) argue that because horizontal accountability rest on the "principle of countervailing ambitions," if different interests and opinions are "improperly" represented in horizontal agencies, horizontal

---

[4] For O'Donnell "horizontal accountability" implies "the existence of state agencies that are legally enabled and empowered, and factually willing and able, to take actions that span from routine oversight to criminal sanctions or impeachment in relation to actions or omissions by other agents or agencies of the state that may be qualified as unlawful" (1999: 38).

[5] The purpose of electoral mechanisms is to reward or punish the policy orientation of representatives rather than the legality of their decisions. In doing so, however, the electorate has the chance to punish or reward the procedures through which those policy decisions were made. Therefore, although electoral mechanisms cannot specifically punish transgressions to the rule of law, they can still make strong signals in this regard. Even though voters do not have judicial entitlements to punish specific acts through the vote, when voting they can choose to reward or to punish representatives who break the law.

accountability will not follow. Thus, in their view the limits of the horizontal controls depend on the institutional design that translates the vertical relationship between voters and legislators. Weingast shows another difficulty that may jeopardize the success of the horizontal controls. If the sovereign is able to collude with specific actors placed in horizontal agencies, this can result in the nonactivation of these agencies and, in turn, in the lack of control of the sovereign's transgressions. In addition to these difficulties, we may find that, even though horizontal mechanisms are in place, they may be difficult to activate if opposition parties do not achieve the electoral majorities needed to use them. Are these examples of the collusion cases described by Weingast or are they something else? Although countermajoritarian institutions, such as the court, can activate some horizontal mechanisms, others, such as some parliamentary controls, depend on the impact of electoral preferences on the distribution of seats in congress. In those cases, when congressional horizontal mechanisms are not activated, are we witnessing the failure of horizontal mechanisms or the success of vertical ones?[6]

How do vertical mechanisms perform in controlling rulers' decisions and what restrictions do they confront? In a recent work Manin et al. (1999) highlight some structural weaknesses that affect vertical mechanisms of accountability. They indicate that electoral institutions face

[6] Let us consider the following example from the Argentinean case. The 1994 Constitution created a new institution, the Consejo de la Magistratura. Article 114 established that its functions include the selection of lower-court judges, the administration of the judicial branch resources, and the application of disciplinary sanctions against lower court judges. The Constitution also established that a law, to be sanctioned by the absolute majority of the members of each chamber, was to decide on the composition of the Consejo. According to the Constitution, its composition should strive for a balanced representation of different actors (members from different representative bodies – executive and legislative – judges, lawyers, and academics). As can be expected, the definition of how the Consejo was to be composed led to long and laborious negotiations. The governing party wanted to assure the presence of more political representatives than judges in the Consejo. The opposition wanted to reinforce the presence of academics and lawyers. Because the governing party had an absolute majority of the votes in each chamber, it had more institutional resources to implement its favored project. How are we to evaluate this case? On the one hand, it is true that the proposal favored by the official party diminished the horizontal control capabilities of the body that was being established. On the other hand, it must be remembered that the horizontal control capabilities were difficult to reinforce because the opposition was not able to attract substantial electoral support. Is this a case of collusion between the ruler and certain sectors of the electorate, or a case that shows the success of the vertical mechanisms in orienting policy preferences? The law was finally approved in December 1997. At that time, most political analysts mentioned that the defeat of the official party in the October elections was critical to overcoming the stalemate that had blocked the negotiations until then (*Clarín* and *La Nación*, 10 December 1997).

intrinsic limitations that make them inadequate as mechanisms of vertical accountability. Basically, they argue that elections are ineffective as an accountability mechanism because we can never know whether they are enforcing prospective or retrospective controls. If that is the case, then voters cannot induce governments to act responsibly. Different factors prevent the vote from being an efficient control mechanism. First, because voters have only one shot at punishing or rewarding various governmental decisions, their representatives know that voters do not have adequate instruments to control each of their decisions. In other words, they know that most of their decisions will not be controlled. A second restriction is related to the fact that voting is a decentralized strategic action (Przeworski 1991). Representatives know that some citizens may choose to use their vote to punish them for past actions and that others may choose to use it to approve promised policies. Because citizens have difficulties in coordinating the orientation of their votes, it follows that the power of voting as a control mechanism ends up weakened.

In sum, while Manin et al. conclude that "citizens control over politicians is at best highly imperfect" (1999: 50), analysts of horizontal mechanisms arrived at a similar conclusion. Acknowledging these difficulties does not imply that these mechanisms are useless. They just point out some fault lines. They show that vertical and horizontal mechanisms are not sufficient to punish and control all rulers' transgressions, and they make us wonder whether additional mechanisms might be at work to make the rule of law rule.

In a recent article, Enrique Peruzzotti and I analyzed alternative mechanisms through which costs are being imposed and oversight of political authorities is being pursued. We have named this type of control "societal accountability" (Smulovitz and Peruzzotti 2000). It involves actions carried out by actors with differing degrees of organization who recognize themselves as legitimate claimants of rights. A wide array of citizen associations, movements, or the media can initiate these actions. They aim to expose governmental wrongdoing, bring new issues to the public agenda, or influence or reverse policy decisions. They employ both institutional and noninstitutional tools. Use of institutional tools involves the activation of legal claims in oversight agencies or participation in institutional arenas for monitoring and policy making. The second scenario encompasses social mobilizations and media denunciations. "Societal accountability" is a nonelectoral, yet vertical, mechanism that enlarges the number of actors involved in the exercise of control. In contrast to electoral mechanisms, societal ones can be exercised

**175**

between elections, and do not depend on fixed calendars. They are activated "on demand" and are being used to oversee and address the procedures followed by politicians and public officials while making policy, as well as to control single issues and the behavior of functionaries and policies.

In contrast to horizontal mechanisms, societal ones perform watchdog functions without fulfilling special majority requirements or having constitutional entitlements. This allows societal mechanisms to give visibility and to articulate demands of actors that may be disregarded in the representative arena. As it is known, the representative arena imposes certain limitations that affect whose and what interests end up being articulated. If actors and interests are unable to show extensive support, they will be excluded and their chances of activating horizontal mechanisms or of having a vertical impact will be low. Societal mechanisms can avoid some of these difficulties because their activation relies on a different principle. Actors do not need to show extensive support; presence rather than extension justifies them. Therefore, societal mechanisms allow actors who are otherwise unable or excluded from playing in the representative arena to reach public attention through an alternative path. When actors excluded from the representative arena are capable of making sufficient "noise" and able to place issues on the agenda, societal mechanisms may force horizontal ones to consider topics that majoritarian requirements could have transformed into "nonissues." Two comments are in order. First, it can be argued that some horizontal mechanisms, such as some parliamentary decisions, also impose costs on the sovereign in a decentralized manner. However, because their activation is limited by the restrictions imposed by the representative logic, their capacity to act in a decentralized and autonomous manner ends up being constrained by the majoritarian requirements that govern this arena. Second, because societal mechanisms do not need to legitimize themselves on representative grounds, their exercise may have ambiguous social consequences in terms of equal representation. Consequently, attention should be paid to the potential tension that results from the conflict between representative and countermajoritarian principles.

Societal mechanisms also differ from horizontal and from electoral (vertical) ones in that they entail not mandatory legal sanctions but rather symbolic ones. Because the imposition of cost is linked to the capacity to enforce decisions, and since these forms of control expose wrongdoing but do not have mandatory effects, some authors regard them more as window-dressing activities than as real checks on power

(Schedler 1999). Although societal mechanisms rely on a soft form of punishment based mostly on public disapproval, this is not necessarily a sign of weakness. Social protest, denunciations of wrongdoings, or monitoring of public activities can modify the available reputational information about public agents. In democratic contexts, representatives need and value their reputation because they know that the strategic and uncoordinated operation of citizens is guided, among other considerations, by this information. Thus, social sanctions can destroy a crucial resource of public officials: their symbolic and reputational capital (Thompson 1997). Experience shows that scandals have not only forced officials out of office, but have also led to a drastic end of their political careers. It is true, however, that societal mechanisms are unable to impose discrete institutional and mandatory sanctions. Nevertheless, it is important to stress that legal and mandatory enforcement of costs is not completely absent from the picture either. Societal mechanisms of control have a rather indirect relation to legal enforcement. Their efficiency is mediated by the evaluation public officials do of the possible reputational and electoral costs they may produce. Although actors exercising societal controls are unable to apply legal punishments themselves, many of their actions commonly trigger procedures in the courts, in the parliament, or in oversight agencies and eventually lead to legal sanctions.[7] In this sense, it can be argued that although costs imposed through societal mechanisms are not mandatory, they can become a condition that enables the imposition of mandatory ones. In other words, the efficiency of the vertical and horizontal controls becomes contingent on the ability decentralized social actors have to organize and impose credible reputational threats. Indeed, what this argument shows is that costs can be imposed if the different mechanisms of control interact: decentralized whistle-blowing imposes reputation costs that activate vertical and horizontal mechanisms that may, in a second round, impose mandatory sanctions. If this is the case, the way in which these costs are produced and imposed is a topic in need of further analysis.

---

[7] Although many oversight agencies (accounting offices, fiscalías, etc.) can be considered as part of the system of horizontal accountability, it must be taken into account that some, such as ombudsman offices, also operate as vertical ones, given that they are activated through specific citizen claims. Another recent development that should be considered is the activation by NGOs or social movements of the oversight mechanisms of international agencies. For example, NGOs like CELS and CORREPI in Argentina have registered complaints about police abuse to the Interamerican Human Rights Commission. These cases involve not only demands for justice but also demands for "due process."

A few examples from the recent Latin American experience can illustrate how decentralized mechanisms impose costs and control the sovereign's actions.[8] Even though law abidance by the rulers is still a pending achievement in many of these countries, cost imposition through decentralized mechanisms is starting to curb sovereigns' transgressions in certain areas of public policy. In Brazil, for example, recently modified legal institutions such as the public prosecutor allow citizens and collective actors to claim and petition for the protection of fundamental rights. Although great variations can be registered across states, in the past five years denounciations regarding administrative wrongdoings advanced by the public prosecutor have resulted in the indictment of 195 public officials throughout the country.[9] In some cases, the public prosecutor office has endogenously activated these actions, while in others they have been triggered by individual or collective actors. According to the newspaper *O Estado de São Paulo* the work carried out by the office of the public prosecutor "is without doubt responsible for a new sense of hope toward ending public impunity."[10] The acts of the sovereign are also being controlled through "soft" mechanisms, such as mobilization of civil society organizations and media denounciations. Civil society organizations have mobilized to demand information about assets of public officials and to denounce electoral frauds, violations of environmental rights, or police abuse. NGOs like Nucleo de Estudos da Violencia and Viva Rio in Brazil, CELS (Centro de Estudios Legales y Sociales) and CORREPI (Coordinadora contra la Represión Policial e Institucional) in Argentina, or Alianza Cívica in Mexico have been able to place these topics on the public agenda and have become, in the process, credible and authoritative voices for controlling the performance of state actions. Recent policy responses, such as the launching of police reform programs or the presence of electoral observers, show that state officials are acknowledging the costs of disregarding denounciations made by these organizations.

The media have also played a central role. Journalists have uncovered wrongdoings involving high-ranking public officials and have conducted investigations denouncing transgressions of the rule of law by the sovereign as well as attempts at collusion with social or political actors. Some denounciations have led to indictments, although others did not

---

[8] An extensive illustration of the way in which these mechanisms operate in six Latin American countries can be found in Smulovitz and Peruzzoti (1999).

[9] VEJA, 6 October 1999. See also Cavalcanti and Sadek (2000).

[10] *O Estado de São Paulo*, 21 February 2000, quoted in Cavalcanti and Sadek (2000: 15).

bring any convictions. In Argentina, for example, different newspapers and television programs have made denouncements implicating high-level public officials that have led to the resignation of the mentioned functionaries and to legal actions.[11] Similar cases in which media denounciations have led to legal processes or to the removal of public officials have taken place in Brazil, when in 1992 press denunciations started the processes that led to the impeachment of Fernando Collor de Melo, and in Venezuela, where in 1993 press denunciations led to the removal of Carlos Andres Perez. In Peru, the newsweekly *Si* published a story known as the case of "La Cantuta" that led to an investigation of the massacre of a group of college students by military squads.[12] Although, with the exception of the legal proceedings, decentralized mechanisms cannot impose mandatory sanctions, these examples show that they still have "material consequences." Decentralized actors with different interests and goals have activated horizontal procedures and imposed reputational and electoral costs. Because the actions of these decentralized actors raise the costs faced by the sovereign in transgressing the law and in devising successful collusions, the benefits of abiding by the law start to increase.

The exercise of societal accountability also faces certain limits and problems that need to be addressed. As was mentioned, the intensity of the voice rather than its extension is critical for the success of societal controls. This feature reveals some of the limits and problems confronted by this type of control. First, controls of rulers' transgressions may center on issues that concern intense but not necessarily majoritarian groups. If controls based on societal mechanisms tend to concentrate on violations that affect the interests of intense and organized actors, the issue of how less organized and less intense actors impose costs still remains unanswered. Second, it is likely that rulers will be more efficiently controlled when their actions affect private rather than public goods. Both points signal that the imposition of costs through decentralized mechanisms results in a certain bias that leaves the interests of some actors and some topics unattended. In spite of these shortcomings, it can be argued that decentralized actions can result in costs,

---

[11] Among the scandals involving public officials that flooded the Argentinian media in the last few years are Yomagate, Swiftgate, IBM-Bco Nación, Carrasco Case, etc. Most of these cases led to the opening of a judicial procedure, some of them are still in process, others led to indictments and others to acquitals. Still others, such as the Carrasco Case, also led to policy reforms (elimination of the mandatory military service). See also Camps and Pazos (1999).

[12] See Smulovitz and Peruzzotti (1999) and Waisbord (1996).

which may lead rulers to evaluate law abidance as a more convenient behavior.

The other condition that needs to be reviewed indicates that for the rule of law to rule, citizens need to share a consensus on certain values. Almond and Verba, for example, assert that for democracy to be stable, a particular "civic culture" that includes, among other values, a consensus on the need "to place limits on politics" is required (Almond and Verba 1963: 490).[13] They consider that, among other things, these values bring about social trust, which in turn keeps a democratic polity operating. They sustain that "Constitution makers have designed formal structures of politics that attempt to enforce trustworthy behavior, but without these attitudes of trust, such institution may mean little. Societal trust facilitates political cooperation among the citizens in these nations, and without it democratic politics is impossible" (Almond and Verba 1963: 490). Weingast, on the other hand, considers that for the rule of law to rule, citizens must share a *consensus on values* regarding "the *appropriate* limits on state action and the rights of citizens." Moreover, he adds that these values must lead to "a *citizen consensus to react* against tomorrow's incumbents if they attempt to rig elections" (Weingast 1997: 255, emphasis added). I do not consider here whether values and culture determine the existence of the rule of law or the stability of democracy. Instead, I focus on whether the positive consequences that consensus on values is to deliver guarantee the self-enforcing character of the rule of law.

Some authors have argued that painful past experiences can bring about consensus on certain values. They assert that after experiencing the ills of the nonexistence of the rule of law, actors start to value the virtues of self-restraint.[14] Although the impact of the cultural dimension in regard to the way actors perceive the importance of the rule of law cannot be disregarded, I do not think it solves the problem. First, there are no guarantees that parties will share these values; therefore there

---

[13] Almond and Verba's argument regarding the connection between culture and democracy is more complex than what is usually acknowledged. They establish multiple and sometimes contradictory relationships between citizens' values and behaviors. I will mention some of their more sophisticated arguments later.

[14] Rustow and Elster mention this adaptive process. The former, for example, mentions how certain nonpreferred values, such as the self-restraint implied by the democratic arrangements, become palatable after resorting to force becomes too costly (Rustow 1970). The latter analyzes how unreachable goals can become "sour grapes," turning values and goals that were originally rejected into preferable options (Elster 1999). In both cases, an originally less preferred option ends up being genuinely favored, a process that may lead to consensus regarding the values and virtues of self-restraint.

can always be a candidate to collude and support future violations of the rule of law. However, even if all actors share values and even if there is an extended consensus on the virtue of self-restraint, actors know that there are no guarantees that all others will act accordingly. Sharing values is not a sufficient condition, because actors may still distrust what the others might do. Actors know that values do not necessarily translate into behavior. Consequently, even if actors share values on the virtue of self-restraint and on the need to sustain the rule of law, this does not prevent them from distrusting how other actors will behave. Therefore, although consensus on values may help, it is not a guarantee.

I argue that consensus on values is not a necessary condition for the imposition of costs by these decentralized actors. Furthermore, it can be sustained that, if values have any impact on the enforcement of the rule of law, a certain amount of dissent over values among citizens is convenient and necessary. It can be argued that if the expected result of sharing values is social trust regarding the actions that others may attempt, it can be expected that the risk of transgressions of the rule of law may increase. It must be remembered that the main problem for the rule of law it is not its foundational establishment but its long-run sustainability. As we mentioned previously, this sustainability depends on the permanent control and oversight of the actions of the rulers and the ruled. Thus, we can speculate that the social trust that results from value sharing weakens citizens' oversight and control capacities of what rulers do and increases, in turn, the chances of opportunistic actions by one of them.[15] Decentralized "whistle-blowing," which multiplies the chances and the sources of control, depends on the existence of multiple actors who distrust what the others may do. For control to be exercised, a certain amount of distrust regarding the actions of other subjects and rulers alike is needed. Therefore, consensus on values, even if it could be achieved, does not appear a sufficient condition insofar as social trust – its predicted return – does not ensure the long-term survival of the rule of law. In contrast to what has recently been asserted regarding the virtues of social trust, it can be argued that unless distrust is also part of the picture, control of the rulers' actions cannot take place. It is true that we can still wonder how much distrust a regime can support; however, this does not imply that social trust that derives from sharing values is the solution that will allow the rule of law to rule.[16]

---

[15] Indeed, as Russell Hardin has noted, "To trust the untrustworthy can be disastrous" (Hardin 1998).

[16] Different authors have considered the issue of how much trust or distrust a society can bear. In a paragraph quoted by Almond and Verba, Berelson warns of the limits that

A second aspect of this problem should also be considered. In Weingast's argument, to enforce the rule of law, in addition to consensus on values regarding "the appropriate limits on state action and the rights of citizens," a citizen consensus to react against rulers' transgressions is needed. As Przeworski indicated, for Weingast two different tasks are needed to enforce the rule of law: coordination of beliefs and coordination of actions (Przeworski 1998). Undoubtedly, this increases the difficulty that citizens face in making the rule of law rule. Even in the case that citizen consensus on values was an achievable goal, a concerted consensual reaction does not necessarily follow. Thus, neither social trust nor coordination of actions is a necessary condition to protect the rule of law. Under certain conditions, both distrust and uncoordinated actions may also do the job, allowing the ruled to bypass the difficulties involved in the articulation of a concerted action.

What are some of the advantages and problems that these decentralized mechanisms confront in imposing costs? Most social and political relationships are governed by rules that are backed by state sanctions. Therefore, the number, places, and opportunities for rulers' transgressions of the rule of law are enormous, and subjects face a technical and physical problem in controlling rulers' transgressions. Indeed, it is unlikely that they will be able to control and impose costs for each transgression. Although societal mechanisms do not completely overcome this problem, the molecular type of control they exercise enables subjects to reach and oversee areas that are usually out of the sight and reach of other control mechanisms.[17] In this case, control of transgressions is not delegated to bureaucratic or representative authorities but is exercised by an array of individual citizens and associations that have a special interest in monitoring the actions of the rulers in specific

consensus over values may imply for the rule of law. He asserts, "Too much agreement would mitigate against the enforcement of elite responsiveness." Yet, if cleavage went too far, "a democratic society . . . would probably be in danger of its existence. The issues of politics would cut so deeply, be so keenly felt, and, especially, be so fully reinforced by other social identifications of the electorate" as to threaten democracy" (Almond and Verba 1963: 491). An echo of this argument can also be found in Hirschman's article, "Los conflictos sociales como pilares de la Sociedad de Mercado Democrática," *Agora* 4 (1996). See also Levi (1996).

[17] As was mentioned, societal mechanisms are able to reach and control topics and actors that are out of reach for the electoral and horizontal mechanisms of control because their activation does not rely on the majoritarian principles. Because decisions based on representative criteria select issues taking into consideration the number of interested subjects, they necessarily leave issues and sectors of the population unattended. This exclusion does not necessarily reveal a failure of representative mechanisms; it only highlights differences in the way they operate.

areas. Decentralization of control not only fragments its exercise but also alters the division of labor among subjects in charge of control and of imposing costs. Control of rulers is not a delegated responsibility of representatives or functionaries, but a task diffused among an indefinite number of interested subjects. Because the actors that intervene have high stakes in the matters being controlled, their attention is more intense. Because they have more knowledge of the issues being controlled, their social control capabilities can be used in a more efficient manner and the chances that rulers implement successful plans to "survive controls" may decrease. In addition, the fragmentation of control allows for the appearance and education of controllers. Finally, because the decentralized exercise of control expands the number of subjects involved, it also expands the areas and issues that can be controlled.

These benefits, however, encounter some problems that jeopardize the effectiveness of this type of control. We have already mentioned that actors performing societal controls cannot completely avoid the problems associated with the way they collectively organize to perform these controls. Let us consider, now, some additional difficulties: the risks of piecemeal collusion, the risks involved in the extended participation requirements, and the risks derived from the nature of the topics that can be controlled.

Years ago, Grant McConnell (1966: 6) noted some of the problems faced by the strategy based on the actions of civil society associations. Because they are organized around a voluntary and homogenous membership with limited purposes and do not have checks on their powers, the risks that their actions can result in special benefits for their members in exchange for acquiescence of rule transgressions is high. In other words, instead of becoming an instrument for the exercise of piecemeal controls, they can become instruments of piecemeal collusion. Therefore, the existence of these decentralized associations for the exercise of control and for the imposition of costs does not alone guarantee the desired result. It is not the proliferation of organizations that determines the effectiveness of their control but the specific type of links they establish with the rulers they control. Indeed, when these associations attempt to influence the orientation of state policies and are thus obliged to confront and negotiate with the state, they run the risk of being co-opted, which renders their control capabilities useless. Consequently, while the decentralization of control in civil society associations may help, it is not by itself a sufficient condition for success.

The operation of decentralized mechanisms implies high levels of participation by those interested in the exercise of control. However, as has been largely demonstrated by different empirical studies on participation, this involves a series of problems. Democratic theory has usually considered civic participation as one of its pillars because it allows citizens to influence policy orientations, to defend their interests, and to control governmental acts. However, empirical studies have shown not only that citizens' participation tends to be relatively low, but also that participation is correlated with social stratification. That is, people with higher socioeconomic status – those with higher education, higher income, and higher status jobs – are more active (Verba, Schlozman, and Brady, 1995). Regardless of the factors that may explain these different participatory behaviors, the phenomenon has an important impact on the type of control that can be exercised through decentralized mechanisms. To be effective, this type of control implies high levels of participation. To exercise control, citizens, as individuals or as members of organizations, must make use of scarce resources. They need to dedicate part of their time, they should use part of their income, and they will need certain knowledge and abilities that will allow them to act effectively. Because the opportunity costs of participating in the exercise of control will be smaller for the richer than for the poorer, it can be expected that the former will tend to be able to use them more frequently and more efficiently than the latter. Therefore, high social inequalities in the access to and use of these decentralized mechanisms can be expected – inequalities that, in turn, affect the orientation and content of the topics that could be controlled.

Finally, it must be remembered that participation is also associated with the intensity of the participants' preferences and with the characteristics of the goods at stake. Participation tends to be higher when the participants have intense preferences and when the issues at stake have private rather than public or collective consequences. Because the activation and effectiveness of controls do not depend on the extension of the demand among those requiring controls, but on their capacity to make themselves heard, it can be expected that vocal individuals and associations will have greater chances of exercising controls than extended but less vocal groups. Moreover, because the noise groups can make depends on their access to monetary and organizational capacities, it can be expected that those topics that mobilize intense, vocal groups will get preferential consideration regardless of their extension. In addition, given the difficulties decentralized citizens face in organizing around the provision of collective goods, it can be expected that the exercise of control through these decentralized mechanisms will tend to focus on those issues that affect private rather than public goods.

**184**

This brief overview of the limitations faced by decentralized mechanisms of control shows that certain policy areas and actors would not be efficiently controlled. At the same time, these limitations highlight the policy areas and actors where it is more likely that transgressions could take place without being punished. Given these restrictions, we must consider whether these decentralized mechanisms can still impose costs in ways that render the rule of law self-enforcing. First, it should be noticed that, in spite of the acknowledged constraints, decentralized mechanisms are still capable of imposing costs in areas and on actors that could remain out of reach to other control mechanisms. In that sense, even though they are not an exhaustive mechanism for the imposition of costs, they do establish additional controls. For that reason, they cannot be completely disregarded. Second, although these limitations signal areas that cannot be controlled, where transgressions could go unpunished, it also should be noticed that rulers do not have perfect information regarding which policy areas and actors will not be reached by these decentralized controls. Therefore, if the actual capacity of these mechanisms to impose controls remains unclear, their virtual ability to exercise control can still be high. Indeed, this will not be very different from the situation that characterizes the imposition of criminal sanctions on law offenders. In those cases, the deterrent effect is also based on the uncertainty offenders have regarding who will actually be punished and what is the actual reach of law enforcers. It is true that these mechanisms create and impose costs in an unequal manner. However, if the cost production and enforcement process remain chaotic and uncertain, preventing rulers from anticipating who and what will actually be controlled, the aforementioned restrictions will not necessarily cancel out their ability to impose costs. Indeed, the decentralized character of these mechanisms makes predictions and anticipations unreliable. If increasing social complexity means the continuous appearance of multiple interests and identities, then rulers will be unable to predict what issues will become the object of subject concerns. If that is the case, predicting which transgressions will go unpunished may end up being a risky and costly business.

In conclusion, the imposition of costs through decentralized mechanisms is a necessary condition for the rule of law to rule. In spite of their acknowledged restrictions, these mechanisms impose reputation costs that rulers in democratic contexts need to avoid. In addition, they may activate otherwise reluctant electoral and horizontal controls that can impose mandatory sanctions on rulers' transgressions. In contrast to what is usually mentioned, the operation of these decentralized mechanisms does not require that actors share values. Indeed, an argument can be made that certain levels of dissent are necessary for their performance. Because their activation is not based on majority or representative grounds, they are able to control issues and actors that are usually out of reach to horizontal and electoral mechanisms. Their decentralized character increases the difficulties rulers face in anticipating where, how, and what will be controlled, and the costs to coordinate actions to bypass these controls. Therefore, and insofar as decentralized mechanisms increase the costs rulers face when transgressing the law and the costs rulers face in bypassing those costs, they lead rulers to conclude that it is in their interest to obey the law. In other words, the decentralized imposition of costs increases the chances for the rule of law to become self-enforcing.

## References

Almond, Gabriel, and Sidney Verba. 1963. *The Civic Culture.* Princeton: Princeton University Press.

Burton, Steven. 1994. "Particularism, Discretion and the Rule of Law." In Ian Shapiro (ed.), *The Rule of Law. Nomos XXXVI.* New York: New York University Press.

Camps, Sibila, and Luis Pazos. 1999. *Justicia y televisión. La sociedaddicta sentencia.* Buenos Aires: Libros Perfil.

Cavalcanti, Rosangela, and Maria Tereza Sadek. 2002. "El Impacto del Ministerio Público sobre la Democracia Brasileña: El Redescubrimiento de la Ley." In Enrique Peruzzotti and Catalina Smulovitz (eds.), *Controlando la política. Ciudadanos y medios en las nuevas democracias latinoamericanas,* 169–92. Buenos Aires: Temas Grupo Editorial.

Elster, Jon. 1999. *Alchemies of the Mind.* Cambridge: Cambridge University Press.

Hardin, Russell. 1989. "Why a Constitution?" In Bernard Grofman and Wittman Donald (eds.), *The Federalist Papers and the New Institutionalism.* New York: Agathon Press.

1998. "Trust." In Peter Newman (ed.), *The New Palgrave Dictionary of Economics and the Law.* New York: Stockton Press.

Levi, Margaret. 1996. *A State of Trust.* European University Institute, Florence. Working Paper No. 96/23.

McConnell, Grant. 1966. *Private Power and American Democracy.* New York: Alfred Knopf.

McCubbins, Matthew, and Thomas Scwartz. 1984. "Congressional Oversight Overlooked: Police Patrols versus Fire Alarms." *American Journal of Political Science* 28, 1: 165–79.

Manin, Bernard, Adam Przeworski, and Susan Stokes. 1999. "Elections and Representation." In Adam Przeworski, Susan Stokes, and Bernard Manin (eds.), *Democracy, Accountability, and Representation,* 29–54. Cambridge: Cambridge University Press.

Maravall, José María. 1999. "Accountability and Manipulation." In Adam Przeworski, Susan Stokes, and Bernard Manin (eds.), *Democracy, Accountability and Representation.* Cambridge: Cambridge University Press.

O'Donnell, Guillermo. 1993. "On the State, Democratization and Some Conceptual Problems: A Latin American View with Glances at Some Postcommunist Countries." *World Development* 21, 8: 1355–1370.

1994. "Delegative Democracy." *Journal of Democracy* 5, 1: 59–61.

1996. "Illusions about Consolidation." *Journal of Democracy* 7, 2: 34–52.

1999. "Horizontal Acountability in New Democracies." In Andreas Schedler, Larry Diamond, and Marc Plattner (eds.), *The Self-Restraining State: Power and Accountability in New Democracies*. Boulder: Lynne Rienner Publishers.

Przeworski, Adam. 1991. *Democracy and the Market*. Cambridge: Cambridge University Press.

1998. "Culture and Democracy." In UNESCO, *Culture Creativity and Markets*. Paris: UNESCO.

Przeworski, Adam, Susan Stokes, and Bernard Manin (eds.). 1999. *Democracy, Accountability, and Representation*. Cambridge: Cambridge University Press.

Rustow, Dankwart. 1970. "Transitions to Democracy." In *Comparative Politics* 2: 337–64.

Schedler, Andreas. 1999. "Conceptualizing Accountability." In Andreas Schedler, Larry Diamond, and Marc Plattner (eds.), *The Self-Restraining State: Power and Accountability in New Democracies*. Boulder: Lynne Rienner Publishers.

Shifter, Michael. 1997. "Tensions and Trade-offs In Latin America." *Journal of Democracy* 8, 2.

Shugart, Matthew, Erika Moreno, and Brian F. Crisp. 2000. "The Accountability Deficit in Latin America." In Scott Mainwaring and Christopher Welna (eds.), *Accountability, Democratic Governance, and Political Institutions in Latin America*. Notre Dame: University of Notre Dame Press.

Smulovitz, Catalina, and Enrique Peruzzotti. 1999. "La responsabilidad pública (Accountability) en las nuevas democracias. ¿Cómo supervisan los ciudadanos a sus representantes?" Universidad Di Tella, Buenos Aires. Unpublished manuscript.

2000. "Social Accountability: The Other Side of Control." *Journal of Democracy* 11, 4.

Solum, Lawrence. 1994. "Equity and the Rule of Law." In Ian Shapiro (ed.), *The Rule of Law. Nomos XXXVI*. New York: New York University Press.

Thompson, John B. 1997. "Scandal and Social Theory." In James Lull and Stephen Hineman (eds.), *Media Scandals*. Cambridge: Polity Press.

Verba, Sidney, Kay Schlozman, and Henry Brady. 1995. *Voice and Equality: Civic Voluntarism in American Politics*. Cambridge, Mass.: Harvard University Press.

Waisbord, Silvio. 1996. "Investigative Journalism and Political Accountability in South American Democracies." *Critical Studies in Mass Communication* 13: 343–63.

Weingast, Barry. 1997. "The Political Foundations of Democracy and the Rule of Law." *American Political Science Review* 91, 2: 245–63.

Zakaria, Fareed. 1997. "The Rise of Illiberal Democracy." *Foreign Affairs* 76: 22–43.

## Chapter Eight

# Dictatorship and the Rule of Law: Rules and Military Power in Pinochet's Chile

Should we associate the rule of law only with democratic legal systems or can we conceive of the rule of law as an independent phenomenon that may equally be associated with other forms of regime? In particular, can we speak of an autocratic or dictatorial rule of law? In this chapter, I discuss two notions of the rule of law and argue that in principle, under specific conditions, both are compatible with nondemocratic forms of rule. Although this association may not be historically all that common, I analyze one case, the military dictatorship in Chile (1973–90), and try to show that a form of rule of law was operative within the regime, particularly during the last nine years of military rule. In developing this argument, I hope to elucidate some general properties of the rule of law and specify conditions under which rules can have force even upon their own makers.

### Two Notions of the Rule of Law

The term "rule of law" is used quite widely in contemporary theoretical and political discussions. Nevertheless two broad conceptions are prominent. One, variously referred to as a "narrow," "formal," or "instrumental" conception of the rule of law, examines the formal characteristics that law must have if a legal system is to provide a nonarbitrary framework around which subjects can form expectations and live their lives. This notion of the rule of law essentially concerns the character of law as a mechanism of mediation between state authorities and social actors. The second notion of the rule of law is more demanding and requires that state authorities and lawmakers themselves be subject to

I wish to thank the participants in the Madrid conference and the anonymous reviewers from the Cambridge University Press for their comments.

law, such that laws and not men purportedly rule. This broader conception dovetails with doctrines of constitutionalism, the separation of powers, and limited government. I proceed by further discussing these two conceptions of the rule of law, their relationships with dictatorship, and finally discuss the Chilean case in light of these perspectives.

## Rule of Law as Rule by Law

The narrow doctrine of the rule of law, which is the notion that occupies most of the legal-philosophical debate on the rule of law, centers on specific formal or procedural characteristics that rules must have if the law itself is not to be a source of injustices. In Raz's words (1979: 224), "the rule of law is designed to minimize the danger created by the law itself." That is, the principles associated with the rule of law stand to eliminate the types of arbitrary power that would arise if the law itself created uncertainty and unpredictability regarding which acts are legal at any given moment and/or how laws will be enforced.[1] From this perspective, by setting and enforcing a clear framework of rules, a legal system that conforms to the rule of law allows actors subject to its terms to develop expectations and to act according to them, regardless of the substantive content of the rules that guide or constrain action.

Although the list of formal characteristics associated with the rule of law often varies from author to author, a general cluster is readily identifiable. These characteristics tend to include that: laws be prospective, publicly promulgated, and clear; laws be relatively stable; the making of particular legal orders (such as administrative regulations) be subject to open, stable, clear, and general rules; laws be consistently applied by an independent judiciary free from extraneous pressures; and law enforcement agencies not pervert the law by applying it discretionarily.[2] The value of these principles of the rule of law can be illustrated negatively: law cannot provide a framework for forming reasonable expectations and allow subjects some degree of security when acts can variously be made illicit after the fact, be subject to secret or imprecise rules, and/or be governed by regulations that depart from known rules.

---

[1] This negative formulation is consistent with Raz's (1979: 242) minimalist argument that the rule of law is "essentially a negative value." As he notes, "conformity to it does not cause good except through avoiding evil and the evil which is avoided is evil which could only have been caused by the law itself."

[2] Here I am loosely following Raz (1979: 212–18) . For other formulations, see Fuller (1964); Oakeshott (1983); Waldron (1989); and Ten (1993).

Similarly, even known, prospective rules fail to provide guides for action when judges apply the law inconsistently or incorrectly or when police and security forces enforce the law upon some social groups and not others or act beyond the limits of their legally authorized powers. In such contexts, individuals can have no certainty or security regarding what is demanded of them by the law.

This notion of the rule of law perhaps may be referred to as "rule by law" insofar as it says nothing about how laws are made or the substantive purposes that laws pursue. This form of the rule of law does require that the subordinate organs and agencies that apply, enforce, and adjudicate the law faithfully abide by its terms, but beyond these limits rule by law does not specify any requirements regarding how laws be made or that lawmakers themselves be subject to law. Rule of law presupposes that some body or office makes laws, but the doctrine does not focus on this process. In theory, then, "rule by law" is independent of whether a regime is autocratic or democratic in the manner of its generation of rules or of whether powers are institutionally limited or unlimited. An example of the conceptual independence of the rule by law from the form of regime and the second version of the rule of law – that state actors themselves be subject to law – is provided in Hobbes's theory of the state. Hobbes, as is well known, discounts that sovereign actors can be subject to rules; nevertheless his account envisages a legal organization of the state in which the law is publicly promulgated, prospective (*nulla poena sine lege*), general, and applied by a public authority, and punishments not founded in such law are explicitly understood to be arbitrary, "act[s] of hostility" (1991: chs. 26–8).[3] This account conforms to this first narrower understanding of the rule of law, yet eschews the second broader understanding of the rule of law.

Despite the theoretical compatibility of rule by law with autocracy, the practice of empirical dictatorships and authoritarian regimes typically deviates from the forms of legal intermediation that define this sense of the rule of law. In fact, the association of dictatorship with the release from legal forms traces to the classical Roman republican dictatorship, which, despite being a constitutional and limited institution, granted the dictator unlimited powers to quell the particular situation warranting his appointment.[4] Contemporary dictatorships similarly stray from the

[3] On Hobbes's conception of law, see Goldsmith (1996). For an interpretation of Hobbes as a theorist of the rule of law, see Oakeshott (1983).

[4] For the argument that dictatorships suspend the law to reinstate the conditions of its efficacy, see Schmitt (1985). On the Roman dictatorship, see Rossiter (1948: ch. 2) and Friedrich (1950: ch. 13).

requirements of rule by law whenever they resort to emergency powers or extralegal forms of repression to impose their order.

Any use of emergency powers, even by constitutional democracies, creates uncertainty for subjects insofar as such exceptional powers grant the executive authority to detain individuals at its discretion, independent of any requirement that an offense have been committed. Whereas constitutional democracies generally inhibit the use of such broad powers by vesting authority to declare a state of siege or emergency in one body (the legislature) and the exercise of the discretionary powers conferred in another (the executive),[5] under dictatorships this institutional constraint disappears whenever both powers are concentrated in a single body or person. Thus, the prior existence of constitutional emergency powers can provide dictators with ready authority to declare states of exception unilaterally and wield broad and continuous powers with which to repress adversaries and deter opposition through the threat and application of administrative detentions.[6] In such situations, executive prerogative displaces any vestige of the "rule by law" in those realms targeted by dictatorial power.

Further removed from any formal basis in law are absolutely extrajudicial acts effected by state organs that neither pursue the repression of a criminal offense nor are authorized by the regime's own public law or positive exceptional powers, such as detentions effected without any judicial or administrative formalities that go unrecognized by the state; extrajudicial executions; the assassination of political opponents; and the kidnapping of individuals, their murder, and illegal interment or destruction of their remains. Such acts usually are effected beyond any law, even the regime's own, and, as in Montesquieu's category of despotism, evince the intention not only to destroy regime "enemies" physically but also to instill fear among the populace.

---

[5] As Friedrich (1950: 581) notes, this separation, which echoes the classical Roman dictatorship, provides a limit only in cases of divided government.

[6] In many situations, emergency powers are the first step toward forms of interrogation and punishment that exceed the particular powers conferred under a specific state of exception and are offenses under standing law. In many such cases, the prior positive regulation of emergency powers provides a protective subterfuge that allows dictatorships to claim that they are merely exercising legitimate powers and to circumvent any judicial interference with their application: on the basis that they are defined as nonjudicial, executive measures, authoritarian incumbents can deflect judicial oversight by insisting that the application of emergency powers is an exclusive political prerogative of the executive. As a result, in those cases where a tradition of separation of powers has resulted in an established jurisprudence of judicial abstinence from reviewing the form and merit of political acts, the administrative character of emergency powers provides a carte blanche onto the avenue of extrajudicial torment just mentioned.

These types of acts, which may be arbitrary even in regards to a given dictatorship's own law, define one extreme in a range of possible modes of autocratic rule, whose other extreme would be a system of rule by laws, even if highly repressive or biased. Intermediate are a range of deviations from "rule by law" that might include the use of emergency powers to effect discretionary detentions, partial or summary judicial procedures, retroactive application of law, and definition of offenses by analogy. None of the points on this range, though, may uniquely characterize a regime's manner of interaction with its subjects. A dictatorship may successively rely on (or fall back on) extrajudicial, administrative, or legal forms of repression, as its perception of the levels of threat and opposition it faces vary, or it may combine these different forms simultaneously. Under some circumstances, authoritarian regimes allow the rule of law to operate to regulate less conflictive areas of social life or to repress moderate opponents, while at the same time applying administrative restrictions or direct extrajudicial force against actors thought to threaten the stability of the ruling group.

This combination of realms governed by norms and others subject only to the prerogative of those in power led Ernst Fraenkel (1969) to characterize the early Nazi state as a "dual state." On this point the limits of autocratic rule by law tie into the second conception of rule of law. In Fraenkel's analysis (1969: 56–7), the jurisdiction governed by law under the Nazi dictatorship always remained secondary to the "prerogative state," as the members of the ruling clique could at their discretion decide whether a case be adjudicated in accordance with law or be handled "politically." As Fraenkel argued, because this group itself is not subject to law, "the jurisdiction over jurisdiction rests with the Prerogative State." This point suggests that, though theoretically compatible with autocracy, stable rule by law in nondemocratic regimes may be contingent upon a broader subjection of state actors to rules, such that jurisdictions are not permeable to discretionary, political manipulation. By most accounts, however, freedom from such limits is precisely one of the properties constitutive of dictatorship.

### Rule of Law as Ruling Bound by Law

Whereas rule by law concerns the properties of law as an instrument with which the state mediates its relations with subjects and citizens, the second, broader notion of the rule of law pursues the objective of subordinating the state and state actors to rules. This intent is often expressed in the imprecise slogan, "the rule of laws, not men." The fundamental idea is that incumbents act not at their discretion but only within legally established limits and are authorized to act because they have been selected according to prior rules whose satisfaction entitles them to legitimately exercise authority. Laws rule because state officials possess no authority other than that conferred by the law. This notion of the rule of law is shorthand for some form of constitutionalism or limited government and therefore can be referred to as "constitutionalist rule of law."

Like rule by law, constitutionalist rule of law is an imprecise concept and can be associated with any number of institutional arrangements, although these usually embody some form of division and/or limitation of government powers. A first version involves separating executive and legislative powers and subordinating the executive to strict execution of rules previously prescribed by the legislative body. Here state powers are divided and government in the narrow sense of executive power is limited but the lawmakers themselves remain sovereign and unlimited. More demanding conceptions and institutional embodiments of the rule of law require that the law-making body also be subject to rules and provide for limits by defining in constitutions the range of valid legislative power (rights) and by establishing institutions to implement these limits, such as courts with constitutional review powers.

Whether any such legal system of constitutional rule of law ought to be cast in terms of an antimony of law and will is a subject of debate.[7] Here, it is important to consider Hobbes's denial of any possibility that actors exercising state sovereignty can be subject to rules since Hobbes's challenge is particularly relevant to whether an autocratic regime can be compatible with constitutionalist rule of law. For Hobbes the impossibility of laws' superseding will as the ultimate basis of a legal-political order is a necessary consequence of sovereignty in the state. The argument is simple. If at the apex of the state there is an actor or organ that is sovereign in that it both possesses the power to make binding rules and is supreme because its authority is not derived from a superordinate rule or body, then this ultimate source of rules cannot itself be subject to rules because if it is truly supreme and not subordinate, no higher legal machinery exists to hold it to rules; and even if it seeks to circumscribe its power to rules, any self-imposed legal restrictions cannot be binding but can be contingent only upon the sovereign's will, given the latter's capacity to decide and make law and therefore to

---

[7] Compare Hampton (1994) and Zuckert (1994).

suppress any legal checks when deemed expedient.[8] In Hobbes's (1991: 184) words, "For having the power to make, and repeal Law, he [the holder of sovereignty] may when he please, free himself from that subjection, by repealing those laws that trouble him." Although subordinate offices and branches of the state may be bound by law, if sovereignty takes this form, rule makers can never be truly subject to rules; under such circumstances constitutionalist rule of law can only be contingent, premised upon the ongoing acquiescence of those actors holding the power to free themselves from limits.

Contemporary political theorists, such as Jean Hampton (1994) and Gregory Kavka (1986), appear to concede this point to Hobbes. Both sidestep the problem of sovereign reversibility and turn instead to arguing, contra Hobbes, that democratic systems of divided and limited powers can be stable and, therefore, provide a foundation for the rule of law.[9] For both theorists, under such institutional arrangements, unconstrained will is displaced from the level of operation of the ordinary institutions of government (as actors at this level are limited by constitutional rules) and enters only at the moment of selection of high-level government officials during periodic elections, which are also rule-bound. For Kavka (1986: 168), the selection of these various officials by multiple, at times overlapping, at times separate, constituencies precludes any absolute sovereign, even a popular one. This is not the place to question whether this grounding of the rule of law in a democratic constitutionalism does not remain open to criticism from the vantage of the logic of sovereignty. For present purposes, it is sufficient to note that Kavka's and Hampton's responses do not address the Hobbesian challenge that sovereignty implies the latent possibility of release from rules, but instead affirm that divided and limited forms deny any one actor or body of the authority to effect this release.[10]

[8] This same argument is restated from a different theoretical perspective in the contemporary literature on credible commitments: actors possessing discretionary authority cannot credibly commit themselves to a set of policies because nothing prevents them from later exercising their discretion to sway from their initial commitment (Shepsle 1991). This general argument is also applied to autocratic regimes (North and Weingast 1988; Elster 1989: ch. 4; and Olson 1993).

[9] On the viability of divided and limited government, see Hampton (1994: 38–42) and Kavka (1986: 165–8, 225–36).

[10] One might argue that divided and limited government merely displaces the problem of sovereign reversibility and the contingency of law upon will to another level. For as long as in principle we can envision the possibility of agreement among the divided powers or of attainment of the quorums required to modify legal or constitutional limits, such a system of divided and limited government remains only contingently subject to law.

Hampton's and Kavka's premising of constitutional rule of law upon democracy concords negatively with the standard definitions of dictatorship as a form of rule in which powers are concentrated, law is imposed from above, and some group or individual at the apex of the regime stands above the law, free from any form of institutional constraint. This characterization of dictatorships as *legibus solutus* may be the one constant that bridges the successive analytical models that have been used to characterize and classify twentieth-century nondemocratic regimes. Whether conceived of as totalitarian, authoritarian, post-totalitarian or bureaucratic authoritarian, despite their many other differences each of these forms of dictatorship has been characterized as involving rule free from legal-institutional constraint.[11] This absence of legal limits does not deny that dictatorships face all sorts of political and material constraints, or that subordinate state organs in such regimes may be subject to law and limited in their powers. The claim is that, insofar as some actor or group within the regime concentrates power and claims for itself the authority to establish and modify rules at its discretion, dictatorial power is absolute and not subject to rules. If this is an accurate account, then dictatorship is incompatible with constitutionalist rule of law.

In other words, even though such levels of agreement and unification may be unlikely, legal and institutional limits are necessarily contingent upon will whenever some body (or bodies) possesses the constituent authority to modify the legal-institutional order. In these cases, legal-constitutional stability is attributable not to subjection of law-making *bodies* to rules, but to heterogeneity among the wills composing these bodies which impedes the formation of the quorums capable of undermining rule-given institutional limits. As Maravall discusses in his essay in this volume, democracy can be turned against the rule of law when governments enjoy strong mandates.

[11] Thus, Ernst Fraenkel (1969: xiii), writing in the late 1930s, speaks of the "prerogative state," which he defines as "that governmental system which exercises unlimited arbitrariness and violence unchecked by any legal guarantees," as one component of the Nazi state. In Franz Neumann's (1957: 233) definition dictatorship refers to "the rule of a person or a group of persons who arrogate to themselves and monopolize power in the state, exercising it without restraint ... and which does not circumscribe either the scope or the duration of dictatorial power." Similarly, Juan Linz (1975: 183) argues, "Nondemocratic regimes ... not only impose de facto limits on minority freedoms but establish generally well-defined legal limits, leaving the interpretation of those laws to the rulers themselves, rather than to independent objective bodies, and applying them with a wide range of discretion." For Guillermo O'Donnell (1999: 334), "the distinctive mark of all kinds of authoritarian rule, even those that are highly institutionalized and legally formalized (a Rechtsstaat, in the original sense of the term), have somebody (a king, a junta, a party committee, or what not) that is sovereign in the classic sense: if and when they deem it necessary, they can decide without legal constraint." Likewise, according to Przeworski (1988: 60), "a particular regime would be authoritarian if there existed some power apparatus capable of overturning the outcomes of the institutionalized political process."

Thus far I have discussed two broad notions of rule of law, each of which points to a different type of relationship. The first, referred to here as "rule by law," centers upon the relationship between the state authorities and subjects as mediated by the law, whereas the second, "constitutionalist rule of law," is internal to the state and concerns the relationship between state authorities, particularly lawmakers, and the secondary rules conferring and delimiting powers. In principle, only "rule by law" appears to be compatible with an autocratic system of rule, notwithstanding the tendency of concrete dictatorships to depart from the requirements of this form of rule of law. Constitutionalist rule of law, on the other hand, is usually viewed as incompatible with dictatorship since the concentration of power within autocratic regimes creates a situation that corresponds to the classical definition of sovereignty.

In these cases, the relationship between state authorities and legal rules that limit the exercise of power reduces to a relationship solely among the officials at the apex of the authoritarian power bloc, given that the rupture with the prior form of rule of law, particularly with once prevailing democratic and constitutional procedural rules, produces a sharp schism between defunct secondary rules and the will of the group in power. Within this vacuum, any subjection of dictatorial rulers to the law, far more so than in ongoing democratic contexts, assumes the form of a relationship between these same actors and their own rules. For precisely this reason a subjection of authoritarian power holders to rules has been argued to be inconceivable: as long as these actors retain the capacity to make and unmake rules, they can always release themselves from rules if they actually bind them.

## Rules and Military Dictatorship in Chile

Notwithstanding this theoretical argument, under certain conditions autocratic rulers can be subject to rules and even be bound by rules of their own making. As an example of how this is possible, I analyze the use and making of rules under the military dictatorship that governed Chile from 11 September 1973 through 11 March 1990. The account presented here differs markedly from the standard interpretations of the dictatorship as a personalist regime dominated by General Augusto Pinochet. In that interpretation, rules conferring powers or limiting the ruler can have no causal efficacy and are absent, as all rules are reduced to being either a codification of prior power or a mechanism for projecting Pinochet's personal power. However, the personalist interpretation, though it mirrors Pinochet's public self-presentation, miscasts both the internal structure of the dictatorship and the manner in which secondary rules actually operated within the regime. As I have documented extensively elsewhere (Barros 2002), the dictatorship was not monocratic but founded on a collective sovereign – the armed forces as separate services – and this collegial foundation gave rise to the need for a dictatorial public law and ultimately provided the foundation for legal-constitutional limits on the power of the dictatorship as a whole.

I analyze two stages in this process of autocratic rule making and dictatorial rule under rules. At a first stage, a set of agreements provided rules defining the scope of executive and legislative powers and the manner and form of legislation and instituted a partial separation of these powers. These rules primarily served to regulate relations among the members of the military junta, to define procedures whereby these men could act jointly, and to protect the initial plural foundation of the regime by preventing any single member from concentrating powers. In this context, rules were self-referential agreements that defined the procedures whereby the heads of formally independent institutions would act together. These rules were constitutive in that they structured a collective will, but they did not limit the power of the dictatorship to make rules at its discretion when the commanders of the armed forces were in agreement. Constitutional constraints upon the dictatorship became effective at the second stage, once the regime's own constitution went into partial force on 11 March 1981. These constraints took the form of a detailed bill of rights and the immediate operation of a constitutional court empowered to uphold the Constitution. At a number of junctures this court held the military regime to the terms of its own rules and on occasion compelled the military junta to enact provisions that it did not otherwise intend to decree. These rulings were hardly inconsequential: they played a major role in providing the opposition parties of the left and center with incentives to participate in the noncompetitive plebiscite that the Constitution stipulated for ratifying or rejecting the junta's candidate for the second presidential term under the new charter. This plebiscite was eventually won by the opposition on 5 October 1988, triggering a transition to civilian rule whose steps strictly followed the military's Constitution and culminated in the charter's full implementation. Strikingly, the course of the dictatorship in Chile is a story in which a limited number of actors seize and concentrate extreme powers, enact legislation to regulate their mutual relations, and, in doing so, set off a conflictive process that results in the promulgation of a constitution to further regulate the terms of their association. This Constitution, in turn, sets into operation institutions that subsequently limit the original rule makers, with the peculiar outcome that the military's immediate political power is eventually dissolved according to procedures contained in its own rules, but with the further result that these rules, with some, though not extensive, modification, live on as the constitutional framework governing political life in Chile.

## The Legal Organization of the Junta

The 11 September 1973 coup d'etat that brought the Chilean armed forces to power brought to a close an extended period of intense economic, social, political, and constitutional crisis, which has been analyzed extensively, if inconclusively. Here, I only want to note that despite the vociferous confrontations over legality and the rule of law that preceded the coup, the military intervention had no foundation in any legal or constitutional norm.[12] The validity of the dictatorship's legal acts rested solely on the force of the military's coercive imposition, backed by the claim that the circumstances provided no alternative but exceptional rule, not a prior positive grant of authority. Thus, the arrogation of power by a four-man junta – composed of the commanders in chief of the three armed forces and the national police force – immediately produced a legal-institutional vacuum that posed the question of how the military would exercise the powers that it put in suspension when it suppressed the constitutional organs of law making and governance.

The first stage of autocratic rule making to structure procedures within the dictatorship occurred only after an initial period in which the commanders of the armed forces ruled without any clear specification of powers or procedures. The day after the coup the new junta gave itself legal form, arrogated to itself the Mando Supremo de la Nación (Supreme Command of the Nation), named Pinochet president

---

[12] Even right-wing jurists who sought to give legal foundation to the coup invariably acknowledged the extraconstitutional character of the military intervention. They located the "legitimate origins" of the junta in a nonpositive, natural right to resistance, which was justified because Allende had purportedly exceeded his constitutional authority and caused the breakdown of the legal order. Although there is considerable evidence challenging this interpretation of Allende's acts, this position remains one pole in the still polarized debate over the reasons for the coup, as can be seen in the debate during the 16 March 2000 special session of the Chilean Senate to address this issue. Natural right justifications are presented in Gaete Rojas (1973) and Larraín (1974). This same justification is given by the Junta in *Bando No. 5*. The most consistent, if farfetched, argument for the constitutionality of the coup is Navarrete (1974). Miranda Carrington (1973) presents the purported constitutional grounds for military intervention in a context of institutional breakdown.

of the junta, and pledged to guarantee the powers of the judiciary and to respect the law and the Constitution insofar as the situation permitted.[13] This decree law (D.L.) did not, however, clarify the powers of the dictatorship or specify procedures for making rules: the term Mando Supremo de la Nación had no meaning within the Chilean constitutional tradition and no powers were associated with the office of president of the junta.[14]

In early November 1973 the junta issued D.L. No. 128, which introduced simple rules that clarified the scope of the dictatorship's powers and the form of its legal acts, but otherwise left the junta largely unstructured. At the request of the Supreme Court, the junta clarified that Mando Supremo de la Nación encompassed constituent, legislative, and executive powers, and that, unless modified in the manner specified in the same law, standing constitutional and statutory law would remain in force.[15] Simple rules stipulated that both constituent and legislative powers would be exercised by the junta by means of decree laws, bearing the signatures of all its members, and that executive power would be exercised by means of supreme decrees and resolutions, in accordance with formalities contained in an earlier decree law. D.L. No. 128, thus, codified secondary rules that defined the rule of recognition that identified the features that the regime's primary legal enactments (decree laws and executive supreme decrees) had to possess to be valid and the rule of change that defined the conditions for their modification, but otherwise did not confer distinct powers among the members of the junta or structure more complex procedures.[16]

For the first nine months after the coup, all members of the junta were simultaneously engaged in executive and legislative functions, and the only differentiation among them was a functional division of labor by policy area. In mid-1974 this informal power sharing among the commanders of the armed forces gave way to a process of rule making

---

[13] Acta de Constitución de la Junta de Gobierno, Decreto Ley (hereafter, D.L.) No. 1, Diario Oficial (hereafter, D.O.), 18 September 1973. The initial junta members were General Augusto Pinochet Ugarte, Admiral José Toribio Merino Castro, General Gustavo Leigh Guzmán, and General César Mendoza Durán, the respective commanders of the army, navy, air force, and Carabineros (the national police force).

[14] The closest referent in the 1925 Constitution to the term *mando supremo de la nación* is the description in Article 60 of the president of the Republic as *jefe supremo de la nación* (supreme head of the nation).

[15] The court requested this clarification of the scope of the military's powers because it was concerned with the status of constituent powers, since if and how the junta exercised this power would directly impinge upon the court's powers of judicial review.

[16] On the concepts of rules of recognition and rules of change, see Hart (1961: 91–3).

that within a year resulted in an explicit delimitation of executive and legislative powers, the introduction of a partial separation of powers, and the institution of an elaborate set of procedures for processing and enacting regular and constituent legislation. I do not reconstruct this sequential process whereby the scope of executive powers was first defined and procedures for enacting decree laws were subsequently regulated, but only suggest some general points about this process of rule making.[17]

First, positive rules conferring powers and defining procedures were necessary among this narrow body to secure for each commander an agreed-upon role within the decision-making process, which otherwise could be unstable in the absence of a positive common rule or standard. This process confirms Machiavelli's insight that, in contrast to monocratic forms, collective forms of rule require some procedural rule to establish what constitutes a decision among the members of the ruling collectivity (Bobbio 1987: 65), and it might be added that individual members of such a collectivity will want such a rule to provide a standard with which to protect their role from circumvention. In this case, rules specifying procedures and delimiting powers were designed only after the commanders of the navy and the air force blocked attempts by Pinochet in the first half of 1974 to undermine the original collegial character of the dictatorship and concentrate executive and legislative powers.[18] Against this backdrop, the agreement that junta decisions would be made by unanimity became the fundamental legal cornerstone protecting the collegial character of the junta.[19]

Second, the procedural organization of the dictatorship was premised on and protected a prior form of organizational pluralism internal to the armed forces. Unlike other cases in which militaries consist of only armies or a single force is dominant, the Chilean armed forces were

---

[17] The respective decree laws are the Statute of the Junta (D.L. No. 527, 26 June 1974) and D.L. No. 991 (D.O., 3 January 1976). This two-stage rule-making process is detailed in Barros (2002: ch. 2).

[18] These moves, which would be repeated in 1977, involved the adoption of majority decision making with the president holding a fifth vote to break ties. This was a formula for a dictatorship of the army, as the head of Carabineros, General Mendoza, was in an extremely weak and dependent position after the coup and rarely, if ever, adopted stances at odds with Pinochet. With Mendoza's vote assured, Pinochet would have been able to force ties and dominate as expedient.

[19] Although in practice the junta immediately adopted the convention of decision making by agreement, as a positive rule decision by unanimity was inscribed in decree law for the first time in June 1974 in D.L. No. 527. D.L. No. 128 had only mentioned that valid decree laws required the signature of all four junta members. The unanimity decision rule was also later inscribed in Transitory Disposition 18 of the 1980 Constitution.

organized as a set of independent branches, each with distinctive conventions, identity, and organizational style, and no tradition of subordination to another branch. In this context, none of the commanders of the particular services could abdicate absolute representation to a single general or admiral and be assured that the institutional interests of his branch would be adequately represented. Thus, after the coup, for the commanders of the different services to assume the form of a unified actor, secondary rules had to be adopted to specify what acts would be sufficient to constitute a joint decision. The rules that established these procedures also reaffirmed and protected the prior organizational format that made rules necessary. Thus, although D.L. No. 527 gave Pinochet control of the presidency, the powers of the president, which largely mimicked those of a constitutional president, were codified restrictively in the area of executive-military relations. Limits were introduced upon the president's regular powers over military promotions; more significant, Pinochet was denied the traditional presidential power of naming and retiring the commanders in chief of the different services. Such restrictions precluded presidential interference within the different services and prevented any executive manipulation of the composition of the dictatorship's rule-making body via the demotion and selection of the commanders who composed the junta. Similarly, the prior plural organizational structure was protected within the junta by the unanimity decision rule, a general property of which is to confer an absolute veto to each member in a group, thereby effectively guaranteeing to each "the right to preserve his own interests against those of the other members" (Mueller 1989: 102).

Third, although the secondary rules enacted by the dictatorship were founded upon this prior structure of military organization, these rules did not merely reproduce a prior structure of power but created procedures that allowed new forms of interaction and coordination that would have been impossible without them. Most generally, these rules made possible joint action. In the absence of rules the only commensurate languages of the armed forces, as separate, hierarchical, coercive organizations, were command and force. These respectively corresponded to logics of dominance and conflict; both were inappropriate as foundations for coordinating among the branches and for jointly creating order. More specifically, the particular institutions adopted created institutional positions and forms of power that would not have been sustained under an unstructured convention of unanimous decision making. These institutions included a partial separation of executive and legislative powers and an elaborate system for processing legislative initiatives.[20] The latter's detailed steps and timetables structured an institutional time and space that enabled each junta member to independently study bills and formulate observations with counsel prior to any joint consideration or resolution, whereas the separation of powers, particularly the removal of the commanders in chief of the navy and the air force and the director general of Carabineros from the immediacy of executive power, structured different institutional positions that allowed the members of the legislative junta to bring distinct perspectives to the review of executive initiatives, often to temper impetuous responses in favor of broader time horizons and legislative stability.

Did this legal organization of the dictatorship imply a subjection of the members of the junta to rules? Can we speak of a dictatorial rule of law under the Chilean military regime? Answers to these questions require distinctions and an identification of stages in the dictatorship. At a very general level, the plural composition of the military junta meant that the dictatorship could not stand unqualifiedly above rules: the junta could act as one only because procedures enabled its separate members to coordinate and arrive at valid joint decisions. These constitutive rules, however, did not impose limits upon the powers of the junta as a body, although some of the rules, such as the separation of executive and legislative powers, did impose constraints upon the president.[21] Nor did surviving institutions set substantive constraints on the will of the junta. After the coup the 1925 Constitution remained nominally in force and the Supreme Court and the Contraloría General de la República (Comptroller General of the Republic) retained their respective powers of constitutional and preventive legal review. However, these institutions posed at best formal constraints given that, when in agreement, the members of the junta could override either body by modifying the Constitution or statutes. This facile supremacy of the junta over the court and Constitution was demonstrated once the Supreme Court declared a decree law unconstitutional in late 1974. The junta responded with a decree law that retroactively constitutionalized its

[20] The legislative system was organized around a secretary of legislation and four legislative commissions that reviewed all projects in the legislative system. The heads of the navy, air force, and Carabineros each presided over their own commission, while a fourth joint commission handled matters of national defense. On the principle of the separation of powers, no legislative commission was created for Pinochet, who until 11 March 1981 participated at the final stage of deliberation and decision within the full junta (after this date he was wholly separated from the legislative system).

[21] For example, in those policy areas subject to legal regulation, the separation of executive and legislative powers subjected Pinochet to laws that he could not unilaterally make or modify.

preceding 787 legislative enactments.[22] Though rules were constitutive of the junta, the junta could at its discretion modify any rules that impinged upon its power.

This situation changed once the 1980 Constitution went into force on 11 March 1981. At its ratification on 11 September 1980 in a questionable plebiscite, the Constitution appeared to be merely a masterpiece of authoritarian constitution making. While the front end of the Constitution structured an essentially republican representative regime, albeit a controverted one, a set of transitory dispositions (hereafter, T.D.s) suspended large chunks of this alternative institutional order and reinstated the status quo of dictatorship. These transitory articles constitutionalized rules governing the junta and the executive, granted Pinochet new discretionary repressive powers, prolonged military rule for one eight-year presidential term, and allowed the junta to nominate the sole candidate in the plebiscite that was to ratify the incumbent for the following presidential term.

In most accounts, this perpetuation of the dictatorship through constitutionalization overshadows the changes that the constitution introduced to the institutional framework of the regime. First, T.D. 18 required plebiscitary approval in addition to unanimity to amend the Constitution. Apparently trivial given the dictatorship's capacity to organize plebiscites, this clause increased the cost of modifications as plebiscites layered an openly political dimension upon a former prerogative of the junta. Second, T.D. 14 perfected the separation of powers through a separation of persons: Pinochet was removed from the legislative junta and replaced by the next ranking army general in seniority (who served at the president's discretion).[23] This modification allowed Admiral Merino to come into his own as head of the junta. Third, the Constitution put into force a detailed, meticulously regulated bill of rights and activated a constitutional court empowered to both decide constitutional conflicts among powers and exercise prior review of organic constitutional laws and laws interpreting the constitution.

---

[22] D.L. 788, D.O., 4 December 1974. In this decree law, the junta committed itself to henceforth enacting only explicit modifications to the Constitution. Henceforth, if a decree law did not lead off with the phrase "The Junta of Government, in exercise of the Constituent Power, decrees the following ...," the Supreme Court would considered it to be merely an ordinary statute and allow it to be subjected to judicial review if challenged in court. Although this requirement was merely adjectival, express modifications forced upon the junta considerations of political prudence that were largely absent from simple legislation, as express modifications drew national and international attention.

[23] This change occasioned the creation of a fourth legislative commission for the army and a reshuffling in the competencies of the legislative commissions.

These changes immediately set into play substantive and procedural constraints upon the junta's prerogative as a body and provided an external mechanism for their enforcement in the form of the constitutional court. Ultimately, this changed institutional context prevented the military junta and Pinochet from unilaterally setting the legal framework for the 1988 plebiscite and indirectly contributed to the opposition's victory as the conjunction of rights, the constitutional court, and prior review of organic constitutional laws ended up giving rise to a relatively level playing field for the plebiscite, less open to bias and manipulation.

## Dictatorship and Constitutional Rule of Law

If the members of the military junta had settled upon a set of rules that enabled joint governance, why was a broader constitution necessary, particularly one that introduced institutional devices that could limit the dictatorship's prerogative power? Although our knowledge of the internal decision-making process behind the Constitution is ridden with gaps, the available primary documentation suggests that the Constitution, like the secondary rules enacted in 1974–5, reflected an interforce settlement that further specified the terms of association among the different services by resolving matters earlier left open, in particular the duration of military rule and the nature of the successor regime. In other words, the Constitution codified the terms of resolution of conflicts that arose because of the incomplete character of the dictatorship's initial public law.

The initial rules defining the institutional framework for the dictatorship were incomplete in that they left open such potentially conflictive questions as how long the military should rule and what type of regime could best assure continuity for the military's laws and policies beyond the life of the junta and its members. D.L. No. 527 provided no mechanism for succession, other than provision for replacement of individual junta members only in event of "death, resignation, or any type of absolute impediment (Art. 18)."[24] Except for such circumstances, the existing composition of the junta was locked in place, particularly after the members of the junta enacted a decree law in 1976 freeing themselves from legal norms requiring retirements upon reaching maximum service limits.[25] In 1974 and 1975 the duration of military rule and the

---

[24] In such situations the same article specified that the remaining members of the junta would designate the succeeding commander in chief.

[25] This was done by D.L. 1,640 (D.O., 30 December 1976). On this decree law, see Arriagada (1985: 138–42).

character of any succeeding regime were not pressing issues, yet during the following years a number of factors gave increasing urgency to these matters.

First, in light of the specific characteristics of Chilean political society and the ferocity of the military coup and the ensuing repression, the Chilean armed forces could not discount the future. This point had immediate consequences for relations among the services. Insofar as the 1970–3 crisis, in which the left gained control of the executive, emerged from within the preceding constitutional order, the armed forces could be indifferent to the future and institutions only at the risk of facing a restoration of earlier institutional arrangements, a reemergence of previous political alignments, and likely demands for retribution by democratic actors. These prospects were the negative payoffs associated with a failure to coordinate and an uncontrolled military withdrawal. It should be noted, however, that this prognosis was not unequivocal in its political implications: the concern to avoid a repetition of the past could bolster either a strategy of prolonged authoritarian entrenchment, premised on the diagnosis that democracy per se was defenseless before the left, or a strategy of constitutional redesign, in turn premised on an evaluation of the earlier crisis as one of particular deficient institutions and not a crisis of constitutional democracy itself.

Second, before difficult conjunctures the members of the junta increasingly acknowledged the strategic value of institutions. Thus, at different moments "constitutionalization" appeared imperative: at times merely as a ploy to allow the dictatorship to claim to be on the road to normalcy; at other times, particularly during severe crises, as a potential institutional alternative should solid evidence of the regime's involvement in particularly egregious crimes precipitate a collapse of the military government or force an opening requiring civilian participation. The latter type of pressure, particularly in the wake of the 20 September 1976 car-bomb assassination of Orlando Letelier and his assistant Ronnie Moffit in Washington, D.C., was decisive in the decision to promulgate the Constitution.

While these two dimensions – the concern to avoid a repetition of the past and the need to stave off international pressure – tended to overlap and could be met by either a hard-line or an institutionalist reaction, any legal or constitutional response that did not involve a break with the internal status quo necessarily had to be mediated through the military junta. Here, the requirement of unanimity was buttressed by the first dimension, which elevated the expected costs of any irreconcilable internal divisions that could produce an uncontrolled transition. Thus, the unanimity rule and the costs associated with noncoordination set a limit to the range of the dictatorship's feasible responses to the political and international challenge faced in the mid-1970s. Within these political constraints, authoritarian entrenchment was inviable since the hard-line course implied modifications to the regime's secondary rules that would have emasculated the junta and structured an absolute dictatorship of the president. This alternative, for reasons already suggested, was unacceptable to the commanders in chief of the navy and the air force, whereas any unilateral move to override their positions could proceed only at the risk of intensifying intramilitary tensions and possibly precipitating a collapse of the dictatorship.

## The Acta Constitucional for the Junta de Gobierno

The particular conflicts that resulted in the decision to enact the Constitution arose in 1977 in the course of a renewed discussion of the legal organization of the junta. This debate was an unintended consequence of an attempt by the junta to stave off international critics by promulgating on 11 September 1976 a series of three Actas Constitucionales (Constitutional Acts). Unlike the Atos Institucionales enacted by successive military presidents in Brazil or Franco's Leyes Fundamentales, these Constitutional Acts were not to regulate or create new dictatorial powers, but were to consist only of norms of constitutional rank, which on a piecemeal basis would anticipate the contours of a future constitutional order. These acts were to allow the military to claim that it was on the road to constitutional normalization.[26]

Although for this reason the junta members wanted to avoid openly asserting the legal organization of the dictatorship in the Actas, the logic of constitutional forms made this unavoidable. While preparing the Actas, legal advisors began to discover that by elevating the Actas Constitucionales to being the sole norms of constitutional rank, they risked diminishing the constitutional status of the many decree laws that gave legal form to the junta and augmented the regime's repressive powers.[27] To avoid this and to foreclose eventual legal challenges, it

---

[26] First announced by Pinochet on 11 September 1975, the complete package was to consist of six or seven constitutional acts; in the end only the three decreed on the third anniversary of the coup were ever promulgated. These were Actas Constitucionales Nos. 2–4, which respectively concerned the "Essential foundations of Chilean institutionality," "Constitutional rights and duties," and "Regimes of emergency." Acta Constitucional No. 1 had been promulgated on the last day of 1975 to create the Council of State, a purely advisory body.

[27] Many of these decree laws had been constitutionalized by D.L. No. 788.

was agreed, at Pinochet's initiative, that decree laws regulating public powers would be repackaged as a constitutional act.[28]

This seemingly simple task ended up reopening conflicts over the structure of the junta. In mid-October 1976 the navy submitted the first proposal for the constitutional act on the junta. Its draft reasserted the standing secondary rules and stipulated additional legal mechanisms to secure the junta's position before the president.[29] Pinochet presented the proposal that precipitated the internal crisis in early January 1977, under the title "Statute of the Government of Chile." As was explained in an accompanying document, this title had been adopted to stress the "permanent goals" of the regime and to avoid giving any impression of "transitoriness," something allegedly conveyed by references to the Junta de Gobierno.[30] The articles of the statute made absolutely clear that the regular character of the new regime was to consist of a dictatorship of the army: for both legislative and constituent acts unanimity was to give way to majority decision making, with the president holding a second tie-breaking vote, and the presidency was to be permanently linked to the army.[31] Some months later, General Leigh replied, insisting that the junta had only agreed to give its earlier laws the form of a constitutional act, not to "change their basic spirit and philosophy," and that the junta had always promised to withdraw once its objectives were realized, a commitment that Pinochet's proposal debarred by seeking to "concentrate total and absolute Power in the person who exercises Executive Power."[32]

---

[28] This obligation was specified in the second transitory article to Acta Constitucional No. 2.

[29] In enumerating the president's powers before attributes whose exercise in D.L. No. 527 had required the "agreement of the Junta," the navy now required "written agreement," and Article 2 specified that unless the supreme decrees that implemented executive acts requiring junta agreement expressly indicated the number and date of the Acta (minute) recording this agreement, the legality of the supreme decree would be impugned by the Contraloria General de la Republica. The draft also proposed a four-year term for the presidency, with allowance for one reelection by the junta. The document, which I have on file, is titled "Acta Constitucional No. *De los Poderes del Estado*." It is undated, but the photocopy I possess has scribbled on it, "Remitted by the Navy of Chile on 14-X-76."

[30] As the fourth "Whereas" clause stated, "The period of transitoriness has come to an end and it is necessary to present the Government of the Nation with a stable character." Oficio CASMIL (R) No. 31000/2 de 04.ENE.77. The document I have on file, stamped "Secret," is a numbered copy, but is undated. The reference I give is the identification given to the document in General Leigh's response; the cross-references in his response fully concord with the copy I possess.

[31] For an explanation why this institutional formula amounted to a dictatorship of the army, see note 18.

[32] Comandante en Jefe de la Fuerza Aerea de Chile, "Emite opinión sobre Anteproyecto de Estatuto de Gobierno," n.d., f. 4. I have this document on file.

These interchanges precipitated a sharp internal crisis, as the navy and the air force refused to go along with Pinochet's proposal. In a departure from usual practices, the general staff of each force was consulted in separate meetings. Within both branches there was no support for permanent authoritarianism.[33] I should stress that in these debates, as in other deliberations, the navy and the air force recurrently invoked standing decree laws, particularly D.Ls. Nos. 1 and 527, as a record of earlier agreements that defined the distribution of powers as well as the sole procedures that could be used to validly modify them.

With the navy and the air force adamantly opposed to Pinochet's bid for absolute dictatorship, institutionalist positions began to gain relevance and prominence within the executive. Apparently as a signal that the hard line would be tempered, on 9 July 1977 Pinochet for the first time publicly announced a plan and timetable for a transition in his *Discurso de Chacarillas*.[34] All of this, including the 1977 conflicts over the junta, took place against a backdrop of increasing international pressure and isolation of the regime. This variable intensified after mid-1977 and fueled pressure within the regime to take steps toward institutional and juridical institutionalization, particularly once strong evidence linking the DINA (the secret police) with the Letelier assassination was established in March 1978. At this juncture the state of siege was allowed to lapse, the curfew was lifted, and the junta decreed an amnesty covering crimes committed during the state of siege. Henceforth, work on a

---

[33] The navy was the branch most cohesively united around a single position. Aside from one admiral, who consistently advocated "not to innovate" on the status quo, the eleven other admirals backed the navy's initial proposal, which apparently had been previously approved by the Consejo Naval, the council of admirals. Positions among the fifteen air force generals were more varied, although the generals overwhelmingly opposed Pinochet's proposal and unanimously rejected fusing the presidency to the army – one air force general did, however, support the adoption of majority decision making. Whereas there is no indication that the admirals explicitly raised the issue of the termination of military rule, an unspecified number of air force generals endorsed setting a deadline for completing the government's task and calling elections. Officers within Carabineros divided equally among generals who did not state an opinion and generals who advocated leaving the status quo intact. Jaime Guzmán, "Sintesis del Resumen Planteamientos Altos Mandos a la Consulta D/L 527," D, Guzmán Papers, Fundación Jaime Guzmán, Santiago. This handwritten document tallies the positions of the generals and admirals at each meeting.

[34] See *El Mercurio*, 10 July 1977. Notes written upon Jaime Guzmán's tally of positions within each service confirm that this announcement was directly related to the tensions precipitated by the constitutional act. These jottings specify that the status quo should remain unchanged and outline a transition formula identical to that announced at Chacarillas. It should be stressed that this announcement was a signal from the executive, not a formula agreed upon with the junta.

constitution accelerated and proceeded through the known stages.[35] On 11 September 1980 the Constitution approved by the junta was subject to plebiscitary ratification and went into force six months later on 11 March 1981.

### The 1980 Constitution and Dictatorship Subject to Rules

The earlier conflicts within the junta over the completion of its secondary rules explain the dualism of the 1980 Constitution and its apparent immediate inconsequence for the structure of the dictatorship. The range of agreement and disagreement within the junta was codified in the dualism of permanent and transitory articles. By postponing the full implementation of the Constitution for at least nine years, the transitory dispositions reflected the interservice consensus that any transition was premature in the short term, whereas the rejection of an open commitment to prolonged authoritarianism appeared in the permanent body of the text in the form of a restructured, strongly constitutional civilian regime. The limits set by the original collegial character of the junta and the navy's and the air force's ongoing defense of their positions also explain why no liberalization ever took place in the form of a designated civilian congress, as had been announced by Pinochet in mid-1977: such a formula required a sharp diminution in the power of the junta, which neither the navy nor the air force could accede to.

Thus, at its promulgation, the components of the Constitution blurred together and the main body of the text appeared as nothing more than an embellishment in an instrument designed to perpetuate military rule. But, as I have already mentioned, the Constitution did have immediate effects on the rules governing the dictatorship: constituent acts now required plebiscitary ratification in addition to junta unanimity; the separation of executive and legislative powers was perfected; and the permanent articles of the text put in force a detailed bill of rights and structured a constitutional court, modeled upon the continental model, whose powers and operation were not suspended in the transitory articles. Through the rulings of this constitutional court the 1980 Constitution grew apart from its makers and at key junctures limited the legislative power of the

---

[35] In October 1978 a group of civilian constitutionalists commissioned within days of the coup, the Constituent Commission, completed its first draft; this then proceeded to the Council of State for review; the council in turn officially presented its revised version to the president in early July 1980; then, in a month of marathon sessions, the junta worked out the final text. On these stages, see Carrasco Delgado (1981).

junta as a body, with major consequences for the outcome of the 1988 presidential plebiscite. Before turning to the operation of the constitutional court, I should explain why institutions with the power to subject the military to its own rules were instituted under the dictatorship, nine years before the Constitution was to govern elected, civilian authorities, as well as why the members of the junta might have wanted to act within the terms of the Constitution.

The activation of the constitutional court during the last nine years of military rule was central to the strategic conception underlying the 1980 Constitution. Contrary to most interpretations of the Constitution, the main body of the Constitution had not been tailored to cloak the dictatorship in constitutional garb but to subject future civilian actors to reinforced constitutional rules. The intent was to circumscribe democracy within clear constitutional boundaries, protected by multiple layers of checks and reinforced organs of legal and constitutional control, as well as demanding requirements for the modification of this framework. Except for one or two articles specifically designed to regulate problems that had arisen during the dictatorship, the concern with rules was fundamentally retrospective: to provide institutional solutions to specific constitutional problems that had emerged during the 1960s and the Allende years and to assure mechanisms for the resolution of any conflicts that might emerge among powers. A fear of democracy drove this concern with rules. Because the right could not reasonably anticipate winning elections, constitutional binds upon democracy were a priority. Among these binds figured prominently a constitutional ban on Marxist parties, a detailed, almost regulatory, enumeration of rights, and a strengthened constitutional court.[36]

This strategic objective of binding future civilian actors explains why the bill of rights and the constitutional court went into force *under* military rule, as well as why the regime limited its authority to modify the

---

[36] Other innovations upon the 1925 Constitution included: (1) the adoption of a second round for presidential elections, (2) a strengthened executive, with expanded regulatory powers, greater autonomy from the Senate in appointments, and power to dissolve the lower house of Congress once a term (though not during the year preceding congressional elections); (3) the nonelectoral generation of slightly less than one-third of the Senate; (4) constitutionalization of the Contraloría's authority to review the legality of executive decrees; (5) restrictions on presidential authority over the armed forces, particularly the denial of any authority (except under duly qualified circumstances) to remove the commanders in chief; (6) the constitutionalization of the National Security Council, with a military majority; and (7) more demanding requirements to modify the constitution (three-fifths majority of all members of Congress and a two-thirds absolute majority in two successive congresses to amend expressly entrenched chapters).

Constitution freely by also requiring plebiscitary ratification. All of these institutional changes were components in a strategy aimed at securing the validity of the Constitution prior to any transition. The underlying idea was that if the junta immediately put into operation as much of the Constitution as possible, the probability of its later wholesale dismantlement would be lower than if the main body went into force only upon a return to civilian rule. Similarly, if a claim to popular support were to bolster the Constitution, after submitting the Constitution to plebiscitary ratification in 1980 the junta could not unilaterally modify the Constitution without vitiating this claim – hence, the requirement of plebiscitary approval for all constitutional amendments.

To a large degree, then, these institutions went into force to assure that other actors would in the future be subject to these rules. Given the change in the amendment rule and the requirement that the constitutional tribunal exercise prior review of organic constitutional laws and laws interpreting the Constitution, the adoption of this framework involved a voluntary, strategic, self-limitation of the junta's powers. The members of the junta accepted these limits on their power to secure the validity of the Constitution. Despite this voluntary aspect, it is unlikely that the commanders expected these changes to limit their authority effectively. Plebiscites could be organized without controls, and all of the members of the constitutional court during the transitory period were to be chosen directly or indirectly by the president, the junta, or the members of the Supreme Court. Notwithstanding these expectations, as I document elsewhere (Barros 2002: ch. 7), the Constitution immediately constrained the junta as a body.

Why then were Pinochet and the different members of the junta willing to subject themselves to rules? One reason was the character of the Constitution itself. As it stood in March 1981, the Constitution could be read to structure a variety of possible medium-term payoffs. These manifold outcomes allowed all branches of the armed forces to accept its terms and provided each commander with incentives to abide by the Constitution, influence its further definition, and pursue its full implementation. This range of possibilities was given by the skeletal character of the constitution – although it fully regulated the contours of a future regime, the Constitution left the regulation of fundamental political dimensions, including many related to the presidential plebiscite, to later regulation in organic constitutional laws. Among others, these matters included states of exception, voter registration, electoral administration and oversight, political parties, and the electoral system. Depending on how these matters were regulated, any number of widely variant regimes and transitions could have emerged from the 1980 Constitution, and the perception that these laws therefore had to be crafted by the dictatorship was another reason to postpone any transition.[37] This openness allowed the Constitution to be seen variously as a vehicle for a second term for Pinochet, for a soft landing for the military institutions after the tumult of military rule, and for postmilitary political institutional stability, which would allow the services to return to a primary concern with defense preparedness. In this context, none of the commanders could be indifferent to the fate of the Constitution, and each had strong incentives to influence its further definition when enacting the organic constitutional laws.

However, at this point the need to further define the terms of the Constitution intersected with the strategy of constitutional entrenchment – prior to their promulgation the organic constitutional laws would be subject to obligatory review by the constitutional tribunal. Again, both institutions – the organic constitutional laws and the constitutional court – had been conceived as mechanisms to bind civilian actors to the military's rules: under democracy the organic laws would require higher majorities for their enactment and modification,[38] and the court's review was understood to provide a safeguard against tacit modification of the Constitution via amendments to the organic laws, particularly as the majority of the court's ministers were to be selected by nonpolitical organs. Despite these expectations that the court would force civilian actors to remain within the Constitution, the operation of the constitutional court under military rule also fundamentally constrained the junta's capacity to unilaterally specify the terms of the Constitution.

During its first four years of operation, the constitutional court posed few problems for the military regime. Except for a first, secret ruling, on the eighteen occasions that it reviewed the constitutionality of legislation enacting or modifying norms of organic constitutional rank, the

---

[37] Pablo Rodríguez Grez, a lawyer of some notoriety as one of the two founders of Patria y Libertad, the extreme-right, nationalist, paramilitary organization that was active in the streets during the Allende government, captures well this potential: "within the present constitutional provisions there fits both a liberal democracy – with very few significant innovations – as well as a neo-organic democracy, capable of reducing the parties to being mere currents of opinion and of preventing the electoral game from being turned into a constant confrontation of social classes" (*La Tercera*, 13 March 1983).

[38] Article 63 set this quorum at three-fifths of the deputies and senators in office. This quorum was lowered to four-sevenths of the deputies and senators in office by the July 1989 constitutional reform that preceded the transition.

constitutional court never declared a norm unconstitutional.[39] Yet, in the succeeding four years, a shift in jurisprudence followed a partial renovation of the court's members and on nine occasions norms approved by the junta were struck down.

Undoubtedly, the courts' 24 September 1985 ruling on the organic constitutional law regulating the Tribunal Calificador de Elecciones (TRICEL), the special electoral court, was politically the most consequential.[40] Regarding the plebiscite that the Constitution stipulated would be held to ratify or reject the junta's nominee for president during the second term under the Constitution, the court struck as unconstitutional a transitory article that left oversight of this contest to an ad hoc electoral court and further ruled that the full electoral system specified in the main body of the text had to be in place for this plebiscite. Like all of the court's rulings, this decision was final and not subject to appeal. This decision meant that the eventual plebiscite would be constitutional only if it took place with electoral registries and independent oversight and counting. These requirements portended an electoral contest far different from the 1980 plebiscite that had ratified the constitution, which had proceeded under a state of emergency with restrictions upon civil liberties, with no electoral registries or independent supervision. The constitutional court's ruling on the TRICEL proved to be only the first in a series of rulings that set a level playing field by creating legal conditions for a fair electoral contest. These decisions, thereby, structured incentives for the opposition to participate in the plebiscite and eventually beat the military at its own game, though at the cost of further validating the constitution.

The constitutional court's rulings establishing a fair, albeit noncompetitive, plebiscite were contingent upon the regulation of rights in the Constitution. Only because Chapter II guaranteed such rights as equality before the law, equal protection of the law, due process, and freedom of association, as well as political rights, could the constitutional court strike norms that introduced biases into the political process. In the period prior to the plebiscite the constitutional court struck from organic constitutional laws any number of articles that established inequalities or enabled arbitrary restrictions of rights at the different stages of the

---

[39] On the court's jurisprudence during the dictatorship, see Zapata Larraín (1991). The secret ruling that I uncovered in my research concerned the organic law regulating the constitutional tribunal itself.

[40] Tribunal Constitucional, Sentencia Rol No. 33 (D.O., 3 October 1985).

political-electoral process – from party formation and registration, internal party organization, voter registration, electoral and plebiscitary campaigns, the convocation of elections and plebiscites, to voting and the qualification of elections. One ruling even compelled the junta to enact further organic legislation to grant both sides equal, free time on television and paid access to the print media and radio, access to which was later widely recognized to have been a major factor in the opposition's victory in the plebiscite.[41]

Thus, once the Constitution went into force, the legislative powers of the dictatorship were effectively constrained. First, the junta no longer held exclusive authority to modify the Constitution; second, the Constitution reserved a clear set of rights from legislative modification; and, third, in addition to the Supreme Court, the constitution put into operation an organ, the constitutional court, with the authority to assure that organic constitutional legislation filling out the Constitution did not contravene its terms. In those areas subject both to judicial review and to prior review by the constitutional court, the dictatorship did not stand above the laws.

I should stress that these constitutional limits upon the military regime did not alter its character as a dictatorship. The norms of the legal system continued to be imposed from above by a body without any electoral mandate, amid a ban upon political-partisan activity upheld by the constitution for most of the period.[42] Furthermore, "rule by law" retained a tenuous status under the constitution. Aside from the repressive legislation administered through the courts (which may be encompassed under the "rule by law"), exceptions to the law, in the form of discretionary authority to restrict individual freedoms without legal justification, were permitted to Pinochet – some upon conferral by the junta (the state of siege), others directly by the Constitution (the state of emergency and the powers conferred under T.D. 24). Furthermore, though on a far lesser scale than during the years 1973–7, a number

---

[41] In particular, see Tribunal Constitucional, Sentencia Rol No. 38 (D.O., 1 October 1986) on the organic constitutional law regulating voter registration and the electoral service; Sentencia Rol No. 43 (D.O., 23 March 1987) on the political party law; Sentencia Rol No. 53 (D.O., 13 April 1988) on the organic constitutional law on popular votes and counts. This last ruling required further legislation granting free media access. The same sentence also established the sole constitutionally valid interpretation of an ambiguity in the Constitution, which, prior to the court's clarification, left open the possibility of a sudden, snap plebiscite.

[42] Under T.D. 10 all such activities were suspended and prohibited until the organic constitutional law regulating political parties went into force. This law was promulgated on 23 March 1987 and went into force ten days later.

of extrajudicial executions occurred, which have been imputed to the regime's security apparatus.

## Rule of Law and Dictatorship

In the preceding pages, I have tried to show that even under a highly repressive dictatorship a form of rule of law is possible. What general conclusions about the rule of law can be drawn from this account? As the principal theoretical challenge concerns what I have called "constitutionalist" rule of law, I focus on how sovereign actors might be subject to rules of their own making. In particular, I want to stress both the importance of pluralism within the body authorized to make rules and the difference between constitutive and limiting rules.

The Chilean case convinces me that a collective sovereign is a condition for any form of constitutional rule of law, whether autocratic or democratic. Only in situations where a plurality of actors compose a rule-making body are procedural rules necessary to define what acts of that collective are sufficient to constitute a decision of the ruling body. Along the same lines, individual actors in such a situation will want rules to secure their positions within the collectivity. In the Chilean case, this pluralism was given by the prior organization of the armed forces as separate services without any tradition or precedent of subordination of one branch to another. This pluralism was amenable to organization as it had a natural foundation in the prior format of the armed forces that allowed for its institutionalization at the peak of each branch without having to foster the downward politicization and fragmentation likely within a junta composed only of officers of a single branch. In this context, rules had to be established to determine how unique decisions would emerge from this pluralism, however narrow, and, as I have shown, specific rules were designed that also protected the prior organizational structure that gave rise to this pluralism and the need for rules. In large measure these rules were stable because the larger, specifically Chilean political backdrop fostered the perception that the armed forces would pay considerable costs if they failed to coordinate and fell into irreconcilable intramilitary conflict.

The type of rules that collective bodies require are constitutive but not necessarily limiting. By providing accepted standards of how and by whom valid decisions or acts may be effected, such secondary rules are constitutive in that they permit forms of action among a collectivity that otherwise would not be possible in the absence of procedural rules. Like the constitutional rules stressed by Holmes (1988), such rules are enabling: if they are stable, they free actors from constantly having to decide how to decide and allow them to focus on substantive matters. Insofar as rules conferring powers and defining decision-making procedures make it possible for a collectivity to act, the actions of such a collectivity, regardless of its irregular origins or unrestricted power as a body, cannot be portrayed as wholly standing above rules. This appears to be a rather weak version of constitutional rule of law, as the powers of the decision-making body as a whole may remain unlimited. The rules that allow the body to act may only be a condition for the exercise of sovereignty – constitutive rules do not have to imply any legal limitation of the powers exercised by the body so constituted.[43] Still, it is worth emphasizing that constitutive rules do, however, limit individual members composing the decision-making body. By defining the standard forms of coordination, they exclude other procedures for decision and provide members legitimate grounds to criticize any deviation from these standards and, under some circumstances, provide mechanisms to uphold these decision rules.

The need for constitutive rules to give form to a collective body does not in itself provide an answer to the question of how a sovereign body may be subject to rules. In Hobbes's challenge the problem is that any body that can make rules can also unmake rules and therefore free itself from limits when expedient. As I have shown, once the 1980 Constitution went into force in Chile, the military dictatorship was subject to substantive legal constraints upon its legislative power and was compelled by an independent organ to abide by the terms of its own rules. To explain autocratic self-limitation fully, then, it is also necessary to explain why a body concentrating absolute powers would set a higher law above itself in the first place. In the Chilean case, the decision to adopt a constitution was driven by perceptions that prolonged direct military rule was inviable and that a failure to impose a new institutional order would have costly consequences for the right and the armed forces.

Still, the question remains, Why didn't the armed forces modify the Constitution once it began to impose limits upon the military's capacity to implement the Constitution at its discretion? Two points are pertinent here. First, even when they turned against the military, the constitutional court's rulings were tolerable because they often ratified positions previously debated within the junta and because the piecemeal implementation of the electoral system meant that the battle never appeared to be irretrievably lost. In fact, only on the night of 5 October 1988,

---

[43] On this point, see Hart (1961: 69–76).

the day of the plebiscite, did Pinochet finally face the fact that he could lose and by then he had lost.[44] Second, the very substantive differences among the armed forces that made secondary rules necessary in the first place also stabilized the Constitution. The constitution provided an institutional framework within which the different commanders could pursue medium-term objectives that did not necessarily coincide. As I suggested earlier, the commanders of the navy and the air force never viewed the Constitution as essentially a vehicle for the perpetuation of Pinochet in power. Insofar as the ends they associated with the Constitution were predicated upon the full implementation of its terms, these actors could accept the court's rulings. During the years 1981–90 institutional limits were stable under dictatorship because the plurality of actors capable of overriding or overturning them was divided in its perception of the relative costs and benefits of accepting limits.

On this basis one might counter that rules were actually insignificant, that if the other commanders had been in agreement with Pinochet, the military could have suppressed the Constitution and the court and held onto power. From this perspective, Hobbes would be right. The junta would not be bound by its own rules. Rather, the junta's subjection to the Constitution was only contingent; it rested upon differences among the armed forces that did not otherwise obviate the junta's capacity to alter the institutional framework (though with the proviso of plebiscitary ratification after March 1981). I accept this argument and think that it points to a general condition of institutional stability and rule of law: when some organ or conjunction of organs has the authority to modify the constituent rules structuring both the institutional framework and mechanisms of legal and constitutional control, the rule of law can be stable only if differences within or among these organs inhibit the formation of overwhelming supermajorities with the strength to modify and suppress constitutional limits. However, it is precisely the point of this chapter that when power is organized on a collective basis, such ongoing differences within the ruling body may arise, be structured by rules, and sustain limiting institutions even in circumstances where the actors that compose the ruling body are not seated by democratic methods of selection. This was the case in Chile during the military period, which strikingly suggests that autocratic rule of law is a historical phenomena and not only a theoretical curiosity. That the Constitution that constrained its own makers with only slight modifications lives on to limit

---

[44] It is notorious that up until the day of the plebiscite close advisors were feeding doctored polling data to Pinochet.

democratic actors in Chile today also begs the question of the potentially ambiguous, as well as partial, character of institutional constraints.

## References

Arriagada Herrera, Genaro. 1985. *La política militar de Pinochet.* Santiago. Unpublished manuscript.
Barros, Robert. 2002. *Constitutionalism and Dictatorship: Pinochet, the Junta, and the 1980 Constitution.* Cambridge: Cambridge University Press.
Bobbio, Norberto. 1987. *La teoría de las formas de gobierno en la historia del pensamiento político.* Trans. José F. Fernández Santillán. Mexico, D.F.: Fondo de Cultura Económico.
Carrasco Delgado, Sergio. 1981. "Génesis de la constitución política de 1980." *Revista de Derecho Público* 29–30: 35–65.
Elster, Jon. 1989. *Solomonic Judgements: Studies in the Limitations of Rationality.* Cambridge: Cambridge University Press.
Fraenkel, Ernst. 1969. *The Dual State: A Contribution to the Theory of Dictatorship.* Trans. E. A. Shils. New York: Oxford University Press, 1941; reprint, New York: Octagon Books.
Friedrich, Carl J. 1950. *Constitutional Government and Democracy.* Rev. ed. Boston: Ginn.
Fuller, Lon L. 1964. *The Morality of Law.* New Haven: Yale University Press.
Gaete Rojas, Sergio. 1974. "Reinauguración de un año académico." *Revista Chilena de Derecho* 1, 1: 124–6.
Goldsmith, M. M. 1996. "Hobbes on Law." In Tom Sorrell (ed.), *The Cambridge Companion to Hobbes.* Cambridge: Cambridge University Press.
Hampton, Jean. 1994. "Democracy and the Rule of Law." In Ian Shapiro (ed.), *The Rule of Law. Nomos XXXVI.* New York: New York University Press.
Hart, H. L. A. 1961. *The Concept of Law.* Oxford: Clarendon Press.
Hobbes, Thomas. 1991. "Leviathan." In Richard Tuck (ed.), *Cambridge Texts in the History of Political Thought.* Cambridge: Cambridge University Press.
Holmes, Stephen. 1988. "Precommitment and the Paradox of Democracy." In Jon Elster and Rune Slagstad (eds.), *Constitutionalism and Democracy.* Cambridge: Cambridge University Press.
Kavka, Gregory S. 1986. *Hobbesian Moral and Political Theory.* Princeton: Princeton University Press.
Larraín, Hernán F. 1974. "El derecho y el uso de la fuerza pública." *Revista Chilena de Derecho* 1, 3–4: 370–5.
Linz, Juan. 1975. "Totalitarian and Authoritarian Regimes." In Fred Greenstein and Nelson Polsby (eds.), *Handbook of Political Science*, vol. 3. Reading, Mass.: Addison Wesley.
Miranda Carrington, Sergio. 1973. "La fuerzas armadas en el ordenamiento jurídico chileno." In Pablo Barahona et al. (eds.), *Fuerzas Armadas y seguridad nacional.* Santiago: Ediciones Portada.
Mueller, Dennis C. 1989. *Public Choice II: A Revised Edition of Public Choice.* Cambridge: Cambridge University Press.
Navarrete, B. Jaime. 1974. "El termino anticipado del mandato presidencial en la Constitución Política de Chile." *Revista Chilena de Derecho* 1, 3–4: 340–8.
Neumann, Franz. 1957. *The Democratic and the Authoritarian State: Essays in Political and Legal Theory.* Ed. Herbert Marcuse. Glencoe, Ill.: Free Press.

North, Douglass C., and Barry R. Weingast. 1989. "Constitutions and Commitment: The Evolution of Institutions Governing Public Choice in Seventeenth-Century England." *Journal of Economic History* 49: 803–32.

Oakeshott, Michael. 1983. "The Rule of Law." In *On History and Other Essays*. Oxford: Oxford University Press.

O'Donnell, Guillermo. 1999. "Polyarchies and the (Un)Rule of Law in Latin America: A Partial Conclusion." In Juan E. Méndez, Guilliermo O'Donnell, and Paulo Sérgio Pinheiro (eds.), *The (Un)Rule of Law and the Underprivileged in Latin America*. Notre Dame: University of Notre Dame Press.

Olson, Mancur. 1993. "Dictatorship, Democracy, and Development." *American Political Science Review* 87 (September): 567–76.

Przeworski, Adam. 1988. "Democracy as a Contingent Outcome of Conflicts." In Jon Elster and Rune Slagstad (eds.), *Constitutionalism and Democracy*. Cambridge: Cambridge University Press.

Raz, Joseph. 1979. "The Rule of Law and Its Virtue." In *The Authority of Law: Essays on Law and Morality*. Oxford: Clarendon Press.

Rossiter, Clinton L. 1948. *Constitutional Dictatorship: Crisis Government in Modern Democracies*. Princeton: Princeton University Press.

Schmitt, Carl. 1985. *La dictadura*. Trans. José Díaz García. Madrid: Alianza Editorial.

Shepsle, Kenneth A. 1991. "Discretion, Institutions, and the Problem of Government Commitment." In Pierre Bourdieu and James S. Coleman (eds.), *Social Theory for a Changing Society*. Boulder: Westview Press and Russell Sage Foundation.

Ten, C. L. 1993. "Constitutionalism and the Rule of Law." In Robert E. Goodin and Philip Pettit (eds.), *A Companion to Contemporary Political Philosophy*. Oxford: Blackwell.

Waldron, Jeremy. 1989. "The Rule of Law in Contemporary Liberal Theory." *Ratio Juris* 2, 1: 79–96.

Zapata Larraín, Patricio. 1991. "Jurisprudencia del tribunal constitucional (1981–1991)." *Revista Chilena de Derecho* 18, 2: 261–330.

Zuckert, Michael P. 1994. "Hobbes, Locke, and the Problem of the Rule of Law." In Ian Shapiro (ed.), *The Rule of Law. Nomos XXXVI*. New York: New York University Press.

Part Three

## Chapter Nine

# Courts as an Instrument of Horizontal Accountability: The Case of Latin Europe

Today, the traditional view according to which democracy implies majority rule in the form of parliamentary supremacy has come under growing criticism. In Europe since World War II, democratic regimes have increasingly incorporated substantive constraints to what the parliamentary majority can do. Not only must public authority be exerted within general rules, but citizens are deemed to be entitled to fundamental rights, whose exercise must remain outside the will of the majority. Therefore, submitting the performance of public functions to the scrutiny of independent judges becomes an effective and essential check on the exercise of political power, ensures the supremacy of the law, and guarantees citizens' rights (Stone 2000).

There is some ambiguity in the concept of judicial independence (Russell 2001). On one hand, judicial independence is understood as institutional independence, that is, as the guarantees judges enjoy vis-à-vis the political branches of government. On the other, the term refers to the behavior of the judges, that is, to their independence on the bench. However, if, as a rule, in order to behave independently, a judge needs to be independent from the parties at the case (and, therefore, also from the executive), it does not follow that institutionally independent judges will automatically behave in an independent way, a point to which we return later.

Historically, in democratic countries, the level of judicial independence as well as the role played by courts in the political system has varied. In general, the role of judges in civil-law countries tends to be far less politically significant (Merryman 1985). In continental Europe the centralization of political authority, including the judicial function, was brought about by the monarchy, to which judges were initially subordinated. In the nineteenth century the constitutionalization of political power and the consequent development of judicial guarantees of independence partially weakened this relationship, but the organizational integration of the judiciary into the structure of public administration was maintained, if not strengthened. In fact, the decline of the monarchy did not radically alter the situation; it merely transferred the power to exert influence over the judiciary to a parliamentary executive.

The situation in Anglo-Saxon countries is different. In England the centralization of political authority resulted in the hegemony of one institution, Parliament. However, the political context of such a development has been more polycentric: the political branches have not been able to monopolize fully the creation of legal norms, and an important role has always been reserved for judicial decisions (Vile 1967). As a result, judges have been able to maintain autonomy in relation to parliamentary statutes: common-law principles developed by judges still remain one of the basic elements of English law. In the United States, a written constitution combined with judicial review of legislation has ensured from the outset that the judiciary would not be subordinate to the political branches. On the contrary, the American judiciary has emerged as an equal power to the legislature and the executive, and its main task has been to balance law-making power in a constitutional system of checks and balances. This was part of the original conception of political power sharing in America, whereby "those who administer each department [are given] the necessary constitutional means and personal motives to resist encroachments of the others.... Ambition must be made to counteract ambition. The interest of the man must be connected with the constitutional rights of the place" (*Federalist* 51). This reflected an early American belief that the judiciary is not only "the least dangerous to the political rights of the Constitution" but also an "excellent barrier to the encroachments and oppressions of the representative body" (*Federalist* 78). A generation later Tocqueville remarked again that "the power vested in the American courts of justice of pronouncing a statute to be unconstitutional forms one of the most powerful barriers that have ever been devised against the tyranny of political assemblies" (1994: 103).

In the past few decades, things have begun to change. In many European countries judicial guarantees of independence have been strengthened. The change has been deeper in the countries belonging to the Latin tradition: Italy, France, Spain, and Portugal (Tate and Vallinder 1995).[1] Here, not only has the institutional setting of the judiciary

---

[1] To this list we should add Belgium, whose judicial system straddles the divide between the Latin and Germanic worlds.

undergone deep changes, but courts have come to play an increasing role in checking the political branches.

## Institutional Conditions

In general terms, in order to be an effective check on the way political power is exercised, judges must be not only independent but also capable of intervening in significant cases. In other words, to assess the role of the judiciary as a political check, not only must the status of the judiciary be taken into account: one should look also at the structure of the judicial system. Therefore, after having analyzed the reforms that have altered the status of European judges, we are going to consider also some changes that have affected the judicial system.

In order to evaluate the guarantees of independence judges really enjoy, we must consider the whole institutional setting of the judiciary – that is, appointments, transfers, disciplinary proceedings, and career patterns, the last constituting the most important variable – in order to characterize the organizational setup of the judiciary. All these elements influence the concrete position of individual judges and allow an assessment of the actual scope of both the internal and the external gradient of judicial independence. To follow a well-known distinction: whereas external independence refers to the relations between the judiciary and the other branches of government, internal independence focuses on personal guarantees aimed at protecting individuals from undue pressures coming from within the organization, namely from other judges (Shetreet 1985: 637–8). Although generally disregarded, the role played by organizational hierarchies is crucial in order to highlight the actual dynamics of the judicial corps and therefore the way courts interact with their political environment.

Judicial organizations in continental Europe traditionally operate within a pyramid-like organizational structure.[2] As could be expected, salary, prestige, and personal influence depend on one's individual position in the hierarchical ladder and can be improved only through promotions. These are granted on a competitive basis and according to a given combination of two concurring criteria, seniority and merit, the latter being assessed by means of evaluations of the judge's professional performance by higher-ranking officials. Here, it is the role of hierarchical superiors that deserves attention. Even when the final decision is up to the Ministry of Justice, or to other institutions, promotions rely heavily

---

[2] For more details on what follows, see Guarnieri and Pederzoli (2002).

on information recorded in personal reports by hierarchical superiors, a fact that highlights the crucial role entrusted to the judicial elite. The "peers' review," a typical device of social control in professional organizations, is here superseded by formal and written evaluations drafted by higher-rank judges. Moreover, the decision-making process leading to promotions often sees the participation of others actors, placed outside the judicial system: especially the executive, that is, the Ministry of Justice. Traditionally, this external intervention, although with different forms, represented the most important institutional channel connecting the judiciary with the political system.

Today, in Latin European countries the prominent role traditionally played by the executive branch has been remarkably weakened, thanks to the creation of new institutions – the Higher Councils of the Judiciary – meant to strengthen the independence of the bench. All Higher Councils share what must be considered their most visible feature: although in different proportions, members of the judiciary are always granted representation therein. The Higher Councils of the Judiciary are indeed a crucial element in understanding how the relationships between courts and politics have evolved in these countries. Despite their common appellation, their composition does vary according to the role they have been assigned in the different systems. It is therefore necessary to take into account their functions and composition – above all, the ratio between judicial and lay members and the ways these groups are chosen. Of course, the level of independence will tend to be higher where judicial members are granted the majority of the seats and are directly elected by their colleagues. In the same way, the guarantees enjoyed by the judiciary will be broader when the functions entrusted to the Higher Councils are more extensive. From this point of view, Italy is undoubtedly the country that has experienced the most radical change.

Since the Second World War a deep transformation of the institutional setting of the Italian judiciary has taken place. As a result, the Higher Council of the Judiciary has been entrusted with the task of taking all decisions related to the status of both judges and public prosecutors. More precisely, their recruitment, appointment, promotions, transfers, and disciplinary proceedings have been removed from the minister of justice – who has been granted only the power to start disciplinary proceedings – and concentrated in the hands of the council that has therefore become the main, if not the only, institutional bridge between the judiciary and the political system. The actual reach of judicial "self-government" in Italy can be better understood by considering the composition of the council. At present, it consists of three members ex officio – the president of the republic, who presides over it; the president; and the prosecutor general at the Court of Cassation (twenty magistrates directly elected by the whole corps and ten "lay" members elected by Parliament from among experienced lawyers and university law professors). In practice, the lay participants are chosen so as to reflect the strength of the different political forces represented in Parliament, including the opposition. Of crucial importance as well in shedding light on the internal functioning of the council is the influence that the various judicial factions are able to exert therein.[3]

In the meantime, the traditional hierarchy has been dismantled step by step. Today, promotions of Italian magistrates depend de facto exclusively on seniority, and promotion is not limited by the availability of vacant positions in higher courts. As a result, any magistrate can attain the highest ranks in twenty-eight years, or at least benefit from the corresponding salary. It goes without saying that such a system removes neither the need to make choices when vacant seats are to be filled, nor the inevitable discretionary power of the appointing authority: they both simply shift when actual functions have to be assigned. Often candidates are chosen only on the basis of seniority, which thus become synonymous with professional merit. However, also belonging to one or another of the judicial factions represented in the Higher Council is far from negligible, a fact that helps explain the need for magistrates to affiliate themselves with such factions.

The Italian case has proved to be particularly attractive to the younger Iberian democracies that emerged from the fall of the authoritarian regimes (Renoux 1999; Magalhães, Guarnieri, and Kaminis, forthcoming). The Spanish judiciary also had a strictly bureaucratic organization, for the most part inherited from the Napoleonic arrangement, that did not undergo radical changes even under the Francoist regime. The 1978 Constitution foresaw the creation of the Consejo general del poder judicial, with the task of securing the independence of the third branch vis-à-vis the executive. Following the Italian model, the Spanish Constitution entrusted the majority of the Higher Council to judicial members, yet limited the functions of this collegial body only to the status of judges. This provision was enacted through the Ley organica of 1980, according to which the Higher Council is chaired by the chief of the Supreme Court and composed of twenty members, with twelve of them being judges

---

[3] From right to left on the ideological spectrum, the most important today are: Magistratura Democratica, Movimento per la Giustizia, Unità per la Costituzione, and Magistratura Indipendente (Guarnieri 1992).

directly elected by their peers and the rest appointed in the same proportions by both chambers of Parliament. As has occurred in Italy, in Spain the minister of justice has seen his competence limited to providing the means for the administration of justice to function. However, in 1985, after the Socialist government had clashed with the conservative majority of the Higher Council, the Ley organica was reformed; as a result, the judicial members of the Higher Council were now elected by Parliament and had their prerogatives partially reduced, leading to complaints from both the judicial corps and parliamentary opposition. As regards its competencies, the Spanish council is in charge of appointments and promotions, according to procedures that vary with the judicial position to be filled. Advancements depend on seniority and, to a lesser extent, merit.

Also in Portugal, since the fall of the dictatorship of Salazar and Caetano, major innovations have taken place. The Higher Council of the Judiciary had been given remarkable latitude, its functions ranging from appointments and transfers to promotions and disciplinary proceedings. Following the 1982 and 1997 constitutional amendments, it consists now of seven judges directly elected by their colleagues through a proportional system, seven members elected by Parliament, and two other members appointed by the president of the republic. The Higher Council is chaired by the president of the Supreme Court, himself elected by his fellow judges, and a crucial role in it is played by the executive council, composed of five judges and three "lay" members. At least so far, advancements depend mainly on seniority.

The French Higher Council is characterized by two main traits, namely the role reserved therein to the executive and the relatively narrow scope of its functions. In the different "versions" of the Higher Council that have followed one another from 1958 to 1993, the president of the republic and the minister of justice have always been present. On the other hand, the tasks assigned to the council do not include judicial selection and training, entrusted to the National Judicial School (whose head, a magistrate, is appointed by the minister of justice), and also its appointing powers appear less incisive, at least from the comparative point of view.

Created in 1946 – inside the framework of the Constitution of the Fourth Republic – in order to preserve the independence of judges, the Higher Council experienced a true mutation under the Constitution of 1958. The newly established setting reinforced the role of the president of the republic inside the Higher Council at the expense of the prerogatives previously assigned to the legislature. All the nine counselors sitting together with the minister of justice and the president of the republic were appointed by the latter, although with some restrictions. The Higher Council functions were also limited, as it could directly deliberate appointments only to the highest ranks, while in the remaining cases it had to give only an advisory opinion to the minister of justice. However, the practice gradually developed for the minister not to appoint judges who had been given a negative evaluation.

The constitutional amendment voted in 1993 has brought about significant transformations. At present,[4] the Higher Council, while being a single body so as to reflect the unity of the judicial corps, consist of two different panels, having competence over judges and public prosecutors respectively. It is formed by twelve members: the president of the republic; the minister of justice; a councillor of state elected by her peers; three lay members appointed respectively by the president of the republic, the president of the Senate and the president of the National Assembly; and six magistrates representing the various hierarchical ranks, elected by their colleagues. It is precisely the composition of this last segment of the Higher Council that changes, according to the type of panel: it consists of five judges and one public prosecutor when measures concerning judges are under consideration, whereas these proportions are reversed in the case of decisions affecting public prosecution. The reform has also increased the functions of the Higher Council. The council now is in charge of judges' discipline and makes direct appointments to all important positions. However, in the remaining cases judges can be appointed only after a recommendation by the council. By contrast, the functions of the panel for public prosecution are more narrowly defined: so far, it can give only noncompulsory advice, and such advice is not even required for appointments to the highest ranks, which are decided directly by the government.

The French Higher Council has been entrusted with functions that are undoubtedly more relevant than they were in the past, although not

---

[4] A constitutional reform has been recently proposed. According to the proposal, in addition to the president of the republic and the minister of justice, the council would have been composed of twenty-one members. Ten would be elected by the judiciary (five judges and five prosecutors) and eleven appointed by different authorities: the Council of State would select a councillor; the president of the republic and the presidents of the Senate and of the National Assembly would appoint two members each; and the vice-president of the Council of State and the presidents of the Court of Cassation and the Court of Accounts would jointly appoint four other members. As in the past, the council would have been divided in two sections with separate jurisdiction over judges and public prosecutors. At present, the process is stalemated, mainly because of the opposition of the right, and the joint sessions of Parliament due to vote on the reform have been postponed indefinitely.

as broad as those vested in its Italian counterpart. Generally speaking, the setup of the French judiciary appears to be still less distant from the traditional civil law type. The position of individual judges, the functions they perform, and their prestige and salary are largely determined by advancements. The multiple steps forming the career path depend not only on seniority but also, and above all, on merit, even though recent reforms have somewhat relaxed the link between function and rank, allowing magistrates to be promoted sometimes without changing their functions.[5]

Thus, the way promotions are organized represents a crucial point in the bureaucratic arrangement: they entail somewhat obseure, diffused constraints. Awaiting a promotion or fearing a rejection is likely to bring about a stronger compliance with the expectations of those in power, be they the minister of justice, the hierarchical superiors, or even a "self-governing" body. We have already remarked the importance for Italian magistrates to affiliate with one or another of the various ideological factions represented in the Higher Council, but empirical research shows that "proximity to power" proves to be a powerful career accelerator in other countries as well. However, the changes introduced in this system in the postwar period have on the whole increased, although to a varying extent, the institutional independence of the judiciary. Not only has external independence been strengthened but the internal gradient has been reinforced, weakening the traditional role played by higher ranks in these judiciaries.

As mentioned before, in order to assess the role of courts as political checks, the organization of the judicial system must also be taken into account. Here we are going to concentrate on two important elements:

---

[5] As regards the procedure of advancements, it is indeed rather complicated: it will suffice here to underline once again the role of the judicial hierarchy. Evaluations of work performances are drafted by higher-ranking magistrates and recorded in personal reports, which are then made available to all actors taking part in the decision-making process. Hierarchical superiors represent, thus, a sort of interface between individual judges and appointing authorities. In this respect, besides the Higher Council and the minister of justice, also the so-called commission for advancements plays a role, for it has the task of drafting every year the list of magistrates who are deemed qualified to be promoted. Because candidates for promotions must necessarily be drawn from this list, the commission represents a delicate element of the appointing machinery. But, while in the past it was staffed by magistrates appointed by the minister of justice, a reform in 1992 has made it possible for the commission to boast a more balanced composition, including not only executive officials but also magistrates directly elected by their peers (Renoux 1999). Recently (January 2001) the chances for promotion have been increased, with more importance given to seniority.

judicial review of legislation and public prosecution. Although the political significance of courts depends also on other elements (Guarnieri and Pederzoli 2002), in this area the changes have been deeper and more visible.

After the ancien régime experience with the *parléments*, it was not until the twentieth century that judicial review of legislation was reestablished on the continent, but only after the Second World War did it begin its cross-national expansion (Cappelletti 1989; Stone 2000). The Italian Corte Costituzionale, foreseen by the 1948 Constitution, was actually instituted in 1956. Two years later, the transition to the Fifth Republic in France brought about the installation of the Conseil Constitutionnel, which, notwithstanding its peculiar features, has come to play an increasing role in the political system. The Iberian countries joined this European trend in 1978 and 1983, with the creation in Spain and Portugal of separate constitutional courts. In all cases judicial review has been entrusted to separate courts.

Constitutional judges are invariably appointed or elected by the political branches: the executive, the legislative, and very occasionally the judiciary itself. As regards parliamentary elections, and often executive appointments, the influence of political parties is always explicit, choices actually being made according to the weight of political forces, including the opposition. In Southern Europe, this fact as allowed elections to become "transitional devices" for constraining the influence of an independent judiciary, whose members often have been recruited during the previous authoritarian regimes (Magalhães et al., forthcoming). In any case, at least so far, constitutional courts have never persistently confronted the political branches.

However, the introduction of judicial review has had a significant impact on the ordinary judiciary. In fact, although centralized review has marked the expansion of constitutional justice all over continental Europe, through the so-called incidental proceeding, litigants have the chance to challenge in court the law that should be applied to their case. If this occurs, the ordinary court has to assess whether the issue is groundless or not and, if not, refer the case to the constitutional court. In other words, courts represent a necessary filter between the litigants and constitutional adjudication. Also important is the fact that, out of any party initiative, courts can raise constitutional issues on their own. As a consequence, one should not overlook the possibility that the proceeding becomes a vehicle of "judicial politics" – a device to affirm personal and even group values that are often represented by union-like associations.[6] In any case, the ordinary judge has become an unavoidable segment of the process of constitutional review, thus balancing to some extent the fact that this function is concentrated in a separate, special court.[7]

Beyond the specific traits of the different political and institutional contexts, it is clear that constitutional courts do not bind themselves to "negatively legislating," according to the wish of Kelsen (Stone 2000). Their task is not only to answer yes or no to a constitutional complaint. The decisional techniques the courts have elaborated – for example, decisions stating only the "partial" or the "conditioned" nullity of a statute, that is, only if interpreted in a specific way – allow them to participate actively in the policy process. In comparison with their American colleagues, European ordinary judges seem to have a reduced role in the constitutional review of legislation, since the final say always goes to special courts. Yet participation, although in an incidental way, in the process of judicial review, together with the establishment and gradual expansion of supranational systems of justice, like those created by the European Community or the European Convention for Human Rights, have opened new areas of intervention that enlarge the scope of ordinary courts as well as their discretionary powers, a fact that must be assessed in conjunction with the previously analyzed decline of hierarchical control. As a result, the traditional deference toward the law as enacted by the legislature has come out radically weakened.

In all Latin European countries criminal courts have begun to play an increasingly important role, leading to what has been defined as the "criminalization of political responsibility" (Sousa Santos 1996: 20). In

---

[6] An interesting example is provided by the Italian case where, since the second half of the 1960s, a group of "progressive" magistrates (Magistratura Democratica) explicitly encouraged judges not only to make an extensive use of incidental proceedings, in order to get the Constitution enforced, but also to apply constitutional rules directly (Guarnieri 1992).

[7] The incidental proceeding produces the so-called concrete review of legislation, because it is triggered by the application of the law in individual disputes. This kind of review can be found in Spain, Italy, and, to some extent, Portugal. The exception is provided by the French Constitutional Council, which deals with legislation not still enforced and whose scope is therefore devoted to only "abstract" review. In the "abstract" review enacted legislation can be challenged only by public authorities, with the exception of the judiciary: the executive, the legislature, the local governments, and even – in Spain and Portugal – the ombudsman. Because no filter is foreseen, the action has to be brought directly to the constitutional court within a given period of time from the moment in which the law has been enacted. Unlike what could be expected, "abstract" review has displayed an impact, especially in France, that appears to have gone well beyond the intentions of its initial supporters.

this development much has to be ascribed to the way the organization of public prosecution has evolved.

The Constitution of 1948 and subsequent reforms have dramatically changed the traditional setup of Italian prosecutors. Nowadays judges and prosecutors enjoy the same independent status: they form a unitary body and govern themselves through the Higher Council of the Judiciary. The minister of justice has lost most of his previous powers over the judiciary. This evolution has been supported by the adoption in the Constitution of the rule of mandatory prosecution: it has been argued that such a rule, by removing from public prosecutors any discretionary power, justified their independent status. In fact, the rule of mandatory prosecution has been interpreted so as to imply the removal of any form of external responsibility, seen as a potential interference with prosecutors' duty to act. This setting has resulted in two main consequences. On the one hand, the political significance of prosecutorial actions has increased.[8] On the other hand, the weakening of the hierarchy, through the practical dismantling of the career and of the traditional chain of subordination to higher units and the minister of justice, has fostered the emergence of a substantially polycentric setting. In fact, today each unit – if not each prosecutor – is more or less free to run a proceeding on the basis of its own assessment.

The status enjoyed by Italian public prosecution has somewhat influenced Spain and Portugal (Magalhães et al., forthcoming). However, Spanish prosecutors are separated from judges, and enjoy a different status, because the top of the hierarchy, the Fiscal General de l'Estado, is appointed by the executive, whereas the Consejo General del Poder Judicial, the self-governing institution of judges, is asked only to give an advisory opinion. Yet, the actual significance of prosecution in the judicial system is limited here by the role played by the examining judge, who is entrusted with all the politically relevant cases.[9] The Portuguese arrangement bears a closer resemblance to the Italian setting. Although retaining the organizational separation of judges from prosecutors, Portugal has recognized the rather strong guarantees of the latter. Prosecutors are administered by the Conselho Superior do Ministerio Publico, the majority of whose members are elected by public prosecutors. The general prosecutor, standing at the top of the pyramid,

---

[8] Thanks also to the increasing influence on the police. See Di Federico (1998).

[9] For instance, the Juez Central de Instrucciòn, working in the Audiencia Nacional, plays an extremely important role with a nationwide jurisdiction over major crimes such as terrorism, drug trafficking, and organized crime.

is appointed – and can be removed – by the president of the republic, acting on the basis of a proposal by the government, but actually enjoys a rather high level of autonomy.

In France, traditionally, the prosecutor has been subject to the executive and, more specifically, to the minister of justice. Prosecutorial units are built into a unitary and hierarchical organization with its chiefs being, at least in principle, subordinate to the minister, although recent reforms have partially released this connection. A trait of the organization in France, as in Italy, is that both judicial and prosecutorial functions are performed by the same corps: it is here commonplace to speak of "sitting magistrates" (*magistrature assise*) with reference to the bench, and "standing magistrates" (*magistrature debout*) with reference to prosecutors, who are also given main positions inside the Ministry of Justice. Actually, although guarantees do vary, transfers from one position to another are not infrequent. Promotions are proposed by the minister of justice, but after the 1993 reform of the Higher Council of the Judiciary an advisory opinion (whose influence must not be discarded)[10] by its panel for public prosecutors is required.

Unlike the situation in other Latin European countries, prosecution in France is grounded on the principle of opportunity: the prosecutor – and, in particular, the chief of the office – is always free to choose whether to start an action or dismiss a case. Because in this latter case the judge is not required to make a decision, the main instrument of control over prosecutorial discretion is the hierarchical structure. However, any attempt to evaluate the overall functioning of the French criminal justice system must also take into account the instructing judge, who handles all relevant cases and enjoys judicial guarantees of independence (Leigh and Zedner 1992). As a consequence, once the examining phase has begun, the treatment of those cases cannot be directly influenced by the government.

In all these countries, although to a different extent, the traditional hold of the executive on public prosecution has been reduced, if not

---

[10] Since its accession, in 1997, the Jospin government has considered these opinions de facto binding, an attitude that has to be related to the fact that the matter has come under the growing attention of the media. Very likely for the same reason the government has also decided not to issue instructions to public prosecutors in individual cases. In the meantime, a further reinforcing of prosecutorial autonomy is presently under discussion in France: as we have seen, a reform of the Constitution has been proposed, changing the composition of the Higher Council of the Judiciary and enlarging its powers. Moreover, the government has presented a project of reform of the criminal code, in which the decisional autonomy of the public prosecutors from the Ministry of Justice is strengthened.

dismantled. The result has been that prosecutors – and investigating judges – have been often able to run investigations involving members of the government as well as top civil servants without real fear of damaging their career. Everywhere criminal initiatives have been supported by the media. The increasing competition in this sector, together with the weakening of the influence traditionally exerted by the government and by political parties, pushes the media to emphasize judicial investigations involving politicians. On the other side, public prosecutors and investigating judges seem to be able, directly or indirectly, to supply the media with valuable information (Jiménez 1998; Pujas 1999).

## Judicial Culture

Judicial interventions in the political process require not only an independent and powerful judiciary but also judges willing to intervene (Friedman and Rehbinder 1976: 33). Thus we have to consider changes in the judicial culture and in the way judges tend to define their role.

The judge as a faithful and passive *executor* of the legislative will has traditionally been influential and is the source of the idea that a judge is only *la bouche de la loi*. Until recently, this view has been dominant in civil-law countries, supported by academic doctrine and widely accepted in the political culture (Merryman 1985; Rebuffa 1993). It developed in conjunction with the institutional transformations of the French Revolution, Napoleonic reforms, and the broadening of political participation. It addressed the potential problem of independent judges opposing a legislature that increasingly represented the political community and, therefore, had stronger grounds for claiming to be the "true" representative of the popular will. However, in the past decades, a different conception of the role of the judge has gained ground in Latin Europe. Judicial creativity – that is, the fact that judicial decisions are not simply taken "on the basis of pre-existing substantive laws" (Cappelletti 1989: 7) – is not only recognized but often advocated. Judges' decisions should also be autonomous from the political branches. In other words, a new, more activist, political role of the judge has emerged. Although only a minority of judges in these countries seems to subscribe to this conception, nevertheless it has exerted a growing influence on judicial decisions. On the whole, Latin European judges are today not only more institutionally independent from the political branches but also more likely to assert their independence when on the bench.

In this process a very important role has been played by judicial associations. The unionization of judges is a relatively recent phenomenon in Europe, notwithstanding the civil-service nature of the judiciary. Until the mid 1970s Portugal and Spain were still authoritarian regimes, where freedom of association was severely restricted. In Italy and especially in France the possibility for magistrates to affiliate themselves with parties or unions was strictly regulated. In recent decades, however, magistrates have increasingly begun to organize themselves in professional associations – de facto unions.[11] Many of the reforms we have analyzed in this chapter – such as the dismantling of the career or the introduction of elective councils – have been brought about under the pressure of these associations. In turn, these reforms have strengthened their significance: they play an important role in organizing the judicial vote for the higher councils as well as in the decision making of these bodies.[12] Moreover, judicial associations tend to exert cross-country influence. For example, the Italian model of judicial independence is today advocated more or less everywhere in Europe (and also in Southern America) by an international association of judges, composed of the left-wing groups of different countries: Magistrats Européens pour la Démocratie et la Liberté (MEDEL).[13]

This phenomenon can also explain the changing attitude of the left. Traditionally, in constitutional matters the left subscribed to the Jacobin tradition. It advocated the concentration of powers in a legislative assembly, directly elected by the people. All devices aiming at limiting the power of the popularly elected legislature were therefore seen as a way of obstructing the influence of the popular will. The distrust toward the judiciary was extremely strong because of the bourgeois origins of most judges and often also because of their role in the repression of socialist unions and parties. Although the experience of authoritarianism had already made some on the left realize the significance of legal and judicial guarantees, the emergence inside the judiciary of groups of left-wing magistrates has further accelerated this process. Courts have become at least potential allies, especially in countries such as Italy, in which the left was excluded from power for a long time.

---

[11] But see the Syndicat de la magistrature in France and the Sindicato dos magistrados do ministério pùblico in Portugal, where the term "union" is employed in order to underline their very connection with the trade-union movement.

[12] Three out of four Higher Councils – in France, Italy, and Portugal – are at least in part elected by the judiciary.

[13] The model has been somewhat received in the proposal of the European Charter of Judicial Status, prepared inside the Council of Europe (Renoux 1999), and has somewhat influenced also the recent (October 2000) recommendation of the Committee of the Ministers of the Council of Europe on the role of public prosecution in the criminal justice system.

## A Tentative Assessment of the Role of Courts in Latin Europe

Although so far systematic research has not been carried out, the political significance of courts seems to have increased everywhere in Latin Europe, at least to an extent higher than in other European countries (Tate and Vallinder 1995). For example, in the past decade in all the countries here considered, members of the government, while still in office, have been put under judicial investigation, often compelled to resign, and sometimes brought to trial and convicted. The number of former cabinet members involved in criminal investigations for reasons connected to their past office is even higher. As for the impact of judicial initiatives, it depends to a large extent on the political context: the role played by Italian courts in the 1990s cannot be understood without taking into account the crisis of political parties, which in the past had played a dominant role in that polity (Magalhães et al., forthcoming). If criminal cases are, without doubt, the most visible, the policy-making role of constitutional and administrative courts cannot be disregarded.[14] This general evolution has been supported by the changes we have previously analyzed. Today, judges – and also prosecutors – are more independent from executive influence while the structure of the criminal process still allows them wide powers. The institution of judicial review has contributed to the growth among judges of a more critical stance toward legislation, and judicial associations have supported the development of more activist definitions of the judicial role.

Latin European judiciaries today are much more decentralized than in the past, and the role of supreme courts has become strongly reduced.[15] As a consequence, judicial interventions tend to be less homogeneous, because the law per se cannot dictate judicial decisions. But the autonomy of courts is a necessary condition for the development of more intense and frequent interactions between the judiciary and its political and social environment. A decentralized judiciary can be less easily controlled by the political branches and therefore can better assure some form of "horizontal accountability." However, exactly because of its decentralized structure it is not easy to detect the interests that tend to be privileged by the judiciary. Some have spotted an

---

[14] The role of constitutional courts has been investigated. See Stone (1992 and 2000) and Volcansek (2000). We have less information on administrative courts, but for Italy, see Predieri (1994).

[15] Continental supreme courts were said to have a "didactic" authority, that is, a capacity to educate lower courts through decisions; this was also aided by the fact that supreme-court judges were able to influence lower-court judges' careers.

increasing use of courts by business interests, a practice often involving both national and European courts (Bancaud and Boigeol 1995). Sometimes, judicial initiatives and their impact depend on local contingencies.[16] In any case, we must take into account that we are dealing with civil-service judiciaries that have come to enjoy some form of self-government. Much of the decision making inside the corps is influenced by the relationships between the different judicial groups and by their relative strength, which in turn depends to a large extent on their capability of satisfying judges' demands in terms of salaries and working conditions. Unlike common-law judiciaries, the influence of the bar is limited. Also, the role of the academic doctrine, once very influential in civil-law systems, has declined as a consequence of the diminishing relevance of merit for promotions. Instead, the role of the media has everywhere increased in the 1990s. The very emergence of judicial populism – often the stepping stone for political careers (e.g., the careers of Thierry Jean-Pierre in France, Baltasar Garzòn in Spain, and Antonio Di Pietro in Italy) – has been made possible, apart from the confusion of judicial and prosecutorial powers, by media coverage and support.[17]

After an initial surprise, the reaction of the political class to the expansion of judicial power has been to try to constrain the power of the judiciary by stopping or reversing the process of institutional reform (as today in France or in 1985 in Spain) and/or by establishing good terms with it at both the individual and group levels. An example is the provision of extrajudicial activities to magistrates, directly or indirectly, by the political class, as well as the increasing practice of appointing or electing judges to executive and parliamentary positions.[18] As for the Higher Councils, they provide an arena for continuous interactions between the judiciary and the political class, their decisions often being the product of exchanges between judicial factions and representatives of political parties (e.g., when appointments to key positions have to be made).

---

[16] For instance, the well-known Clean Hands investigations started in Milan, where the left-wing group Magistratura Democratica had always had a strong following. On the other hand, Milan was also the political stronghold of the Socialist leader Craxi. This partly explains why the Socialist Party was so strongly affected by the investigations.

[17] This is maybe the reason why in Italy prosecutors seem to have been more cautious when dealing with interests controlling significant media, for example, in the case of the Fiat and De Benedetti groups, whose newspapers have always supported Clean Hands investigations (Colajanni 1996).

[18] Italy is the best but not the only example. Spain can also provide a good case of collusion between judges and politicians (see Maravall, Chapter 11 in this volume).

The erosion – and, in the case of Italy, the dismantling – of the traditional career structure has brought about a new situation. As we have seen, while judges continue to be recruited among relatively young and inexperienced law school graduates, the traditional instruments of professional evaluation have lost much of their effectiveness. Seniority has increasingly replaced merit, and promotions are in the hands of a body in large part elected by those that have to be evaluated. Therefore, the traditional setting that once in some way ensured the professional qualifications of the judiciary is declining, but this change has not been matched by a corresponding increase in the selectivity of the recruitment process.[19] As a result, the judicial setting is less able to provide consistency in decision making. In European continental countries the career system was once the functional substitute for the lack of *stare decisis*: lower-court judges followed high-court rulings because they knew that their career was at stake (Friedrich 1950). In this way, conformist and conservative attitudes were obviously encouraged, but one can wonder whether the rule of law can be achieved without some degree of consistency in judicial decisions.

In general terms, the ability of a bureaucratic judiciary to sustain the rule of law can be questioned. It is not only that a political system bound to follow the rule of law must be reasonably sure of what the law is. If the interpretation of the laws becomes the exclusive domain of self-appointed bureaucrats, the risk for democracy is evident. In common-law countries the recruitment process is the main way through which the political system and the legal profession can exert an influence on the judiciary. In the tradition of the civil law a similar influence was achieved through a hierarchical setting, based on merit, and the power of the executive over top appointments. The need to strengthen judicial independence has led Latin European countries to increasingly transfer executive powers to collegial bodies such as the higher councils. However, when judges are in control of the councils, corporatist interests tend to be privileged, and sometimes the power of the judicial factions becomes a threat to the independence of the individual judge. On the other hand, when political or parliamentary appointees are in the majority, it is not such a great gain over the past situation of executive predominance.

The capability of the judiciary to ensure some form of accountability cannot be taken for granted. The way judges are selected and socialized,

---

[19] The relation between initial selection, internal socialization, and organizational control is pointed out by Gross and Etzioni (1985).

and therefore the values they tend to share, must be considered. Judicial independence is not a value in itself but a means toward achieving judicial impartiality (Shapiro 1981). Therefore, it must be balanced against other significant considerations. Judicial independence cannot become a bar to an effective evaluation of judges' professional qualifications. Above all, it should not divorce the judiciary from the political system. It is not only that the significance of judicial decisions in contemporary democracies requires judges to be made in some way accountable. There is more than that. As judicial power expands, an incentive is created for political groups to put pressure on the judiciary, exploiting all the available channels of influence. Because it is impossible to make politics vanish, it seems wiser to channel political pressure in institutional ways. In this manner, the way political influence is exerted can be better exposed, and consequently constrained, while judicial power is also checked: in order to prevent abuses, all power must be checked, and the judiciary is no exception.

## References

Bancaud, A., and A. Boigeol. 1995. "A New Judge for a New System of Economic Justice." In Y. Dezelay and D. Sugarman (eds.), *Professional Competition ad Professional Power*, 104–13. London: Routledge.
Cappelletti, M. 1989. *The Judicial Process in Comparative Perspective*. Oxford: Clarendon Press.
Colajanni, N. 1996. *Mani pulite? Giustizia e politica in Italia*. Milan: Mondadori.
Di Federico, G. 1998. "Prosecutorial Independence and the Democratic Requirement of Accountability in Italy." *British Journal of Criminology* 38: 371–87.
Friedman, L., and M. Rehbinder (eds.). 1976. *Zur Soziologie des Gerichtsverfahrens*. Opladen: Westdeutscher Verlag.
Friedrich, C. J. 1950. *Constitutional Government and Democracy*. Boston: Ginn.
Gross, E., and A. Etzioni. 1985. *Organizations in Society*. Englewood Cliffs, N.J.: Prentice Hall.
Guarnieri, C. 1992. *Magistratura e politica in Italia*. Bologna: Il Mulino.
Guarnieri, C., and P. Pederzoli. 2002. *The Power of Judges*. Oxford: Oxford University Press.
Jiménez, F. 1998. "Political Scandals and Political Responsibility in Democratic Spain." *West European Politics* 21, 4: 80–99.
Leigh, L. H., and L. Zedner. 1992. *A Report on the Administration of Criminal Justice in the Pre-Trial Phase in France and Germany*. London: HMSO.
Magalhães, P., C. Guarnieri, and G. Kaminis. Forthcoming. "Democratic Consolidation, Judicial Reform, and the Judicialisation of Politics in Southern Europe." In Richard Gunther, Nikiforos Diamandouros, and Gianfranco Pasquino (eds.), *The Changing Role of the State in Southern Europe*. Baltimore: Johns Hupkins University Press.
Merryman, J. H. 1985. *The Civil Law Tradition*. Stanford: Stanford University Press.
Predieri, A. 1994. "Potere giudiziario e politiche." In *Italia fra crisi e transizione*, 227–63. Bari: Laterza.

Pujas, V. 1999. "La 'scandalisation' en France, en Italie et en Espagne." Paper presented at the XVI Congress of the Association Française de Science Politique, Rennes, 28 September–1 October.

Rebuffa, G. 1993. *La funzione giudiziaria*. Turin: Giappicchelli.

Renoux, T. 1999. *Les conseils supérieurs de la magistrature en Europe*. Paris: La documentation Française.

Russell, P. 2001. "Toward a General Theory of Judicial Independence." In P. H. Russell and D. O'Brien (eds.), *Judicial Independence in the Age of Democracy*, 1–24. Charlottesville: University Press of Virginia.

Shetreet, S. 1985. "Judicial Independence: New Conceptual Dimensions and Contemporary Challenges." In S. Shetreet and Deschenes (eds.), *Judicial Independence: The Contemporary Debate*. Dordrecht: Nijhoff.

Sousa Santos, B. 1996. *Os tribunais nas sociedades contemporaneas: o caso portugues*. Lisbon: Afrontamento.

Stone, A. 1992. *The Birth of Judicial Politics in France*. Oxford: Oxford University Press.

2000. *Governing with Judges: Constitutional Politics in Europe*. Oxford: Oxford University Press.

Tate C. N., and T. Vallinder. 1995. *The Global Expansion of Judicial Power*. New York: New York University Press.

Tocqueville, A. de. 1994. *Democracy in America*. London: Fontana.

Vile, M. J. C. 1967. *Constitutionalism and the Separation of Powers*. Oxford: Clarendon Press.

## Chapter Ten

# Rule of Democracy and Rule of Law

Rule of law and democracy are both desirable attributes of a political system. Scholars writing of democratic transitions from authoritarian rule usually argue that the goal of such a transition is the establishment of democracy with the rule of law, implying that both may be achieved simultaneously. Perhaps that is so. What is often meant by rule of law is no more than the notion that government should work its will through general legislation, legislation to which the governors themselves are subject, rather than through irregular decrees and ad hominem proclamations. But rule of law may require more than this: it may require that people are able to foresee accurately the legal consequences of their actions and not be subject to sudden surprises whether or not these take the form of legislation, or perhaps that the law contain, or at least not violate, certain substantive principles and rights.

Democratic rule minimally requires government by the people or their representatives, elected on a broad franchise. But, in some conceptions, it too may require more than that. Perhaps, democracy demands that the range of choice open to government be broad and not constricted by externally imposed restraints (such as legal protections for minorities). We expect, for example, or hope, that our government can correct inequities arising from markets or social interactions. Such interventions can involve confiscatory taxes or draconian regulations, either of which can threaten claims for minority rights. Or perhaps, democracy requires that the people be regularly and genuinely consulted on fundamental legal changes so that institutions or practices of deliberation and consultation are in place and functioning. On some accounts, courts should be prepared to enforce such requirements by striking down legislation. Clearly, the more capacious definitions of democracy and rule of law, as values or aspirations, can bring them into conflict with one another.

Moreover, democracy and rule of law are embodied in distinct institutional systems. Democracy principally concerns electoral institutions, governments, and legislatures. Law operates through courts, police, and lawyers. To be sure, there is an intersection – the legislature, and perhaps the jury trial – where democracy and law come into close contact. But this contact is brief, and, for the most part, law takes on a life of its own once it issues from the legislative process. So, the fact that legislation passes from one set of institutions to another, each operating according to its distinct norms and expectations, suggests the likelihood of more mundane tension between democracy and law. Where legal institutions successfully claim broad authority to regulate and structure social interaction, democratic rule seems somewhat restricted. And the converse seems true as well: where parliament claims sovereign authority to make whatever law it chooses, judicial institutions are relegated to a subservient status – judges become, at best, agents of the legislature and interpreters of its commands.

## Law and Democracy: Boundaries

The fact that democracy and law are institutionally embodied leads to characteristic problems of agency. Insofar as the operation of law requires independent judges, able to hear and resolve disputes more or less impartially, judges will have latitude to behave opportunistically: to render decisions for private or biased reasons, or at least reasons not acceptable to the public or its representatives. This is a reason for putting in place controls that attenuate to some extent the degree of judicial insulation from political officials. But, if those political officials are able to interfere with judging, they can abuse that capacity by interfering opportunistically in pursuit of their own partisan or pecuniary objectives.[1] These twin issues of agency may be illustrated in two sharply drawn political controversies.

In 1788 the anti-Federalist Brutus argued that the most important danger presented by the proposed Constitution was not that it imposed a dominance of law over the will of the people; rather, it was that the judges – those presumably charged with articulating and enforcing the Constitution – would be completely unrestrained by law. He argued that "the real effect of this system of government will ... be brought home to

---

[1] Elsewhere, one of us has argued that the resolution of these two agency problems is theoretically intractable and requires political resolution that accommodates fair dispute resolution and democratic control. See Ferejohn (1999).

the feelings of the people, through the medium of the judicial power."
And the judges who were entrusted with this power would be placed in
an unprecedented situation. "They are to be rendered totally independent, both of the people and the legislature, both with respect to their
offices and their salaries. No errors they may commit can be corrected
by any power above them ... nor can they be removed from office for
making ever so many erroneous adjudications" (Ketchum 1986: 293).
By so insulating its judges, Brutus worried that the proposed Constitution would create a government in which the judiciary would rule
without legal or popular restraint. Thus, for Brutus, judges rather than
legality itself were the problem for a democracy. Brutus was right to see
that, because democratic and judicial institutions necessarily worked
over a common ground, the important issue for a constitution was how
to achieve an institutional balance among politicians and judges.

Nearly two centuries earlier a very similar issue was framed in an
argument between James I and his chief justice of the Court of Common
Pleas, Edward Coke. The dispute arose when Common Pleas asserted
the right to regulate the jurisdiction of the Ecclesiastical Court; the High
Commission and the archbishop of Canterbury, as head of that court,
appealed to the king for support. Coke argued that the king could not
decide the issue. He acknowledged that the king was the chief justice
of England in the sense that he sat in King's Bench and presided in the
upper house of Parliament, but he was not competent to decide cases at
law himself. However, judgments of these courts (King's Bench and the
House of Lords) "are always give per curiam; and the Judges are sworn
to execute justice according to the law and custom of England ... the
King cannot take any cause out of any of his Courts, and give judgement
upon it himself" (12 Coke's Reports 63 [1607]). The king could not lawfully, therefore, overrule Coke's court. The dispute might go before the
King's Bench and the judges there might well rule for the High Commission. But the king himself had no individual judicial role even in that
venue.

The archbishop of Canterbury, Coke's opponent, argued that, because
the authority of judges is only a delegated authority, "the King may
take what causes he shall please to determine, from the determination
of the Judges and may determine them himself." In his extended attack
on the common lawyers (especially Coke), Hobbes's philosopher put the
king's position dramatically: "I cannot believe that Sir Edward Coke ...
could mean that the King in the King's Bench sate as a Spectator only,
and might not have answered all motions, which his Judges answered,
if he had cause for it: For he knew that the King was Supreme Judge

then in all causes ... and that there is an exceeding great penalty ordained by the Laws for them that shall deny it" (Hobbes 1971: 88–9). Indeed, on the philosopher's argument Coke was doing no more than employing the authority that had been delegated to him, and such delegated power could always be recalled and employed directly.

Although Coke admitted that his powers as chief justice were delegated by the king, he claimed that he sat to resolve matters by law, which was the application of a kind of "artificial reason" acquired through years of professional training and practice. While the king might command those who possessed this artificial reason, he did not himself possess such reason. If the king were to sit on the bench and decide cases, therefore, he would be issuing merely sovereign commands, at best exercising legislative powers, and not applying law. His decisions would be, in that respect, arbitrary acts of will (though binding as sovereign commands) and not lawlike or, at any rate, not dictated by preexisting law of which the people might have previous knowledge.

But it is unclear whether Coke meant that the king was forbidden to act as a judge – that would surely have been grounds for indictment and severe punishment – or was instead making what we would now term a constitutive argument: that, if he decided a case as a judge, what the king would be doing would not be applying law. This is essentially the same as saying that, though the king could surely (legally) take the violin from the musician in his court and begin sawing away on it, he would not thereby be making music rather than noise. Acting as a judge requires a special kind of ability that can be gained only through training and practice. Common lawyers and judges learn how to discern which legal rules are applicable to particular situations, develop methods to cognize factual circumstances relevant to conflicts, and determine which legal decision best resolves the conflict at hand. The practices by which these steps are accomplished are technical and arcane but are utterly foreseeable and stable to practitioners of the legal arts.

Thus, whereas Brutus famously feared uncabined discretion in judges, Coke celebrated their reliability and predictability. This reliability was rooted in the fact that judicial authority was rooted in legal expertise. For Coke, it was the sovereign whose commands, while sometimes necessary for the health of the kingdom, threatened legal stability and predictability. A wise sovereign would exercise forbearance and let the law work its way whenever at all possible. This was Coke's advice to James; and James famously did not want to hear it. Of course, no sovereign wants to hear of the limits of his authority since those limits mark out what may permissibly be accomplished by government.

**245**

Unlike Brutus, then, Coke saw the conflict as one between types of authority: sovereign authority, essentially acts of will by an authoritative lawgiver, versus the orderly discovery and application of preexisting legal rules and principles. Coke's notion partially foreshadowed Montesquieu's conception of the separation of judicial and legislative powers. Drawing on Coke's principle articulated in Bonham's case that no man should be judge in his own cause, Montesquieu asserted that the essence of tyranny was the combination of the judicial and legislative powers, whether in the hands of the judiciary or the sovereign. Coke would have half-agreed: tyranny would follow if the sovereign exercised judicial powers (this is precisely what he resisted in Bonham's case), but he thought that judges were too restrained (by artificial reason) to threaten legislative power. Coke would have agreed with Montesquieu that the judicial power is a null power in that it did not create or extend any new authority but merely worked out the consequences of previous legislation for individuals in conflict. As such, judges acting in their judicial capacity posed no real threat to the sovereign.

Brutus, taking a more cynical psychological perspective, emphasized the potential conflict between legal officials and the people. He thought that the proposed Constitution would make judges so independent as to be uncontrolled by anything beyond their own interests. There would nothing – certainly internal legal or moral restraints would be insufficient – to stop judges from simply taking over rule-making authority as it suited them. In this sense, Brutus predicted that the new Constitution would inevitably lead to combining legislative and judicial powers but in the hands of the judge rather than the legislature. Brutus, it seems, echoed another strand in Montesquieu – the idea that the judicial authority is properly subordinate to the popular sovereign (that it is the mouth of the law) and that judicial decisions should be appealable to the people or their officials.

Obviously, nothing fundamental turns on the nature of the sovereign; whatever tension there is between sovereign commands and law carries over directly to our topic: the relationship between democratic and legal authority. And in Coke and Brutus we can see two visions of judicializing politics. On Coke's side we see a normative defense of judicialization: a theoretical perspective that emphasizes the differences between the impetuous or will-driven exercise of sovereign power and the normatively restrained actions of judges and lawyers guided by artificial reason. On the other side we see Brutus's fear of judicialization: the notion that judges, like anyone else, will inevitably yield to the temptation to expand their powers if they are unrestrained by elected officials or by the people themselves.[2] Underlying this fear is the suspicion that people, including judges and other legal officials, cannot be reliably restrained by norms such as Coke's artificial reason.

## The Displacement of Democratic Rule

An important instance of the institutional struggle between democracy and legality was described by Alexis de Tocqueville in 1835. He observed that "Scarcely any political question arises in the United States that is not resolved, sooner or later, into a judicial question." He was describing not only that judges, juries, and courts had become important loci of social decision making but also a tendency for people "to borrow, in their daily controversies, the ideas and even the language peculiar to judicial proceedings.... The language of the law thus becomes, in some measure, a vulgar tongue."[3]

In many respects, the political influence both of judges and legal discourse has grown more prominent since Tocqueville's time. Not long after he wrote, for example, the Supreme Court undercut the fragile sectional compromise that had helped keep the union from collapsing. Then, for more than half a century the courts effectively prevented Congress and the states from significantly regulating economic activity. And, for the last seventy years, even while loosening the restrictions on economic regulation, the courts have erected an increasingly elaborate system of protections for an expanding list of civil rights and liberties that places severe limits on the policies governments can undertake and the way permissible projects may be pursued. And, even as courts were elaborating doctrinal schemes to regulate legislatures, American private life has become increasingly litigious, so that Americans live under the constant specter of legal processes. In fact, one might even describe the arc of American political and social history as bending toward the displacement of both social and political governance by legal rule.

The growing importance of law and courts in American life no doubt struck Tocqueville as ironic. He was well aware of the institutional

---

[2] Whether judicialization of politics is attractive depends on how one views what we might call the prepolitical status quo. If one thinks that, without governmental interference, the status quo exhibits much social and economic injustice – of the sort that could be corrected by governmental action – the notion that sovereign authority should be tightly bound by legal restraints is bound to seem unattractive.

[3] Tocqueville (1945: 290). Subsequent page references are given in parentheses in text.

limitations of American courts: that judicial power is passive and specific rather than active and general.[4] Indeed, he argued that it was precisely because of the passive and specific nature of judicial power that law had become so powerful in the United States.[5] "When a judge in a given case attacks a law relating to that case, he extends the circle of his customary duties without, however, stepping beyond it, since he is in some measure obliged to decide upon the law in order to decide the case" (p. 103). "If a judge, in deciding a particular point, destroys a general principle ... he remains within the ordinary limits of his function" (p. 103). Tocqueville goes on to emphasize the power that passivity and specificity create: "If the judge had been empowered to contest the law on the ground of theoretical generalities, if he were able to take the initiative and censure the legislator, he would play a prominent political part" (p. 106). "If the judge could attack the legislator only openly and directly, he would sometimes be afraid to oppose him.... The laws would be attacked when the power from which they emanated was weak, and obeyed when it was strong" (p. 107).

This phenomenon – the displacement of the political by the juridical – has not been restricted to the United States but has become common throughout the advanced democracies, especially since World War II. For example, Alec Stone Sweet argues that over the course of the Fifth Republic, and especially since 1971 when the Constitutional Council successfully extended its authority to review statutes supported by the government, French politics has become increasingly judicialized in both senses. For example, in 1981 when the Socialists enacted legislation that would have nationalized several industries, the Constitutional Council blocked the proposals. Ultimately, after the French legislature redrafted the statutes, the council permitted the legislation to proceed but only after the legislature had taken account of its constitutional theory requiring more substantial compensation for shareholders. While the Constitutional Council did not, and perhaps could not, finally stop the nationalizing legislation, it did slow down the

---

[4] "... an action must be brought before the decision of a judge can be had" (103). And judges act on specific cases rather than general principles.

[5] Tocqueville himself traced the power of legal discourse to a sociological process. He argued that because jury trial was central to the everyday administration of justice, and ordinary people were often called to serve on juries, people naturally learned to respect lawyers and, especially, judges. Lawyers and judges became, said Tocqueville, the natural aristocracy of American society and, as such, a principal source of its order and stability. In turn, the people learned to see and resolve social and political conflicts in legal terms, whether or not those disputes are settled in courtrooms.

process, force the Parliament to address its constitutional objections, and substantially reshape the legislation itself.

In the next section we describe the development of constitutional adjudication, which is, in various ways, transforming the role of parliaments in Europe. Throughout Europe both national and supranational courts have begun to play a much more active and important role in deciding important and controversial social questions, questions traditionally decided by governments and parliaments. This is a particularly striking development on a continent so opposed to judicial review of legislation for most of the past two centuries. Although there are important difference among the European states, in all of them we can witness the creation of a structure of fundamental rights and liberties that are protected by courts, often with the collaboration of political institutions as well.

Tocqueville, famously, argued that egalitarian and democratic values were at the root of the displacement of politics by law. But if judicialization has been occurring in postwar European societies (which are hardly as egalitarian as Tocqueville's America) as well as throughout American history, there is reason to be skeptical of this explanation. We cannot, of course, deny the possibility that American and European judicialization have different causal roots. But we think it best to defer that possibility until we consider the possibilities of a more parsimonius account. And we can find suggestions of just such an account in *Democracy in America*.

Early in his book, when describing American local government, Tocqueville argued that some of the roots of judicial authority could be found in the fragmentation of authority among elected officials. The effective operation of government depends, he said, on the coordination of these separately elected officials, but each is subjected to removal only through electoral defeat. Therefore, "The communities . . . in which the secondary officials of the government are elected are inevitably obliged to make great use of judicial penalties" (p. 76). If they do not, an "elective authority which is not subject to judicial power will sooner or later either elude all control or be destroyed" (p. 76). In this respect, the growth of judicial authority might be traced not so much to democracy (the use of elections to fill all offices) or to equality (the requirement that no one is to be given more weight than another) as to political fragmentation.

In what follows we pursue Tocqueville's argument that the existence of a fragmented, indecisive, or gridlocked political system is the primary explanation for judicialization. While it is true that courts are passive

**249**

institutions that depend on others to come to them with issues to decide, courts are also generally able to take decisive action.[6] Whether courts are made up by a single judge or as a collegial body, they generally adopt decision procedures that enable them to settle the disputes before them. Thus, when they cannot get decisive action from their political leaders, people can turn to courts and judges instead. And where the legislature cannot act, these judicial settlements will tend to stand. We argue therefore that indecisive or gridlocked legislatures are likely settings for the development of an enhanced-scope judicial authority. And, insofar as judges make policy for legal reasons, ordinary people whose actions are being regulated have reasons to anticipate judicial discourse. Moreover, because of the possibility that judges may intervene, political officials have reason to anticipate the kinds of reasons that are likely to weigh in judicial proceedings. Thus, issues come to be framed and debated in juridical (or constitutional) terms and the decisions taken for legal reasons.

## Constitutional Courts and the Expansion of Legality in Postwar Europe

The introduction of constitutional courts in postwar Europe has fundamentally changed its political-legal landscape, but the manner in which this has occurred has varied among countries. In all cases, the constitutional court has developed a jurisprudence aimed at, and increasingly effective at, protecting fundamental rights. As such, these courts have placed important limits on the ordinary political processes. Indeed, by American standards – especially by standards of the early American republic – these courts have been extraordinarily active in striking down and modifying legislation. In that sense, constitutional courts have introduced an increase of judicial policy making – albeit by constitutional rather than ordinary judges. But in some countries activist constitutional courts have permitted ordinary judges to become more involved in checking and disciplining legislative processes. In others, the constitutional court has forced changes in internal legislative deliberations.

While most European legal systems have parliamentary sovereignty traditions – in the sense that both the executive and the judiciary are

---

[6] This is not to claim that courts cannot find ways to avoid taking decisions. But, in a country with many courts, those with persisting disputes can usually find some judge to listen and the hierarchical structure will then work to resolve differences in the resulting patterns of interpretation.

subordinated to parliament – developments in the twentieth century, particularly following the two world wars, have tended to erode these commitments. Thus, Austria after the World War I, and Germany and Italy after World War II (and Spain and Portugal after the collapse of fascist regimes), adopted constitutions that departed from the hierarchical parliamentary model in important ways.[7] For convenience, we may call all of these regimes Kelsenian, after the eminent Austrian jurist who invented their distinct institutional form. Each of the European constitutions reflects, in various ways, Kelsen's central idea that constitutional adjudication is more of a legislative than a judicial function. When a constitutional court strikes down a statute, it is not only legislating in the negative sense of abolishing a law but, insofar as it must reconstruct the legal situation before the statute, legislating positively as well.[8]

While constitutional adjudication involves a kind of legislating, this legislative action is of a particular kind. The role of constitutional adjudication is exclusively to maintain and enforce an accepted hierarchy of norms and specifically to ensure that the legislation and administrative actions do not encroach on constitutional values. Within the quasi-federal structure of post–World War I Austria, this constitutional adjudication was largely aimed at protecting the federal structure and, in that respect, it tended to police jurisdictional boundaries rather than to protect individual rights. But political developments in the twentieth century have tended to place the protection of individual (and group) liberties in an increasingly important position within the hierarchy of constitutional norms needing institutional protection.

Kelsen's notion of constitutional adjudication emphasized its legislative aspect by conceiving it as involving a comparison of a statutory and a constitutional text. Such abstract review arises not out of a fact-specific case with real (harmed) litigants claiming rights, but as an a priori and abstract comparison of texts. Constitutional adjudication seen this way seems inherently political, in the sense that a constitutional court must deliberate and choose from among alternative normative rules for

---

[7] Austria was the first country on the European continent to introduce (in 1920) a constitutional court. Hans Kelsen played a crucial role in establishing this institution. It is important to take into account that historical antecedents of such an organ were courts adjudicating conflicts between the central government and the *Länder* in the Austro-Hungarian Empire, as well as in the Holy German Empire (*Reichskammergericht*).

[8] This is even more clearly the case when a constitutional court construes a statute in light of constitutional values. Kelsen hesitated in defining the role of the constitutional court. At the beginning he spoke of "negative legislation," but later on, answering C. Schmitt, he accepted in his book *Wer soll der Hüter der Verfassung sein?* (1931) that the court plays a positive legislative function. See Pasquino (1994).

regulating social conduct. As a result, Kelsen thought that constitutional courts should be placed outside the judiciary as well as the other governmental departments. Their powers were to be exercised by politically appointed judges, usually drawn from people particularly competent at making abstract comparisons among texts, and with the capacity to deliberate about norms and explain decisions, and not necessarily from those with judicial experience.

## Constitutional Adjudication in Postauthoritarian Regimes

Kelsen's ideas have proved especially attractive to postauthoritarian regimes. Not only were they adopted in Austria, Germany, Italy, and Spain, but they have also taken root throughout Eastern Europe. Each of the postauthoritarian constitutions put in place institutions of constitutional adjudication that permitted constitutional review of legislative, executive, and judicial acts.[9] But in each of these cases, the very fact that there was a transition under way from an old and distrusted regime to a new one, meant that judges were viewed with particular suspicion, as potential holders of constitutional review authority.[10] As a result, there were powerful political reasons, in addition to the theoretical arguments that Kelsen offered, to place constitutional adjudication outside the judiciary – in effect the reviewing body was placed above each of the other institutions in position to review any governmental action from a constitutional perspective – and give it to a specialized and politically appointed body.

While Kelsen emphasized abstract constitutional review, all of the modern postauthoritarian constitutional courts have been given concrete a posteriori review powers as well. Access to these courts is controlled not only by governments and political minorities, but also by ordinary litigants in the context of specific cases or, as in Italy, by ordinary lawcourts. Thus courts may be asked, in a Kelsenian fashion, to compare constitutional and statutory texts abstractly (by direct referral of constitutional issues), or they may be presented with a constitutional issue that arises in an ongoing case before a lower court, or they may be presented with a whole decided case (as happens in both Spain and

---

[9] Perhaps the same distinction would be illuminating in postauthoritarian regimes in Latin America or Eastern Europe.

[10] The judiciaries of each of these systems are essentially closed career hierarchies that are particularly insulated from outside influence. This extreme insulation of judges made it even less likely that important additional powers would be vested in them following the collapse of authoritarianism.

Germany).[11] In any of these situations, the actual authority to nullify or modify legislation is generally concentrated in the constitutional court and not dispersed throughout the judiciary. If an ordinary court doubts the constitutionality of a law, it must stay the proceedings before it and refer the question to the constitutional court for determination.[12]

The makeup of these constitutional courts is distinctive as well. Because the separation-of-powers systems tend to have dispersed and concrete review, ordinary judges can be expected to develop competence in constitutional adjudication. In postauthoritarian systems, however, where constitutional review is concentrated and often abstract, ordinary judges have no special claims to position. Moreover, because of their authoritarian pasts, judges in these systems were at least initially distrusted as arbiters of constitutional and democratic values. Thus, in all of the postauthoritarian systems, law professors tend to occupy many of the seats on the court together with some judges.

### Preserving Parliamentary Sovereignty: The French Conseil Constitutionel

The institution of constitutional review in the French Fifth Republic is worth considering separately. The French republican tradition is solidly in the parliamentary sovereignty tradition and it has been hostile to constitutional adjudication since the Revolution.[13] But De Gaulle and his supporters insisted on placing institutional restraints on Parliament, and one of these was the Conseil Constitutionel. Within the parliamentary sovereignty system, the only way that this could be done was to place the court effectively within the legislature. Thus, to a greater extent than Kelsen recommended, this placement emphasized the Conseil's legislative function. It is permitted to review statutes only prior to their promulgation, and then only on referral from the government or significant political minorities of deputies or senators. Thus, legislative proposals cannot become law if the Conseil strikes them down. But, the Conseil has no capacity to review a statute after it has become law, and regular courts are not empowered to undertake constitutional

---

[11] This is the traditional practice also for appeals to the European Court for Human Rights in Strasbourg, which reviews cases only after litigants exhaust domestically available remedies. With the incorporation of the European Convention on Human Rights, domestic courts increasingly give direct application to human rights law.

[12] The same practices are followed by courts applying European Community Law.

[13] The Convention unanimously rejected in 1795 a project presented by Sieyes of introducing a *jury constitutionnaire*. See Pasquino (1998: 95).

review in the course of ordinary litigation. In the French view, the legislature is sovereign and subject to no external checking, certainly not by judges, and not by a constitutional court either. Rather, the constitutional court, by acting as part of the legislature itself, plays an essential role in preserving the idea of legislative sovereignty. Legislative action cannot occur in the presence of an objection by the Conseil and, once it takes place, is unchecked by constitutional mechanisms.

Because French legislative proposals cannot become law in the presence of Conseil refusal, if it is requested (and this virtually always at the request of a political minority appealing against government sponsored legislation), constitutional review must take place immediately after the legislative action and in the face of a sitting government whose proposed law has been challenged. This means such review has to happen quickly and, in view of the majoritarian nature of French political institutions and political culture, in a potentially politically charged situation. By contrast, constitutional challenges to U.S. statutes must await a case raising the issue in a genuine manner, and this often occurs long after the legislature that enacted the statute has disappeared. In postauthoritarian systems, such as Germany, Spain, and Italy, constitutional courts cannot prevent a law from going into effect, even while reviewing it a priori. Thus, unlike the French situation, because the government is enforcing the disputed law, there is not much political pressure to resolve constitutional issues quickly (indeed, political pressures might work in the opposite direction), and so even a priori review may take place after the heat of political battle is somewhat dissipated.

### A Summary Overview of Constitutional Adjudication in Europe

Roughly speaking, we may describe the institutional situation of constitutional courts as situated along a single dimension, with pure parliamentary sovereign regimes, such as Britain or the French Third and Fourth Republics at the left and a Montesquieuian separation-of-powers regime on the right. Between these two poles is a variety of constitutional systems that mix aspects of legislative supremacy with other more or less independent institutions. Parliamentary sovereignty regimes, by definition, regard both the executive and the courts as subordinated to the legislature, implementing and enforcing its commands. The notion of judicial review of legislation is, for this reason, completely alien to such legal regimes and, as a result, the way in which legal institutions can lead to statutory revision takes on a particular institutional form in such settings.

By definition, a parliamentary sovereignty regime must place any constitutional review that takes place inside the legislature. Otherwise the parliament would not be sovereign. This implies that in parliamentary sovereignty regimes constitutional review can only be *a priori* – prior to the promulgation of a legislative proposal as law – and *abstract*, in the sense of involving only the comparison of legislative and constitutional texts. Moreover, in such systems, while advice as to constitutional principles may be widely sought, the authority to invoke constitutional principles will have to be concentrated in a small number of hands internal to the legislature. Thus, traditionally, in Britain, France, and Sweden whatever constitutional review takes place must occur wholly inside the legislature. Constitutional norms lack direct legal authority (unless they are embodied in statutes). Such review may be concentrated in an upper chamber, which may have some kind of negative legislative authority (such as a suspensive veto), or in a judicial committee of some kind, or perhaps in a separate institution such as the French Conseil d'Etat, which can advise the legislature on constitutional issues.

And as we have seen, the French Fifth Republic has devised what some observers have termed a third legislative chamber – the Conseil Constitutionel – that can modify or veto proposed legislation before it may be promulgated as law (Stone 1992: 209–21). While the Conseil was originally invented by the Gaullists as a way of "rationalizing" or controlling Parliament, it has evolved to permit general constitutional review of governmental legislative proposals.[14] In any case, parliamentary sovereignty requires that, wherever the review or advice originates, the authority to apply constitutional principles to legislation rests with the legislature itself.

Division-of-powers regimes, again by definition, hold the legislative, executive, and judicial powers to be separated horizontally rather than

---

[14] This transition occurred at two critical moments in recent French history. First, in 1971 the Conseil asserted the authority to strike down governmental legislation based on broad (and uncodified) constitutional principles. In the particular case, the Conseil asserted that there was a right to free assembly that could be discerned from the "fundamental principles underlying the republic." In the same opinion, the 1789 Declaration of the Rights of Man and the preamble to the 1946 Constitution were elevated to the status of constitutional norms that could be used to overturn legislative proposals. The second critical moment occurred in 1974 when the government, fearing electoral defeat, successfully urged a constitutional amendment permitting any sixty members of the legislature to refer legislation to the Conseil Constitutionel. Thus, after 1974, the Conseil focused increasingly on reviewing governmental initiatives with the powerful constitutional tools it created in 1971.

vertically, and such regimes tend to attribute constitutional authority to institutions exercising each of these powers. Montesquieu, of course, famously defined tyranny as a circumstance without separated powers, arguing that undivided powers inevitably produced arbitrary and unpredictable rule. He thought it particularly important that courts, when applying law to particular cases, were not legislating in any important sense. The judicial power was, in this sense, a *pouvoir null*. But this did not mean that judges (or, perhaps more precisely, juries) exercised no discretion in applying the laws. A court could refuse to apply a law to a particular case if its application would produce injustice. This would not nullify or abolish the law but would set its effects aside in the case. This kind of review authority, the power to interpret law and facts in application, produces a characteristic kind of judicial review that is quite distinct from that found in parliamentary sovereignty regimes. Review authority is dispersed throughout the judiciary – any court must interpret the law, constitutional or statutory, in order to apply it. It is exercised in the context of concrete cases and is neither abstract nor a priori. Finally, it is not legislative in the sense that laws are not abolished but only refused application to the case (and, depending on the legal system, to "similar" cases).[15]

As an example, Article III of the U.S. Constitution places the Supreme Court at the head of the federal judicial department and permits the federal judicial power to be exercised only in genuine cases or controversies.[16] When Congress created other federal courts, the judicial power – which includes the power to review statutes – was vested in them as well. The U.S. system of constitutional adjudication is, in this respect completely different from the French and most other European models. Courts, in applying statutes, must always read them in view of the Constitution and never apply them in ways that would violate constitutional protections. In view of these requirements statutes are often given interpretations fitting them into the constitutional scheme and are occasionally given no authority at all. Although such actions may have something like legislative effects, they do not formally change or eliminate

---

[15] The "nonlegislative" character of judicial review is a theoretical idea. Judicial systems with dispersed review will typically give order and predictability to judicial actions by devising methods of hierarchical control of lower courts that create coherent rules or doctrines out of diverse decisions. The effect of such developments is to make judicial action more legislative as statutory rules are supplemented with judicially crafted ones.

[16] In many respects, the Norwegian system of constitutional adjudication resembles the American in that such review takes place in concrete cases and is dispersed throughout ordinary courts.

statutory texts in the manner of the French system. Unconstitutional statutes are not repealed or eliminated. They are simply given no application to particular disputes. Putting matters this way emphasizes the judicial rather than legislative aspects of judicial review.[17]

## Political Conflict and the Rule of Law

However vague they may be as concepts, democracy and legality represent very widely shared values. So it is common and natural for political disputants to invoke them in aid of their own arguments. For example, the recent fight over the Clinton impeachment was frequently put by the Republicans as a matter of rule of law. They saw blatant populist hypocrisy in the willingness to overlook the illegal actions of a popular president. But, given the nature of the alleged transgressions and the issue of whether they would justify the particular "legal" sanction sought, the case suggests that the real issues were much more mundane and political. Even though the president did lie in various legal settings, it is a fundamentally political question whether such action justifies conviction and removal from office.

Perhaps of more constitutional significance was the conflict between the New Deal Congresses and Supreme Court during the mid 1930s. A majority on that Court saw New Deal legislation as threatening profound constitutional values, and these justices regarded themselves as obliged to strike down many of these statutes. But it seems clear that the reading of the Constitution advanced by these justices – one that placed protection of property rights and freedom of contracting at its core – was only one possible (and politically controversial) reading and not at all required by adherence to rule-of-law values. As these justices were replaced and their substantive reading of the Constitution faded, the conflict between legal and democratic values diminished – at least for a time. Putting things this way seems to place the onus for the conflict on ideologically conservative judges, but the blame might as well be put on Roosevelt and his allies for advancing a populistic conception of democracy that licensed trampling on fundamental rights of property by mere acts of majority will. The point is that the conflict is better understood as one between defenders of property rights as central to the Constitution, and those who wanted to permit majorities to regulate and manage those rights.

---

[17] It is a matter of some uncertainty whether an unconstitutional statute may be revived or whether the legislature is required to act again.

Later on the development of constitutional theories that placed civil liberties and civil rights as core constitutional values produced new tensions of roughly the same sort. Courts attempted to protect certain kinds of rights against majoritarian incursions. This time, however, it was a liberal Court that tried to restrain popular majorities that sought to limit freedoms of speech, religion, and political association. The rapid inversion of the ideological placement of the Court and political institutions, where the court was shifted away from economic to political liberties, shows that the issues were not so much conceptual but were institutional manifestations of more fundamental political disagreements. In a word, the makeup of the Court had shifted sharply in a liberal direction.

There is a second, institutional, source of conflict between politicians and judges that may also, misleadingly, be attributed to the tension between democracy and legality. Politicians want to build popular support for themselves and their policies. They attempt this by making or proposing policies (depending whether they are in or out of office) aimed at convincing others to support them. To do this, they need to fight a battle on two fronts. First, they need to compete with opposing politicians for political support. Second, while in office they need to establish the power to make or change policies. Here is where they may come into conflict with law and judges. Because judges value legality both intrinsically and as the principal source of their own authority, they are particularly disposed to take an expansive view of legal requirements. This desire is independent of any particular ideological values they may have. Because their desire for expansive authority conflicts with the interests of political officials capable of diminishing judicial authority, its pursuit must (in any political system) be tempered by institutional considerations. Like the first (ideological) conflict, the institutional conflict is political in the sense that it is rooted in desires to maintain or increase authority and is not necessarily connected to norms of legality themselves.

A few other observations seem worth making. Politicians and judges have interests as individuals as well as institutionally defined interests so that one would not ordinarily expect a head-on or sharp dispute between the two organizations. Most often, we would expect ideological and institutional interests to be crosscutting so that neither judges nor politicians will be able to pursue their common institutional interests in a single-minded fashion. Moreover, each organization will experience collective action problems as well. Second, it seems likely that judges will find it easier to act on the basis of common institutional interests than legislators. This is so for two reasons. Judiciaries are more or less hierarchically organized so that higher level courts are in position to coordinate the actions of other courts.[18] Moreover, because of common training and general expectations about appropriate judicial behavior, judges are probably likely to express and be motivated by more or less shared norms of legality. Even though many of these norms are disputed, even within the judiciary, there seems likely to be more overlap among them than among the values shared by competing politicians.

Still, despite these organizational differences, political conflicts are often articulated as disputes about democracy and legality. Indeed, we think that the tendency for such articulation is probably increasing over time, in Europe as well as the United States. Part of the reason for this is that, as we have argued, the rule of democracy – policy making by a preeminent and unchallenged legislature – has been losing ground pretty steadily over the past fifty years and probably longer. The causes of this loss have been various, but the widening acceptance of some kinds of fundamental human rights that can be vindicated in courtrooms surely must play a part. But it is important to recognize that as we place legal restraints on legislatures, we pay a price. That price is in diminishing the capacity of the legislature to intervene forcefully in the economy and social system in order to correct the inequities and dislocations that occur there. Rights can be threatened by private (social or economic) sources too, and legislative remedy has been, historically, the only road to correcting these interferences. Such intervention invariably involves threatening claimed rights – of property holders, or of possessors of social privilege – and so often raises constitutional objections. A good example of this was the attempt of the French government to nationalize various industries following the Socialist victories in 1981. The French Constitutional Council promptly stalled this attempt and required that the government pay more adequate compensation to achieve its objective. While this demand might have been justifiable, it surely raised the price of the nationalizations to the government.

Perhaps legal institutions can do some of the job of protecting rights from private interference as well as governmental infringement. Constitutional courts in Europe have proved to be remarkably effective in expanding the range of constitutionally protected rights. But managing "private" action seems to require legislation in order to define rights that courts can help protect. If injustice arises as much from private as

---

[18] This is probably true even in court systems without a *stare decisis* norm and in which constitutional courts are separated from the regular court system.

from public activity, therefore, we have a need for rule of democracy as well as rule of law.

## References

Coke, Edward. 1670. *An Exact Abridgment of the Two Last Volumes of Reports of Sir Edw. Coke*. London: H. and T. Twyford.

Ferejohn, John. 1999. "Independent Judges, Dependent Judiciary." *Southern California Law Review*, 72, 2–3: 353–84.

Hobbes, Thomas. 1971. *A Dialogue between a Philosopher and a Student of the Common Laws of England*. Chicago: University of Chicago Press.

Ketchum, Ralph (ed.). 1986. *The Anti-Federalist Papers and the Constitutional Convention Debates*. New York: Mentor.

Pasquino, Pasquale. 1994. "Gardien de la constitution ou justice constitutionnelle? C. Schmitt et H. Kelsen." In M. Troper and L. Jaume (eds.), *1789 et l'Invention de la Constitution*, 141–52. Paris: Bruylant L.G.D.J.

1998. *Sieyes et l'invention de la constitution en France*. Paris: Odile Jacob.

Stone, Alec. 1992. *The Birth of Judicial Politics in France: The Constitutional Council in Comparative Perspective*. New York: Oxford University Press.

Tocqueville, Alexis de. 1945. *Democracy in America*. Vol. 1. New York: Vintage.

## Chapter Eleven

# The Rule of Law as a Political Weapon

Let us assume that politicians want to be in office and to maximize their autonomy in decision making. On the other side, citizens want to avoid abuses by politicians. Citizens have two instruments to protect them: first, to throw the rulers out of office at election time; second, to enforce, through institutions, legal limits to the political discretion of incumbents between elections. The first protection is provided by democracy; the second, by the rule of law.[1] Prima facie they complement each other. Citizens are not just interested in electing politicians who, once in office, are controlled only by the prospect of future elections; they are not interested either in unelected, nonrepresentative rulers, even if bounded by laws passed by an undemocratic assembly.

I use here a minimalist definition of the rule of law. It consists of the enforcement of laws that have been publicly promulgated and passed in a preestablished manner; are prospective (*nulla poena sine lege*), general (like cases are treated alike), stable, clear, and hierarchically ordered (the more particular norms conform to the more general ones); and are applied to particular cases by courts independent from the political rulers and open to all, whose decisions respond to procedural requirements, and that establish guilt through the ordinary trial process. This definition makes no reference to fundamental rights, democracy,

---

[1] Democracies operate under binding laws that guarantee the rules of the game. These laws not only limit the discretionary power of politicians; they also enable them. If, for instance, a law empowers parliament with the possibility of bringing down a government with a motion of no confidence, it introduces control over the latter but enables the former. Yet, all enabling laws establish limits: the three conditions of the minimalist, "rulebook" conception of the rule of law that restrict politicians' decisions.

I wish to thank Andrew Richards, Carlos Maravall, Belén Barreiro, Sonia Alonso, Ignacio Sánchez-Cuenca, and Adam Przeworski for their comments.

equality, or justice: it corresponds to what Dworkin (1985: 9–32) has termed the "rulebook" conception of the rule of law.[2]

My intention is to discuss how, under particular political and institutional conditions, politicians can turn democracy against the rule of law, and vice versa. Their strategic instruments are majoritarianism and judicial independence. I shall examine, more particularly, the strategic use of judicial decisions by politicians in order to subvert democracy and the rules and conditions of political competition. The focus will be on politicians and judges as the main actors in the scenario: on the strategies of the first, on the political independence and impartiality of the second. The media and economic actors will also play an important role. Citizens will be in the shadows, standing in the background of the stage, trying to figure out with incomplete information what politicians do in order to react with their votes at election time. The relation of forces, then, will mostly have to do with institutions (and the elites that inhabit them), rather than with the distribution of electoral support.

I understand by "judicialization of justice" something very different from "judicial activism." The latter refers to courts expanding their decisions to matters that corresponded to political agencies, or acting as arbiters between political contenders. Judicial activism will expand in situations of political gridlock: this is what Ferejohn and Pasquino (Chapter 10 in this volume) study. Politics becomes judicialized when courts become actors in political strategies that alter the rules of democratic competition. Such strategies include the use of courts to criminalize political adversaries.

The conditions for democracy or the rule of law not to be an equilibrium have been discussed by models à la Przeworski (1991) and Weingast (1997). We know much less about situations in which politicians judicialize politics in order to modify the results of democratic competition, while democracy and the rule of law are maintained. I use three arguments to interpret such situations. These arguments do not refer to conditions that are both necessary and sufficient: that is, politicians may or may not embark on the actions that I examine, but if they do, the conditions should be present. In the first two arguments, the judicialization of politics is a strategy of the opposition; in the third, the government carries the initiative.

---

[2] This definition in no way assumes that the rule of law is better served when the legal limits to the incumbent's powers are more extensive. Its operation requires only that the law is systematically enforced according to the mentioned three conditions, not that politicians have their hands tied.

The first argument is that, if the accountability of politicians is limited, the probability that politics becomes judicialized increases. Incentives for the opposition to embark on such a strategy will be great, unless it colludes with the government or fears reprisals. Institutions that provide insulation to strong executives or promote coalitions hardly removable by elections may restrict the accountability of incumbents. If elections are the only mechanism for enforcing political responsibility, if politicians turn electoral victories into exonerative devices, and if between elections they respond only to legal responsibilities, then parliament becomes irrelevant and political confrontation is transferred to a judicial terrain. If politicians collude, independent judges will take the initiative if they have powerful support from media and interest groups; if politicians do not collude, the strategy will be launched by the opposition. The likelihood of collusion increases if the opposition expects an electoral victory: in that case, it may be interested in preserving the conditions of limited accountability (an insulated executive, the control of public television, and so on).

The second one goes as follows. Suppose that government and opposition do not collude, and that the latter complies with democratic outcomes because it expects to have some chance of winning the elections in the future. Yet, when that expected future (i.e., the best imaginable conditions for electoral victory) arrives, the opposition loses again. This opposition may conclude that it cannot win under the present rules of competition. This may or may not be due to a lack of accountability of the government. Different circumstances can give a persistent advantage to the incumbent: elections may be strongly ideological and the median voter may be with the government; the leader of the ruling party can be very popular. The opposition, however, does not turn to dictatorship: it introduces new dimensions of competition in which judicial activism becomes instrumental.[3] In Riker's (1982: 209) terms, "this is the art of politics: to find some alternative that beats the current winner."

In the third argument the strategy is carried out by the government. Under particular political and institutional conditions, with independent but not neutral judges, a government may manipulate judicial activism in order to consolidate its power and weaken the opposition. This strategy depends on whether the government finds stronger support within the judiciary than in the electorate and believes that its

---

[3] This is related to Przeworski's (Chapter 5 in this volume) argument on the manipulation of rules. Party A will prefer democracy with new, more favorable rules to the extent that party B is indifferent to democracy or dictatorship.

electoral vulnerability will persist in the future. Hence the value that the government attaches to the probability of winning in the future under the present conditions of competition is lower than the value attributed to the probability of winning after the politicization of the judiciary minus the risk of failure.[4] A government can then try to modify in its favor the balance of power and influence, using the rule of law against political opponents. The target may be the parliamentary opposition, hostile interest groups, or critical media.

## Beyond Stereotypes

If politicians can undermine the rule of law with democratic instruments, subvert democracy, or alter the conditions of competition with strategies that use the independence of judges, then the combination of democracy and the rule of law will simply be a normative stereotype, not reflecting well the real world of politics. This rhetorical stereotype is, however, routinely reiterated in the constitutions of new democracies.[5]

For instance, the Spanish Constitution of 1978 defines the new regime as a "social and democratic state of law"[6] (article 1, paragraph 1). And the Russian Constitution of 1993 speaks of a "democratic federative rule-of-law state" (article 1). We also find this normative stereotype in many political analyses. Thus, O'Donnell (1999: 321, 318) writes that

> Democracy is not only a (polyarchical) political regime but also a particular mode of relationship between state and citizens, and among citizens themselves, under a kind of rule of law that, in addition to political citizenship, upholds civil citizenship and a full network of accountability.... All agents, public and private, including the highest placed officials of the regime, are subject to appropriate, legally established controls of the lawfulness of their acts.

---

[4] The risk of failure includes the judicial rejection of the strategy, as well as retaliation by the adversary if it can find sympathies within the judiciary. The assessment of risks becomes more uncertain when the judiciary is very decentralized (and "judicial power" is an attribute of every individual judge).

[5] Examples, among many, can be found in the 1991 Constitution of Bulgaria (preamble); the 1991 Constitution of Slovakia (chapter 1, article 1); the 1992 Constitution of the Czech Republic (chapter 1, article 1); or the 1997 Constitution of Poland (article 2).

[6] The expression used is that of *Estado de Derecho*, the translation of the German *Rechtsstaat*. I shall not differentiate between this concept and that of the "rule of law."

We know the components of this normative ideal. Nobody will be above the law; citizens will be protected against discretionary abuses of politicians; the use of power will be predictable; the vertical accountability of democracy will be complemented by the horizontal accountability of divided powers, the checks and balances typical of political liberalism. Moreover, the rule of law will reinforce the control of citizens over their rulers' representativeness in two ways.[7] First, independent courts will correct the myopia of democratic governments, mitigating "the influences of the short term ... (the) violent swings and panic measures of legislatures concerned with re-election" (Raz 1994: 260). Second, independent courts will facilitate the monitoring of rulers, providing citizens with information via the mutual vigilance of separate powers. In this ideal world, democracy and an independent judiciary do not just coexist in harmony: they support each other.

This appears to be the happy end of two institutional arrangements that were historically in conflict. Born in the common-law tradition[8] when the British parliament imposed legal limits to the power of an already weakened crown in order to protect private rights (and, more particularly, private property), the rule of law became an instrument to protect individuals from the "tyranny" of majorities. That is, it became a countermajoritarian, antidemocratic device. In Madison's famous statement, "democracies have ever been spectacles of turbulence and contention; have ever been found incompatible with personal security or the rights of property" (*Federalist Papers* 10). Elected governments, in the name of the majority, could infringe individual rights, expropriate property, redistribute resources, intervene in the economy. The law was an instrument to prevent political intrusions in personal freedoms and private property. As Tocqueville (1969: 287) put it, "the courts correct the aberrations of democracy." The view of democracy as a threat and of the rule of law as a guarantee against redistribution was reiterated from Dicey's original definition in 1885 onward. Remember Hayek (1994: 87–8): "any policy aiming directly at a substantive ideal of distributive justice must lead to the destruction of the Rule of Law.... It

---

[7] I consider a politician to be "representative" when his decisions are taken in the best interests of voters: that is, voters would have made the same choice, if their information was symmetrical, and their preferences were not time-inconsistent or myopic. See Manin, Przeworski, and Stokes (1999: 29–54).

[8] In the civil-law tradition of continental Europe, the law was an instrument that the state used to expand its power, rather than a restriction on public officials. The two major state builders, Napoleon and Bismarck, massively expanded the legal systems of France and Germany.

cannot be denied that the Rule of Law produces economic inequality."
Democracy and economic redistribution were the dangers to be avoided.
This is why, over a long time, the left distrusted the rule of law (Shklar
1987): any strategy of transforming capitalism had to challenge the rule
of law as a bourgeois device. It was only after a long experience of dictatorships and violations of civil rights that the left defended the rule
of law as the self-binding of rulers, compatible both with majority rule
through elections (democracy) and with socioeconomic reforms (social
democracy).

Democracy and the rule of law, however, can provide opportunities
and incentives for politicians to subvert each other. Either majoritarianism or judicial independence will provide the instruments. That is,
the original institutional conflict may be activated by politicians' strategies: the rule of law and democracy can undermine each other through
politics. The central point of this chapter is the political manipulation of
judicial independence.[9] To quote Madison again, "if men were angels,
no government would be necessary. If angels were to govern men, neither external nor internal controls on government would be necessary"
(*Federalist Papers* 51). But why would membership of the judiciary be
restricted to angels? Judicial independence has generally been seen as
protection from the government or the legislative majority: if rulers are
to be controlled, the checks provided by the rule of law must be immune
to their influence. But the protected checkers are unchecked. *Quis custo-
diet ipsos custodes* is the weak spot in the role attributed to the rule of
law in liberal democratic theory. Examining judges in America in 1835,
Tocqueville (1969: 206) wrote that "The arbitrary power of democratic
magistrates is even greater than that of their counterparts in despotic
states.... Nowhere has the law left greater scope to arbitrary power
than in democratic republics, because there they feel they have nothing
to fear from it."

In the legal tradition of continental Europe, the limit to the power of
judges was the law. Judges were to act just as *la bouche de la loi*; their
power was to be "as null" (Montesquieu 1951: 401). The Enlightment

[9] Judicial independence usually means that judicial decisions cannot be overturned by
retroactive legislation or by appeals to the parliament or the government; judges cannot be removed or promoted by decisions external to the judicial system; judicial
procedure must be stable, not under constant revision by the legislature or the government; legislative and executive acts must be open to judicial review; and the "doctrine of precedent" and *stare decisis et not quieta movere* must be respected (previous
decisions by superior courts are binding and contain a *ratio decidendi*: what has been
settled must be applied to subsequent cases, and can only be reviewed by a higher
court).

and Jacobinism, reacting against the despotism of the crown, also mistrusted the magistrates of the ancien régime. The inheritence transmitted from the French Revolution was the supremacy of the legislature. And in order to avoid the excessive power of an unelected judiciary, the application of the law was to be a mechanical execution of the will of parliament.

But this limit to judicial power is a very loose one. First, constitutional control of legislation increased such power. Exerted by the United States Supreme Court since the beginning of the nineteenth century, this control was introduced in many civil-law countries when democracy was reestablished: for instance, in the German Federal Republic and Italy after 1945; in Greece and Spain in the 1970s. Second, laws often do not have a clear, univocal meaning. If judges must interpret norms that carry a "penumbra of uncertainty" (Hart 1958: 607), their interpretation may come close to legislation.

It is obvious that differences remain between judicial interpretation and legislation. For example, judicial decisions are framed in preexisting and publicly known laws (principle of legality); they must be justified by facts and norms (principle of impartiality); judicial activity follows an initiative undertaken by an external actor (*ne precedat judex ex officio*); sentences are preceded by hearings of the parties involved in the case (principle of contradiction). But the judiciary contributes to creating law, in civil-law countries as well; it is not just a brake on political power, but exercises political power – hence, the problem posed by unchecked checkers in democracies.[10]

The accountability of the judiciary has been examined from two additional, very different perspectives. One is normative: if we see the rule of law as inseparable from a political theory of rights, judges do not just enforce laws but follow principles. That is, they use their discretion deciding on legal issues according to the best theory of justice; they are constrained by an ideal of law, based on "an accurate public conception of individual rights" (Dworkin 1985: 11–21). Besides, because of their public visibility, judges may be the object of criticism by public opinion, which limits their discretion (Raz 1994: 358–9). We know, in fact, that judicial decisions generally reflect public opinion: either judges are influenced by it, or they seek popular acquiescence with their

---

[10] To quote Radin (1989: 796), "If rules do not tie judges' hands with their logical or analytical application, the traditional view is that judges will have personal discretion in how to apply the law.... It will also confer on judges a realm of 'arbitrary power' and undermine democracy.... The government is a Leviathan to be restrained. Yet ... judges are even more in need of restraint."

decisions.[11] Judges must also stay "attuned to the support and expansion of the polyarchy" (O'Donnell 1999: 317). No instruments, however, ensure that these exhortations are followed; principles of justice alone would be seen as a weak protection if the suspects were politicians. And the control of judges by public opinion is not of great relevance in most of the strategies that I examine here. These strategies are based not on recurrent judicial decisions but on exceptional ones, with effects intended to be lethal for the adversary.[12]

The other perspective is administrative: checks on the checkers are internal. These checks refer in particular to the divisions between, and the hierarchy of, courts; also to corporatist guarantees, such as the training, recruitment, and professional incompatibilities of judges; finally, to disciplinary action and legal liability that restrict prevarication. But these checks are always enforced by the checkers themselves: if the rule of law limits abuses by politicians, no democratic accountability exists for judges.

Judges, invulnerable to political pressures from other branches of the state, may have political interests of their own. We do not know why the judiciary – protected, unchecked, and unaccountable – would be politically impartial and neutral. Yet losers may still accept biased judicial decisions if they expect that the composition of the judiciary, and its partial activism, can be reversed in the future, and if they consider other alternatives (i.e., noncompliance) to be worse. Judges operate in scenarios where other actors play: politicians in government or in opposition, individuals who control mass media or vast economic resources. Multiple interests crisscross in this scenario. As Guarnieri and Pederzoli

---

[11] On the first reason, see Rehnquist (1986: 752, 768): "[I]t would be very wrong to say that judges are not influenced by public opinion.... judges go home at night and read the newspapers or watch the evening news on television; they talk to their family and friends about current events. Somewhere 'out there' – beyond the walls of the courthouse – run currents and tides of public opinion which lap at the courthouse door." On the second, remember Justice Frankfurter's words: "The Court's authority – possessed of neither the purse nor the sword – ultimately rests on sustained public confidence in its moral sanction" (*Baker v. Carr*, 1962). Evidence on the U.S. Supreme Court shows that "the individual justices follow shifts in public mood" (Flemming and Wood 1997: 493), the lag involved in that influence is debated, and the effect seems to be more noticeable in moderate judges that hold critical swing positions within the Supreme Court (Mishler and Sheehan 1993, 1996). A different view, of course, is that judicial decisions influence public opinion: the public listens to courts and supports their decisions. See Dahl (1957), Franklin and Kosaki (1989), Hoekstra and Segal (1996). In this case, the judiciary would hardly be controlled by public opinion.

[12] That close to 60% of voters disapproved of Kenneth Starr's methods as independent counsel and that less than one-third supported the impeachment of Clinton did not stop Starr. See Sonner and Wilcox (1999: 554–7).

(1999: 57) put it, "The rupture of most institutional connections with the political system and the looser hierarchical links have indeed ensured particularly high levels of internal and external independence; they have not prevented, but rather facilitated, a network of connections, often hardly visible and with little transparence, that can undermine the autonomy of the magistrature."

Politicians, either in government or in opposition, will devise strategies and search for allies to achieve their political goals. Such strategies cannot ignore judges, these unchecked agents whose decisions are binding. I do not discuss in this chapter why politicians comply or do not comply with the law, but why and how they will deploy to their advantage strategies of conflict between the rule of law (more particularly, an independent judiciary) and democracy (majoritarian political support). We know well two kinds of strategies: one in which politicians use democracy to subordinate the judiciary and to overcome the limits set by the rule of law; another in which politicians use existing norms and independent judges to undermine democracy as a regime. In both, either the rule of law or democracy are not an equilibrium: they are subverted by politics. We know much less well strategies in which, although democracy is preserved, the independence of judges is turned into a political instrument to get rid of an opponent if the rules of democratic competition are not enough. I therefore concentrate more on the latter.

Politicians will politicize the independence of judges when the payoffs of this strategy appear to be higher than those of the alternative – respecting the mutual autonomy of judges and politicians. The probability of success will be assessed, together with the risk of costs, particularly a future effective retaliation by the adversary. Probabilities and risks ultimately depend on the political balance of forces: votes when the target is the rule of law; sympathies and complicities that politicians may have within an independent but not neutral judiciary when the target is either democracy as a regime or the conditions of political competition. The strategies of two actors, an opposition and a government, can be analyzed as a dynamic game with complete information: that is, as a sequential-move game in which the players' payoffs are known, and whose outcome can be established by backward induction. Strategies and payoffs are represented in the following game tree (Figure 11.1), in which actor 1 is the opposition (O) and actor 2 is the government (G).

Because a strategy of retaliation, whatever its outcome, involves costs, the order of preferences of actor 1 is $O_4 > O_2 > O_3 > O_1$. The reverse order is that of actor 2. A subgame-perfect equilibrium constructed

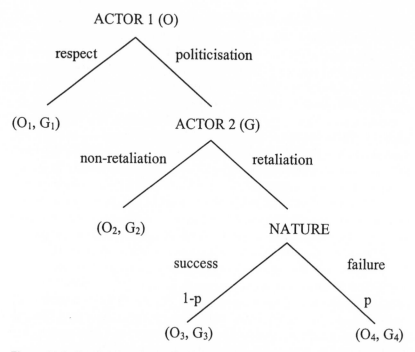

Figure 11.1. Strategies and payoffs in a sequential-move game in which actor 1 is the opposition (O) and actor 2 is the government (G).

in the following manner captures the former arguments. To start with, payoffs are assigned in the third stage in case actor 2 retaliates. The probabilities (p) of success and failure of retaliation depend on the balance of forces, which is given by nature (i.e., it is unrelated to the strategies of the actors). For actor 2 (G), the payoff is $pG_4 + (1-p) G_3$. Hence, in the second stage, actor 2 (G) will not retaliate if $G_2 > pG_4 + (1-p) G_3$. Finally, in the first stage, given the assumed payoff structure so far, actor 1 prefers politicization to respect, as $O_2 > O_1$. Thus, by construction, a subgame-perfect Nash equilibrium is politicization (by actor 1) and nonretaliation (by actor 2).

## Subverting the Rule of Law on the Grounds of Democracy

In democracy, if rulers confront independent courts, they will do so when they enjoy a broad mandate, the opposition is weak, and the credibility of the legal system and the courts is low. The probability of success of their strategies will then be high, and the risk of retaliation limited.

The institutions of the rule of law will be presented as opposed to democracy, to what Tocqueville (1969: 246) called "the absolute sovereignty of the will of the majority."

This is the liberal nightmare about democracy: when no boundaries of legality contain the whims of the majority. This is also a central mark of "delegative democracies": for governments, "other institutions – courts and legislatures, for instance – are nuisances.... Accountability to such institutions appears as a mere impediment" (O'Donnell 1994: 60). The usual suspect is the plebiscitarian populist politician, of which there are endless examples. A well-known one is President Juan Domingo Perón in Argentina, on whose behalf crowds shouted in the streets "even if a thief we want Perón" (*aunque sea un ladrón queremos a Perón*). Another one, also from Argentina, is President Carlos Menem: enjoying an overwhelming mandate, he changed the composition of the Supreme Court. With two-thirds of its members under his command, the Court was no longer independent but an obedient instrument.[13] Menem incarnated for this Supreme Court the "sovereign will of the nation";[14] as one of its members put it, "my only two bosses are Perón and Menem.... I cannot have an interpretation which is contrary to the government" (Larkins 1998: 428–9). This subordination of the judiciary contradicted hopes that, with democracy, courts would become an independent and effective instrument to redress abuses and solve claims.[15] As a result, the prestige of courts collapsed: while in 1984 42% of citizens had little or no confidence in them, in 1991 the percentage had risen to 71%, and in 1996 it had reached 89% (Smulovitz 2002). A third example is President Hugo Chávez in Venezuela. Following his 1999 electoral landslide, Chávez and his parliamentary majority embarked on a purge of judges. A decree of judicial emergency allowed the new Assembly

---

[13] Menem also changed the attorney general of the state and most members of the Tribunal of Public Accounts.

[14] Sentence of the Argentinian Supreme Court on decree 36/90 that introduced the Bonex Plan. According to this plan, savings in private bank accounts exceeding one million australes ($610) had to be invested in state bonds, in order to finance the internal public debt.

[15] Such hopes led to a multiplication of claims presented to different courts, to the National Ombudsman Office (Defensoría del Pueblo de la Nación), and to the Municipal Ombudsman Office (Controladuría General Comunal). Judicial cases also became widely publicized by the media. On this discovery of courts by citizens and media, see Smulovitz (2002). The Argentinean judiciary resisted its political subordination with initiatives such as the investigation of three ministers of Menem for an illegal sale of arms to Ecuador and Croatia between 1991 and 1995; and of the minister of labor's and the secretary of the intelligence's service under the presidency of Fernando de la Rúa, for allegedly buying votes in the Senate to support a reform of the labor market.

(la Soberanísima) to investigate magistrates of the Supreme Court and of the Judicial Council, as well as every judge in the country. The president of the Assembly, Luis Miquilena, warned against resistance: "Anybody who opposes the decisions will be eliminated. If the Supreme Court of Justice were to take any measure, and it is likely that it will do so, you may be certain that we shall not hesitate for a moment to suppress the Supreme Court of Justice" (*El País*, 21 August 1999: 8).

These politicians used mobilized majorities in democracies to suppress limits to their powers. Another type of politician has similarly undermined the rule of law in new democracies: anticommunist politicians implementing lustration policies after 1989, in order to eliminate competitors in the political arena. Lustration means purification by sacrifice: that is, purges within institutions, screening individuals who had political responsibilities in the former communist regimes. Demands for punitive retroactive laws were made by conservative politicians, usually backed by the Catholic Church, as communism crumbled. In the former Czechoslovakia a law was passed in 1990; Bulgaria, Germany, Hungary, Lithuania, and Russia followed. In Poland, lustration was introduced under the government of Hanna Suchocka in 1992. Parliamentary initiatives of AWS (Solidarity Electoral Action) and UW (Freedom Union) in the Sejm backed the purges, with the argument that the judiciary should "meet the needs of society."[16] In the former German Democratic Republic, lustration led to the replacement of 70% of civil servants of the Justice Department of Brandenburg by West German imports.[17]

Demands for lustration were made in the name of democracy. This contrasts with the argument that *garantismo* (Di Palma 1990: 44–75) and pacts of coexistence make new democracies more stable (O'Donnell and Schmitter 1986: 37–47; Karl and Schmitter 1991: 280–2). The usual prescription for democratization has been "to forgive, but not to forget," as long as compromises do not make democratic competition or the agendas of governments irrelevant. It may be argued that this prescription is valid only for postauthoritarianism, not for postcommunism: as Linz and Stepan (1996: 24) put it, "in comparison to post-communist Europe, some of the long-standing authoritarian dictatorships we have considered in Franco's Spain, Salazar's Portugal, and Pinochet's Chile left more to build on in the way of a constitutional culture. . . . In all three

---

[16] The demand for purges included the prohibition of the SLD (the Democratic Left Alliance). Leszek Kolakowski, Jacek Kurón, and most members of the KOR (Committee for Workers' Defence) would have been victims of lustration.

[17] This information is reported by Linz and Stepan (1996: 251, n. 38).

cases most of the principles of Western democratic law, while abused or put in abeyance in practice, were not fundamentally challenged."

According to this argument, because of the confusion between legality and politics and the overlapping between state and regime, democracy could be sustained only in postcommunist countries with a new judiciary. An analogy is sometimes established between postcommunist lustration and denazification after 1945 (Morawski 1999). But this analogy is unconvincing. First, the Nuremberg trial was part of an investigation of the whole German population following a world war, and it was grounded on legally based charges of crimes against humanity by an international tribunal. Second, lustration served politicians to get rid of political competitors and policies which they simply disliked: for instance, because they opposed a market economy, defended abortion, or public education (Kaniowski 1999). Finally, politicians who defended lustration in the name of democracy subverted two basic principles of the rule of law (Esquith 1999): that no guilt can be established through association, and that no offense can exist without a preexisting norm (*nullum crimen sine lege*).

The strategies of politicians in postcommunism promoted tensions between democracy and the independence of courts. Thus, when communist politicians were confident that they would win the first elections, they cared little about the independence of the judiciary and defended the supremacy of the legislative. On the contrary, when they feared defeat, they tried to protect the existing judiciary from a future political majority, granting independence to the former. As for conservative and liberal politicians, they defended the subordination of the existing judiciary to the newly elected representatives and were ready to accept an independent judiciary only after a political purge by a democratic majority had taken place (Magalhàes 1999). Both anticommunists and plebiscitarian populists subordinated the rule of law to the "will of the majority."

## Subverting Democracy with the Rule of Law

If politicians use independent judges as an instrument against democracy, they will do so when the political institutions are weak, society is divided in its support to the regime, and a judiciary beyond the control of parliament and government is hostile to democracy. In these circumstances, the probability of success of subversive strategies increases, while the threat of retaliation is hardly credible. If politicians create a divorce between democracy and the rule of law that opens up an opportunity for regime subversion, the conditions will be the opposite of those of the earlier case: the executive is fragile, powerful actors hostile to democracy have not been discredited, and judges are accomplices of the strategies rather than victims.

This scenario is likely in new democracies that inherit norms and independent, but partial, judges from the past. As Friedrich (1958: 139–40) put it, if "a large part of judges come from a precedent regime, and are maintained due to the principle of non-removability of judges, the loyalty of courts to the new government can become suspect." But established democracies may also be subverted through this type of strategy when the vital interests of potential veto groups are threatened, or when the country is in a deep political and economic crisis. A patriotic savior has an opportunity to emerge and, in the name of the "national interest," find support to attack the regime.[18]

Politicians may use the rule of law against democracy: the former only requires the observance and enforcement of any law, whatever its content. That is, it does not protect democratic political rights; it ensures only that, because laws are general, the consequences of actions can be predicted and individuals may enjoy greater security from arbitrary sanctions. But the rule of law can still be the rule of "bad" laws (i.e., norms that well-informed citizens would not have passed) as long as a government remains within the limits of a hierarchically ordered and logically consistent legal system. As we know, Kelsen's theory of the *Rechtsstaat* simply required a principle of legality, that the actions of governments were limited by existing laws, that the legal system had a logical structure deduced from the *Grundnorm*, and that constitutional review should be a responsibility of courts.

> We do not conceive the *Rechtsstaat* as a state order with a specific content . . . but as a state whose acts are carried out in their totality on the basis of the legal order. . . . Every state must constitute an order, a coercive order of human behaviour, and this coercive order, whatever the method of its creation may be – autocratic or democratic – and whatever its content, must be a legal order, that gradually becomes more concrete, from the hypothetical fundamental law to the individual legal acts, through the general norms. This is the concept of the *Rechtsstaat*. (Kelsen 1977: 120)

---

[18] Remember Schmitt's (1985: 27) argument that, if a dictatorship suspends the law, it is only to reestablish the conditions of its efficiency: "[A]lthough it ignores the law, it is only to achieve it." This is a characteristic of the *Kommissarische Diktatur*, as opposed to "sovereign dictatorships."

The nature of the political regime is indifferent;[19] democracy or dictatorship is irrelevant, as long as the laws are respected and enforced. As Raz has argued (1979: 211, 219, 225), if the rule of law is to have any meaning, it cannot overlap with a theory of justice or normative political philosophy: "A non-democratic legal system, based on the denial of human rights, on extensive poverty, on racial segregation, sexual inequalities, and religious persecution may, in principle, conform to the requirements of the rule of law better than any of the legal systems of the more enlightened Western democracies.... Conformity to the rule of law also enables the law to serve bad purposes."

Politicians may use the rule of law against democracy. If what matters is the respect and implementation of the law, political instability under democracy may be a reason to subvert it in the name of the rule of law. The regime can be subverted from within if it has inherited norms and courts from the authoritarian past, or if "bad" laws were passed under democracy that can be used to overthrow it. There are abundant historical experiences of such strategies of subversion. Two well-known cases are the Weimar Republic and Salvador Allende's Chile: the first was a new democracy with authoritarian legacies; the second, an apparently well-established democracy.

The German judiciary played a decisive role in the collapse of German democracy in the 1930s. Whereas the Second Reich had purged the judiciary of liberal members from 1878 onward, no relevant changes were introduced after the First World War. The Weimar Republic inherited a very conservative judiciary, trained in the Historical School, more loyal to a German *Volksgeist* than to the regime and the 1919 Constitution (Ehrmann 1987). Its organization was bureaucratic, and its internal, vertical controls very strong; its political autonomy was very great, due to legal independence, unstable governments, and a polarized parliament. But if the judiciary was autonomous from democratic political institutions, it was not neutral: it repressed the left and, on the contrary, tolerated an extreme right increasingly subversive and violent. While right-wing militants committed 308 murders between 1918 and 1922, and only 11 resulted in convictions, the corresponding numbers for leftist militants were 21 and 37 (Ott and Buob 1993: 94): that

---

[19] Kelsen accepted that legal coercion under democracy does not assume that the majority has the truth and keeps open the possibility that the minority becomes the majority (1979: 472–3). But, as Heller (1972: 71, 216) pointed out, the "normative logicism" of Kelsen attributed "an authority to law deprived of any ethical or sociological content." The context of the debate between Kelsen and Heller was the dramatic collapse of the Weimar Republic.

is, courts were 47 times more likely to convict a left-wing activist. In Müller's (1991: 21) words, the judiciary "encouraged the radical right and undermined the confidence of the supporters of democracy." The crisis of Weimar democracy was used by antidemocratic politicians to destroy it, and in this strategy the courts were crucial: they allowed the use of article 48 of the Constitution to dispossess the Prussian government, led by the social democrats, in July 1932 (Dyzenhaus 1997); to pass the emergency decree of 28 February 1933; to appoint, and later dismiss, Heinrich Brüning, Franz von Papen, and Kurt von Schleicher as successive chancellors; and, eventually, to surrender power to Adolf Hitler. The Nazi access to power used and manipulated democratic means; it also respected the rule of law. As Lepsius (1978: 56) has written, "pseudo-legality was transformed into a nominal legitimacy, which in turn was used to destroy constitutional legality and to establish an undemocratic rule." Politicians and courts subverted democracy by legal means.

The judiciary may facilitate antidemocratic strategies in established democracies as well. The typical situation is one where the interests of key actors appear to be threatened, a political or economic crisis exists, and the democratic parties are weak. The success of subversion becomes more likely, while the risk of retaliation is low. Chile under Allende was such a case. The country had a long tradition of judicial independence, but this did not guarantee the political neutrality of courts under a left-wing government. On the contrary, courts were very hostile toward the government of Unidad Popular.

The higher courts, and particularly the Supreme Court, had never been committed to democracy. They also had a tight control over judges in the lower echelons of a unified, hierarchical system. As Hilbink (n.d.: 7) puts it after studying judicial performance in Chile since 1964 in high-profile civil and political rights cases, "a judiciary, even one recognized as relatively independent, will not automatically serve the values and principles of a meaningful democratic system." In the confrontation between the government of Unidad Popular and the conservative opposition over legality and the rule of law, the judiciary was mostly an ally of the latter. This confrontation started when the government, with a legislative minority, used what were called *los resquicios legales* (the legal interstices) in order to implement its program. These were old norms that had survived in a chaotic and contradictory legal system.[20]

---

[20] The term *resquicios legales* was used by the newspaper *El Mercurio* after August 1972, to disqualify this strategy of Allende.

Thus decree law 520 of 1932 and the Ley Orgánica de la Corporación de Fomento de la Producción of 1939 (Organic Law of the Corporation to Promote Production) were used by the government as the legal bases for nationalizations. The right attacked this strategy from mid-1971 onward, on the grounds that it violated the Constitution and the rule of law. The Consejo de Defensa del Estado and the Constitutional Court remained neutral; the Contraloría General de la República,[21] the Supreme Court, and a large number of courts and judges did not. While hundreds of terrorist actions in 1972–3 were never investigated, the judiciary became a crucial actor in the campaign to undermine the government (Novoa Monreal 1992: 61–71, 95–105).

Although no constitutional or legal grounds existed for a military intervention, the judiciary was eventually ready "to support the coup and defer to the armed forces on issues of personal liberties" (Valenzuela 1989: 190). Following the 1973 military coup, on imposing the presidential band on General Pinochet, the president of the Supreme Court declared: "I put the judiciary in your hands."

General Augusto Pinochet did not need to interfere with the independence of this politicized judiciary. The first decree law of the dictatorship, of 18 September 1973, manifested that the new regime, which had bombed the presidential palace, closed Parliament, and purged the state bureaucracy, would respect judicial power. The exception was the Constitutional Court, under attack before the coup because its sentences often supported the legal initiatives of the Allende government: it was dismantled in November 1973 (Silva Cimma 1977: 63–78, 209–16). This respect for the judiciary was very different from what had happened in Argentina and Brazil.[22] Although the military junta controlled the judicial budget, and human rights cases were transferred to the jurisdiction of military courts, decree law 527 of 1974 reaffirmed the independence of the courts. The judiciary never questioned the military legality[23] or tried to prevent violations of human rights. On the contrary, the Supreme Court complained against the protection of *habeas*

---

[21] The Contraloría General de la República (General Controller of the Republic) had the preventive control of the legality of executive actions. The controller general was Héctor Humares, who held a life-long appointment and responded to no institution.

[22] In Argentina, the dictatorship purged 80% of judges. In Brazil, the Supreme Court was changed.

[23] This position was often justified on positivist grounds. Thus, in an interview in the conservative newspaper *El Mercurio* (20 January 1985), Hernán Cereceda Bravo, magistrate of the Supreme Court, declared: "You are using the words 'even if they are unjust laws.' I do not believe they are unjust, because if they are laws that have been duly enacted, they are there to be enforced."

*corpus*: of 5,400 writs presented by the Vicariado de la Solidaridad (the church-sponsored Vicariate of Solidarity), it accepted only 10. In the inaugural speech of the 1975 judicial year, the president of the Supreme Court stated that "As to torture and other atrocities, I can say that we do not have executions or iron walls here, and that such information is due to political media committed to ideas that have not, and will not, prosper in our country" (Correa Sutil 1993: 91).

When President Patricio Aylwin took office in March 1990, after nearly seventeen years of military dictatorship, the new democracy inherited a legality framed by the 1980 Constitution and a rule of law based on these independent, nonneutral courts. Fourteen out of the seventeen magistrates of the Supreme Court had been appointed by Pinochet. The political interference of an independent judiciary was a threat to the new democratic government. The problem was not the absence of "horizontal" checks, the inexistence of a rule of law to contain governmental abuses. It was, on the contrary, a judicial system that accepted democracy as long as conservative political interests were not challenged; in order to protect them, it was ready to destabilize democracy. Eventually, the composition of the Supreme Court changed: seventeen of the twenty magistrates were appointed under the presidencies of Aylwin and Eduardo Frei: when this court had to decide on whether to withdraw parliamentary immunity from Pinochet, fourteen magistrates voted in favor, and six against. The situation had been reversed: rather than the judiciary subverting democracy, the rule of law was modified by democratic politicians.

## The Judicialization of Politics in Democracies

I have examined so far situations in which either democracy or the rule of law was not in equilibrium. Due to their resources in one or the other institutional areas, politicians chose not to comply either with the rule of law or democracy, and turned to subversion. I now discuss situations in which politicians respect both: democracy and the rule of law are in equilibrium, because neither the government nor the opposition is better off with a different option given the anticipated strategies of the adversary. Yet, under particular political and institutional circumstances, politicians or judges may judicialize politics. Thus, while democracy is maintained, politicians can try to improve their position by devising strategies in which an independent judiciary becomes an instrument of power.

278

I first examine institutional reforms that may transform judges into a potentially destructive political weapon. The legal control of politicians varied over a long time in the different traditions of the common and the civil law.[24] In the tradition of the common law, judges are a crucial part of the system of checks and balances; they can prevent the majority of the day from passing laws that infringe the constitution; and they operate with adversarial procedures. They are also recruited through direct or indirect popular elections.[25] In the tradition of the civil law, on the contrary, judges were not to interfere with the popular will, represented in the elected bodies; they were simply expert civil servants, whose task was to apply a body of written laws, with inquisitive rules, and in order to solve conflicts. The judiciary was supposed to be anonymous, person-proof, powerless. As civil servants, judges were selected mostly through a competitive entrance examination, with or without a subsequent stage at a judicial school.[26]

Mostly following dictatorships and the experience of compliant courts, institutional reforms were introduced in several civil-law countries. Reforms were a reaction to the political subordination of the judiciary and were intended to increase controls over governments. Jurisprudence (i.e., the binding interpretation of norms by judges) achieved an unprecedented importance; constitutional courts and judicial review were established; the independence of judges was reinforced by their self-government via judicial councils (first in Italy, then in France, Spain, Portugal, and many Latin American countries); hierarchical controls were suppressed. These institutional reforms brought the civil- and common-law systems closer to each other, yet they did not introduce in the former the checks on the judiciary that exist in common-law countries (Guarnieri and Pederzoli 1999). These institutional reforms created the conditions for the judicialization of politics by particularly unchecked checkers.

---

[24] On the two judicial traditions, see Toharia (1999).

[25] In the United Kingdom judges are appointed by the lord chancellor, who is a member of the cabinet. In the United States, the election is direct or indirect depending on whether it is to a state or federal court. The election of judges in state courts was introduced in the second quarter of the nineteenth century; in 1994, 70.5% of all judges in the fifty states had been directly elected on partisan or nonpartisan ballots. As for judges in federal courts, their election is indirect: it consists of a presidential nomination and confirmation by the Senate.

[26] France, Spain, Portugal, and Uruguay have competitive entrance examinations, followed by judicial school; Italy, Belgium, Peru, and Brazil share the entrance examinations but do not have judicial schools. Germany, Argentina, Chile, and Ecuador select judges through practical training, without entrance examinations or judicial schools.

**279**

What can initiate this judicialization of politics is a restricted democratic accountability of governments. If electoral competition or parliamentary controls are unable to shed light on the actions of governments, the new powers of the judiciary may now be used to make politicians legally, if not democratically, accountable. The judicialization of politics is often the consequence of a limited political accountability of governments. The initiatives will be taken by judges[27] when the opposition fears retaliation or colludes with the government (for instance, on the illegal financing of parties). When politicians lead the strategies, they will first consider their electoral impact. Their incentive is to win office: by judicializing politics, they hope to discredit an adversary difficult to defeat at the polls. I consider these strategies led by the opposition later.

French and Italian politics have been examples of judicialized politics in which politicians played a passive role. A drastic change in the relationship between democracy and the rule of law in both countries was facilitated by institutional reforms and the limited political accountability of rulers. The reasons for the latter were different in the two cases. In France, the 1958 Constitution allocated significant power to the executive – including vast competences to the president of the republic and the minister of justice over judicial matters.[28] The two-ballot electoral system manufactured solid majorities over many years. In Italy, restrictions to political accountability were due to multiparty coalitions, in which the Democracia Cristiana (DC) was the pivotal member: voters were hardly able to throw politicians out of power.

In both countries, politics became judicialized when the executive became weaker, but hardly more accountable due to interparty collusion and/or the capacity of incumbents to survive in power through coalitional strategies. In France, this was the case in the last period of Valéry Giscard d'Estaing as president,[29] and also in the first *cohabitation*

---

[27] Under a nonhierarchical, decentralized judiciary in which each and every judge embodies "judicial power," assumptions about a "unified" judiciary are not needed. A single judge may be instrumental for a political strategy. It is, however, reasonable to think that judges prefer to make binding legal decisions with autonomy and independence (whatever the content of such decisions, the conception of justice that they reflect, or their congruence with democracy). And also, that judges have political preferences: their willingness to participate in political strategies will depend on their aversion to risk, which will be lower the greater their independence.

[28] To the president, regarding the appointment of judges; to the minister of justice, over their promotion or their removal from politically delicate cases.

[29] Giscard d'Estaing had been in a comparatively weak position from the beginning. His victory in May 1974 was by the narrowest of margins, 50.8% of the votes in the second ballot, against 49.2% for Mitterrand. He headed a very uneasy coalition of conservative parties: his confrontation with Jacques Chirac (leader of the strongest party in the

(1986–8) between a president of the republic (François Mitterrand) and a prime minister (Jacques Chirac) elected by opposite majorities. In Italy, where collusion between judges and politicians had been a feature of the political landscape for a very long time (Pizzorno 1992), politicians became vulnerable in the 1990s. *Mani pulite*, the investigation into the illegal financing of parties, was initiated by Milan judges before the 1992 elections, but was intensified when the DC and the Partito Socialista Italiano (PSI) lost ground and after the murders of judges Giovanni Falcone and Paolo Borsellino by the Mafia were seen as evidence of an impotent executive. It has been convincingly argued (Burnett and Mantovani 1998: 261–3) that, in the Italian case, *Mani pulite* was the contingent outcome of a tacit alliance among independent magistrates, powerful industrialists, and influential media controlled by the latter.[30] Judges, even independent ones, need support and resources to confront governments. Important Italian businessmen provided this, reacting against illegal financial demands from the parties that had grown exorbitantly since the mid-1980s, and against increased taxation. Besides, politicians could no longer deliver their part of an implicit deal that had existed for decades: protection against outside competition in a European economy now integrated. And the public deficits and vast national debts of Italian governments threatened their economic future after the 1991 Maastricht treaty.

Political collusion between parties was also evident in both countries. In France, the scandals extended to left and right.[31] Over five years, two prime ministers and nearly twenty first-rank politicians were prosecuted. Eventually, Parliament passed in January 1990 a retroactive law that granted amnesty to the prosecuted politicians: this cover-up by politicians from left and right provoked widespread anger; it also stimulated increased judicial activism to make politicians legally accountable

coalition, and prime minister from 1974 to 1976) was publicly known. The first legal scandal in the Fifth Republic, an alleged gift by the president of the Central African Republic, Jean Bedel Bokassa, to Giscard, appears to have been due to information provided by Chirac and his party, the RPR (Rassemblement pour la République).

[30] Thus, *L'Expresso*, which played a crucial role in the *Mani pulite* strategy, was owned by Carlo De Benedetti (Olivetti). The Agnelli family (Fiat) controlled *La Stampa, Corriere della Sera*, and *Il Mondo*. Confindustria, the Italian confederation of industry, owned *Il Sole 24 Ore*.

[31] The first scandal of the Parti Socialiste (PS) was the illegal funding of the party by Carrefour du Développement and Urba. The minister of justice removed Judge Thierry Jean-Pierre from the Urba affair, exacerbating the politicization of justice. The first scandal in the 1980s affecting the conservatives was the case of Michel Noir, member of Parliament and mayor of Lyon. See *Le Nouvel Observateur*, nos. 1759 (23–9 July 1998) and 1766 (10–16 September 1998).

(Roussel 1998). In Italy, judicial investigations led to 2,381 sentences for political corruption between 1991 and 1996.[32] The consequence was a political earthquake: the DC, the PSI, the Social Democrats, the Liberals, and the Republicans disappeared from the political scene. Not all judges were, however, beyond suspicion. Collusion between judges and politicians was claimed in the investigation of 203 judges in 1998. After studying the Italian experience, della Porta (2001: 13) concludes that "institutional autonomy is hardly enough to ensure the success of investigations into corruption."

Judicial strategies had similarities in both countries. Judges brought the cases under criminal law and used imprisonment without bail, which could last several months, to extract information. One of the Milan magistrates, Francesco Saverio Borrelli, defended this practice in the following terms: "[T]he shock of preventive detention has produced positive results ... are we then to be scandalized if it is said that detention before trial can have the effect of drawing us closer to the truth?" (interview in *La Repubblica*, 19 February 1995). Judges also sought support from the mass media, providing them with secret information from the judicial proceedings. As one of the most active French judges, Eric de Montgolfier,[33] declared, "to bring the media inside justice is necessary, because justice will hardly be possible in darkness." In the case of Italy, Guarnieri and Pederzoli (1999: 147) have also argued that "the mass media are interested in the actions of courts because they offer a precious material, and they can amplify the impact of an action." Of course, media have interests of their own: greater political influence and increased sales, rather than justice. They are also connected to powerful economic empires, affected by governmental decisions.[34] An alliance between the judiciary and the press does constitute a formidable political weapon.

---

[32] The annual numbers went up steadily until 1996: 159 in 1991, 185 in 1992, 263 in 1993, 369 in 1994, 549 in 1995, 856 in 1996 (della Porta 2001: 12).

[33] Eric de Montgolfier was the *procureur* in the case of Bernard Tapie. See his defense of the use of prison without bail and leaks to the press, on the grounds that the end justifies the means, in *Le Nouvel Observateur*, no. 1766 (10–16 September 1998).

[34] In France, one group controlled Aerospatiale, Matra, *Europe 1*, *Journal du Dimanche*, *Paris-Match*, *Elle*, Hachette, Fayard, Grasset, Stock, Calmann-Lévy, *Livre de Poche*; another group, Vivendi-Havas, *L'Express*, *L'Expansion*, Canal +; another one, Pinault (Printemps) Redoute, *Le Point*, TF-1, FNAC. In Spain, one group, whose center was Telefónica, controlled Antena 3 Televisión, Onda Cero, Vía Digital, *El Mundo*, and *Expansión*; another group, Santillana de Ediciones, *El País*, the SER radio network, Canal +, Canal Satélite Digital.

In the French and Italian experiences of the judicialization of politics, the role of politicians was largely passive: they were the victims or beneficiaries, but hardly devised active political strategies to use to their advantage. I now turn to Spain to examine how politicians can undertake this type of political initiative, which turns the independence of judges into an instrument for judicializing politics.

## Getting Rid of Adversaries through the Rule of Law

The Spanish legal system, following the 1978 Constitution, corresponded to the reformed civil-law model. The transition from dictatorship to democracy had introduced profound changes in the norms and the judicial structure, although none in the personnel. No purges were carried out, but the special courts that had jurisdiction over political matters were suppressed.[35] The Constitution allocated judicial review and the protection of fundamental rights to a Constitutional Court, and the self-government of judges to a Judicial Council (Consejo General del Poder Judicial). Judges became independent and unaccountable: only judges could recruit, organize, govern, or sanction judges. Judicial power was seen as an expression of the people's will; its decisions regarding legislation, as grounded on "the judicial conscience of the community" (Rubio Llorente 1991: 32).

Opposition to the dictatorship had hardly existed in the judiciary. Only in the last years of the regime did a group of judges set up an anti-Francoist organization, Justicia Democrática. Under the new regime judges were overwhelmingly conservative: of the 1,369 that were affiliated with a professional organization in 1994, 54% belonged to the reactionary Asociación Profesional de la Magistratura, 18% to the right-of-center Asociación Francisco de Vitoria, 24% to the progressive Jueces para la Democracia. The majoritarian association had opposed the creation of the Constitutional Court, defended the principle that appointments to the Judicial Council had to be strictly corporatist, and

---

[35] It has been argued that legal reforms under Francoism subordinated politicians to the rule of law. This is misleading: only bureaucrats were responsible vis-à-vis citizens, according to the 1956 Ley de la Jurisdicción Contencioso-Administrativa and the 1957 Ley de Régimen Jurídico de la Administración del Estado. Franco was responsible only "to God and History." The Code of Military Justice of July 1945 attributed judicial powers to the generals in command of the military regions, naval departments, and air zones. The Court of Public Order had jurisdiction on illegal political activities that did not affect the military, either directly or indirectly.

demanded criminal sanctions against public criticisms of judicial decisions. A 1985 law of the socialist government that gave to Parliament the competence over appointments to the Consejo General del Poder Judicial was seen by the conservative judiciary as undermining the rule of law.

Satisfaction with the judiciary was limited to less than two out of ten citizens.[36] Skepticism over its independence was also widespread: in 1997 statements that "judicial decisions are independent from the interests and pressures of the government," "from the interests and pressures of economic and social groups," and "from the pressures and comments of the media" were rejected respectively by 57%, 58%, and 55% of citizens (Toharia 1999: 18). The view that judges were independent from the government also declined with time: from 40% in 1986, under the socialist (PSOE) government, to 28% in 1998, under the conservative (PP) government.[37]

Let us now turn to politics. I have already argued that the judicialization of politics depends on the political accountability of governments and on the unlikelihood of an electoral victory of the opposition. If rulers limit their political responsibility to the verdict of elections and between elections are only ready to accept legal responsibilities for their actions, political confrontation will be transferred from parliament to courts. My second argument is that if politicians in opposition have been losing elections for a long time, value office highly, and believe that their chances of winning in the foreseeable future are negligible under the routine rules of democratic competition, they will be likely to turn to strategies of judicializing politics in order to dislodge the incumbent. They will do so if the costs of such strategies are low: that is, if they have powerful allies, and the risk of retaliation by the adversary is small. I examine an illustration of such strategy, before turning to strategies in which a government (rather than an opposition) uses judicial actions for its political advantage.

### Dislodging the Incumbent

In June 1993 the Spanish socialists, led by Felipe González, unexpectedly won their fourth consecutive election. One year later, a judiciary

---

[36] Eurobarometer survey, May 1997. In France, Portugal, and Belgium the percentage of satisfied people was similar. In Italy, it was less than 10%. On the contrary, in Austria, Denmark, and Finland the percentages were greater than 50%. See Toharia (1999: 17).

[37] The data are from surveys by Demoscopia. See *El País*, 11 May 1998, 20.

investigation into a "dirty war" against the Basque terrorist group Euzkadi Ta Azkatasuna (ETA), carried out by secret Grupos Armados de Liberación (GAL), suggested that it was organized or protected by the Ministry of the Interior. This investigation overlapped from the very beginning with a political strategy of the opposition. We must, therefore, disentangle the judicial investigation of what had happened, on the one hand, and the political strategy devised to bring down the government, on the other. As Fish (1993: 738) has argued, "the difference between reaching political conclusions and beginning with political intentions is that if you are doing the second you are not really doing a job of legal work." Years later, one of the main organizers of the political strategy recalled it in the following terms: "It was naturally an operation of the opposition party.... It included some financial institutions, some newspapers.... An operation was carried out in depth to put an end to the 13 and a half years of González in power" (interview of Luis María Ansón, *Onda Cero*, 16 February 1998).

Some information is needed about the antecedents. The Basque terrorist organization ETA, set up in 1959, became much more active under democracy. In the three years that followed the first general elections in 1977, 287 people were murdered. Underground anti-ETA terrorism started in early 1975, organized by members of the Francoist secret service (the Servicio Central de Documentación), following a strategy called Operación Diana. Until the socialist electoral victory in October 1982, successive groups (Batallón Vasco-Español, Tripe A, Anti-Terrorismo ETA) murdered 40 ETA members or supporters and wounded 128. Under the conservative governments of UCD, from 1977 to 1982, strong suspicions existed that the Ministry of the Interior might be involved in these anti-ETA actions.[38]

The "dirty war" against Basque terrorism persisted after the socialists won the elections. The same police officers continued in charge of antiterrorist policies. The first underground action against ETA was in October 1983: in this first year of socialist rule, ETA murdered 44 people,[39] wounded 31, kidnapped 5, and committed 28 armed attacks.

---

[38] For instance, three members of the Batallón Vasco-Español, who were arrested after murdering two people in a hotel in Hendaye, were later released following orders from Manuel Ballesteros, a high-ranking police officer in the Ministry of the Interior.

[39] Of these, eighteen were civilians; twelve, Civil Guards; eleven, policemen; three, military officers. One of the latter was general Víctor Lago, who commanded the Brunete Armored Division in Madrid and had played a crucial role in the defeat of the coup against democracy on 23 February 1981.

The underground anti-ETA terrorism was carried out by a group with a new name, GAL, but the continuities with past groups were clear.[40] From the first action until the end of the "dirty war" in 1986, the GAL murdered 28 ETA members or supporters. Judicial investigations were started in 1988, under the socialist government, by Judge Baltasar Garzón. As a result, two policemen were sentenced to 108 years in prison for organizing the GAL. In the 1993 elections Garzón was elected to parliament in the socialist lists but was careful to keep the case open. When he resigned from office one year later, he was able to resume the investigation of the GAL.

The results of the 1993 elections were a surprise. Although the socialists had been trailing the conservative party (PP), "the González effect" (Barreiro and Sánchez-Cuenca 1998) was decisive in the new socialist victory. This result provoked a strong political reaction among the leaders of the PP. They were aware that the position of the median voter ensured the reelection of the socialists, unless ideological voting was neutralized by the introduction of new dimensions of competition and issues that would cut across ideological cleavages.[41] They also believed that the possibility of an electoral victory was remote unless extraordinary means were used to weaken González. They were not ready to wait patiently for the next election. They also had important resources, as well as strong allies who shared the same views and were similarly impatient: militant newspapers, a network of radio stations with a large audience,[42] and a very powerful banker, under judicial investigation after the Bank of Spain had discovered a fraud of $4 billion under his presidency of the Banco Español de Crédito, one of the largest Spanish banks. An alliance, then, of politics, media, and money. Although the

[40] For instance, Jean Pierre Chérid organized the "dirty war" against Basque terrorism from 1975 until 1984, when he was killed while setting a bomb. That is, he was first recruited by the Francoist secret service and ended up in the GAL. A dozen terrorists were successively members of the *Batallón* Vasco Español, Triple A, Anti-Terrorismo ETA, and GAL (Belloch 1998: 113).

[41] I owe this argument to Belén Barreiro and Ignacio Sánchez-Cuenca.

[42] One of the newspapers, ABC, had a long antidemocratic tradition: it mixed reactionary Catholicism and monarchist loyalties. The latter had led to its acceptance of democracy. Its director was Luis María Ansón. Another newspaper, *El Mundo*, was different: it was created in 1989, with a populist orientation, particularly aggressive toward González. It was partly owned by the banker Mario Conde and its director was Pedro J. Ramírez. The newspapers had, respectively, 321,573 and 307,618 readers. The main radio network was the COPE, owned by the Catholic Episcopate, and with an estimated audience of 3.4 million. The data are for 1995, and the sources are the official *Oficina de Justificación de la Difusión* (OJD) and *Estudio General de Medios* (EGM). See *El País*, 14 April 2000, 42–3.

contours of the strategy were known from a very early stage,[43] its intention was fully revealed several years later by one of its chief organizers:

> There was no way to beat Felipe González with other weapons. This was the problem.... González had won three elections with an absolute majority, and won again a fourth time when everything indicated that he was going to loose. We had to raise our criticisms to levels that, on occasions, destabilised the state.... González was a man whose political strength was of such a caliber that it was necessary to go to the limit.... We had to bring González to an end, that was the question.... Not so much for the possible abuses that he had perpetrated, if they had existed at all, but because of the risk that alternance would not be viable. (interview with Luis María Ansón, *Tiempo*, 23 February 1998, 24–30)

This was the difference between the judicial investigation into what had happened, and the political strategy to dislodge the incumbent that judicialized politics as a political weapon. The goal of the latter was set from the beginning: to bring Felipe González to jail, to weaken decisively the PSOE, and to finish the "democratic abnormality" of socialist rule, to use the words of Francisco Álvarez-Cascos, the deputy leader of the PP.[44] The "dirty war" was presented, and judged, as a creation of the socialist government: of the eleven years of anti-ETA terrorism, only the last three were investigated; that anti-ETA terrorism had come to an end in 1986 under this government was ignored. No responsibility was attributed to the former conservative governments:[45] earlier

---

[43] For instance, in an article published in *La Vanguardia* (the main Catalan newspaper) on 22 August 1994, José Luis de Vilallonga wrote that "the operation will be deployed in different stages. First, the government will be destabilized, with an all-out attack on Felipe González, who is at his lowest ebb.... This will be in parallel with a strong campaign in favor of Aznar (the leader of the PP, JMM). It will be carried out by a well-known newspaper, with scarce ethical scruples, (and) a former banker who regularly finances the antigovernment campaigns undertaken by this newspaper." Vilallonga was an aristocrat who wrote the authorized biography of King Juan Carlos.

[44] Speech of Francisco Álvarez-Cascos in the Senate, 25 February 1998. As a sociologist who was also an important member of the Workers' Commissions wrote, the politicians and their allies in the strategy were "fully disposed to use every nonviolent means as far as they could reach their goal, to get rid of González" (Fernández Enguita 1998: 10).

[45] These governments included four different ministers of the interior. The first was Manuel Fraga, from December 1975 to July 1976 – that is, when anti-ETA terrorism started. Fraga was the founding father of the PP. The second was Rodolfo Martín-Villa, in the UCD government from July 1976 to April 1979. The third, Antonio Ibáñez Freire, was also in the UCD government, from April 1979 to May 1980. The fourth was Juan José Rosón, in the UCD government from May 1980 until the socialist government. The death of

actions were presented as sporadic, disconnected, disorganized – different from those of the socialist-inspired GAL.[46] In fact, responsibilities for such actions had been prescribed when the GAL affair was investigated. The sequence of steps was also carefully timed.[47] Judges, as in the French and Italian cases, used the threat of prison without bail in order to extract confessions: those under accusation faced either jail or conditional freedom if they transferred responsibilities upward (in which case, they could also adduce the extenuating circumstance of "due obedience"). Judges also filtered to the sympathetic press secret information from the proceedings. The political strategy aimed to provoke a "popular judgment" rather than establish the judicial truth: thus, Álvarez-Cascos declared that "Public opinion has every day a clearer verdict on the GAL affair.... If the sentence was not to correspond with the verdict of citizens, it will be to the loss of justice" (public statement to the press, 10 September 1995).

Rosón, the main link with the past, was important: he could have provided information that was essential for the socialists.

[46] The opposite interpretation was, however, well supported. General Antonio Sáez de Santamaría, for instance, declared that "the dirty war that existed before the socialists came to power has been presented as consisting of isolated cases, and then the GAL as organized by politicians. This was not so. The groups were the same, there was no discontinuity.... The dirty war was not organized: it was a reaction, an uncontrolled response to an unbearable situation due to the sheer number of murders, 89 in 1980. Not everybody has a cool head to carry the antiterrorist struggle through its due course" (interview in *Cadena Ser*, 17 February 1998). This general was one of the army officers who defeated the coup against democracy in February 1981. He held political appointments both under the UCD and the PSOE governments: among others, that of chief representative of the government (*delegado del gobierno*) in the Basque country, and that of director of the Civil Guard.

[47] The sequence of events was as follows. On 5 May 1994, Judge Baltasar Garzón resigned as a member of Parliament and resumed the investigation of the GAL. On 4 December, the deputy leader of the PP, Francisco Álvarez-Cascos, promised a pardon by a future PP government to the two policemen sentenced to 108 years in jail for organizing the GAL, on the condition that they accuse socialist politicians in the Ministry of the Interior (the meeting was organized by the director of *El Mundo* and the offer was made to the lawyer for the two policemen). For several days in December 1994, Judge Garzón met the director of *El Mundo*. On 16 December, the two policemen made a voluntary statement to Judge Garzón, accusing the minister of the interior (José Barrionuevo), the secretary of state for security (Rafael Vera), the *gobernador civil* of Biscay (Julián Sancristóbal – the top representative of the Ministry of the Interior in that Basque province), and the general secretary of the PSOE in Biscay (Ricardo García Damborenea). On 19 December, Judge Garzón put Sancristóbal in prison without bail and gave the two policemen conditional freedom. On 23 December, the banker Mario Conde was imprisoned due to the fraud in the Banco Español de Crédito (Banesto) and joined Sancristóbal in the prison of Alcalá-Meco. A brother of Judge Javier Gómez de Liaño (who shared with Judge Garzón the investigation of the GAL and was later in charge of the Sogecable case) was also under judicial accusation, as an accomplice of Conde. On 27 December, *El Mundo* started to

The verdict of citizens, however, distinguished between a judicial investigation of what had happened and a partisan strategy of judicializing politics. In 1995,[48] 47% of people believed that "after such a long time, to open again the GAL affair can only be due to political interests"; only 22% disagreed with such a statement. This majoritarian view existed among all voters, although its incidence was greater among the former socialist supporters (54% against 43% among the nonsocialist voters), who also disagreed less with the statement (13% against 26%). A majority (46%) also thought that "some media are carrying out a parallel trial to discredit the government and end with Felipe González" (22% rejected this view). This majority was again larger among PSOE supporters: 58% against 41% in the nonsocialist electorate (only 11% of the latter, and 7% of the socialist voters, disagreed with this view on the conservative press). While citizens detected the political strategy, they also rejected the actions under judicial investigation: 59% of voters condemned the operations of the GAL (52% of the socialists, 62% of the nonsocialists); 16% were comprehensive: they disapproved, but found excuses (the percentages were 17% and 15% for each of the two groups of voters); and, finally, 10% supported the "dirty war," declaring that their priority was to end up with ETA (14% of the socialist voters, 9% of the nonsocialists).

A few months later, in March 1996, the PP won the general elections. The socialists had been weakened by an economic crisis and growing unemployment in 1993 and 1994. The economic recovery that followed was not enough to renew their electoral support; besides, they were deeply hurt by economic scandals. With voting intention for the socialist government coded as a dichotomous dependent variable, the following logit regression estimates whether the probability of such

publish the memoirs, and the accusations, of the two policemen. On 18 April 1995, Judge Garzón accused Sancristóbal and García Damborenea of organizing the GAL: Sancristóbal remained in prison, and García Damborenea was left in conditional freedom. On 12 June, *El Mundo* started to publish alleged documents of the Centro Superior de Información de la Defensa (CESID, the Spanish secret service), obtained by a high-ranking officer related to the banker Conde and to the PP. On 17 July, Sancristóbal made a voluntary statement to Judge Garzón, accusing the minister and the secretary of state. On 20 July, García Damborenea made a voluntary statement to Judge Garzón, accusing the prime minister, Felipe González. On 20 July, *El Mundo* published that "Aznar spoke with Damborenea before his first statement to Judge Garzón" (the author of the article later became director of the cabinet of the secretary of state for communication in the 1996 PP government). On 27 July, *El Mundo* published in its entirety the statement of García Damborenea to Judge Garzón accusing Felipe González. On 27 September, García Damborenea reiterated to the Supreme Court the accusation against González.

[48] Survey from the *Centro de Investigaciones Sociológicas*, no. 2133, February 1995 (national sample of N = 2,500).

**Table 11.1.** Probability of Voting for the Socialist Government

|  | Logit Coefficients | Standard Error |
|---|---|---|
| Constant | −1.094* | .653 |
| Variable |  |  |
| *Past vote* | 5.361*** | .426 |
| *Assessment of the economy* | −.676*** | .121 |
| *Evaluation of corruption* | −.274** | .094 |
| *Views on the GAL affair* | −.256** | .105 |
| Chi 2 | 782.353 |  |
| Pseudo R2 | .43 |  |
| Number of cases | 1053 |  |
| % of correct predictions | 87.7 |  |

* Significant at 10%.
** Significant at 5%.
*** Significant at 1%.

support increased or decreased as a result of four independent variables (Table 11.1). The variables are the vote in the former general elections, the assessment of the economy, the evaluation of political corruption, and the views on the GAL affair.[49] The four variables are statistically significant: the probability of voting for the government increased when voters had supported the socialists in former elections; and it decreased when their assessment of the economy was negative, when they thought that political corruption was a problem of great political importance, and when they rejected the GAL more strongly. That is, the GAL affair influenced the voting intention, regardless of whether the individual had previously supported the government.

An electoral victory was not the only goal that mattered for the conservative strategy: after all, the victory had been by a mere 1.3% of the vote. The question now was how to stay in power for as long as possible.

[49] The survey is that referred to in note 48. Vote intention was coded as 1 = support for the government, 0 = any other alternative (support for any other party, blank vote, and abstention). Vote in the former general elections had the same values. Assessment of the economy went from 1 (very good) to 5 (very bad). No reference to corruption as a serious political problem was coded as 0; reference as 1. Views on the GAL went from 1 (approval) to 4 (unqualified rejection). Interviewees who did not know or did not answer questions referring to their vote intention or any of the four independent variables were excluded. Ideology, which was initially included in the model as an independent variable, was eventually excluded due to its correlation with past vote (r: −.28, with a statistical significance at the 0.01 level), in order to avoid problems of multicollinearity.

Once the PP was in government, the two top politicians in charge of the Ministry of the Interior in the 1983–6 period were sent to prison on the grounds of their responsibility in the GAL affair. But the main target was González: if he were to be brought to jail, the PSOE would be disabled as a serious political contender for the foreseeable future. On 29 September 1996 Álvarez-Cascos, now deputy prime minister, declared in a public speech in Mérida that "the GAL were orchestrated by Felipe González"; this charge was only one of a string of accusations against the former prime minister made by leaders of the PP. The general attorney, appointed by the government and following its instructions, tried to extract a prison sentence from the Supreme Court. However, González was exonerated in November 1996. But, in the course of a decade of investigation, the socialists never provided an articulate story of the "dirty war" against ETA.[50]

The strategy was successful in polarizing attitudes toward González: he evoked both profound hostility and passionate support in Spanish society, dividing it in two camps. Believing that this antagonism was politically explosive, González did not stand for reelection as leader of the party in the PSOE congress of June 1997. Why a moderate politician would produce such polarization was an intriguing question: the answer to this, and to other similar questions, is that political hostility does not depend so much on ideological distance as on the electoral appeal of the antagonist. Similarities were often pointed out between González and Clinton:

> The most relevant parallelism between the ferocious oppositions to the centre-left governments of Clinton and González has been the use of the judiciary to achieve what was impossible through the ballot box. There are two key questions.... One is that the right has found in courts an instrument to brutally harass left-wing governments. The other, that capable left-wing politicians can help their defeat if they do not accept the political responsibility for scandals that took place under their mandate. (Jackson 1998: 9–10)

---

[50] Felipe González only argued that the GAL, which operated in French territory, damaged the antiterrorist cooperation of the French government, which started after a bilateral meeting between González and Mitterrand on 20 December 1983 (the first action of the French police against ETA was on 10 January 1984). The French government actively supported González. An additional argument favorable to González was that in 1994, before Garzón had resigned from his seat in Parliament and the GAL investigation had advanced, he appointed as minister of the interior a prestigious, independent magistrate (Juan Alberto Belloch), whose personal political ambitions were much stronger than his solidarity with the government, and who was decisive in the clarification of the GAL.

The end of this story raises two counterfactual questions, which affect democracy as an equilibrium. The first is, What would have been the reaction of an exasperated right if González had won again in 1996 (as he nearly did, being later exonerated by the Supreme Court) – that is, if neither the votes nor the extreme politicization of the rule of law had led to the demise of the adversary? The answer to this question lies in the political withdrawal of González: it would have taken place even if he had won. A surviving González, a fortiori if in government, could have led to a greater radicalization of the right and to regime instability.

The other question is, What would have been the reaction of the PSOE if its leader had been put in prison? A strategy of judicializing politics, while preserving the rule of law as an equilibrium, has as its outcome that the victim of such strategy is indifferent to compliance or noncompliance: the Spanish socialists came close to that outcome. When the former minister of the interior and the former secretary of state for security were sentenced by the Supreme Court to ten years in prison in July 1998 for their responsibilities over the GAL affair, the official newspaper of the PSOE declared: "[W]e believe in their innocence.... We cannot ask the magistrates of the Supreme Court to be heroes, to judge and sentence according to what has been presented in the proceedings.... A lot of courage is necessary to go against the current" (*El Socialista*, 618, August–September 1998). The position of the executive committee of the party was that, while the socialists acquiesced with the sentence, the court had been influenced by pressures from the government and some media. The leaders of the party organized in 11 September 1998 a large demonstration in front of the jail, to support the two politicians. Only gradually did the PSOE overcome this traumatic political experience and normalize its relationship with the judiciary.

This political reaction of the socialists damaged their electoral support. In July 1998, voting intentions for the PSOE and the PP were similar: 23.8% and 23.9%. In October, the PP had surpassed the socialists: 26.1% versus 22.9%. In January 1999, the difference had increased: 26.7% for the PP versus 20.3% for the PSOE. That is, in six months marked by the resistance of the socialists to a politically damaging judicial sentence, the conservatives had built a difference of 6.4 percentage points in voting intentions. The PSOE lost ground until the general election of March 2000; with the socialists no longer led by Felipe González and with a difficult leadership succession, under a prolonged economic expansion, the PP won a confortable majority of the votes (44.5% against 34.1% for the PSOE) and an absolute majority in parliament.[51]

Thus, punishment by voters at election time is one reason why politicians comply with judicial decisions. Besides, the PP knew well that the socialists lacked support in the judiciary to retaliate and that past responsibilities for anti-ETA terrorism fell outside the statute of limitations. Also, the socialists would not carry out a strategy that, in their view, could destabilize democracy – that is, lead to a worse payoff. The PSOE had to accept the destructive effects of the conservative strategy and comply with the rule of law, whatever the damage. It could only hope for a better future under a democracy whose rules of competition had nevertheless been transformed. This was probably the calculation of the conservatives when they launched their strategy. Thus, the rule of law remained an equilibrium, even in a case of a politically nonimpartial justice and a selective use of the law, because the losing actor was worse off under any other option (in terms of electoral support, judiciary battles, or regime stability). While the loser acquiesced today, increased electoral support in the future might eventually change the balance of forces in the judiciary – that is, lead to greater impartiality.

## Silencing Opponents

Politicians in government often try to modify to their advantage the balance of power that exists in society, that is, to fortify their position and to erode the influence of their critics. When rulers devise strategies to this effect, they believe that the electoral risks are minimal, they have powerful allies in society, and failure does not pose great political threats. Unsympathetic media are a usual target.

My illustration comes again from Spanish politics and flows directly from the preceding one. Remember that the conservative party (PP), led by José María Aznar, had won the 1996 elections with a difference of 290,328 votes only. Expecting an absolute majority in parliament, the leaders of the PP attributed this resilience of the socialists not only to what remained of the "González effect" but also to the influence of a liberal-left media group, PRISA.[52] Thus, PRISA became, together with

---

[51] The data are from surveys of the *Centro de Investigaciones Sociológicas*, no. 2294, July 1998; no. 2307, October 1998; no. 2316, January 1999 (national samples of N = 2,486; 2,489; 2,493).

[52] PRISA owned *El País*, the SER radio network, and the private TV channel Canal +.

González, the major political target of the new government. The judiciary was again the instrument of a strategy later described by one of its main victims, the founding director of *El País*, as "a formidable aggression of the government against media that it did not see as obedient" (Cebrián 1999).

The political strategy started in December 1996, a few months after the elections. PRISA was to launch a TV digital platform (Canal Satélite Digital), shared by two private channels (Canal + and Antena 3 Televisión) and the public television of Catalonia (TV-3). The government decided to veto this initiative and to create its own TV digital platform (Vía Digital), using a telecommunications giant[53] that was under its control (Telefónica). The transmission of soccer matches (particularly those of the Real Madrid and Barcelona) was the most treasured resource for the two competing TV platforms: Canal Satélite Digital had already signed a contract with the clubs and was from the beginning the most powerful of the two platforms.

The political strategy tried, first, to stop Canal Satélite Digital through executive and legislative initiatives; and, second, and more important, to bring to an end the influence of the PRISA media group by judiciary means. Thus, the government declared illegal, as a start, the decodifier for the new TV, passing a decree law on the grounds of "exceptional urgency";[54] it then increased by 10 percentage points the value-added tax that this new TV was required to pay; and, finally, a law was passed that snatched soccer matches from this TV on the grounds of the "public interest." Simultaneously, PRISA was left without partners. Antena 3 Televisión was bought by Telefónica, and the nationalist party (CiU), which governed Catalonia and provided parliamentary support to the PP government in Madrid, forced TV-3 to abandon Canal Satélite Digital.

The most serious political attack was launched at the beginning of 1997. The actors and their steps were the following. First, the government: it commissioned a legal and economic report in order to bring a criminal case against PRISA.[55] Politicians of the PP accused,

---

[53] Telefónica had been a public monopoly. The new PP government appointed as president of the company a close friend of Prime Minister José María Aznar; it then privatized the company, ensuring that it would be controlled by friendly hands and that it would be protected from socialist governments in the future.

[54] The decree law was finally suspended by the European Commission. No other kind of decodifier existed in the market, and the intrusion of the government was contrary to European Union rules.

[55] The report was written by two economists and a lawyer, closely associated with banker Conde.

in Parliament and in the press, PRISA of being a group of "swindlers" and "counterfeiters." Second, the press: the report of the government was published by the magazine *Época*[56] on 24 February 1997; subsequently, the director of the magazine took the board members of PRISA to court. Also, the conservative press mounted a massive campaign to undermine the economy of PRISA and to build up a "verdict of public opinion." Third, the judiciary: Judge Javier Gómez de Liaño,[57] with the support of the general attorneys depending on the government, started criminal proceedings against PRISA. The judge withdrew the passports of the board members and established an individual bail of 200 million pesetas for the chairman. The proceedings were declared secret; leaks to the press were, however, constant.[58] As one of the general attorneys declared, "They (the board members of PRISA, JMM) will be forced to do the 'little promenade' [*el paseillo*], up and down the stairs of the Court. We shall carry out a judicial revolution from the Court [*la Audiencia Nacional*], in order to finish with this corrupt political system and with *Felipismo.*"[59]

The judicial investigation lasted a year. The director of PRISA avoided prison without bail thanks to Jordi Pujol, the president of the nationalist party that governed in Catalonia and supported the PP government in Parliament. Eventually the High Court declared that the accusations were unwarranted. The director of PRISA retaliated, bringing Judge Gómez de Liaño to court on charges of prevarication. The government

---

[56] *Época* was an extreme right-wing magazine. Its director had been president of a Francoist trade union (the Sindicato Vertical del Espectáculo) and director of *Arriba* (the newspaper of Falange, the single party under the dictatorship). Banker Mario Conde financed the magazine.

[57] On Judge Javier Gómez de Liaño see note 47. He had been a member of the Judicial Council (Consejo General del Poder Judicial) proposed by the PP. The state attorneys who were part of the concerted strategy were the Fiscal General del Estado, Jesús Cardenal, appointed by the government; the fiscal general of the Supreme Court, José María Luzón (who also played an active role in the GAL affair); the fiscal jefe de la Audiencia Nacional, Eduardo Fungairiño; and two fiscales de la Audiencia Nacional, Ignacio Gordillo and María Dolores Márquez de Prado, married to Judge Javier Gómez de Liaño.

[58] The media were again *El Mundo* and ABC, the Catholic radio network COPE, the two public televisions, and the private TV network Antena 3 Televisión. See note 42.

[59] The declaration of the general attorney (*fiscal*), María Dolores Márquez de Prado, was made to Judge Baltasar Garzón. The latter revealed it while declaring under oath to the high court (Audiencia Nacional) on 16 September 1999. The "little promenade" (*paseillo*) referred to the humiliating arrival at the court of the accused, photographed and recorded by TV. *Felipismo* was a pejorative reference to a network of power, which included PRISA, supposedly controlled by Felipe González. A former minister of the economy under the conservative UCD government, Jaime García Añoveros, also testified to the high court that the goal of "this process would be the end of the present political system."

and its party, as well as the conservative media, supported the judge; his lawyer was a PP politician; the general attorneys also defended him, following instructions from the government;[60] the same media carried out a campaign of intimidation of the Supreme Court magistrates. But this was the end of the "mafia-like operation of politicians, media, and judges" (Pradera 1999: 4). Two years after the strategy was launched, on 15 October 1999, Gómez de Liaño was found guilty of prevarication and lost his job. The Supreme Court used this case to establish limits to judicial independence within a reformed civil-law system: "The judge cannot transform his will or conviction into law. This task can only correspond to Parliament.... Decisions based solely on the conviction of a judge, without a rational foundation in the law, are incompatible with a modern *estado de derecho*" (*El País*, 16 October 1999, 17–20).

The politicians who took part in the strategy were, however, unaffected, either legally or politically. Voters viewed the conflict as a clash of powers and did not care much about it: the government suffered no electoral costs. In March 2000 the PP won the general elections, obtaining now an absolute majority of the seats. And scarcely one year after the Supreme Court sentence, on 1 December 2000, the PP government pardoned Gómez de Liaño, who got back his job as a judge. The whole strategy was thus costless, not just for the incumbent politicians but also for the judge who served as their instrument.

Only the hierarchical control by higher courts, whose composition was carefully attuned to democracy, prevented judges from becoming destructive political weapons. Judges as *bouches de la loi* seemed to better guarantee that the rule of law would respect the rules of democracy. Reforms that made judges not just independent, but also unaccountable and unchecked, did not introduce impartiality: they opened the possibility that judges could be transformed into instruments to destroy competitors, rather than to protect democracy.

## Conclusions

I have questioned in this chapter the thesis that democracy and an independent judiciary, a central component of the rule of law, are two institutional arrangements that reinforce one another. I have not discussed their institutional maladjustments but politicians' strategies. My

---

[60] The politician who acted as lawyer was Jorge Trías, a PP member of Parliament. The general attorneys were those of note 57.

arguments have rested on the old question of an independence of the judiciary that does not guarantee its political impartiality or neutrality. Przeworski (1991: 35) has argued that "we tend to believe that an independent judiciary is an important arbitrating force in the face of conflict." Yet there are no serious reasons that guarantee such a position of the judiciary above politics. Judges are "nonelected quasi guardians," to use Dahl's term, who limit the democratic process: but, as he argues, these "nonmajoritarian democratic arrangements by themselves cannot prevent a minority from using its protected position to inflict harm on a majority" (Dahl 1989: 156).

In this chapter, however, strategies are led by politicians, not judges. The exception is when politicians collude, as was the case in France and Italy. Independent but not neutral judges may be instrumental in promoting initiatives by politicians and create opportunities for a conflict between courts and democracy. Two of these strategies are well known. In one, politicians try to rule unfettered by judges, courts, and norms: they use votes against laws and robes. These strategies affect not just the plebiscitarian populist politician that we know well, but also postcommunist politicians who want to get rid of the power of the judiciary, also in the name of democracy. This latter case poses the question of what kind of judges should be granted independence. That is, do checkers need to have a particular identity before they become autonomous and start checking politicians? The second strategy in which politicians exploited a conflict between the judiciary and democracy was the destabilization of regimes helped by instrumental judges. The problem in such a case was not weak institutions of "horizontal accountability" against powerful executives; it was rather the reverse.

The rule of law also provides extraordinary resources to politicians when democracy is an equilibrium, particularly when institutional reforms lead to a lack of responsibility on the part of a decentralized and independent judiciary and create conditions for unrestricted judicial activism. Such reforms have been introduced in both common-law[61] and civil-law countries, but this chapter focuses on the latter. Institutional reforms, in countries where the judiciary was hardly independent from past authoritarian regimes, have resulted in an unchecked judicial power. If rulers are scarcely accountable politically and reduce their

---

[61] An example is the introduction of the independent counsel in the U.S. system. First, Archibald Cox, followed by Leon Jaworski, with Watergate in the Richard Nixon presidency; Lawrence Walsh, with the Iran-Contra affair under Ronald Reagan; and finally, Robert Fiske, Kenneth Starr, and Robert Ray with Whitewater and the Monica Lewinsky cases, in the Bill Clinton presidency.

political responsibilities to legal liability, incentives for a judicialization of politics will be strong. If an opposition has been losing elections for a long time, and its prospects for the future are not hopeful, it will have incentives to introduce this new dimension of competition in order to undermine its adversary. A government that wants to reinforce its hold on power can also judicialize politics and use independent, partial judges to weaken opponents.

Politicians can transform a decentralized, independent judiciary into a political weapon against their adversaries if they have a strong urge for power now, they have little fear of retaliation, partial judges are available, and their opponents will be substantially weakened as a result of the strategy. The latter will comply for the opposite reasons: if they value the long term under democracy, even with rules of the game that are now unfavorable; if they cannot find similar resources in the judiciary but hope to compensate for this unbalance with the votes some time in the future; if voters punish resistance to judicial decisions. I have examined two strategies of this kind: in one, the judicialization of politics is used to dislodge the incumbent; in the other, to silence opponents. In both strategies, what ultimately limited the destructive capacity of the selective use of the law as a political weapon were the political credentials of the higher court on which the final verdict rested.

When the rule of law becomes a political weapon, some of its principles are eventually undermined. Thus, the end justifies the means; cases are selected for political reasons; "judicial populism" leads to violations of the presumption of innocence and legal guarantees; cases last several years and become general inquisitions in search of causes; secret proceedings become public (López Aguilar 1999). A network of complicities develops among judges, the media, and politicians. The judicialization of politics does not just end with political conclusions; it starts with political intentions.

Skepticism toward the rule of law and "the assumption of its overriding importance" has been expressed by Raz in the following terms: "[O]ne should be wary of disqualifying the legal pursuit of major social goals in the name of the rule of law.... Sacrificing too many social goals on the altar of the rule of law may make the law barren and empty" (Raz 1979: 210, 339). The skepticism expressed in this chapter, however, does not stem from the prevalence of economic security against social reforms, but from the disconnection between judicial independence and political impartiality. That is, it stems from the risk that such a formidable weapon can pose to democracy as a regime or to the rules of democratic competition.

**298**

The answer to such risk does not lie in an impotent judiciary, abusive majorities, or unchecked politicians. What this chapter asserts is that the different limitations to judicial impunity of common law and civil law systems should not be carelessly eliminated – and also, that politicians must accept democratic accountability and political responsibility if they want to avoid the judicialization of politics.

## References

*Baker v. Carr.* 1962. 369 U.S. 186.

Barreiro, B., and I. Sánchez-Cuenca. 1998. "Análisis del cambio del voto al PSOE en las elecciones de 1993." *Revista Española de Investigaciones Sociológicas* 82: 191–211.

Belloch, S. 1998. *Interior.* Barcelona: Ediciones B.

Burnett, S. H., and L. Mantovani. 1998. *The Italian Guillotine.* Lanham, Md.: Rowman & Littlefield.

Cebrián, J. L. 1999. "El fin del silencio." *El País,* 15–16 October.

Correa Sutil, J. 1993. "The Judiciary and the Political System in Chile: The Dilemmas of Judicial Independence during the Transition to Democracy." In I. P. Stotzky (ed.), *Transitions to Democracy in Latin America: The Role of the Judiciary,* 90–106. Boulder: Westview Press.

Dahl, R. A. 1957. "Decision Making in a Democracy: The Supreme Court as a National Policy Maker." *Journal of Public Law* 6: 279–95.

1989. *Democracy and Its Critics.* New Haven: Yale University Press.

della Porta, D. 2001. "A Judges' Revolution? Political Corruption and the Judiciary in Italy." *European Journal of Political Research* 39, 1: 1–21.

Di Palma, G. 1990. *To Craft Democracies.* Berkeley: University of California Press.

Dworkin, R. 1985. *A Matter of Principle.* Cambridge, Mass.: Harvard University Press.

Dyzenhaus, D. 1997. "Legal Theory in the Collapse of Weimar: Contemporary Lessons?" *American Political Science Review* 91, 1: 121–34.

Ehrmann, H. W. 1987. "Judicial Activism in a Divided Society: The Rule of Law in the Weimar Republic." In J. R. Schmidhauser (ed.), *Comparative Judicial Systems,* 75–92. London: Butterworth.

Esquith, S. L. 1999. "Toward a Democratic Rule of Law. East and West." *Political Theory* 27, 3: 334–56.

*Federalist Papers.* 1961. New York: New American Library.

Fernández Enguita, M. 1998. "Mirando hacia atrás sin ira." *El País,* 29 July.

Fish, S. 1993. "On Legal Autonomy." *Mercer Law Review* 44: 737–41.

Flemming, R. B., and B. D. Wood. 1997. "The Public and the Supreme Court: Individual Justice Responsiveness to American Policy Moods." *American Journal of Political Science* 41, 2: 468–98.

Franklin, C., and L. Kosaki. 1989. "Republican Schoolmaster: The U.S. Supreme Court, Public Opinion, and Abortion." *American Political Science Review* 83, 3: 751–71.

Friedrich, C. J. 1958. *La démocratie constitutionelle.* Paris: Presses Universitaires de France.

Guarnieri, C., and P. Pederzoli. 1999. *Los jueces y la política. Poder judicial y democracia.* Madrid: Taurus.

Hart, H. L. A. 1958. "Positivism and the Separation of Law and Norms." *Harvard Law Review* 71, 4: 593–629.

Hayek, F. 1994. *The Road to Serfdom*. Chicago: University of Chicago Press.

Heller, H. 1972. *Teoría del estado*. Mexico: Fondo de Cultura Económica. Spanish translation of *Staatslehre* (1934).

Hilbink, L. N.d. "Exploring the Links between Institutional Characteristics of the Judiciary and the Substance of Judicial Decision-Making." University of California, San Diego. Unpublished manuscript.

Hoekstra, V., and J. Segal. 1996. "The Shepherding of Local Public Opinion: The Supreme Court and *Lamb's Chapel*." *Journal of Politics* 58, 4: 1079–102.

Jackson, G. 1998. "Los destinos de Clinton y González." *El País*, 5 August, 9–10.

Kaniowski, A. 1999. "Lustration and Decommunization." In M. Krygier and A. Czarnota (eds.), *The Rule of Law after Communism*, 211–47. Aldershot: Ashgate.

Karl, T. L., and P. C. Schmitter. 1991. "Modes of Transition in Latin America, Southern and Eastern Europe." *International Social Science Journal* 128: 269–83.

Kelsen, H. 1977. *Esencia y valor de la democracia*. 2d ed. Madrid: Guadarrama. Spanish translation of *Grundrib einer allgemeinen Theorie des Staates* (1926).
        1979. *Teoría general del estado*. Mexico: Editora Nacional. Spanish translation of *Allgemeine Staatslehre* (1925).

Larkins, C. 1998. "The Judiciary and Delegative Democracy in Argentina." *Comparative Politics* 30, 4: 423–42.

Lepsius, R. 1978. "From Fragmented Party Democracy to Government by Emergency Decree and National Socialist Takeover: Germany." In J. J. Linz and A. Stepan (eds.), *The Breakdown of Democratic Regimes: Europe*, 34–79. Baltimore: Johns Hopkins University Press.

Linz J. J., and A. Stepan. 1996. *Problems of Democratic Transition and Consolidation*. Baltimore: Johns Hopkins University Press.

López Aguilar, J. F. 1999. "¿Hacen política los jueces?" *Claves de Razón Práctica* 96: 8–15.

Magalhàes, P. C. 1999. "The Politics of Judicial Reform in Eastern Europe." *Comparative Politics* 32, 1: 43–62.

Manin, B., A. Przeworski, and S. C. Stokes. 1999. "Elections and Representation." In A. Przeworski, S. C. Stokes, and B. Manin (eds.), *Democracy, Accountability, and Representation*, 29–54. Cambridge: Cambridge University Press.

Mishler, W., and R. Sheehan. 1993. "The Supreme Court as a Counter-Majoritarian Institution? The Impact of Public Opinion on Supreme Court Decisions." *American Political Science Review* 87, 1: 87–101.
        1996. "Public Opinion, the Attitudinal Model, and Supreme Court Decision-Making: A Micro-Analytic Perspective." *Journal of Politics* 58, 1: 169–200.

Montesquieu, C. L. 1951. *De l'esprit des lois*. Vol. 2. Paris: Gallimard (Pléiade).

Morawski, L. 1999. "Positivist or Non-Positivist Rule of Law?" In M. Krygier and A. Czarnota (eds.), *The Rule of Law after Communism*, 39–54. Aldershot: Ashgate.

Müller, I. 1991. *Hitler's Justice*. Cambridge, Mass.: Harvard University Press.

Novoa Monreal, E. 1992. *Los resquicios legales*. Santiago: Ediciones BAT.

O'Donnell, G., 1994. "Delegative Democracy." *Journal of Democracy* 5, 1: 56–69.
        1999. "Polyarchies and the (Un)Rule of Law in Latin America." In J. E. Méndez, G. O'Donnell, and P. S. Pinheiro (eds.), *The (Un)Rule of Law and the Underprivileged in Latin America*, 303–37. Notre Dame: University of Notre Dame Press.

O'Donnell, G., and P. C. Schmitter. 1986. *Transitions from Authoritarian Rule:*

*Tentative Conclusions about Uncertain Democracies.* Baltimore: Johns Hopkins University Press.

Ott, W., and F. Buob. 1993. "Did Legal Positivism Render German Jurists Defenceless during the Third Reich?" *Social & Legal Studies* 2, 1: 91–104.

Pederzoli, P., and C. Guarnieri. 1997. "Italy: A Case of Judicial Democracy?" *International Social Science Journal* 152: 253–70.

Pizzorno, A. 1992. "La corruzione nel sistema politico." In D. della Porta (ed.), *Lo scambio occulto.* Bologna: Il Mulino.

Pradera, J. 1999. "La Alegre Muchachada." *El País*, 17 October.

Przeworski, A. 1991. *Democracy and the Market.* Cambridge: Cambridge University Press.

Radin, M. J. 1989. "Reconsidering the Rule of Law." *Boston University Law Review* 69, 4: 781–819.

Raz, J. 1979. *The Authority of Law.* Oxford: Clarendon Press.

——— 1994. *Ethics in the Public Domain.* Oxford: Clarendon Press.

Rehnquist, W. H. 1986. "Constitutional Law and Public Opinion." *Suffolk University Law Review* 20, 4: 751–69.

Riker, W. H. 1982. *Liberalism against Populism.* Prospect Heights, Ill.: Waveland Press.

Roussel, V. 1998. "Les magistrats dans les scandales politiques." *Revue Française de Science Politique* 48, 2: 245–73.

Rubio Llorente, F. 1991. "La igualdad en la jurisprudencia del Tribunal Constitucional." *Revista Española de Derecho Constitucional* 31: 9–36.

Schmitt, C. 1985. *La dictadura.* Madrid: Alianza Editorial. Spanish translation of *Die Diktatur: Von den Anfängen des Modernen Souveränitätsgedankens bis zum Proletarischen Klassenkampf* (1922).

Shklar, J. N. 1987. "Political Theory and the Rule of Law." In A. C. Hutchinson and P. Monahan (eds.), *The Rule of Law: Ideal or Ideology.* Toronto: Carswell.

Silva Cimma, E. 1977. *El tribunal constitucional de Chile (1971–1973).* Caracas: Editorial Jurídica Venezolana.

Sonner, M. W., and C. Wilcox. 1999. "Forgiving and Forgetting: Public Support for Bill Clinton during the Lewinsky Scandal." *PS. Political Science & Politics* 32, 3: 554–7.

Smulovitz, C. 2002. "The Discovery of Law. Political Consequences in the Argentinian Case." In Y. Dezalay and B. Garth (eds.), *Global Prescriptions: The Production, Exportation, and Importation of a New Legal Orthodoxy.* Ann Arbor: Michigan University Press.

Tocqueville, A. de. 1969. *Democracy in America.* New York: J. P. Mayer.

Toharia, J. J. 1999. "La independencia judicial y la buena justicia." *Justicia y Sociedad* 3: 9–32.

Valenzuela, A. 1989. "Chile: Origins, Consolidation, and Breakdown of a Democratic Regime." In L. Diamond, J. J. Linz, and S. M. Lipset (eds.), *Democracy in Developing Countries: Latin America*, 159–206. Boulder: Lynne Rienner Publishers.

Weingast, B. 1997. "The Political Foundations of Democracy and the Rule of Law." *American Political Science Review* 91, 2: 245–63.

## Chapter Twelve

# The Rule of Law and the Problem of Legal Reform in Michel de Montaigne's *Essais*

The nature of the law – in the sense of both customary human practices and positive, written law – is a central theme in Montaigne's
*Essais*, though, like any other major subject in his work, it is difficult to present systematically without imposing a somewhat arbitrary
order on the text.[1] There were basically three dimensions in which
Montaigne developed this subject: the first one was the broad anthropological reflection on the nature of social norms and moral conventions
within human societies, no doubt the best-known aspect of his contribution to this issue and one that is generally regarded as distinctly
representative of his skeptical approach. The second dimension was
the devastating critique of contemporary French legislation and of the
judicial machinery responsible for administering it – a reality Montaigne
was intimately associated with in his capacity of *conseiller* first, between 1554 and 1557, at the Cour des Aides de Périgueux, and then,
from 1557, at the Parlement of Bordeaux until his decision to sell

---

[1] To make the reading less stressful for non-French speakers I have confined all passages
from Montaigne's French text to the annotation, giving at the same time a reference to
the English translation by Screech (1987). In all quotations from the *Essais* I give first
the number of the book and of the chapter of the work (in Roman numerals); then the
volume and page number in the edition by Villey (1999); finally the page number in
Screech (1987). It is practically impossible to confine any large topic in the context of
the *Essais* to a particular section of the text; however, I have mostly used the following
chapters: book I (ch. XXIII, "De la coustume et de ne changer aisément une loy receue");
book II (ch. XVII, "De la praesumption"; ch. XII, "Apologie de Raimond Sebond"; ch. XIX,
"De la liberté de conscience"); book III (ch. I, "De l'utile et de l'honneste"; ch. II, "Du
repentir"; ch. IX, "De la vanité"; ch. XIII, "De l'experience"). Montaigne continued to
work on the *Essais* throughout the 1570s and 1580s until his death in 1592: though it
is possible to recognize in the text the additions made to the different editions (between
1580 and 1588) it is often difficult to follow the evolution of certain opinions and put
them in relation to external events.

his post in 1570.[2] Finally, the third dimension was the evaluation of the impact of the Reformation and of religious conflict upon the French legal order, a retrospective assessment that Montaigne attempted at various points in the *Essais* but which was more fully developed in the 1588 edition of the work (the one that contains book III), published when the prospect of peace and of a durable settlement with the Protestants under Henry of Navarre was finally in sight.

After sketching briefly the first dimension of Montaigne's analysis, I focus mainly on the second and third: it was, in fact, in reflecting on the conditions of the French legal system and on the crisis of the religious wars that Montaigne was forced to think more sharply about the efficacy of the law as an instrument of governance and about the interaction of political authority, legal structure, and opinion.

Montaigne's overall view on the origin of moral norms and collective rules that govern human societies was that these were the product of custom and habit. Habit led people to adopt precepts and practices, which in themselves were arbitrary, accidental, or even aberrant, without questioning them. The same attachment to habit and tradition made people mistake these conventional arrangements for moral imperatives dictated by nature. The great variety of human customs across space and time – a major theme in the *Essais* – offered the best illustration of how different and often contrary practices would appear to those who subscribed to them in the light of natural, universal precepts.

This principle – that social norms were founded upon local agreements – applied to both religious practices and legal systems. Religious beliefs, even the true Christian faith, were generally accepted by people as part of a package that came with their membership in a particular community: one was a Christian in the same way in which he may be German or from the Perigord.[3] Similarly, positive laws were simply the elaborate transcription of old customs (either existing locally or

---

[2] On Montaigne's legal career, see Frame (1994, ch. 4), a translation of *Montaigne, a Biography* (this French translation has an updated bibliography and annotation, which makes it more user-friendly than the original English version). There is proof that Montaigne continued to function as legal adviser for the Bordeaux Parlement after his resignation in 1570, though unfortunately no comprehensive study of his activities in this field, including all the documentary evidence, has ever been produced.

[3] "Nous sommes Chrestiens à mesme titre que nous sommes ou Perigordins ou Alemans" (book II, ch. XII; vol. 2, p. 445; Screech, p. 497).

imported by foreign conquest), although the passing of time and the evolution of language may contribute to blurring their origin. Montaigne did not deny that somewhere beyond these conventional arrangements there was such a thing as a law of nature and, with it, a kind of natural and universal justice, different from the particular justice of nations.[4] This natural justice, unlike its ghostly shade embodied in human institutions (the representation of justice as "umbra et imago" was borrowed from Cicero's *De officiis*, III.17), was accessible to human beings only through the exercise of individual judgment. Reason could help each individual to see the limits of his prejudices, but in practice this critical effort was bound to produce a variety of conflicting opinions rather than a system of shared truths. Each individual would judge by himself and judge differently; indeed, it was not even sure that the same person would be consistent in her judgment at different points in time. Given the impossibility of attaining a shared view of justice, Montaigne suggested that it was generally advisable to submit to the current customs and laws of the country one lived in, even if one happened to believe privately that they were indifferent, worthless, or positively bad. He also stressed that established beliefs and practices, however questionable, would prove very difficult to change without causing widespread disruption, so that in the end the damage inflicted to the community by innovation may be greater than the evils associated with the bad old rules.

The combination of these two positions – the invitation to conform to the existing rules and the insistence on the dangers of novelty – has contributed to establishing the image of Montaigne as a conservative skeptic, an image reinforced by his outward fidelity to orthodox Catholicism and his hostility toward the ideological postures of the Reformation. This conservative interpretation of the political message of the *Essais* – which presents the wise man according to Montaigne upholding authority in spite of his misgivings about it – though still widely accepted, has recently come under attack. According to some scholars the conservative views expressed in some passages of the *Essais* are undermined by other sections of the same work in which the author develops a radical critique of the existing order and confesses his readiness to

---

[4] "La justice en soy, naturelle et universelle, est autrement reiglée, et plus noblement, que n'est cette autre justice speciale, nationale, contrainte au besoing de nos polices" (book III, ch. I; vol. 3, p. 796; Screech, p. 898). On the concept of "natural justice," see also Alberti (1995).

disobey both the law and the prince's command if these are in conflict with his own conscience.[5]

The artful ambiguity that characterizes Montaigne's discussion of crucial political issues (such as freedom of conscience, political obligation, or raison d'état) is undeniable, and it is very difficult to imagine that it was not deliberate, whether the author's "real" intention was to disguise excessively provocative opinions, to awake skeptical doubts in the reader, or to express a genuine ambivalence. Moreover, Montaigne's supposed attachment to tradition and mistrust of political action was patently contradicted by his intimacy with Protestant intellectuals, by the somewhat risky personal choice of supporting Henry of Navarre, and, more generally, by his active involvement in the cause of peace and national reconciliation.

Setting aside the general question of Montaigne's political outlook, the remarks in the *Essais* about the great inertial power of habit and about the unforeseen consequences of promoting change do not simply offer a broad anthropological view, or express an individual preference for stability; they also articulate a specific historical judgment about the experience of reform in contemporary France.

Whenever he describes the variety of human customs, Montaigne adopts a characteristically detached, even amused tone, relating with gusto the bizarre diversities of manners, tastes, rituals, and superstitions across present and past, real and imagined nations, relishing the conclusion that there is no "faintasie si forcenée" not to have been adopted somewhere as a public norm. This detachment disappears altogether whenever he talks of the laws of his own country, giving way to a tone of icy sarcasm or passionate indignation.

In his reconstruction, an unfortunate combination of Roman law and feudal custom had produced in France an aberrant result, a judicial monstrosity that subsequent royal interventions had only succeeded in making more useless and unmanageable. To begin with, France had far too many laws, as if jurists had pursued the insane design of creating a specific law for each particular case that could conceivably present itself, not just in this world, but "in all the worlds imagined by Epicure." Predictably, a hundred thousand laws of this kind would still be too few to legislate for "the infinite diversity of human actions." Moreover, a lot of these laws were obsolete, many repeated or contradicted one another,

---

[5] For a classical formulation of Montaigne's conservatism, see Brown (1963); cf. the discussion of this theme in Schaefer (1990: 153–76).

and all were expressed in a characteristically cryptic jargon, so that the French language, which proved adequate for all other purposes, became obscure and unintelligible in as simple a document as the drafting of a will or a contract: on balance, not having any laws at all would be preferable to this state of affairs.[6]

Montaigne did not take sides in the dispute that opposed at the time the partisans of Roman law and those jurists who supported French common law. He just stressed that the accumulation of interpretations and commentaries had turned the practice of the law into an idle philological exercise on which unfortunately the lives and property of the subjects had come to depend. Roman law had at least the advantage of being accessible to the Roman people, who could read the codes inscribed on tables in the public square: the French were not so lucky, because they were governed by laws that were not even written in their own language.[7] But the most odious feature of French law in Montaigne's eyes was the unnecessary cruelty of its penal code, with its ferocious tortures and executions. If the customs of those distant tribes who ate human flesh, wore rings through their lips and noses, and sacrificed slaughtered animals to the gods seemed savage and barbarous, how should one qualify the behavior of those Christian magistrates who manifested their religious zeal by inventing appalling new torments to inflict on their victims?[8]

The incoherence and barbarity of French law found a natural counterpart in the "disorder and corruption" of the institutions responsible for its interpretation and administration.[9] Like many of his contemporaries, Montaigne was strongly opposed to the venality of judicial offices and to the payment of fees (*épices*), which characterized the French legal system. Although officially the French crown continued to forbid the sale of posts in the magistracy, since 1551, under the reign of Henry II and his successors, the financial crisis brought about by the Italian campaigns and, later, by the religious wars had led to a steady growth

---

[6] "Les plus desirables (loix), ce sont les plus rares, plus simples et generales; et encore crois-je qu'il vaudroit mieux n'en avoir point du tout que de les avoir en tel nombre que nous avons" (book III, ch. XIII; vol. 3, p. 1066; Screech, p. 1208).

[7] On this debate and its implications, see Franklin (1963); see also Bodin (1941), Desan (1987), Couzinet (1996, 114–20).

[8] "De la cruauté" (book II, ch. IX; vol. 2, esp. pp. 431ff). On Montaigne's critique of violence and cruelty (also as part of aristocratic education), see Quint (1998).

[9] "Les nostres (loix) françoises present aucunement la main (cannot but favour), par leur desreiglement et deformité, au desordre et corruption qui se voit en leur dispensation et execution. Le commandement est si trouble et inconstant qu'il excuse aucunement (entirely) et la desobeyssance et le vice de l'interpretation, de l'administration et de l'observation" (book III, ch. XIII; vol. 3, p. 1072; Screech, pp. 1216–17).

of this market, which the monarchy itself promoted and encouraged in its eagerness to secure a steady supply of cash.[10]

In Montaigne's view the practice of turning the law into a commodity available only to those who could pay for it undermined any claim to impartial justice. If laws were often made by idiots (*sots*), they were even more often made by men who could not be impartial because they simply hated equality (book I, ch. XXIII; vol. 1, p. 177). In France the Robe represented a powerful cast, a "fourth estate," but in practice only commoners were subjected to its authority, because the nobility followed a code of honor of its own, which was often contrary to and above ordinary legislation. As to the third estate, the rich were forced to pay to obtain justice, while the poor alone would suffer the rigors of the law.

Here some peasants who had discovered the body of a man viciously attacked would not give him assistance or report the crime for fear of being accused of it – fear that Montaigne thought fully justified; in a town nearby some "pauvres diables" would hang for a crime they had not committed because the court acquired the proof of their innocence only after some other tribunal had sentenced them to death, and both sets of judges would prefer to see them dead that to confront an embarrassing conflict of jurisdiction. Magistrates – Montaigne actually calls them contemptuously "gens maniant des procés" (book I, ch. XXIII; vol. 1, p. 118) – were tested for doctrine and knowledge of the legal codes, but not for common sense or honesty. Everywhere justice was sacrificed to greed, to stupidity, to social privilege, and to empty legal forms, producing as a result "condamnation(s) plus crimineluse(s) que le crime" (book III, ch. III; vol. 3, p. 1071).

If the laws, Montaigne concluded, still had some credibility, it was not because they were just but because they were laws: this was the only mystical foundation of their power; they had no other. Such credit was so undeserved that people were fully justified if they ignored or disobeyed them; indeed, in some cases it was only by disobeying them that individuals could follow the principles of justice dictated by their conscience. For his part, Montaigne confessed his incapacity as a magistrate to apply the law whenever this seemed contrary to common feelings of humanity and mercy. He also admitted that he would not hesitate to emigrate to another country if the laws he served were to limit his liberty or threaten his physical integrity.[11]

---

[10] See Mousnier (1971: 35ff.).
[11] See book III, ch. XIII; vol. 3, p. 1072; cf. "De la physionomie" (book III, ch. XII, vol. 3, p. 1062).

If Montaigne's passionate critique of French law had especially radical undertones, his views on the corruption of the Robe were shared by many of his fellow magistrates. The problem was: could the system be reformed, and if so, how, by what means, given that the monarchy was hostage to its financial needs while the courts resisted all attempts to interfere with their corporate interests?

In 1561, just before the beginning of the civil war, a last attempt in the direction of a general reform of the judiciary had been undertaken by Chancellor Michel de l'Hospital with a set of *ordonnances* issued at the request of the Estates of Orléans. This document sketched an ambitious plan of reorganization of French institutions in which the suppression of a series of abuses in the administration of ecclesiastical benefits was combined with measures designed to fight against the corruption of the magistracy. These measures called for, among other things, the abolition of all offices created after the death of Louis XII in 1515 that should become vacant, as well as of a variety of redundant posts; they suppressed all "perpetual" offices and forbade the payment of the *épices* to magistrates as well as any other direct or indirect form of compensation (pensions, benefits, etc.); they made it impossible for two members of the same family to sit on the same court and established a practice of control over the financial conditions and the "morality" of judges and *conseillers*; they also introduced a principle of appeal against the decisions of a particular magistrate or court through resort to an independent review.

In de l'Hospital's view, a substantial reform of the law was as vital as the reform of the church to restore the credit of the crown and to fight against the menace of religious dissent.[12] In this respect the *ordonnances* of Orléans were the necessary complement to the edict of toleration known as the "édit de janvier" of 1562, the last attempt made by the moderates to forestall the civil war.[13] Predictably the chancellor found it increasingly difficult to enlist supporters for such a broad and radical project: after encountering the opposition of the Estates, he turned to the sovereign courts and finally – following a procedure that was not, strictly speaking, constitutional – resorted to a consultative assembly of notables to promote the *ordonnances* of Moulins in 1566. Like those of the "édit de janvier," these measures were never enforced,

---

[12] "L'on dit bien qu'il est besoin de reformer l'Eglise, mais la justice a aussi grand besoin de reformation que l'Eglise.' Michel de l'Hospital, 'Harangue au Parlement de Rouen" (17 August 1563), in Descimon (1993).

[13] On Montaigne and the "édit de janvier," see Smith (1991).

since by then all chances of political intervention had been sunk by the outbreak of the war. Victim of the intrigues of the Guisard party, de l'Hospital resigned and retired from politics in 1568.[14]

The failure of de l'Hospital's project of legal reform – an experience that Montaigne had closely followed[15] – helps us to understand the account given in the *Essais* of the Reformation as a large-scale ideological fraud, a collective delusion. Montaigne's judgment did not derive from the persuasion that the Protestants were necessarily wrong in their religious beliefs (he certainly thought that their theological views were possibly as plausible as any others ) or generally in bad faith. But he felt that religious reform was a very unsatisfactory substitute, some kind of ersatz reform, for a legal reform that had failed to materialize.

To begin with, if changing the laws of men was a difficult and hazardous enterprise, the reformers were guilty of an even greater folly, which was the ambition to change the laws of God, by submitting public constitutions and practices to the instability of a "private fantasy."[16] In Montaigne's view, this undertaking was especially perverse and absurd because it caused much real damage to people's lives and property on account of things (religious truths) that were completely beyond human experience and out of the grasp of human reason, an argument he developed at length in book II in the "Apology of Raimond Sebond." Moreover, this exercise eliminated what the author of the *Essais* saw as the major advantage of the Christian religion, the separation that the Christian doctrine established between spiritual and secular power.

Although Montaigne was guarded in expressing sentiments that may be interpreted as Epicurean or materialistic, a recognizable theme in the *Essais* was the necessity for humans to pay closer attention to their concrete, bodily needs rather than to spiritual or symbolic factors (see, for example, his account of the trial of the Arginuse, where able generals who had just saved Athens from a Persian invasion were executed for abandoning at sea the bodies of their dead sailors) (book I, ch. III; vol. 1, p. 20). Unsurprisingly, given its far too ambitious scope, the Reformation had only scratched the surface of the corruption of French society,

---

[14] On de l'Hospital's reforms, see Crouzet (1998: 429ff.).

[15] De l'Hospital visited Bordeaux and addressed the local *parlement* in 1562: see Nakam (1993: 211ff.).

[16] "me semblant tres-inique de vouloir sousmettre les constitutions et observances publiques et immobiles à l'instabilité d'une privée fantasie (la raison privée n'a qu'une jurisdiction privée) et entreprendre sur les loix divines ce que nulle police ne supporteroit aux civiles, ausquelles encore que l'humaine raison aye beaucoup plus de commerce, si sont elles souverainement juges de leur juges" (book I, ch. XXIII; vol. 1, p. 121; Screech, p. 137).

affecting political rhetoric rather than political practices, or, in other words, changing the appearance of things rather than their substance.[17]

This effect was especially apparent if one looked at the evolution of French legislation during the troubles. The anxiety of the crown to control religious dissent had accentuated the worst features of French law, its uncertainty and instability. The monarchy in particular had been unable to develop a coherent line of conduct, hesitating all the time between repression and toleration: as a result, the law, Montaigne observed, kept changing, just like fashion in clothing.[18]

Montaigne disapproved very strongly of religious persecution, which he considered both inhuman and practically ineffective; he also thought that, in this as in other cases, punishment fell almost exclusively upon people of modest condition, who paid for the ambitions of their social superiors, sacrificed to beliefs they did not even understand and to the intrigues of unscrupulous leaders. Much as he hated persecution, he did not think, however, that a permissive legislation was necessarily an effective means to ensure peace, at least not in the short term. In his account of the experience of the Emperor Julian in the chapter on "Liberté de conscience" (book II, ch. XIX), he suggested that the immediate effects of toleration were generally to increase conflict and disorder, while its beneficial effects would be felt only in the long run, once people had become accustomed to a degree of freedom and the religious sects had learned to coexist. On the whole, however, Montaigne saw this as a rather murky area of causal explanation, one in which it was difficult to establish simple and direct connections: if the religious settlement that had proved impossible in the early 1560s had become feasible in the late 1580s, this probably depended on different factors, rather than being the direct result of legislative intervention.

In any case the French crown had been unable to pursue consistently any kind of strategy, and the gradual acceptance of a coexistence with the Protestants had been the product less of political design and legal prescription than of the progressive loss of power and consensus of royal

---

[17] "Ceux qui ont essaié de r'aviser les mœurs du monde, de mon temps, par nouvelles opinions, reforment les vices de l'apparence; ceux de l'essence, ils les laissent là, s'ils ne les augmentent: et l'augmentation y est à craindre; on se sejourne (dispense) volontiers de tout autre bien faire sur ces reformations externes arbitraires, de moindre coust et de plus grand merite; et satisfait-on par la à bon marché les autres vices naturels consubstantiels et intestins" (book III, ch. II; vol. 3, p. 811; Screech, p. 914).

[18] "Le pis que je trouve en nostre estat, c'est l'instabilité, et que nos loix, non plus que nos vestemens, ne peuvent prendre aucune forme arrestée" (book II, ch. XVII; vol. 2, p. 656; Screech, p. 745).

authority. In practice, rather than imposing a given pattern upon reality, the law had simply followed the evolution of events, adjusting from time to time to the fluctuating fortunes of the contending parties. As proof of this shift, Montaigne indicated the changes in the language of the edicts issued to discipline religious dissent, in which "public vices" had gradually acquired, in tune with the dominant rhetoric, "gentler names."[19]

In other words, having failed to get what it wanted (crushing the Protestants), the French crown had prudently decided to want what it could get, a compromise with them. Similarly (the same formulation is used in different chapters), it seemed wiser in the end to make the laws will what they could do, since they could not do what they willed.[20]

Was the lesson to be learned from the French experience that the law could only endorse a status quo, changing with the evolution of power relations within society? After a long civil war, the old order, in which heretics were excluded from the political body, had been replaced by a new one in which the same heretics – under the new "gentler" name of "religionnaires" – after gaining control of significant portions of French territory, had established their entitlement to be part of the French state and had forced the French crown to inscribe this entitlement in the law. This new order was not necessarily more just, equitable, and transparent than the old one, but it had the advantage of reestablishing a shared rule.[21] Although this interpretation seems to follow from Montaigne's notion of the law as "convention" (as well as expressing the kind of conservative pessimism generally attributed to him), I believe it would be a partial and misleading rendering of the argument of the *Essais*.

Montaigne thought that the rule of law was a necessary condition for the existence of political society: without it there was no sovereign (for the king was unable to protect his subjects and to be obeyed by them) and no subjects to follow his command (since disobedience was the natural response to the corruption of authority). In this respect what had happened in France during the religious wars, the collapse of a fragile and corrupt order, could be truly described as a "civil death."

---

[19] "On lict en nos loix mesmes, faites pour le remede de ce premier mal, l'apprentissage et l'excuse de toute sorte de mauvaises entreprises; et nous advient, ce que Tucidides dict des guerres civiles de son temps, qu'en faveur des vices publiques on les battisoit des mots nouveaux plus doux, pour leur excuse, abastardissant et amolissant leurs vrais titres" (book I, ch. XXIII; vol. 1, p. 120; Screech, p. 135).

[20] The formulation appears in book I, in ch. XXIII on custom and then again in book II, ch. XIX on the freedom of conscience.

[21] One could argue that it was more equitable because it recognized the religious freedom of Protestants; yet Montaigne obviously thought that this kind of equality was less relevant than, say, the equality of rich and poor in front of the law.

However, one could not generalize from the French case to conclude that the law must necessarily be the function of power relations. First, the "rule of law" had been virtually nonexistent in France even before its absence was made obvious by the collapse of royal authority. Second, the new status quo that had been gradually imposed would not be truly accepted or prove durable unless it satisfied certain conditions – witness the difficulties that first Henry III, then Henry IV encountered in building up the process of peace even after military resistance on both sides had subsided).[22] One would think that any kind of settlement was preferable to the war, but the quality of consensus mattered: a new order imposed by force, accepted from exhaustion or from calculation, in view of some future redress, would never last.

In considering the future prospects of France, the focus of Montaigne's argument shifted decisively from the role of political institutions to that of individual agents. All members of a political community were individually responsible for its corruption, though in different ways and degrees according to their personal inclinations and their position within society: some – those who had power – would be guilty of active vices, such as greed, cruelty, and deceit, whereas others, among them the writer himself, would give their contribution in the form of laziness, cowardice, and the passive acceptance of evil.[23] In this respect there was no qualitative difference between the moral position of governors and governed. Even the most humble member of society had always, as a last resort, the option to disobey what he should regard as an unjust rule, and the "homme de bien" was never morally obliged to do just anything that the prince should command.[24] The echo of Etienne de La Boétie's "Discours de la servitude volontaire" was not entirely lost in the *Essais*, even if its political implications were never made explicit.[25]

---

[22] On Navarre's strategy to gain consensus across French territory, see Finley-Crosswhite (1999); also De Waele (2000).

[23] "La corruption du siècle se faict par la contribution particulière de chacun de nous: les uns y confèrent la trahison, les autres l'injustice, l'irreligion, la tyrannie, l'avarice, la cruauté, selon qu'ils sont plus puissans; les plus faibles y apportent la sottise, la vanité, l'oisiveté, desquels je suis" (book III, ch. IX; vol. 3, p. 946; Screech, p. 1071).

[24] "... l'interest commun ne doibt pas tout requerir de tous contre l'interest privé, et ... (que) toutes choses ne sont pas loisibles à un homme de bien pour le service de son Roy ni de la cause generalle et des loix ... Ostons aux mechants naturels, et sanguinaires, et traistres, ce pretexte de raison; laissons là cette justice enorme et hors de soy, et nous tenons aus plus humaines imitations" (book III, ch. I, vol. 3, pp. 802–3; Screech, pp. 905–6).

[25] De La Boétie (1983); originally Montaigne intended to publish the text of the discourse with his essays: the reasons why he abandoned this project have never been conclusively established; the classical reference remains Armaingaud (1910).

Naturally the individual who had the greatest responsibility of all was the king: the exceptional circumstances of war and rebellion offered the sovereign an easy excuse to pursue a vicious line of conduct under the pretext of necessity: yet this Machiavellian temptation (the trap by which the Valois monarchy had fallen to its ruin) must be resisted at all costs, before it became a collective alibi for generalized licence and abuse.

Building upon the traditional theory of royalty – which saw the monarch as the custodian at the same time of the laws of the kingdom and of the law of God[26] – Montaigne admitted that the king might if necessary depart from traditional law if this appeared surpassed and inadequate, but this departure from the letter of the law could not be a departure from the rule of justice. If the king adopted a logic of duplicity and crime in the name of public interest, his actions would be submerged by the rising tide of vice and corruption around him.[27] On the contrary, the winning strategy for the monarch was to turn the tide by being the first to give an example of clemency, goodness, and justice: only in this way could he hope to reconquer the loyalty and confidence of his people.[28]

That in writing about the need for "bonté et justice" Montaigne did not simply appeal to some ideal image of royalty but also indicated an immediate political strategy is shown by a letter he addressed to Henry of Navarre on 18 January 1590: congratulating the king on his recent victory at Arques, he deplored the violence that had been used during the Toussaint of the previous year to repress the resistance of the Parisian *faubourgs* controlled by the Catholic League. If the king's cause could be advanced "par armes et par force," only clemency could perfect his victory and make it complete. The care that Navarre himself, now the official successor to the French crown, invested in building up a reputation for clemency, avoiding useless bloodshed of prisoners and civilians, also shows the relevance of this issue.[29]

---

26 See, for example, de Seyssel (1961: 22ff.).

27 See Montaigne's discussion of Machiavelli's views in Book III, Chapter I; on Montaigne and Machiavelli, cf. Nakam (1984: 245–50), Shaefer (1990: 347–65), Statius (1997: 243–62), Berns (2000).

28 "Et ne fut jamais temps et lieu ou il eust pour les princes loyer plus certain et plus grand proposé à la bonté et à la justice. Le premier qui s'avisera de se pousser en faveur et en credit pour cette voye là, je suis bien deçu si, à bon conte, il ne devançe ses compaignons. La force, la violance peuvent quelque chose, mais non pas tousjours tout" (book II, ch. XVII; vol. 2 p. 646; Screech, p. 735).

29 "Si s'est-il toujours vu que les conquètes par leur grandeur et difficulté ne se pouvaient parfaire par armes et par force, elles ont été parfaites par clémence et magnificence, excellentes leurres à attirer les hommes spécialement vers le juste et légitime parti." Montaigne to Henry of Navarre, 18 January 1590, in Montaigne (1962: 1398).

In conclusion, if Montaigne did not believe that in practice natural justice and the particular justice of nations could ever coincide, he could not bring himself to edit out of the text of the *Essais* the sustained tension between the two. No doubt people were generally blinded by prejudice and inclined to accept authority without questioning it: but there were moments when they would be able to tell deceit from sincerity, vice from virtue. Under the "wrinkled mask" of the law, the real face of justice would continue to show to those who were prepared to recognize it.

## References

Alberti, Antonina. 1995. "The Epicurian Theory of Law and Justice." In A. Laks and M. Schofield (eds.), *Justice and Generosity: Studies in Hellenistic Social and Political Philosopy*, 161–90. Cambridge: Cambridge University Press.

Armaingaud, Arthur. 1910. *Montaigne pamphlétaire, l'énigme du contr'un*. Paris: Hachette.

Berns, Thomas. 2000. *Violence de la loi à la Renaissance: L'originaire du politique chez Machiavel et Montaigne*. Paris: Editions Kimé.

Bodin, Jean. [1566] 1941. *La methode de l'histoire*. Trans. and ed. Pierre Mesnard. Paris: Les Belles Lettres.

Brown, Frieda S. 1963. *Religious and Political Conservatism in the Essais of Montaigne*. Geneva: Droz.

Couzinet, Marie-Dominique. 1996. *Histoire et méthode à la Renaissance; une lecture de la "Methodus" de Jean Bodin*. Paris: Vrin.

Crouzet, Denis. 1998. *La sagesse et le malheur, Michel de l'Hospital Chancelier de France*. Seyssel: Champ Vallon.

de Seyssel, Claude. [1519] 1961. *La Grande Monarchie de France*. Ed. Jacques Poujol. Paris: ***.

De La Boétie, Etienne. 1983. *Discours de la servitude volontaire*. Ed. S. Goyard-Fabre. Paris: Flammarion.

De Waele, Michel. 2000. *Les relations entre le Parlement de Paris et Henri IV*. Paris: Editions Publisud.

Desan, Philippe. 1987. *Naissance de la méthode (Machiavel, La Ramée, Bodin, Montaigne, Descartes)*. Paris: Nizet.

Descimon, Robert (ed.). 1993. *Discours pour la majorité de Charles IX, et trois autres discours*. Paris: Editions Imprimerie Nationale.

Finley-Crosswhite, S. Annette. 1999. *Henri IV and the Towns: The Pursuit of Legitimacy in French Urban Society, 1589–1610*. Cambridge: Cambridge University Press.

Frame, Donald M. 1994. *Montaigne, une vie, une œuvre*. Paris: Champion.

Franklin, Julian H. 1963. *Jean Bodin and the Sixteenth Century Revolution in the Methodology of Law and History*. New York: Columbia University Press.

Montaigne, Michel De. 1962. *Œuvres completes*. Ed. Albert Thibaudet and Maurice Rat. Paris: Gallimard.

1987. *The Complete Essays*. Trans. M. A. Screech. Harmondsworth: Penguin Books.

Mousnier, Roland. 1971. *La vénalité des offices sous Henri IV et Louis XIII*. Paris: PUF.

Nakam, Géralde. 1984. *Les Essais, miroir et procès de leur temps*. Paris: Nizet.
1993. *Montaigne et son temps*. Paris: Gallimard.
Quint, David. 1998. *Montaigne and the Quality of Mercy: Ethical and Political Themes in the "Essais."* Princeton: Princeton University Press.
Schaefer, David Lewis. 1990. *The Political Philosophy of Montaigne*. Ithaca: Cornell University Press.
Smith, Malcom C. 1991. *Montaigne and Religious Freedom: The Dawn of Pluralism*. Geneva: Droz.
Statius, Pierre. 1997. *Le réel et la joie: Essai sur l'œuvre de Montaigne*. Paris: Kimé.

# Author Index

# Subject Index

accountability, 9, 172–81

checks and balances, 10–12, 88, 200–2
  and limited government, 10–12,
    194–5, 202–4
constitution, 9, 109, 138–9
constitutive rules, 6, 65–90, 102, 139
culture
  and democracy, 116–29, 140–1
  and the rule of law, 112, 114

democracy, 37–9, 129–30
  as an equilibrium, 129–41
  and majority rule, 147–65, 223
  survival of, 115, 131–5
dictatorship
  and the rule of law, 188, 204–18

independent judiciary (also judicial
    independence), 12, 223–40
  organization of, 225–34
  origins of, 25–8, 247–50, 263
  and the rule of law, 12–15, 104–7,
    262–99
institutional equilibria, 4–12, 84–5,
    139–40

judicial discretion, 104–7, 266–8
judicial review, 14, 237–40, 250–6

law, 1, 68–9, 96, 168, 261–2
  compliance with (also obedience of),
    2, 40–1, 65–90, 94–5, 169
  and coordination, 5, 9–10, 110–13,
    170–86
legislatures and courts, 13, 257–60

majority rule (also democracy)
  and limited government, 153–62
  and the rule of law, 9, 12–15, 147–52,
    242–6, 257–60, 264–99
  and separation of powers, 9, 148–52

*Rechtsstaat*, 95–101
  and the rule of law, 96
rule by (through) law, 3–4, 8, 22–3, 49,
    189–92, 196
rule of law, 3–4, 62–3, 67–71, 192–6,
    242–3, 261–2
  emergence of, 19–60
  as an equilibrium, 2–3, 109–13,
    140–1, 169
  and individual autonomy, 2, 95
  normative conception of, 1–2
  and political conflict, 36, 257–60
  and political equality, 21–3, 47–53
  and predictability, 2, 32–4
  and separation of powers, 9, 147–50,
    194–6